TURGOT

AND THE *ANCIEN RÉGIME* IN FRANCE

A. R. J. TURGOT

From the Engraving by le Beau, after Troy, 1774, in the Bibliothèque Nationale

TURGOT
AND THE
ANCIEN RÉGIME IN FRANCE

by

DOUGLAS DAKIN

OCTAGON BOOKS

A DIVISION OF FARRAR, STRAUS AND GIROUX

New York   1980

Originally published 1939, by Methuen & Co. Ltd.

Reprinted 1965
by special arrangement with Methuen & Co. Ltd.

Second Octagon printing 1972
Third Octagon printing 1980

OCTAGON BOOKS
A DIVISION OF FARRAR, STRAUS & GIROUX, INC.
19 Union Square West
New York, N.Y. 10003

LIBRARY OF CONGRESS CATALOG CARD NUMBER: 65-16771
ISBN 0-374-92033-8

Manufactured by Braun-Brumfield, Inc.
Ann Arbor, Michigan
Printed in the United States of America

PREFACE

No comprehensive study of Turgot's life and administration has appeared in English during the last forty years. Of the nineteenth-century works upon him in our language none is really of great value to-day. Hodgson's *Turgot : his Life, Times and Opinions* (1870) was written long before Foncin brought to light many important sources for his scholarly narrative, *Essai sur le ministère de Turgot*, which was published in 1887. Morley's chapter in the *Critical Miscellanies, Second Series*, 1877, gives a fairly full account of Turgot's early years and a résumé of his philosophical and economic thought ; and it also devotes a section to Turgot as intendant, though it does not, apparently, draw upon the valuable material in d'Hugues's excellent monograph, *L'Essai sur l'administration de Turgot dans la généralité de Limoges*, which had appeared in 1859. By far the most satisfactory work on Turgot in English is Stephens, *The Life and Writings of Turgot* (1895), which, in as far as it is concerned with his political career and administration as Comptroller-General, is based mainly on Foncin's *Essai*. From that source it reproduces a number of inaccuracies ; yet what makes it more out of date is the standpoint from which it is written—that of the nineteenth-century liberal's veneration for one of the founders of his creed. It tends, too, to simplify the political, administrative, and economic history of Turgot's age.

During the present century our knowledge of Turgot's life and work has grown considerably ; and the output of literature on the *ancien régime* has been so great that the background to a new biography must necessarily take a different form from that of earlier studies. The present century, too, has given us a new edition of Turgot's works—Gustave Schelle's *Œuvres de Turgot* in five large volumes (1913–1923), containing not only the Editor's own researches but also those of scholars who worked before him—d'Hugues, Foncin, Neymarck, Lafarge, and others. Needless to say this edition (see Bibliographical Note on page 307), which leaves nothing to be desired, can never be superseded. A

v

few odd documents may yet be unearthed (my own small discoveries are mentioned in my Bibliography and Notes); but, it is safe to assume, there is nothing remaining to be revealed that can possibly call for any drastic revision of the facts of Turgot's life and work. My task, therefore, has been less one of collecting material first hand than of studying a vast and highly controversial literature and of giving my own interpretation of Turgot's career and the age in which he lived.

In this biography I have paid considerable attention to the general history of the *ancien régime*. I have done this in the belief that it is impossible to say precisely what Turgot attempted, accomplished, and failed to do, and what were the reasons for his failure, without describing in more detail than is usual in biographies some aspects of the economic and administrative history of the man's age and also some phases of its thought and politics. It is also my purpose—and this seems to me a very essential one in view of the misconceptions concerning Turgot's administration—to explain exactly what he did not attempt in order to define clearly what he actually attempted. The fulfilment of this aim necessitates, as I think my study will show, the devotion of much space to the general setting of his life and work. There is another reason for following such a course : when a man fails where no one could have succeeded, it goes without saying that the verdict must take into account not only the shortcomings of the man himself but also the conditions of his environment that frustrate him. But this is not all. As I hope to show in my conclusions upon his political career and administration (pages 266–72), the many failings usually ascribed to him as a statesman (most, though not all, of which are admittedly true) did not contribute either to his disgrace or to the defeat of his programme of reform. For all these reasons, then, this biography becomes, as far as space allows, a general work upon the *ancien régime*.

As such, although it must lack the completeness of an outline history, it may, perhaps, in describing certain aspects of the *ancien régime* in detail, be able to bring out clearly a number of ideas which cannot be adequately stressed in a work of a purely general character. In Turgot's administration at Limoges we have an illustration of the system of government by intendants, and we may watch the French bureaucracy actually working in a province, its efforts constantly frustrated by other institutions ; we shall see, too, the fiscal machine in action ; and we may gather also some idea of the problems of government in studying the economic conditions in a particular region, which, though admittedly more backward and poverty-stricken than many, is nevertheless fairly typical of a large part of France. When we come to speak of Turgot as Minister of State, we shall examine the working of the central bureaucracy, and we shall see this government in relation to the politics of the age : the party struggles at the Court, the conflicts between the Crown and Parlements, the religious quarrels, and the efforts of the liberals of the age to bring about changes in the administration of the realm. In other words, a study of Turgot's career affords the opportunity of bringing together upon a scene limited in extent and in duration the economic and political forces of the age, the administrative machinery in its social setting, the new ideas and ancient prejudices, and of watching their interplay far more closely than is possible in a panoramic survey. It may be objected that to do this is to single out an exceptional man and unusual events. The reply must be that the *ancien régime* displayed one of its chief characteristics in its resistance to the man who attempted to reform it.

Much indeed of what is true of the *ancien régime* during the years 1774–1776 holds good again in 1789. To some extent, therefore, this book touches upon and may suggest answers to those vexed questions concerning the origins of Revolutionary thought, the actual part played by ideas in bringing about the Revolution, and also the historical processes issuing in that great upheaval. But although I have necessarily assumed answers to these problems, I have not attempted any proof of my assumptions, first because space does not permit, and secondly because I do not hold any version of that view which simplifies the origins of the Revolution by apportioning them arithmetically among economic, political, ideological and personal causes. Believing that historical events may often come about independently of economic forces and widely held ideas, and that one incident may lead casually to another ; convinced also that prevalent ideas may one day have no power to issue in action and the next may be so organized as to assail the existing order ; and persuaded that the Revolution might have broken out in 1776 and, in the form we know it, might never have occurred, I take it that although a study of the *ancien régime* in Turgot's day may throw light upon that event it cannot explain it, since much of the explanation must lie in the happenings between 1776 and 1789. For these same reasons, I have also refrained from attempting to estimate Turgot's share in preparing the Revolution. In the chapter upon his economic and philosophical thought I have indeed asserted that his writings, though obviously in themselves a part of Revolutionary thought, contributed very little, if at all, to the formation of Revolutionary opinion, and I have also taken the view that although certain widely held ideas may have played a considerable part in Revolutionary politics the growth of those ideas was not the simple product of a few literary works. I have also argued that Turgot's programme of reform met with the approval of the masses ; but I have not assumed that he therefore converted the multitude to Revolutionary thinking or that he necessarily increased the probability of Revolution. In fact I hold that he accomplished neither the one nor the other.

I first began this study under the supervision of Mr. Arthur Jones, M.A., Reader in History and Head of the Department of History at Birkbeck College, London. I must thank him sincerely for the interest that he has taken in my work and for the help that he has given me. I have also to express my gratitude to the Rev. J. M. Thompson, M.A., of Magdalen College, Oxford, who kindly read my first draft and who solved for me many difficulties, particularly a number concerning the arrangement of material. I should like to make it clear, however, that I alone am responsible for the views and statements contained in this book. For the Sketch Map on page 34 I am indebted to Mr. A. W. Harding, B.A., of Birkbeck College. I must also thank my wife, who has helped me at every stage in my work. Finally, I would like to acknowledge my debt to the Birkbeck College Publications Committee for generous assistance in the publication of this book.

DOUGLAS DAKIN

February, 1939

CONTENTS

ILLUSTRATIONS

TURGOT
AND THE *ANCIEN RÉGIME* IN FRANCE

CHAPTER I

EARLY YEARS, 1727–61

(1)

ONE day Mme Du Hausset was dining at the *Entresol* at Versailles, a suite of rooms then occupied by the celebrated economist, Doctor Quesnay, who enjoyed the patronage of Mme de Pompadour and the pleasant sinecure of physician in ordinary to Louis XV. The gathering was a large one, and among those present was a tall, well-proportioned, impressive young lawyer, a *maître des requêtes*. Mme Du Hausset had forgotten his title, but she remembered him as being the son of Michel-Étienne Turgot, the late *Prévôt des marchands* in the city of Paris. The general conversation ran upon administrative problems, and Mme Du Hausset paid little attention. But later there began a discussion upon the love of the French nation for their king. The young Turgot ventured an opinion. To his mind the love of the monarchy was really something more than a blind and superstitious veneration for a man and an office. And, strange as it may seem, his argument, which was generally appreciated for its subtlety, was the somewhat crude assertion that the adoration of the monarch derived from a memory of the great material benefits of kingly rule. He went on to explain himself more fully : France, Europe, even humanity at large owed their liberty to a king of France (whose name Mme Du Hausset could not remember). This king had established communes in the cities of his realm, had given a multitude of men a civil existence, and had freed them from the bonds of feudal authority. But in doing this he had been following his own self-interest ; he had wanted the support of the towns against over-mighty feudal subjects ; he had needed money to govern his kingdom ; and he had therefore compelled the burgesses to pay for their rights. But whatever the motive, the outcome was laudable. Out of self-interest accrued a good to humanity.

Here was a fashionable argument. Here was the brilliant thought of a young intellectual who had already foretold with confidence the secession of the English colonies in America.

1

Here was the voice of reason, which seemed to speak for reason
itself, and not for archaic, unreasonable assumptions. Here was
history, itself an oracle, and no longer a perplexing chronicle of
divine revelations. Here was a mode of thought which promised
to explain how the universe explained itself. Here, indeed, was
the language of a revolutionary.

But let Mme Du Hausset continue her story. From a discussion
of the French monarchy in general, Quesnay's guests went on to
consider particular kings of France. Finally they talked of
Louis XV. Again the young Turgot ventured an opinion. What
a pity it was, he remarked, that Louis XV lacked faith in his own
good sense, which he so frequently displayed in the Council
Chamber ! What a pity that he failed to place his confidence in a
prime minister approved by the nation ! These were mild words
for a revolutionary. But here again was the voice of reason, no
longer speaking for itself, but for tradition, which seemed so
reasonable. Here again was history's revelation: yet what was
revealed was not an untried form of government, but an ideal
picture of that which was known. Here again was the revolutionary
keeping true to the political heritage of his family. These sentiments were pleasing to Mme Du Hausset. And she, determined
that the King should hear such a profession of loyalty, asked
Quesnay to write down what Turgot had said. She showed the
paper to Mme de Pompadour, who brought it to the notice of the
King. Louis, who was reputed to know every noble house within
his kingdom, quickly recalled Turgot's family, and, appreciative
of the compliment that had been paid, remarked: ' C'est une
bonne race.' [1]

The comment was particularly apt. For generations the
Turgots had belonged to a group of families whose associations
with the monarchy had been especially close. It was not that
they had lived in idle elegance at Versailles, showing their devotion
in hollow phrases. Their loyalty found its expression in serving
those institutions that tended to enhance the monarchical authority.
By a tradition which began when Louis Turgot became a master of
requests under François I, the sons of the family had usually
found a career in the royal bureaucracy or, to speak more
accurately, in a branch of the legal profession which, having
particular administrative and extraordinary judicial duties to
perform, upheld the royal authority against the republican
principles of the legal corporations. The English analogy is not
a very close one: but the Turgots subscribed to the Baconian
view of the magistracy and looked upon the judges as lions beneath
the throne. For over two centuries they had aided the Crown in
its struggle against the claims of the courts to limit the King's
executive, legislative and judicial authority. Like Louis Turgot,

most of the subsequent Turgots became masters of requests. Originally these magistrates used to receive and hear petitions addressed to the King and, from mediaeval times onwards, had been attached rather to the Court than to those branches of the magistracy that in the thirteenth century had begun to form in fact, if not in theory, tribunals with little contact with the King.

It is no wonder, then, that Louis XV recalled the Turgots with the greatest satisfaction. It is still less to be wondered that the young Turgot revered the monarchy which his ancestors had served. Reason might have led him to other conclusions. History might have revealed to him a record of the irreparable crimes and follies of monarchical rule. But his mind did not run to political extravagance. Tradition was too strong. And his ideal was an enlightened monarchy ruling in the interests of the masses, unimpeded by aristocratic faction and legal conservatism. He would have agreed with Bodin (whom he and his contemporaries seem never to have read) that Venice had been the only tolerable republic, and he believed that where the King's will was limited by the mediaeval estates, there precisely was the rule of self-seeking aristocratic factions.

(2)

The Turgot family [2] had long been famous, but its early history is obscure. According to one story, it was of Scandinavian origin, having been founded by Togut, a Danish prince, long before Rollo settled with his warriors in Normandy. But another account, which is probably the true one, is that the family came originally from Scotland. One of the Turgots became Bishop of St. Andrews, almost certainly wrote that treasured chronicle, *The Life of Queen Margaret*,[3] and later attained the position of minister-in-chief to Malcolm III. What became of those ancestors who remained in that outlandish region will never be known. Nor is it certain who was the adventurous son to forsake his homeland to fight under the banner of the Norman dukes and to found a feudal dynasty in the north of France. All that is certain is that from the twelfth century onwards the Turgots were one of the most noted Norman families, and such they remained at the beginning of the modern ages.[4]

During the sixteenth century the Turgot family divided into several branches, and from that time onwards almost every generation sent sons into the King's service as masters of requests. Towards the end of that century and during the early years of the next these magistrates were often despatched to the provinces as intendants. Among them was Jacques Turgot, son of Antoine, the founder of the youngest branch, the Turgots of Saint-Clair.

He saw service in several provinces in turn (the intendant being at this time a special commissioner rather than a permanent governmental agent), and he was finally appointed to the intendance of Normandy. When, during the reign of Louis XIV, government by intendants became a regular system, it was only to be expected that members of the Turgot family should be called upon to take provincial office. One of them, Dominique Turgot de Sousmont, became intendant of Touraine, remaining there until his death at the early age of forty. His son, Jacques-Étienne Turgot, the grandfather of Anne-Robert, followed the same career, first as a master of requests, then as intendant of Metz in 1697, of Tours in 1704, and finally of Moulins in 1710. At that same time another Turgot, Marc-Antoine of Saint-Clair, was also an intendant, and it was he who succeeded his relative at Moulins in 1713. In all their *généralités* (or fiscal regions for which the intendants were responsible) these two Turgots left behind them a record of faithful service to the Crown. They did nothing outstanding. But they performed competently that multiplicity of administrative and judicial tasks by which the royal authority was gradually asserted in regions where for generations it had been ignored. They facilitated the movements of the armies, evoked cases from the feudal, municipal, and the older royal courts, built roads, made provisions against famine, and, like all other intendants, kept the newly-organized bureaucracy in Paris fully informed of the condition of the provinces.

Jacques-Étienne's son, Michel-Étienne Turgot, acquired much greater fame, not because he had greater gifts or because he was more assiduous, but because he held an office which brought him notoriety. First of all a master of requests, an employment which was now the stepping-stone to important posts in the bureaucracy, in 1729 he was appointed by the King to the highest administrative office in the city of Paris—that of *Prévôt des marchands*. Bougainville has recorded for us the man and his work in the *Éloge de Michel-Étienne Turgot*. Michel-Étienne was a benevolent and enlightened official. He showed always a deep concern for the poor of Paris, and during the disastrous famine of 1738, it was largely through his fearless and timely measures that the hungry masses were supplied with bread. He was the Hausmann of his day. He constructed the great sewer on the right bank of the Seine; he enlarged the Quai d'Horloge and connected it by a bridge with the opposite bank; and he caused to be erected the beautiful fountain that can be seen to-day in the rue Grenelle de Saint-Germain. It was he, too, who engaged an architect to begin a five-years' task of making a pictorial plan of Paris in twenty sections. The map is a noble and artistic work, and a social document of great value. A note upon it explaining the

purpose of the undertaking shows that Michel-Étienne wanted the
new Paris that was growing to take a pleasing shape, and not a
sprawling and untidy form.[5]
  Michel-Étienne retired from his office in Paris in 1740. But
to the day of his death he remained in the service of the King.
He was already a Councillor of State ; and, in recognition of his
great administrative work, he was made a president of the *Grand
Conseil*, a tribunal of monarchical partisans which at the King's
bidding often heard cases evoked from other chambers of the
Parlement of Paris. All the same, after 1740 he enjoyed the
leisure to devote attention to his private estates situated in a
region bounded by Caen, Falaise, Bayeux, and the Channel—a
part of Normandy known to-day as Calvados. His actual dwelling
was some little distance from his chief estates of Sousmont, at a
small village named Bons, where he held also the domains of
Mondeville and Brucourt. Not far from these properties was
situated the Château de Lantheuil, which, in Anne-Robert's time,
belonged to the elder branch of the Turgots of Saint-Clair. Here,
some time after his death, a great number of Turgot's papers, some
of which had been in the keeping of his great friend, the tragic
Malesherbes, were finally deposited ; and it was here that his
disciple and biographer Du Pont de Nemours, upon returning
from his exile in America, studied them when, from 1808 to 1811,
he published the *Oeuvres de Turgot*, in nine volumes.
  Michel-Étienne Turgot married a noble, engaging, and intellectual woman, Dame Magdelaine-Françoise Martineau, who
bore him one daughter and three brilliant sons. The daughter
married the Duc de Saint-Aignan. The eldest son became first
a master of requests and later a *président à mortier* (a senior judge
entitled to wear the mortar-board) of the Parlement of Paris.
The second son, the Chevalier Turgot, was a noted army officer
who, in recognition of his military services, was appointed
governor of Guyane. He was a botanist of great reputation, and a
number of his letters to da Costa are preserved in the British
Museum.[6] The youngest son, Anne-Robert-Jacques, was born
in Paris on 10 May 1727.
  Their mother—at least this is the verdict of a later generation
which had read Rousseau's *Émile*—ruled her family firmly, almost
tyrannically, and certainly unwisely. From her, no doubt, two
of her children, the Duchesse de Saint-Aignan and Anne-Robert,
inherited their domineering characters. But their upbringing had
also given them, and especially Anne-Robert, a somewhat conflicting trait—that of excessive modesty and shyness. When
visitors called at the Turgots' house in Paris, the young Anne-
Robert would run away and hide ; and if ever by chance he was
taken unawares, he would sulk, his face hidden in the flounces of

his mother's skirts.[7] These two characteristics produced a curious effect. To those who hardly knew him his retiring disposition accentuated his inflexible nature and he appeared disdainful, cynical, and supercilious. Du Pont tells us that he involuntarily concealed his benignant disposition. He had the habit of allowing a half-smile to steal across his face, which gave the impression that he was arrogant and overbearing. And although as he grew older this mannerism became less and less pronounced, his general appearance, his tall and well-proportioned figure, his piercing brown eyes, his massive forehead, his majestic features, the very poise of his head, a dignity like that of Roman statuary, all expressed the severer rather than the gentler parts of his character.[8] But his was a kind of arrogance which disappeared in the company of those who came to know him well. No longer shy, he was no longer cold and distant: much more sure of himself, he was less overbearing, and at times even gracious. And when he spoke, his voice expressed his kindly disposition, his utmost sincerity, and his benevolent mind. On occasions, however, he could speak with fire and fervour, as on that when he was a member of the tribunal that heard the appeal against the sentence of the Parlement upon the Protestant, Calas, who had been condemned to be broken on the wheel. But usually he preferred to make his influence felt rather by the quiet impelling logic of his argument than by the effusions and the passion of the orator. On lighter topics he conversed naturally and clearly, but on more serious subjects he had so much to say and so many niceties to expound that he was difficult to follow. He, himself, was rarely satisfied with his words in public and, as Du Pont informs us, ' he loved rather to write, for then he was sure of expressing the whole range of his thought '. [9] Yet he never found it easy to speak the language of reason to those who argued from other basic assumptions or to those of little, shallow minds. ' It is as well to turn to first principles '—this is a phrase which appears in many of his writings. And so he wrote always fearing that no one would fully understand him, and always determined that no one should contradict him. He had the annoying habit of answering arguments in advance; he had a condescending turn of phrase; he laboured the point; he was dogmatic, always serious, and sometimes ponderous. He could never believe that he was in the wrong: and he had no patience with those who were frivolous and unreflecting.[10] The Abbé de Véri, a friend of his student days and confidant at the time when he was minister of state, records that he was almost incapable of gentle argument. He had views on every topic, and these he aired whenever the occasion presented itself. Véri tells a story which is typical. Returning to Paris a few days after Turgot had been dismissed from the ministry, Véri found him helping his successor, Clugny, to pick up the threads of administration. His motive was the best in the world, for he knew from experience the difficulties confronting a successor. But when Véri entered the room, he found Turgot holding forth on the only methods of stamping out the cattle plague. Véri smiled to himself: it seemed as though Turgot were still Comptroller-General, and Clugny a mere subordinate in the Finances. Later, Véri remarked on this; but Turgot could see nothing incongruous in the situation; and he was quite prepared to defend himself by saying the same things again for the Abbé de Véri's benefit.[11]

Nature, perhaps, had been a little whimsical in thus fashioning a mind which proclaimed itself the product of reason. And it seemed most careless that a man who—as Malesherbes once said—was endowed with the heart of a l'Hôpital and the head of a Bacon, should lack the full armoury of the politician of his age—the social graces, the courtly smile, a way with mistresses, and the gift of turning intrigue to his purpose. But perhaps it mattered little in the long run. The language of reason must usually sound detestable to those who do not want to hear it. And reasonable measures, when they involve an attack upon vested interest, inevitably cause an uproar, no matter who attempts to introduce them. Judged by the ordinary standards of the age, Turgot was a clumsy politician. Yet he was never so maladroit as is commonly assumed. At times he used the existing political weapons tolerably well, with very little effort and with no enthusiasm. But as these were obviously inadequate to his purpose, he would not have profited by employing them more often. A wit once said that Turgot did good things badly. It could hardly have been otherwise. What is surprising is that the administrative and political institutions did not curb him more, that he did not remain a thinker only, saying what ought to be, perhaps what must be. It is also remarkable that a man who thought so deeply never lost himself in a world of his own making and never came to love ideas for their own sake alone.

(3)

Turgot's early schooldays were passed at the Collège Duplessis in Paris.[12] Later he entered the Collège de Bourgogne. This institution introduced him at an early age to modes of thought not then current in the Schools: one of its most gifted teachers, the Abbé Sigorgne, had displaced the *Vortices* of Descartes by Newtonian physics, and, owing to his influence, the sensational philosophy of Locke was systematically studied. Turgot's mastery of these two English thinkers was amazingly rapid and thorough, and it was while he studied under Sigorgne that the general scaffolding of his thought was constructed. In his spare time he read widely. Voltaire was his favourite, but he probably found Montesquieu, though less entertaining, much more stimulating. He already displayed a mind in which all branches of knowledge were quietly and easily finding their place. Morellet, a fellow-student, wrote of him at this time: 'The dominant features of his mind were penetration, which enabled him to detect relations among ideas seemingly unconnected, and a range of view which took them all in systematic order. . . . His memory was prodigious, and I have heard him repeat as many as one hundred and sixty lines of verse after he had heard them only twice, or even once.' [13]

His feats of memory once nearly earned for him an ignominious detention in the Bastille, where scribblers and prodigal sons who outraged unduly public decency and family honour were sent to reflect upon their misdeameanours. One of his fellow-students, the Abbé Bon, had composed impromptu a scurrilous poem on the occasion of Prince Edward Stuart's expulsion from France in 1748. The verse contained also a scathing reference to Mme de Pompadour. Turgot, hearing it only once, repeated it to Sigorgne, who wrote it down and later dictated it to his pupils and his friends. All the world came to know of it, and one sniggling wit passed it to another at the Court. This was the famous epigram for which at first the minister Maurepas was held responsible. Yet another man of great powers of memory, he loved to repeat the satirical verses that came his way. His part in circulating the Abbé Bon's poem was never proved. But all the same he was dismissed from the Marine and exiled to his estates at Ponchartrain, where he remained for a quarter of a century, a raconteur who was never surpassed, until with the accession of Louis XVI he was recalled to place at the disposal of the King his vast knowledge of people and parties. The police continued their search for the author of the libel. Sigorgne was traced and was sent to the Bastille ; but for a long while he refused to disclose that he had heard the verses from Turgot. Finally—probably at Turgot's own request—the truth was told, yet no action was taken against him, his family being too respectable and his own conduct up to that time much too decent to warrant sterner measures. The matter was allowed to drop. But the author, the Abbé Bon, was for ever on tenterhooks. He left Paris to hide himself at Bourges. He had—according to the Abbé de Véri, who tells this story—lost his poetic nerve ; he would not write another verse ; and when asked to recite, he would tremble all over, much to the amusement of his old fellow-students. Turgot was bolder. Some years later, greatly incensed at the Treaty of Versailles of 1756, he composed and circulated a pointed satire on the negotiator, Cardinal Bernis.[14]

Here, however, ends our record of Turgot's frivolities and indiscretions. It is only by chance—only because his friend the Abbé de Véri treasured good anecdotes—that these stories were recorded. Turgot's youth was serious, and the only excitement he deliberately sought was intellectual. Moreover he had to think carefully about a future. For a long time it had been the Turgots' intention that Anne-Robert should follow an ecclesiastical career, which in eighteenth-century France was the surest means of advancement for one whose fortune was small but whose family was influential. As long as his father lived, Anne-Robert could count upon a small income only, which was insufficient even for the upkeep of the establishment of a master of requests, and totally inadequate for that of an intendant. Turgot accepted a younger son's lot. He studied for the Church and, as Du Pont maintains, the choice was good, for he possessed those very qualities which would have assured him a high position.[15] Accordingly, in 1743, at the age of sixteen and a half, he entered the Séminaire de Saint-Sulpice, where he applied himself seriously to the study of theology. So rapid was his mastery of this subject that he was allowed to submit his thesis for the degree of bachelor at an earlier age than was usually the custom. The subject of the thesis is not known ; but according to a letter which Michel-Étienne wrote to his second son, the Chevalier Turgot, the dissertation, lasting fully five hours, was delivered in one of the large halls of the Sorbonne, in the presence of the Archbishops of Paris and Tours, of the Doctors of the Sorbonne, and of many of the representatives of the clergy, who were holding an assembly in the city. The next day the Archbishop of Tours met the King at Versailles and informed him that he had never in his life heard so brilliant an oration for the degree of bachelor.[16]

In view of his distinguished career at Saint-Sulpice, Turgot was admitted to the Sorbonne as a resident student in June 1749 to read for his *licence*. This famous institution was the theological faculty of the University of Paris ; it was organized as a residential college, with thirty-six suites of rooms, its own chapel, its own library, and its own gardens. Its total membership was about one hundred, including regular and secular clergy. As a number of the latter were provincial *curés*, performing parochial duties outside Paris, the vacant rooms were allotted to theological students, ten to twelve of them being in residence at a time. Among Turgot's contemporaries were the Abbés de Cicé, de Boisgelin, de Brienne, Morellet, and de Véri. He easily surpassed them all in academic study. Only six months after his admission he was elected a *prieur*, an honour generally awarded to distinguished young scholars or to sons of distinguished parents. The *prieurs* presided in turn over the assemblies of theological students, and it was one of their duties on those occasions to pronounce an address in Latin. Two of the *discours* which Turgot delivered in 1750 have been preserved, the first entitled *Les Avantages que l'établissement du christianisme a procurés au genre humain*, the second *Tableau philosophique des progrès successifs de l'esprit humain*.[17] They were brilliant orations : they reveal a mind which had mastered itself and which knew the way that it was striking. Turgot had proclaimed himself an apostle of progress. History was no longer a series of patterns, but a bold design revealing its shape.

The Sorbonne was, at this time, notorious for its censorship of liberal writings, but it permitted an extraordinary degree of freedom to its members, so that Turgot and his fellow-students were able to extend their studies beyond the narrow bounds of the prescribed curriculum. Already in 1748 at Saint-Sulpice he had composed a reply to Buffon's theory of cosmic and geological changes, basing his arguments upon Newtonian physics.[18] His first economic writing dates also from this time, consisting of a long letter written to the Abbé de Cicé refuting a pamphlet published some twenty years earlier by the Abbé Terrasson, who upheld John Law's policy of issuing paper money during the Regency. To the argument that money was the mere sign of wealth, Turgot replied that money was itself a part of wealth, becoming the medium of exchange because its comparatively small bulk enabled it to be carried about and stored conveniently.[19] In a note upon this treatise, Du Pont points out the moral that, had the members of the Constituent Assembly taken to heart this truth propounded by Turgot, France would have been saved from the economic disasters which accompanied the excessive issue of *assignats* during the Revolution.[20]

It was also while he was in residence at the Sorbonne that Turgot planned a vast history of the progress of humanity. Only the copious notes of a few sections of this project survive, but from them it is possible to see that he contemplated the study of all branches of human knowledge : religion, mathematics, physics, economics, sociology, psychology, and language. His studies at the Sorbonne he arranged with a view to collecting materials for this work, and the few writings from this period of his life are obviously the outcome of this undertaking.[21]   In 1750 he composed a long critique of Maupertuis' *Réflexions philosophiques sur l'origine des langues* ;[22] a refutation of the philosophy of Bishop Berkeley ;[23] and a discourse entitled *Recherches sur les causes de la décadence du goût dans les arts et les lumières dans les sciences*,[24] which he delivered to the Académie de Soissons. His reading, moreover, extended to seven languages—Greek,

Latin, Hebrew, Spanish, German, Italian, and English, the last three of which he spoke fluently.[25] He made translations from all these languages, and—a rare accomplishment in those days— he translated easily from English into German and from German into English. He began also the study of Greek and Latin versification, a pursuit which later became the occupation of his few hours of leisure and the subject of many letters which he wrote to Caillard, who was for a short time his secretary. From this period date several of his translations from the classics— fragments of Homer, Ovid, Cicero, and Horace, the *Eclogues* of Virgil, and the whole of the fourth book of the *Aeneid*, which he rendered into non-rhyming hexameters. He wrote French verse, too, and, using alternate long and short syllables, he endeavoured to reproduce the melody and cadences of the classics.

Early in 1751, when nearly twenty-four years of age, he suddenly announced his intention of abandoning an ecclesiastical career and of entering the service of the Crown. Du Pont holds that his fellow-students endeavoured to persuade him to remain with the Church, and in the *Mémoires* reports the following dialogue :

Abbé de Cicé : ' We all think that you are about to act in a way quite at variance with your interest and with your remarkably good sense. You are the youngest son of a Norman House, and consequently you are poor. The magistracy requires a considerable fortune, without which you cannot be considered for advancement. Your father has a great reputation ; your relations have influence. If you abide by the career that they have assigned you, you are certain to obtain excellent livings, and to be a bishop early on in life. . . . Then your fine dreams of administrative power may be realized, and, without ceasing to be a churchman, you may be an administrator at your leisure. . . . If, however, you shut the door against yourself . . . you will be doomed to try cases at law ; you will waste in petty, private business a genius fit to deal with public affairs of the highest moment.'

Abbé Turgot : ' I am deeply touched by your zeal on my behalf. . . . In what you say there is much truth. Take to yourselves the counsel you offer me, since you can follow it. I respect you all, but I cannot fully appreciate your view of this matter. As for me, I cannot possibly resign myself to wear, all my life, a mask over my face.' [26]

Exactly at what period in his life he came to this decision, it is impossible to say, for there is no record of his motives, and never during his later years did he reflect upon this event. Such lack of evidence, however, is in itself significant and need occasion no surprise, for his decision, although momentous in its results, was not at all unusual, except for the sense in which his friends discussed it : he had abandoned a career in which he might have reached the highest office for one in which he was handicapped by lack of means. In all probability, from the very beginning his attitude to the career chosen by his family was neither one of fervour nor of apathy, and, like the majority of the clergy of the *ancien régime*, he was ready to enter the Church as a matter of course, to utilize its facilities for advancement, and to secure a standing in society which would have been denied him had he remained a provincial *seigneur* managing his private estates and occupying some inferior office in the magistracy. According to the standards of the age, there was nothing hypocritical in his position. In the eighteenth century, the Church both in France and England attracted men of many types : there were those who felt the deeper emotions of religious experience ; there were place-hunters who found satisfaction for their worldly and their social needs ; and finally there were intellectuals who enjoyed the opportunity and security afforded for academic study. It was to this last class that Turgot and his fellow-students at the Sorbonne belonged. Such valuable intellectual gifts as he possessed—the inquisitive and powerful mind, the passion for systematic and synthetic thought, the yearning to relate all facts and ideas with ultimate principles— these may lead men to the study of theology, but at the same time encourage them to transcend its narrow bounds. ' My dear Abbé,' Turgot used to say to Morellet, ' it is only we, who have studied for our *licence* who know how to reason accurately.' [27]

It is unnecessary, then, to postulate any deep or agonizing mental conflict to explain Turgot's decision to seek advancement outside the Church. Although he had found an outlet for his intellectual gifts in his studies at the Sorbonne, it is highly probable that from the beginning he would actually have preferred to follow in the footsteps of his father and his eldest brother. Du Puy, who wrote the official *Éloge de Turgot*, and who probably consulted the family, states that as early as 1744 Anne-Robert wrote to his father making the tentative suggestion that he should enter the administration. Michel-Étienne advised him to continue his studies, to avoid making irrevocable vows, and to leave the decision until a later time.[28] This advice he readily followed. And it was not so much a dislike for an ecclesiastical career, as an intense passion for administrative office which prompted him ultimately to leave the Church. ' He believed then,' says Du Pont, ' and he continued to believe for a long while, . . . that administrative office offered the best means of serving his country and humanity.' [29] The date of his announcement to leave the Sorbonne is highly significant ; his decision was not made public until February 1751, a few days after his father's death, when he inherited an income from the family estates.[30]

(4)

Turgot's career as a magistrate [31] began in January 1752 with his appointment as a substitute attorney-general; in the following December he became a Councillor in the Parlement of Paris; in March 1753, by special dispensation from the law which required as a qualification three years' service in a superior court, he bought the office of master of requests, thus following family tradition and entering a particular branch of the high magistracy which, as we have seen, involved administrative as well as legal duties. In this office he quickly earned the reputation of an impartial and painstaking magistrate. Soon after taking up his duties he was employed in proceedings against a subordinate official of the *contrôle général* and, being convinced of the defendant's innocence, he had the case adjourned in order that further evidence might be produced. The delay proved to be considerable. Meanwhile the accused could not receive the salary from his office. Turgot not only secured the man's acquittal, but paid out of his own pocket the loss that his client had sustained; and when a fellow-magistrate complimented him upon his action, his reply was that his was not a gesture of generosity, but one of justice.[32]

Turgot's entry into the magistracy coincided with one phase of that fierce struggle between the Crown and the Parlements which was renewed early in the century and which lasted up to the outbreak of the Revolution—a struggle which was the constitutional outcome of the religious conflicts of Jesuits and Gallicans, of Molinists and Jansenists. From 1746 onwards the French bishops, who adhered to the Bull *Unigenitus*, issued orders to their clergy to refuse the sacraments to those who were suspected of Jansenism, and also to those who were unable to produce evidence that they had made adequate confession to a priest subscribing to the constitution embodied in the Bull. That same year the Parlement of Paris instituted proceedings against a priest who had refused the last rites to a Jansenist named Coffin. Again, in 1752 the Parlement ordered Bouettin, *curé* of Saint-Étienne-du-Mont, to pay a fine and threatened to confiscate his effects if he persisted in his refusal to administer communion to an aged Jansenist priest, named Lemère. The King's Council overruled this judgement, and Lemère died without having heard the last offices of the Church. Ten thousand people attended his funeral, and the Parlement took the occasion of this popular demonstration to order the arrest of the offending *curé* and to take proceedings against numerous other clergy who had complied with the instructions issued by their bishops.

On 22 February 1753 Louis XV addressed to the Parlement of Paris letters patent by which he evoked to the King's Council all affairs relative to the sacraments. These the magistrates refused to register, and replied to the King with their famous remonstrances of April 1753, in which they claimed once more to be the sole depository of law, drawing that distinction, so familiar in legal history, between their constant loyalty to the institution of the monarchy and their obligation to oppose the personal aberrations of the monarch. Upon the second refusal on the part of the magistrates to register the letters patent, the presidents and the councillors of the *Chambres des requêtes* and of the *Chambres des enquêtes* were exiled, some to their domains, some to specified towns, and others to Mont-Saint-Michel, the Château de Ham, the Pierre-Encise, and to the island of Sainte-Marguerite. At first the *Grand' Chambre* was spared, but when its members had for a second time declared their sympathy with the exiles, it, too, was ordered to leave Paris and to remain at Pontoise until further notice. The remaining central courts, the *Châtelet*, the *Cour des aides* of Paris, and the *Chambre des comptes*, addressed congratulatory messages to the *Grand' Chambre* upon its defiance of the King, and the provincial Parlements took up the struggle against the Church, that of Rouen going so far as to condemn the Bishop of Évreux to pay a fine of 6,000 *livres* for having instructed his clergy to refuse the sacraments to all suspected Jansenists.

During the exile of the Parlement of Paris the Government organized a special tribunal known as the *Chambre Royale*, composed of eighteen councillors of state and forty masters of requests. This court sat at the Louvre; it was divided into two chambers, the one dealing with civil and the other with criminal cases. But the experiment was short-lived; for, although the former tribunal worked successfully, the latter proved a failure. As, moreover, the Government feared that a foreign war might break out at any moment, and as consequently an increase of taxation might be necessary, it was thought advisable to recall the Parlement, and in October 1754 a royal declaration was issued to that effect, with the proviso that the magistracy should maintain silence on all matters pertaining to the Church. This condition was not observed, and during the next year the Parlement of Paris, the provincial Parlements, and many of the inferior courts instituted proceedings against the Ultramontanes, imposed fines upon the lesser clergy who complied with the instructions of their bishops, and distrained upon the temporal effects of a number of offending prelates.[33]

The outcome of this struggle does not concern us here,[34] but

the conflict deserves mention, since Turgot was one of those
forty masters of requests who served upon the *Chambre Royale*.
His action on this occasion gave rise to a life-long feud with the
high magistracy of France. Twenty years later the Parlement
of Paris recalled the incident and, according to Condorcet, prevented his appointment to the office of *président à mortier*.[35]
The whole incident, particularly Turgot's willingness to serve
upon the *Chambre Royale*, requires some explanation, since at
first sight it would appear that in order to find favour with the
King and Ministry, he was prepared to support the intolerant
Ultramontanes in their struggle with the Jansenists. The matter,
however, is not so simple. Turgot believed in toleration ; already
he had expressed himself convincingly in its favour. ' No
religion ', he wrote, ' has the right to any other protection than
that of its liberty. . . . If a State chooses a religion, it is because
it is useful, and not because it is infallible. . . . What offends
conscience is punishable only because it violates the public
order.' [36] But, by serving upon the *Chambre Royale*, he in no
way acted at variance with his principles, for the Gallicans, the
Jansenists, and the Parlements were all as intolerant as the higher
clergy. Ever since 1732 the Gallican clergy, supported by the
Parlements, had endeavoured to suppress the Protestant congregations that, under the ministry of Fleury, had enjoyed
immunity from persecution. Men had been sent to the galleys,
women had been imprisoned, and their children had been placed
in convents to be instructed in the Catholic faith. Therefore,
all things considered, the struggle that had resulted in the exile
of the Parlement was not one for religious liberty, but one of
contending factions for the right to persecute. Hence it was
that Turgot's decision to serve upon the *Chambre Royale* was
made upon other considerations. In the remonstrances of 1753
he saw with alarm the extravagant claims of a self-seeking magistracy to sovereign power within the State. He believed then—
and later he had frequent cause to express this belief in very
definite terms—that the courts should confine their activities
solely to the administration of the law. In serving upon the
Chambre Royale he was therefore acting in accordance with that
tradition of a group of families which gave their sons to the royal
administration ; he was following in the footsteps of his ancestors ;
and he was also acting in accordance with his faith in the absolute
monarchy of France, which alone of all the institutions in the
kingdom he considered at this time to be capable of enlightenment.

(5)

From March 1753 to August 1761 [37] Turgot held no other
office than that of master of requests, and, as the duties of this

position were not at all arduous, he enjoyed the facilities to continue the studies of his youth, and to take an active part in the intellectual life of Paris, which since the 'thirties was centred in the *salons*.[38]   While still in residence at the Sorbonne, Turgot with his friends Cicé and Morellet had visited frequently the *salon* at Mme de Graffigny's, where, Morellet tells us, his profound learning and his unassuming manner quickly won for him the respect of every one assembled there.   It was here, too, that he made his life-long friendship with Mlle de Ligniville, Mme de Graffigny's charming niece, familiarly known to the *salon* as ' Minette '.   In the outcome of this attachment (Turgot had not taken irrevocable vows) Morellet was perhaps a little disappointed. ' I was often astonished ', he wrote, ' that this friendship did not give rise to a true love-marriage, but, whatever were the causes of (Turgot's) excessive reserve, there remained always a tender affection of the one for the other.' [39]   No other writer of the time refers to the matter.   As a fact, Minette married the financier and philosopher, Helvétius, and Turgot remained a bachelor.

Another *salon* which Turgot visited frequently at this time was Mme de Geoffrin's, to which he had been introduced by the Abbé Morellet.[40]   It was here that he made the acquaintance of d'Alembert, Condorcet, Grimm, d'Holbach, and Mlle de Lespinasse, who later founded her own *salon* in the rue Saint-Dominique ;   here, too, he probably met David Hume and Edward Gibbon.   For Mme de Geoffrin's *salon*—and the same is true of those founded by Mlle de Lespinasse and by d'Holbach, ' the personal enemy of the Almighty ',—attracted especially the *philosophes* and the *encyclopédistes*, from whom Turgot ultimately dissociated himself because of their cynical, shallow, and atheistical doctrines.   ' I am not an encyclopaedist,' he is reported to have said, ' since I believe in God.' [41]   But he allowed himself to be persuaded by d'Alembert to contribute five articles to the *Encyclopédie* : *Etymologie*, *Existence*, and *Expansibilité* in 1756, *Foires et Marchés* and *Fondations* in 1757.   It had also been arranged that he should write upon *Mendicité*, *Inspecteurs*, *Hôpital*, and *Immaterialité* for 1759, but in the March of that year the Government, in deference to the attacks of the Parlement of Paris, prohibited the *Encyclopédie*, and although publication was actually continued, Turgot was not prepared to jeopardize his position in administration in supporting a group of writers with whom he had but little sympathy.[42]   He found much more in common with the *économistes*, or Physiocrats, who in 1757 began to meet regularly at Quesnay's rooms to hear the *Patriarche* expound his economic theory.   That very year Quesnay had contributed two articles to the *Encyclopédie*, the first *Fermiers*, and the other *Grains*.   He had not then published his more famous works, the *Analyse du Tableau économique* and the *Maximes générales du gouvernement économique d'un royaume agricole*, which did not appear until 1760. But already his ideas, though a little inconsistent here and there, were beautifully clear: he was teaching that land was the source of wealth, that all taxes fell in the long run upon the landowners, that capital must be allowed to flow freely back to the fields whence it came, and that the State, if it is to be prosperous, must tax in moderation. To these ideas Turgot was listening carefully and critically. At Quesnay's he sometimes gave his own opinions, as on that day when Mme Du Hausset heard him expressing his views upon the monarchy of France. And he made many acquaintances among those who attended the *meute des chiens*, as the court wit named the assembly at the *Entresol*. Here he encountered Mirabeau, that half-feudal, half-democratic character, *l'ami des hommes*, as he came to be known; the Abbé Baudeau, for a while editor of the *Journal de l'agriculture*, a physiocratic publication which the Government supported; Mercier de la Rivière, formerly intendant of Martinique; and later Du Pont, of whom Quesnay used to say, 'We must take care of this young man, for he will speak when we are dead.' Here, too, Turgot met Adam Smith, who was making his first visit to Paris as tutor to the young Duke of Buccleuch. According to Morellet, Turgot was profoundly impressed by the intellectual abilities and the conversation of the Scottish philosopher. Condorcet maintains that the two econonomists subsequently corresponded, but no trace of these letters has been found either in Scotland or in France.[43]

Different from these friendships formed with the followers of Quesnay were those which Turgot made with a few members of the administrative class, men who were content neither to confine themselves entirely to official duties nor to regard the existing régime as perfect and immutable. Soon after leaving the Sorbonne, Turgot had come to know Vincent de Gournay,[44] who was then an inspector of manufactures. Gournay was born at Saint-Malo in 1712, and at the age of seventeen was sent by his family to Cadiz for a commercial training. He became, not only a successful man of business, but also a profound student of economics, and in the course of his travels studied the commercial systems of most European countries, acquiring in particular an intimate knowledge of Dutch and English trade. In 1748, after inheriting the domain of Gournay, he retired from business and went to live in Paris. Soon afterwards, owing to the influence of the Minister Maurepas, he was appointed intendant of commerce, and it was not long before there had gathered round him a group of enlightened administrators which met at his house, a circle which included Malesherbes, the liberal magistrate who managed the business affairs of the *Encyclopédie*; Daniel Trudaine, then intendant of commerce, and Trudaine de Montigny, his son, who later became the chief official for the grain supplies of Paris. For Turgot, Gournay had a great affection, and the two would spend countless hours in discussion of economic problems. When from 1753 to 1756 he was occupied in making an official inspection of trade and manufactures in Bourgogne, Dauphiné, Lyonnais, Provence, Languedoc, Maine, Anjou, and Bretagne, he invited Turgot to accompany him in an unofficial capacity. And so for the greater part of three years Turgot assisted Gournay in inquiring into the conditions of trade and industry and in hearing the complaints of industrialists and merchants. The experience was extremely valuable in every way. When later he began to frequent Quesnay's circle, which too often neglected problems of industry, he had the means of avoiding a number of Quesnay's extravagances and—what was more important—of building economic theory on a firm rock of fact.[45] The result was that his economic thought was much more profound than that of his contemporaries who were less informed.

Shortly upon returning, Gournay fell ill and after long suffering died in 1759. Marmontel, wishing to write a memoir of Gournay's life, asked Turgot for notes upon his master's work and doctrines. A few days later Turgot had complied with the request. He had composed an economic treatise expounding briefly and clearly the free-trade opinions he had heard from Gournay during their eight years' friendship. This was the work which in 1808 Du Pont published under the title of *Éloge de Gournay*. Along with the *Réflexions sur la formation et la distribution des richesses*—a short treatise hurriedly written in 1766—it provides the general outlines of Turgot's economic theories.[46] This later work marks no advance upon, and no change in, those ideas that he held in 1759. He could have written the *Réflexions* just as readily in that year as seven years later. Moreover, in neither treatise was he expressing the full range of his opinions. In the *Éloge* he was merely giving a graphic summary of Gournay's teaching: in the *Réflexions*, within the compass of one hundred paragraphs, he was merely composing a simple text-book. He was greatly surprised when this trivial effort acquired European fame. 'That morsel', he explained to Dr. Tucker, 'was written for the instruction of two Chinese who are staying in our country.'[47] These were Ko and Yang, whom the Jesuits had brought to France to educate, and whom the Physiocrats had made it their business to interest in economic doctrine. When they returned to China they were given pensions on the understanding that they should correspond with Bertin, the Minister. As a parting gift Turgot gave them books. He also furnished them with a list of over fifty questions on the economic and social conditions of their country. The *Réflexions* was intended as an explanation of the theories upon which these were based and as a clue to providing relevant answers.

Up to the time when Turgot hurriedly composed the *Éloge de Gournay* he had published very little.[48] Apart from the articles in the *Encyclopédie* he had given to the world only one [49] of his works, *Questions importantes sur le commerce* (1755), which was a translation with notes of Dr. Tucker's *Reflections on the Expediency of a Law for the Naturalization of Foreign Protestants* (1751-2). The remainder of his writings were fragments upon a variety of topics in the form of letters, essays, and rough outlines for larger works.[50] His *magnum opus*, that history of human progress, had not been written. For he had taken all knowledge to be his province and, always learning, he was writing only as a means towards those vast contemplative ends. Therefore his early compositions were mere flashes of his brilliant thought: they do not reveal the whole mind, but merely the directions which it was striking. They do indeed tell us much, and Condorcet, speaking of the *Discours* of 1750, pertinently comments, ' One can find in them, so to speak, his intellectual beliefs in their entirety, and it would seem that his thinking and experience of later times have only developed and strengthened them the more '.[51] Grimm, too, had noticed how very little basic difference there was between Turgot's philosophical ideas when he was at the seminary and those which he held when he became Comptroller-General.[52] But those early writings (and this is true also of a number of his later works) do not fully reveal the true depths and the rare quality of his thought. Voltaire, after meeting him for the first time at Ferney in 1760, wrote to d'Alembert, ' I did not know he had written the article *Existence*. He is even better than his article. I have scarcely seen a man more lovable or better informed.' [53] He was better than all his writings. But how much better it was impossible to tell—impossible until in the years that followed he began to write his *magnum opus*, not, however, as he had dreamed of it and planned it, but in official correspondence—in lengthy footnotes, as it were, to his more general compositions. This was a work, as Du Pont tells us, which would have filled three ordinary life-times. And yet it was written during the course of a strenuous life of public service, much of it after a hard day's riding, sometimes at the abominable country inns at which he was staying. In it he reveals the true range and quality of his thought—his thought in action.

CHAPTER II

INTENDANT OF LIMOGES: THE MONARCHY AND THE BUREAUCRACY

(1)

In 1760, shortly after returning from a tour of Switzerland and the French Alps, Turgot arranged to spend a few months with La Michodière, the intendant at Lyon. It was understood that he should give assistance in making a statistical survey of the *généralité*, and that he should also have the opportunity to acquire experience of provincial government. While still serving this apprenticeship he was seeking employment in the administration. In April 1760 he applied for the intendance of Grenoble. ' I take the liberty ', he wrote to Choiseul, ' to ask you to propose me to the King for this intendance. I am the senior master of requests who is without office, and I may say that I have worked as hard as any not only upon commissions of the Council, but also in acquiring useful experience for the career for which I am destined.' [1] But he had no influence with Choiseul. A little later he asked for the intendance of Bretagne, but this was an office usually reserved for older men who had spent their best years elsewhere, for, as Bretagne was a *pays d'états*, the intendant escaped the arduous task of levying royal taxation. Early in 1761 Turgot was a candidate for the post of *Prévôt des marchands* at Lyon. His experience with La Michodière, and also the knowledge gained when he accompanied Gournay upon his tour, had rendered him admirably fitted for this employment. But, as on previous occasions, Choiseul replied that he was too young for such responsibilities. To Voltaire, who had come to take a great interest in his career, he complained : ' M. Choiseul maintains that to fill such an important office I must go back to school for several years.' Actually, he was nearly thirty-four years old : most men received their commissions at a much earlier age. But he had not long to wait. Pajot de Marcheval was appointed to Grenoble, and Turgot was offered the vacancy at Limoges.

This intendance was generally considered as a starting-point, and most intendants of Limoges left after a few years for other,

20

more congenial, and more remunerative positions. Turgot's commission was issued on 8 August 1761. He entered Limoges a disappointed man. He was parted from his friends—destined to live in an outlandish province, one of the most backward in the whole of France, among a boorish race of peasants and among a poverty-stricken and uncouth nobility who had been accustomed to regard the intendance as a country club where they went to drink and gamble. ' I have the misfortune ', he wrote to Voltaire shortly after receiving his commission, ' to be an intendant. I say the misfortune, for in this age of quarrels and remonstrances, there is happiness only in living the philosophic life among one's books and one's friends.' Voltaire replied, ' You are going, then, to win the hearts and the purses of the Limousins ! . . . I believe that an intendant is the only person who can be useful. Can he not have the highways repaired, the fields cultivated, the marshes drained, and can he not encourage manufactures ? ' [2] True, he could do all these things. But to build the highways he had to impose the *corvées* on his people ; the few acres he reclaimed from waste and fen could never make good the grave deficiency of food ; and the manufactures he encouraged the masses could not buy. For he had to take their hard-earned money. Turgot was right, though perhaps at the time not altogether serious. He was later to learn how truly he had spoken. After fifteen years in the service of the monarchy, he was to spend a brief retirement among books and savants, disillusioned, perfectly happy, still optimistic, but still deceived, for he believed that reason, by its mere quality, by being what it was, would ultimately conquer calmly the minds of man.

(2)

The monarchy that Turgot served, although to all outward appearances a Leviathan, was, from a more critical point of view, limited by its environment, by surviving institutions, and by the social habits of the age.[3] Monarchical theories, the outlines of monarchical administration—indeed, the cursory surveys of all types of constitutions—are frequently misleading in their simplicity. It is a commonplace, of course, that in democratic countries, much more important than the mere mechanisms of government are those less easily definable political influences—the nature of judicial bodies, the traditions and habits of the civil service, the methods and ethics of party organization, the power of newspapers and of moneyed interests. In past ages the subtle impulses imparted by Society at large to the mechanism of government were just as vital.[4] From the day when Clovis had been crowned by St. Remi, through all the changing ages, the French monarchy had derived at once its grandeur and its weak-

ness from Society. Those very forces that raised the kingship to
its proud position, prescribed vaguely, but none the less effectively,
the limits to the kingly power. The holy oil from the sacred phial
at Rheims had a two-fold significance : the King was divine, but
he was a servant of God, and therefore of the Church. The town
charter was never so much an act of authority as the price for the
support of the growing *bourgeoisie.* In more recent times a
moneyed aristocracy—the sixty Farmers-General, numerous other
financiers, and all their avidious underlings—had come to manage
the greater part of the State's finances. The credit of the
monarchy was in their keeping, and they often dictated conditions
to the Crown. Even more influential was the proud aristocracy
of birth, ranging from the Princes of the Blood to the poverty-
stricken provincial nobility whose ancestors of feudal times had so
frequently defied the King from their strongholds. In the later
seventeenth century the Crown, profiting from an economic
revolution which undermined their feudal power, had been able
to curb the violence of the nobles and to transform the higher ranks
into courtiers at Versailles, where, to use Taine's phrase, they
became the quintessence of everything exquisite. The lesser
nobles—the *hoberaux,* as they were called—once banded together
in powerful *clientèles,* thus lost their leaders and settled down to
enjoy the remnants of their feudal power, for some the rusty
ancestral sword being the only outward sign of their nobility.
But the siegneurs, in thus surrendering to the royal authority,
had made the King the figurehead of noble society, and had come
to look upon the organs of monarchy as existing exclusively for
their own advantage. The epigram of a genteel society had
replaced the sword of rougher ages ; public opinion at Versailles,
distorted and refracted a thousand times, a never-ending whisper,
now spoke with all the authority of feudal law and the commands
of God ; and the factions of the Court furtively fought the party
battle without oratory, sometimes without decency, often without
principles.

   When all things are considered, the parties at Versailles were not
so fundamentally different from those across the Channel at St.
James's. In both kingdoms an aristocracy, substantially
unanimous in basic ways of thinking, was endlessly divided on
secondary and usually trivial issues. In England, Whigs and
Tories—parties, or rather groups of parties, surviving the causes
they once served—formed in different combinations throughout
the eighteenth century, occasionally on religious issues, sometimes
on economic, frequently on no particular issue at all, but according
to personal allegiances and political self-interest. In France,
too, religion often determined parties : more frequently, however,
the factions simply determined themselves. Yet in both countries

there was never an interest—not even the Whigs in England—with the primary object of depriving the monarch of the royal authority. Rather, the factions first endeavoured to persuade the King to employ the royal power for their own advantage. Only when particularly disgruntled did the factions revive those time-worn mediaeval theories of limits to the royal prerogative. In doing this, however, they could never conceive of absolute limits to the Crown, any more than they could imagine an authority which was absolutely sovereign. And whatever the factions did—whether they concurred in a power being exercised in their interests or whether they opposed a king who was ignoring their demands— their fundamental assumption was always the same : the royal authority exists for a purpose, of which their own wants and desires were the most essential part.[5]

Those fundamental interests of the aristocracy were never seriously violated either in France or in England. They were always recognized, even though the King showed favour to one faction and dislike of another. Politics had ceased to be tempestuous ; and it was a light breeze that ruffled St. James's and Versailles. Whig lords might be republicans without ceasing to be aristocrats : Princes of the Blood might be democrats while attempting to revive the power of the greatest noble houses. Only on occasions, when the Church was in danger or when political adventurers called out the grain mobs or aroused the city 'prentices to action, did political intrigue lose its delicate patterns and assume a more romantic and bolder form. Usually Ministers rose and fell in response to the chatter of many tongues, and to a constant shifting of petty interests. No king could raise himself above contending parties. The more he tried, the more they made him the focus of their constant struggles.

It mattered little at the time that in France there was no Parliament like that in England. The checks to the French monarchy, when circumstances demanded them, were just as real as those imposed upon the royal will across the Channel, and they came invariably into play in all their subtle forms. Even the restrictions upon the power of the King which may be called constitutional seem to have been as effective in France as in England. It is too frequently assumed that the English Commons had come to control the royal expenditure. But in reality, not only were the systems of appropriation of supply and audit of accounts most perfunctory matters, but, as the King could influence the composition of the House, in effect the members were often voting sums of money from which they derived their own rewards. In France, on the other hand, an aristocracy of lawyers curtailed in a very definite way the powers of the King to extend taxation. While Turgot was at Limoges, two Comptrollers, Bertin and

d'Invau, who tried to impose a small tax on the privileged, fell
from power because the monarchy dared not risk a conflict with
the courts.[6]

This aristocracy of lawyers, the *noblesse de la robe*, stood at the
head of a vast legal profession ranging from the great magistrates
of the superior courts down to the petty judges, advocates, and
notaries who swarmed in the provinces and who made a hard-
earned, but nevertheless an adequate, livelihood at the expense of
the peasantry and smaller *bourgeoisie*. In the upper ranks the
magistrates formed a guild, or rather a series of corporations,
somewhat like the Inns of Court of seventeenth-century England,
and enjoyed considerable autonomy. During the eighteenth
century, though still preserving a caste-like character, the high
magisterial families mixed freely with those of the nobles of the
sword and also with those of the great financiers. Between all
these aristocracies there were frequent intermarriages. There
was, too, an institutional association between the magistracy and
the nobility. It was never so close as that in England, but the
Princes of the Blood and the Peers of France had the right to
assist at the superior tribunals, and a large number of the old
nobility made for themselves careers in the courts.

In all there were thirteen Parlements of France, the premier
court of Paris sitting in the capital, and the others (created at
different times) in the provinces. Each court may be defined as a
sovereign judicial body dispensing ultimate and appelate justice,
both criminal and civil, which was vested in the King. But
though such a definition is strictly accurate from the standpoint of
absolutist doctrines, it conveys a false impression, since it omits
all mention of their claims, their traditions, and their actions. As
early as the fourteenth century the Parlement of Paris was demanding the right to examine, to modify, and to reject the King's
decrees, asserting, like the Courts of Common Law and the Parliament in England, that the King must govern in accordance with
the fundamental law of which the Parlement itsc'f was the depository and custodian. During the second part of the eighteenth
century the conflict between the Crown and Parlements became
particularly serious. The magistrates not only voiced the discontent of lawyers who claimed for their profession a voice in the
affairs of government, but also championed the privileges and
immunities enjoyed by the nobles, the financiers, the *bourgeois*
investors in public stock, the office-holders, the towns, and also
the guilds. On occasions their legal conservatism coincided with
the prejudices of the peasantry and the urban working classes, and
this gave some credence to their claim to represent in the absence
of the States-General the opinion of the nation. Behind them,
too, was that great following of Jansenists who increased in

numbers throughout the century. Every religious demonstration, every grain riot in the *faubourgs*, brought credit and influence to the magistrates. Their claims were universal : upon all matters—taxation and economic regulation, public assistance and affairs of police, education and ecclesiastical discipline—they pretended to a supreme authority. Véri noted in his *Journal* : ' They knew how to employ the name of the public weal in all their acts of obstruction. . . . There was never a conflict in which the magistrates did not base their arguments upon the sanctity of fundamental laws, upon their zeal for the good of the people, upon the sacred duties of the magistrature, upon their loyalty to the King, their disinterested service and continual sacrifice—even at the times when their actions travestied all these good principles.' [7]

Alongside of the Parlements and the courts subordinate to them, the *sénéchaussées* and the *présidiaux*, were a series of financial tribunals, the *cours des aides* (three of them with an independent existence, the others being departments of the Parlements), the *bureaux des finances* and the *élections*. The *cours des aides* claimed a sovereign judgement in all affairs relative to the assessment and collection of impositions of mediaeval origin, the chief of which were the *taille*, the *octrois*, and the *aides*. During the seventeenth and early eighteenth centuries the monarchy and its agents had succeeded in curtailing considerably the financial administration of the *cours des aides*. Much of their administrative work, and also much of the judicial business connected with it, was withheld from them and allotted to the intendants, while taxes of more recent origin, the *capitation*, the *vingtième* and the *dixième*, were never allowed to come within their scope. The share of the *bureaux des finances* and of the *élections* in financial administration had been likewise reduced, though the *élus* (the petty officials of the *élections*) still retained much of their judicial work and continued to favour their friends, to make false statements, and to involve the wretched peasantry in lengthy, and consequently ruinous, litigation. But it is impossible to state in general terms the actual share that the officers of the *élections* enjoyed in financial administration, for, though they still possessed in theory considerable powers, it was the practice of the greater number of intendants to ignore, in varying degrees, their work, and often the findings of their courts.[8] Thus, a number of these officials who met at Bordeaux in 1789 complained that ' they had seen parishes and communities unjustly assessed, the wealthiest individuals taxed separately by the intendants and subdelegates at modest rates, the reports of their *chevauchées* (tours to ascertain the value of the growing crops) disregarded, their statistics of the farmers' losses ignored, the rebates . . . distributed by favour and caprice and the making of the rolls entrusted to agents who were without both character and probity '. In most *généralités*, the report continues, the intendants and their agents had virtually control of the administration of taxation.[9]

In nearly all branches of government the bureaucracy, strengthened and reorganized during the later seventeenth century, had encroached gradually upon the preserves of other institutions. The towns, for example, and the guilds, too, had been subjected in varying degrees to administrative tutelage, and the liberties of the provincial Estates had been curtailed. But though the monarchy might supervise these prescriptive authorities, and though it might withhold from them the newer forms of administrative business, it could not abolish them. For one thing, the bureaucracy itself was not sufficiently developed to take over all affairs of government. To have fashioned an engine of despotism appropriate to such a task would have required untold wealth upon the part of the monarchy. And it would have necessitated also a social revolution : for an office, whether in the Parlement, the *élection*, or the town, was a form of property as sacred and imprescriptible as that in land. It was easier for the monarchy of old-world France, as for governments of to-day, to develop new forms of administrative machinery than to eradicate the old. In the modern world the State may without difficulty multiply social services and economic regulations : it may subject older, and in their origin private social institutions to governmental supervision ; but it will find it almost impossible to extend its activities to the limits that logic and the common good demand when private property and wealth must be seriously violated. Similarly in eighteenth-century France : the bureaucracy could sometimes assume control of affairs formerly the concern of other institutions ; it could increase gradually the scope of its paternal rule ; it could take upon itself new tasks of government ; but all this it could accomplish only upon the understanding that it did not seriously infringe rights of property in offices and land. That is why the prescriptive powers in the kingdom retained their vigour, and that is why the royal authority, as expressed in its more recent creations, was continually in conflict with its more ancient institutions.

On two occasions in the eighteenth century the monarchy, with the backing of important interests at the Court, attacked the high magistracy of France. The first was in 1753, when the Parlement and other courts were exiled, the second in 1770, when Maupeou and his following, employing the wiles of the Du Barry, abolished the Parlements and organized a new system of justice.[10] But both times the Parlements were ultimately recalled—a shifting of the factions, the influence of the magistracy even when in exile, the clamours of a populace ignorantly following false leaders and interests, the power of financiers, the fears of the ministers, insinuating whispers to the King, all contributing to the reversion to more normal conditions.

(3)

Such were the limitations to the proud monarchy that Turgot now must serve in a remote and hilly province—several days' riding from the capital. But all has not been told. For the bureaucracy, which at first sight was so impressive, was never the powerful machine that de Tocqueville has imagined, only to denounce as a vicious tyranny. To all outward appearances it was indeed a masterpiece in centralization, coming into contact with every minute detail, teaching, for example, the peasant to sow his crops, permitting a parish to repair its steeple, imprisoning for a family its prodigal son, condemning to the galleys the unwary criminal and smuggler, and shutting up base scribblers in the Bastille. Says de Tocqueville : ' . . . the administration of the country was highly centralized, very powerful, prodigiously active. It was incessantly aiding, preventing, permitting. It had much to promise, much to give. . . . A single body or institution placed in the centre of the kingdom regulated the public administration of the whole country ; the same Minister (the Comptroller-General) directed all the central affairs of the kingdom : in each province a single government agent (the intendant) managed all the details . . .' [11] But this description is merely an outline of the form of government, and not a revelation of its inner working. A more critical examination will reveal that the pulse of government was often weak, fitful, and uneasy.

Even writers who have praised the intendants of the eighteenth century, both as a body and as individuals, emphasizing the benevolence of their work, eulogizing their humanitarianism and their enlightenment, have too frequently forgotten the limits to their powers, or rather they have failed to draw a distinction between their ceaseless activity in attacking a multiplicity of abuses singly and their constant frustration when more comprehensive and more drastic measures were attempted.[12] The very multiplicity of the intendant's duties, which had increased throughout the century, would have prevented him from executing large measures of reform even had the Central Government desired to introduce them. He was committed to a perpetual drudgery in administrative bad habits, to a wearisome tidying of endless lumber. He had to collect direct taxation under a system which was archaic, bizarre, wasteful of effort ; he had to rectify justice which so frequently miscarried ; he must promote the arts of agriculture among an ignorant, surly, and beggarly peasantry ; he was called upon to encourage industry and commerce to satisfy a Government whose economic wisdom was merely the time-worn prejudice of a mediaeval town. To all these duties he must add many more: he must make himself a continual busybody. Everything came within his scope—sanitation and public order, morality and poor relief, the recruiting and billeting of soldiers, military equipment, rations and transport, religious processions and the repair of churches, colleges and libraries, parochial and municipal finance. Indeed, it is difficult to mention any matter with which the intendant was not in some degree concerned. Even in the administration of indirect taxation, which came under the control of the Farmers-General, the excise officials, and the fiscal agents of the domain, he might be called upon to intervene, especially in checking the cupidity and sharp practice of their rapacious underlings. In origin a magistrate rather than an administrator, the intendant always retained indefinite judicial powers, and he was for ever instructing local magistrates, judging suits himself, or evoking cases to the King's Council. He carried, as it were, the appelate jurisdiction of the Crown to the extremities of the kingdom. To his competence there were no definite bounds. In so far as his power was limited, it was not so much because there were administrative matters which were withheld from him as because, since he had so much to do, much had necessarily to be left undone.

The very extent of the area under his administration (for the *généralité* was much larger than the average English county) made his tasks more onerous, and tended, as the work of government increased, to thrust upon him much dull routine. It was a small nation that he was called upon to govern. And although he could appoint a number of subdelegates or *subdélégués* (there were thirty-one in the *généralité* of Limoges [13]), who performed much of the executive routine, and although he had also a staff of clerks who worked at the intendance, the local civil service—that is to say, the agents who held appointments by revocable commissions as distinct from the swarms of officials who bought their benefices—was everywhere far too weak numerically to enable the intendant, even had other circumstances been favourable, to make radical readjustments in provincial administration. And there was nothing to compensate this grave numerical deficiency of the civil service. Local self-government did indeed exist in rudimentary forms: in the parishes there were assemblies which elected officials, or rather imposed unpleasant duties upon those powerless to resist; and in the towns there were oligarchical governments and an hereditary ruling caste. But where local self-government flourished, it was local misgovernment requiring constant correction; it was a petty tyranny of rich over poor, a never-ending parochial feud in which sworn enemies overtaxed one another, or in which the unwilling holder of office took what revenge he could upon a heartless community.

Yet, though condemned to spend much of his time in an exhausting drudgery, the intendant was never the complacent and narrow-minded departmental bureaucrat of more recent ages. So multifarious were his duties that he never became merely a judge, a tax-collector, a recruiting sergeant, or a poor-law overseer. Since he came into contact with provincial life at every point, he possessed at once a more thorough knowledge of administrative problems and a more sympathetic attitude to the masses than did ill-informed superiors in the Ministry. Though government by intendants was a bureaucratic system, the intendants themselves were never mere functionaries. Since custom prescribed that they should be chosen from a relatively small group of administrative families, they had come to form an official caste with a mind of its own. A century of provincial government had given the dynasties of intendants an outlook which was much more liberal than that of other bodies in the realm. Had Montesquieu been as thoroughly objective as he professed to be, had he been less influenced by those ideas of the magisterial caste to which he himself belonged, he might have found in the families of intendants yet another intermediary power which mitigated a capricious and arbitrary despotism in ways often more laudable than those of the self-seeking judicial corporations. The fact is that the intendants had come to play an important part in determining the decisions of the Council, a body which had tended since the days of Louis XIV to lose its arbitrary and despotic character, which had ceased to be a mainspring of governmental action, and which had become rather a decorative and formal institution, important decisions really emanating from the central and provincial bureaucrats.

It is not to be inferred, however, that these officials were able to ride rough-shod over other interests in the realm, or that as a body they always wished to do so. But on the whole they were far more enlightened than other classes. Not that they were all inclined towards the new philosophical ideas, or that they were imbued with a desire for liberty (one form of which the parliamentary magistracy might have a greater claim to champion); but their close contact with administrative problems led them to work for secondary social reforms, to mitigate economic hardships, and even to attempt attacks on privilege.

The day had long passed since the intendant was a stranger to his province. Always a king's man, he had come also to be the representative of his people, interceding with the Ministry on their behalf and compelling it at times to lend a helping hand. Far from being a docile servant of the Crown, he often goaded the Central Government to action. Because he was in possession of social facts and better able to envisage plans in all their bewildering detail, he was ready to advance where officials in the capital feared to tread. And since he must be consulted not only on matters of local interest, but also upon those of national importance, he and his colleagues could influence considerably the decisions of the Government. Or sometimes, when Ministries were apathetic, he could carry on in his own sweet way, soften harsh measures he was called upon to execute, and in planning his own small reforms could risk a mild rebuke or wait for retrospective sanction and applause. His superior in Paris, the Comptroller-General, held a precarious office (there were no less than nineteen Comptrollers between 1754 and 1789), and even if not altogether inexperienced, this Minister usually encountered considerable difficulty in managing his subordinates in the Finances. He was over-whelmed by a flood of official correspondence; his time was occupied in trivial business and in endless routine; and therefore he could not for ever be prying too closely into provincial affairs. But the intendant remained for a lifetime in office, it being not unusual for him, refusing all offers of more lucrative intendances, to stay upwards of ten years in one *généralité*. Many intendants had their own estates in the provinces they ruled. They came to know their people and to be adored by them. Undoubtedly they were popular, as a reading of the *cahiers* and other documents will reveal; medals were struck in their honour, they were fêted when they left for other regions, and when they died monuments were erected in their honour. If in a number of *cahiers* and elsewhere we also read that they were tyrants and ought to be suppressed,[14] we shall usually find that such accusations originate from the nobility and the parliamentary magistracy, which in their hostility towards the intendants repeated the old charges that dated from Louis XIV's despotism.

For between the intendants and subdelegates on the one hand and the Parlements and lesser courts upon the other there was an intermittent feud. The tribunals were for ever claiming a large degree of executive authority as a corollary to their judicial powers, and it was not uncommon for them to issue ordinances conflicting with those of the intendants, or even with the decrees of the Council. In such circumstances the majority of intendants were usually more tenacious than the Ministers in upholding the royal authority against magisterial opposition. But they sponsored absolutism only in the interests of good government. Some-times—and this as we shall see is true of Turgot—they collaborated with the courts, with municipal authorities, and, in the *pays d'états*, with the provincial Estates in frustrating despotic measures which they considered baneful.

The intendants were never the tyrants of common birth whom

de Tocqueville, attaching too much importance to magisterial censures, has grossly caricatured in his picture of the *ancien régime*. Like Turgot, they were almost all members of the old aristocracy, and though a number were indeed descended from families newly ennobled, they could hardly be considered as plebeians in a society which was quickly losing many of its rigid class distinctions based upon birth. Office gave them power and responsibilities, but never rank and wealth, for these they possessed already. Even many of the subdelegates were drawn from the old aristocracy, or they were chosen from the provincial magistracy, which, like that of the highest rank, was connected by marriage with the nobility. And far from being tyrants, with very few exceptions the intendants of the second half of the eighteenth century were not only benevolent, but also enlightened—enlightened, that is to say, by the liberal ideas that had gained in strength as the century proceeded. The intendants became citizens of the republic of letters. Every year they transferred their households to the capital for weeks on end, and a great number came closely into contact with the intellectual life of the *salons*, those like Montyon and Sénac de Meilhan, not to mention Turgot himself, achieving considerable fame in the world of literature. The philosophical vocabulary of the *salons* gradually permeated the official correspondence that passed between the intendants and the Government, and also found its way into the ordinances by which they executed the laws of the State. Indeed, the attempt of the physiocratic school to enlighten the administration in economic science was not at all fantastic when so many of the bureaucrats had displayed a readiness to break away from routine. As we shall see, when Turgot introduced reforms at Limoges, he could make little claim to originality. Others had attempted similar measures before him. And when he became Comptroller-General, the reforms that he introduced were almost all sponsored by the intendants, and in some degree based upon provincial experience.

But the intendants toiled in an age when efforts to bring about social reform met with a meagre reward, when accomplishments, as contrasted with what remained to be done, were trivial victories only, when amelioration on a large scale was not to be accomplished by ordinary means—hardly by any means at all, short of a general upheaval and convulsion of society. Even to make a relatively small adjustment in financial administration was a task fraught with difficulties: to rectify a parish roll, to give the peasants relatively just rebates on their assessments when storms had destroyed their crops, to save them from distraints, from hunger, from the direst poverty ; to build a road ; to drain a fen— all these were no mean achievements when everything—famine, plague and pestilence, foreign war and loss of trade, lack of communications, ignorance and suspicion, a conflict of classes in the realm and powerful vested interest, all conspired to defeat the good intentions of officials. Turgot setting out for Limoges might leave his books behind him. He would have little time to read them. Nor could he console himself that he was on the road to fame. He seemed doomed to write his life in a chronicle of despair—in official correspondence to the bureaucrats in Paris.

CHAPTER III

THE *GÉNÉRALITÉ* OF LIMOGES

(1)

The *généralité* of Limoges[1] included the greater part of the ancient province of Limousin, about two-thirds of Angoumois, a small area of Basse Marche, and a morsel of Poitou.[2] In terms of present-day divisions it comprised the departments of La Haute Vienne and La Corrèze, a portion of La Creuse, and the larger part of La Charente. It extended over 853 square (common) leagues—that is to say, 1,686,000 hectares.[3] Within its confines were five *élections*, or financial divisions dating from mediaeval times—Limoges, Tulle, Brive, Angoulême, and Bourganeuf, the first three subject to the appellate jurisdiction of the *Cour des aides* of Clermont, the other two to the *Cour des aides* of Paris. In the province of Limousin there were six *sénéchaussées*, three of them—Limoges, Tulle, and Brive—being also *présidiaux*, or intermediate courts of appeal for the *sénéchaussées* of Uzerche, Ussel, and Saint-Yrieix, and also for similar courts at Dorat and Bellac in the province of La Marche. The supreme appellate jurisdiction in all the regions depending on these tribunals was the Parlement of Bordeaux. It was here that Roman Law or *droit écrit* obtained.[4] But in Angoumois, which was under the jurisdiction of the *sénéchaussée* and *présidial* of Angoulême, and also in the *élection* of Bourganeuf, customary law prevailed, and the appellate tribunal was the Parlement of Paris. Other administrative areas—the dioceses, the *eaux et forêts, bureaux des postes, lieutenances, ponts et chaussées*—similarly failed to coincide either with the financial and judicial regions or with one another. No map could be drawn to make clear the administrative divisions of the *ancien régime*—to say nothing of the multiplicity of tolls and customs barriers—so chaotic were they. But the barrier of the Five Great Farms, encircling Poitou, Normandy, Picardy, Champagne, Bourgogne, Berry, Bourbonnais, and Anjou, might be made to stand out, and it would be found to skirt the *généralité* of Limoges where Limousin touched Poitou, and to approach within a few miles of its north-eastern boundary.[5]

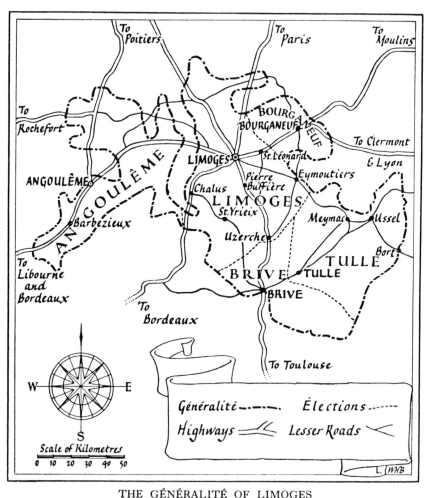

THE GÉNÉRALITÉ OF LIMOGES
Based upon maps by Corunan (1783), Jaillot (1719), and de Vaugoudy (1780)

Within the *généralité* of Limoges there were in all 976 civil parishes,[6] their total population amounting, as far as can be ascertained, to 580,000 souls.[7] Of these inhabitants 85 per cent. at least were peasants; ½ per cent. were clergy and religious; 2½ per cent. were nobles.[8] All told, only 75,000 people dwelt in the towns. Limoges, with 14,000 inhabitants, and Angoulême, with 12,000, were the only cities of any size; Brive and Tulle had populations ranging between 4,000 and 5,000; and there were four other towns with over 2,000 citizens; but the remainder were only large villages, some with as few as 800 inhabitants. Among this urban population there were many who were the domestic servants of the wealthier *bourgeoisie*. In the very small towns most of the inhabitants belonged to the peasantry, and some perhaps to a slowly-growing class which divided its attention between agricultural and industrial occupations. Marmontel, who was born of peasant parents at the little town of Bort, tells us that ' a little property combined with some industry or small trade with neighbouring districts furnished the means of subsistence to almost all its inhabitants '. His own family possessed a small garden, an orchard (in the shade of which he used to read Virgil), and the tiny farm of Saint-Thomas. They kept a few sheep and they cultivated a small plot of flax. The wool was spun by Marmontel's aunts and the flax dressed by young neighbours in the evenings by oil-light, the oil, we are told, being obtained from the nut-trees.[9] But these semi-industrialists, who were quite numerous in certain parts of France, were not a large group in the *généralité* of Limoges. Only in these small towns and in the parishes in the vicinity of Limoges, Angoulême, Tulle, and Brive does the peasantry seem to have supplemented its earnings by industrial occupations.[10] Rural industry as a whole was little developed in Limousin, and this is somewhat surprising, seeing that it usually flourished in those places where agriculture was backward, thus meriting the censure of Arthur Young. But it would seem that the towns were too small, too few, and not sufficiently developed industrially to bring about any rapid extension of ' outwork ' industry. The larger and more progressive manufactures were, indeed, taking such a form as in other parts of France.[11] Of the 1,800 people of both sexes for whom La Forêt, the manufacturer of *cotinades*, claimed to give employment without cost to the Government, only sixty actually dwelt in Limoges, and the remainder, including the 150 spinners in Éymoutiers, lived scattered in the small towns and the parishes around. Again, the manufactures of druggets which were to be found in several of the small market centres were also organized upon an ' outwork ' system, the craftsmen being supplied by the merchant-industrialist not only with materials, but also with wheels and looms.[12]   But when all is told, industry in the *généralité* of Limoges was of relatively little importance, and when Arthur Young visited the region he found only 1,000 cotton-spinners in the whole of the province.[13]

Among the remaining town-dwellers were the *bourgeoisie*, a varied class, composed chiefly of large farmers and landowners, who were often office-holders (one may count from a list which makes no claim to be exhaustive 267 in Limoges, 160 in Angoulême, forty in Brive and twelve in the small town of Éymoutiers); of merchants ranging from wealthy men like Joseph Touvenin, who dealt in wine, down to small hawkers and pedlars; of large and small industrial masters and of shopkeepers.[14]   By way of contrast to the nobility, the *bourgeoisie* formed a class growing in numbers and in riches.   In the *élection* of Angoulême by the year 1703, about sixty *bourgeois*, including a number of magistrates, had acquired fiefs the value of which amounted to one-fourteenth of the land remaining in the hands of the nobility.[15] As in Bretagne, their estates were mostly situated near the larger towns, in which they had their houses and sometimes their trade or employments.   In all, the *bourgeoisie* accounted for 8 to 9 per cent. of the population.

It follows, then, that the industrial wage-earners formed at the outside only 4 per cent.   They were centred chiefly in Limoges, where they were employed in the textile manufacture, the nail-making industry, in the porcelain and enamel works, and in several lesser industries, and also in Angoulême, where there were paper-mills and where shipping provided steady employment.   Others were to be found in towns like Brive, which, in Arthur Young's time, had sixty to eighty looms, each providing work for five people, including women and children. The remainder were employed in other paper-mills (there were seventy in the *généralité*, each with twelve to twenty men), in the forty forges, some of which provided work for 100 men, and also in the building trades, which were to be found in nearly all the towns.[16]   But it would be an error to suggest that all engaged in these industries were simple wage-earners: a number, though how many exactly cannot be determined, were small master craftsmen, journeymen, and also apprentices.   A large proportion of the small industrial proletariat must have been casual labourers, and where to any degree these were concentrated in a town, they provided a spectacle of wretchedness and squalor.

(2)

It was, then, a race of peasants that Turgot was called upon to rule.   Descended from the Celtic Limovices, and preserving in their mountain fastnesses their primitive racial characteristics and many of the words of their ancient language, they (particularly the hill-men) were small in stature, but wiry and robust. They were notorious for their churlishness and stubbornness, for their apathy to innovation and, though moderately industrious, they toiled doggedly with lack of enterprise. They were proverbial for their poverty, the butts of men of fashion : the *masche raves*, as Rabelais once called them. Bernage, the intendant at the end of the seventeenth century, described them thus : ' Generally speaking, the Limousins are outwardly devout, but sinful in their lives. They have no compunction after having joined in a procession of the penitents in sauntering immediately into inns and other places of debauchery. They have a superstitious veneration for the saints of their own country, among others Saint-Martial and Saint-Léonard, whom they worship to the extent of forgetting other saints and their duty to God Himself.' The inhabitants of Angoumois were a different breed : they were less uncouth and less industrious, but more defiant. They ' owe their livelihood more to the natural fertility of the soil than to their own endeavours. Generally speaking, they are idlers and given to pleasure, working only when necessity compels them.' [17] Bernage was writing over sixty years before Turgot became intendant of Limoges, but in the meantime the inhabitants had not changed. ' In the Limousin ', remarks Turgot, ' there are hardly any peasants who can read or write, and very few upon whom one can count for intelligence or probity ; they are a stubborn race, opposing even changes which are designed for their own good.' [18]

This ignorant and obdurate peasantry enjoyed a prescriptive, an economic, and indeed a form of legal ownership of just over half the soil of the *généralité*. Peasant proprietorship, though the term does not imply the ownership of freehold, which was rare in France, was one of the forms of tenure that arose as a consequence of the break-up of manorialism. Lords of the land in need of ready money leased their estates for perpetual *rentes*, a contract known as the *bail à rente*, by which, according to an eighteenth-century jurist, ' one of the parties leases and cedes to the other a heritage ... and obliges him to take the title of proprietor, under the provision that the latter pays an annual rent of a certain sum of money or of a certain proportion of productions.' [19] Such a contract was not so much a lease as a purchase of certain elements in land upon perpetual instalments ; and the one who acquired the *domaine utile*, as it was called, had the right to cultivate the land freely, to alienate it, and to bequeath it. The lord of the land retained the *domaine direct*, which carried the right to exercise feudal justice and to levy various duties known under a variety of names—*surcens, gros cens, croit de cens, arrière cens, censives* (all of which should be distinguished from the strictly feudal *cens* which was a servile payment of earlier origin), *capascal, rentes seigneuriales et emphytéotiques, champart, targe, terrage, arage, agrier, complant,* and *soëte.*[20] The land might also be burdened with other obligations known as *rentes secondes, rentes foncières,* or *rentes constituées,* some the result of loans raised upon the security of land, some arising out of bequests to religious corporations, and others the outcome of a growing practice for younger sons to renounce a share in their father's patrimony and to take instead a perpetual annuity.[21] Not every peasant domain was necessarily subject to all these charges; but it might be saddled with other burdens—*lods et ventes* (dues on transfer); *rachat* and *acapte* (fines on succession); *ban des vendages* and *droit de banvin* (duties on sale of wine); *fouage* (hearth tax); and *banalités* (payments for the compulsory use of the lord's mill, oven, or wine-press), to mention only a number of the more common ones.[22] From all these rents and dues, for which the peasants of a domain were conjointly responsible, the seigneurs in Limousin derived the major part of their incomes,[23] and it was to their advantage if these charges continued to be paid in kind, commuted rents, owing to the fall of the value of silver, yielding an ever-decreasing return.

The remainder of the soil was held by the clergy (3 per cent.), the nobility (15 per cent.), and the *bourgeoisie* (26 per cent.).[24] But, as a general rule, these classes did not farm the whole of their possessions. Retaining only a small home-farm, they sometimes leased their other domains to middlemen, who in turn sublet it to farmers and *métayers,* or more often they engaged these tenants directly themselves. The farmers paid a money-rent for their land and buildings alone, but the *métayers,* who received also implements, stock, and seed, contracted to give their masters a percentage of the produce. These *métayers*—a sure sign of wretched husbandry—were far more numerous than the lease-holders. All told they formed just over one-third of the peasant population of the *généralité.*[25] Some of them, like the day-labourers employed on the home-farms and upon the land belonging to the richer peasants, and like the rural artisans, owned tiny plots of land which were their share in small patrimonies several times divided among inheritors. Indeed, it is impossible to draw a hard-and-fast line between the peasant proprietors proper and those who were labourers, *métayers,* and artisans. There were many who held part of their land in *métayage* and the remainder in ownership; and there were large numbers of very small peasant proprietors who worked for wages for part of the year, or who were engaged in part-time industrial occupations. In the taxation rolls it was the practice to distinguish the *laboureurs* (the peasant farmers working on their own account), the *vignerons*, the *journaliers* (day-labourers), *métayers*, *artisans*, and *industriels*. Loucthisky's study of these documents has shown that the day-labourers owned 5 per cent. and 7·2 per cent. of the soil in the *élections* of Tulle and Brive respectively, the average size of their holdings being roughly from six to six and a half English acres. In these same regions those engaged in industrial occupations held about 3 per cent. of the soil in portions which on an average were slightly smaller. As for the *métayers*, however, Loucthisky's figures are, as he himself admits, entirely unreliable, because in all probability by far the greater number are not included in the rolls, it being a common practice for the masters to contract to pay the *taille*.

But while the multiplicity of small-holdings was an essential part of the agrarian economy of Limousin, the important agricultural unit, whether the land was owned by peasants or leased to farmers and *métayers*, was the family domain. A contemporary description of a *métayer's* farm in Angoumois would hold good also of that belonging to a peasant proprietor. ' The *métairie* of two oxen '—so it runs—' is composed of a dwelling for the *métayer* consisting of a little passage, a room on each side, and granary above running the whole length. It has also a barn for storing hay and straw, a stable for the oxen . . . an oven and a wash-house . . . pens for pigs, sheep, and poultry, a shed for handcarts and ploughs, twenty acres of arable, five of meadow, three of vineyard, five of copse for providing firewood, hedges with oaks and elms in them for furnishing acorns, leaves, and fences for the garden. The farm has also fifteen to twenty nut bushes, apple, pear, and cherry trees, two acres of chestnut wood and sixteen of stubble for pasturing the sheep during the winter and the spring.' [26] In most parts of Limousin there would be a difference or two : cows and fat cattle would take the place of sheep, and, instead of vineyards, there would be larger chestnut woods and meadows.

That farm, one of fifty or more English acres, was above the average size, especially for Angoumois. There were, indeed, many which were larger—in all, it has been estimated, between one-quarter and one-third of all those supporting a family. But the more extensive farms were usually to be found in the higher regions where the soil was thin, in the heath districts of the *généralité*, in parts of the *élections* of Tulle and Brive, and almost everywhere in Bourganeuf. Many of these were upwards of 100 acres in size, yet large proportions of them lay fallow, sometimes for several years on end. In these regions even the fields belonging to the day-labourers, *métayers*, and rural artisans were relatively large, sometimes exceeding forty or fifty acres.

In the valleys, on the other hand, a more intensive agriculture obtained, and the prevailing farm was between twenty and forty acres.[27]   In Angoumois the domain of fifty acres was the exception rather than the rule: here the soil, owing to the customs governing inheritance, was minutely divided and, even though a peasant was relatively prosperous, it was not uncommon for him to hold his patrimony in 100 tiny plots.[28]   Here, too, as in parts of Limousin, there were many vine-growers; but these, like the day-labourers, craftsmen, and *métayers*, possessed quite small holdings of ten acres usually, though often under five.

Such, in brief, was the agrarian organization of Limousin and Angoumois.   It was known as *la petite culture*, as distinct from *la grande culture* or the exploitation of large farms by workers receiving daily wages.   'The regions of *la petite culture*,' wrote Turgot, 'that is to say at least four-sevenths of the kingdom, are those where there exist no *entrepreneurs* in agriculture, where a landowner who wishes to exploit his lands finds to cultivate them only poverty-stricken peasants with nothing but their hands, where he is obliged to take upon himself all expenses, provision of capital, animals, implements, and seed, to advance food even to *métayer* until the first harvest. . . . It is in this province (Limousin) that the proverb, *Tant vaut l'homme, tant vaut sa terre*, is precisely true, for the land itself here has no value.'[29]   What Turgot means is that most of the farms had no value which could be expressed in terms of money-rent, for they could be leased only to these wretched *métayers*, the landlord's profit depending entirely upon the exertions of a type of tenant notorious for laziness, improvidence, and ignorance.

Yet the farms of the peasant proprietors were little better cultivated.   Arthur Young's claim that ownership turned sand into gold did not hold good of Limousin, where even the rich loams bred a beggarly race.   And Young himself admitted that the province was 'disgraced by a miserable husbandry, though possessing the advantage of good climate, and a soil almost everywhere good.   The produce', he added, 'instead of being 31*s.* (per English acre) ought to be 50*s.*, for the whole country I saw is enclosed, and wants little more than a skilful variation in the course of crops.'[30]   'When I came to this province', wrote Turgot's predecessor, 'I soon realized its meagre resources. Probably for centuries the peasants have cultivated their farms in the same old way.'[31]   Their method of ploughing was extraordinarily primitive.   'The husbandmen and *métayers* of these provinces', a contemporary explains, 'do not use a real plough; they till the land with an implement called a *hero*.   It is a poor affair without wheels, without a colter, and without a ploughshare, composed merely of a frame from which runs a pole to

which the oxen are harnessed and under which is fastened ver-
tically a pointed stock about one foot and one-half in length.
This point is driven hard into the soil, but actually it does not so
much plough the land as make a trench. . . . It is the custom
to plough as many as nine times in all directions, but such energy
is merely to provide so many dressings for weeds and roots,
which are thus made free to grow in all their vigour.' [32]   Repeated
ploughings of nine times over, up and down as well as across the
hill slopes, were the ideal rather than the practice.   The peasant
was content to scratch the soil at odd intervals, and clung to the
prejudice that ' a field which is ploughed too deeply becomes
unproductive, even for several years '.[33]

The arable received hardly any manures.   Poor bastard grain,
which was often mildewed, was sown thickly broadcast in the
hopes that some would germinate ; was buried at unequal depths
by means of the *hero* ; and was left to struggle for existence
against healthy weeds and bracken.   The better loams were often
left untilled in the belief that they were far too moist.   Much of
the poorer land lay fallow for two, three, and even four years
at a stretch, but the richer fields were cropped excessively and
thoroughly exhausted.   A yield of three to one was normal :
that of four to one the exception, and that of five to one very
rare indeed.[34]   ' The harvests ', wrote Bernage—and conditions
had not changed—' are never abundant, and are sufficient only
for the needs of the province.'   As a result the corn trade within
the *généralité* was very small in bulk and very localized.   An
abundant harvest of one district was fed to the cattle : a few
miles away the peasants starved because a summer thunder-
storm had ruined the crops.   Sometimes the grain supplies,
following a general failure of the harvests, were completely
exhausted, even before the winter months began ; but, as Bernage
informed the Council, the peasants could still keep body and
soul together if it happened that they had small stores of maize
and buckwheat, a few coarse raves, and chestnuts in abundance.[35]
Turgot, in sending his first annual report upon the crops to the
Comptroller-General, had a similar tale to tell : ' The inhabitants
are very poor, and their poverty prevents them from investing
money in growing the more valuable crops.   Consequently they
are obliged to cultivate buckwheat, maize, and raves, all of which
cost little to sow, require little attention, and give sufficient
nourishment.   They utilize chestnuts, which they dry round
their stoves and which they consume throughout the winter,
the only preparation being to boil them.   These four kinds of
food are of vital importance, since they supplement bread made
from wheat and rye, of which the majority of the poorer peasantry
never eat.   Rye is consumed by the more prosperous farmers

and small quantities are sold, and in default of this crop the cultivator is ruined and cannot pay his taxes.'[36]

Turgot was describing the arable farmers of the higher regions rather than the cattle-breeders in the valleys and the vine-growers of Angoumois and of parts of Brive. ' The principle income of the Limousin ', so runs Bernage's *Mémoire*, ' is derived from the sale of live stock, and especially oxen. . . . Many cattle are sold in neighbouring provinces, but a still greater number to the merchants of Paris. It is the custom to fatten them again in Normandy, since they lose weight considerably on the journey. In recent times those responsible for laying in provisions for the armies of Italy have made large purchases of beasts in the *généralité*, and this trade has enabled the peasants to pay the heavy taxation occasioned by the wars.'[37] But by the time that Turgot went to Limoges the cattle farmers were no longer prosperous. ' At one time ', Turgot reported, ' oxen were reared in these regions and sold for slaughter in Paris. . . . Hence the fame of the fairs of Limousin—the real origin of the excessive burden of taxation of which this province complains. For many years these fairs have lost their renown, perhaps because the consumption of cattle in Paris has decreased, or perhaps because the merchants of the capital prefer the more accessible fairs of Normandy. In past wars the provisioning of the armies has compensated the reduced purchases of Paris ; but during the present war (the Seven Years' War) the armies are far afield, and the ease with which the purveyors obtain meat supplies in Germany and Switzerland has given the last blow to the prosperity that the province used to derive from this trade, and the only hope that is left is the bounty of the King.'[38] What had really happened, as Turgot later discovered, was that a cattle-breeding industry had gradually developed in Normandy as an outcome of the practice of fattening cattle reared else-where.[39] Against the Norman farmers the peasants of Limousin were unable to compete, for the cost of driving a beast from Limoges to Paris was 20 *livres*, and each animal, moreover, lost from 60 to 80 lb. weight on the journey. To make matters worse, the Paris market had contracted owing to the fashion among the aristocracy of spending a season in the country.[40] Such was the fate of a province in which formerly 600 head of cattle were sold in one of the larger fairs in a single morning.[41]

In Angoumois there was hardly any cattle-raising on a large scale. The peasant here used to keep a cow or two. These he tethered on his scattered plots of meadow so early in spring that he ruined his hay-crop, and obliged himself to spend most of the summer in collecting odd bundles of grass while his fields recovered to produce a meagre rick for winter feeding. He reared also half a dozen sheep, which he turned out ' at all seasons of the year, at all hours . . . when winds were biting and the sun was scorching. But it does not matter : it is the custom thus to drive them out in all winds and weathers. The animals fare no better in the sheep-pen ; they are thin and their wool is coarse and dirty.' [42] Better specimens than these were to be found on the heathlands near Éymoutiers, their wool, which was fine and valuable, being sold to the textile merchants at Limoges and Saint-Léonard. Yet, on the whole, the *généralité* was under-stocked with sheep. That was so in Bernage's day, and it was still true of Turgot's. But pigs—those angular, mathematical shapes that amused Arthur Young—were common enough : every one kept them, and these, along with a few dirty sheep, provided a little ready money for the very small farmers and part-time labourers. They were to be seen rooting in the woods, feeding on chestnut husks, and devouring the refuse that even peasants throw away. Epidemics frequently carried off the pigs and sheep ; and when this happened it was a family calamity, for the *taille* could be paid only by selling a portion of the winter's food.

Even among the richer peasantry there was a serious shortage of money. For they, too, had experienced economic depression at a time when they were called to meet the increasing burdens of taxation. The few peasant horse-breeders had lost what at one time was a reasonably lucrative occupation. But for the most part it had been the nobles who in better days had made an honest penny, and even a fortune, by rearing and training horses for the cavalry. The horse fairs of Limoges and Châlus had once been famous, but by 1761 they were in decline ; and when the Government later renewed its policy of offering bounties, only the nobility were able to take advantage of the revival. [43]

Much more serious was the fate of the vine-growers in the *élections* of Angoulême and Brive. In the seventeenth century the wine trade had flourished to the extent of promoting over-production. Arable was turned into vineyards, and throughout Angoumois there sprang up thousands of small presses from which the merchants collected wine. [44] But as time went on the better wines of Bordeaux captured the foreign market, those of Angoumois being at yet another disadvantage in that their price was greatly enhanced by a heavy toll on the Charente ; and though for a while the merchants avoided ruin when they took to making brandy, which put courage into English sailors, the markets were finally irretrievably lost, the price of wine being too low to cover the expenses of production. [45] ' The vines have failed badly this year,' mentions Turgot shortly after his arrival at Limoges, ' but the condition of this province is such that failure is preferable to abundance, for it means that the costs of harvesting and wine-making are decreased at a time when there is no sale. Trade with foreign countries has been curtailed by the War; the market provided by the port of Rochefort has been lost ever since hostilities began, and the local sale, in spite of low prices, is so mediocre that nearly all the peasants have two years' wine upon their hands.' [46] But these indolent men of Angoumois would not turn their vineyards back into arable. They would have lost nothing by scrapping their vines, which had greatly deteriorated, and which were to provide a sorry sight for Arthur Young. [47]

Nothing would sell: timber, melons, peaches, haricots, dried plums, nuts, flax, hemp, dye-products had no market. The province was a backwater cut off from the swifter streams of economic change. [48] Agrarian capital was lacking: for over three-quarters of a century it had been drained away in royal taxation. Arthur Young contended that in Limousin the invest-ment of working-capital was barely 20s. the English acre, as compared with 60s. to 100s. in England. [49] According to Turgot, the gradual decline of the rate of interest on money from 12 to 5 per cent. throughout the seventeenth and eighteenth centuries had produced no visible effect upon agriculture in Limousin. In some parts of France this supply of cheap money had led to an influx of capital into agriculture, since it had become more profitable for the larger farmers and landowning *bourgeoisie* to develop their domains than to lend their surplus money to merchants in the towns. In Limousin the return from agri-cultural land had always been so poor that even the more pros-perous agriculturalists had never acquired surplus capital to invest elsewhere, so that when the rate of interest fell, there was no returning flow of money into land. Nor was capital attracted from outside, for to the *bourgeois* speculator other regions promised more lucrative rewards.

Turgot himself calculated that on many of the domains in Limousin, when expenses of production, *rentes*, tithes, and royal taxation had been paid, there remained only 125 to 150 *livres* (about six English pounds) out of which a family of five had to be fed and advances made for the ensuing year. [50] According to Arthur Young, who had travelled through England twenty years before touring France, the annual wage of English agri-cultural workers was nearly £20. [51] But comparisons in cold figures are apt to be misleading. It does not necessarily follow that the peasant proprietor was infinitely poorer than the English rural labourer. Out of his wages the latter had to pay rent for his house, while prices, especially that of bread, were higher in England than in France. [52] What is more, Turgot probably based his calculations upon an estimate of the consumption of various foods—chestnuts, for instance, and buckwheat—which in Limousin had hardly any value in exchange. Therefore, these poorer peasants were not so badly off as the figures would suggest. And much the same holds good of the majority of the day-labourers in Limousin, and even of a large proportion of the industrial wage-earners : their wages, which ranged from 9 *sols* in some districts to 15 *sols* [53] in others, were low indeed, and they worked usually for less than 200 days in the year ; but on their small holdings they often raised those cheaper foods which spared them from buying large quantities of rye, and in times of famine they had greater powers of resistance than the more prosperous urban day-workers, who were compelled to buy the better grains in rising markets. [54]

In the main, however, the standard of life of the average peasant family in Limousin must have been below, if only a little, that of the English rural labourer. The trouble was that a mediaeval husbandry was carrying several burdens : that of the eighteenth-century military State, that of the remnants of feudal government, and also that of a mediaeval Church. Arthur Young conveys a wrong impression when he states that tithes were heavier in England. [55] These charges, being a portion of gross produce, were heaviest precisely where the cost of production in proportion to the yield was high. Normally a twelfth of agricultural produce, and not a tenth as in England, the tithe in France nevertheless sometimes consumed from 40 to 50 per cent. of profits. Feudal dues and *rentes foncières*, the next charge upon the domain, took on an average another twelfth of what was left. Only in exceptional cases did these exactions amount to 34 per cent. of profit—a figure which Kowalewsky, basing his study upon the unreliable evidence of the *cahiers* of 1789, suggests as an average for the whole of France. [56] Of the remaining profits, at least one-half disappeared in taxes to the State, [57] the burden of the *taille*, as we shall see, falling particularly heavily upon the regions of *la petite culture*. With the greatest hardships were all these payments made, in trivial sums to the bailiff and to the unhappy functionary, the parochial collector of the *taille*.

Only with difficulty, to use Taine's metaphor, did the peasants keep their chins above the water level, the slightest ripple causing them to drown. In Limousin, where Nature promised much, yet gave so little, the husbandmen experienced the waves of seasonal variation and pestilence with all their force. Unable to obtain credit, lacking the money to buy even the cheapest grain, having defaulted in the payment of dues and taxation, there was only one course left for the unfortunate : to sell out

and tramp the roads. The population had been declining for
over half a century. 'Every year', writes Turgot's predecessor,
'men leave their homes for Spain to become unskilled labourers,
or for Paris to take up casual work in the building trades. Fathers
of families return every year to give the receivers of taxation the
fruits of their labours. But the young men never return.' [58]
Only two out of every ten, says a parochial petition, ever made
a decent livelihood in their exile. [59]

CHAPTER IV

FINANCIAL REFORMS, 1761–74

(1)

TURGOT arrived at Limoges in August 1761. There was much to be done, for the new financial year began on 1 October, and all those creaking wheels of the fiscal machine had necessarily to be stirred to greater activity.[1] The levy of that degrading tax, the *taille*, upon nearly five million peasant households in the kingdom was a tremendous, never-ending task. Early in the summer the Council of Finance, having decided upon the sum it was necessary to impose upon the *pays d'élections*, divided the quota among the twenty *généralités*. The writs, signed by the King, were then sent to the intendants, who, in collaboration with the treasurers of the *bureaux des finances*, divided the sums to be imposed upon the *généralités* among the *élections*. The next division of the tax among the parishes and the individual contributors did not take place until some time afterwards. For in July, while the crops were standing, the officers of the *élections* toured their districts to ascertain the promise of the harvests and to obtain information of particular agrarian misfortune, the damage by floods and tempests, the ravages of pests, and disease among the cattle. At the same time the intendant made a similar survey. Obviously he could not see everything for himself; but he trusted to the reports from the subdelegates and to those tales of woe which stricken parishes prevailed upon their priest to cast in the form of a petition; and sometimes he himself would ride the dusty tracks in the blazing summer heat to investigate thoroughly those regions where losses had been heavy. Using this information, he then composed a report (*état des récoltes*), and this, along with those drawn up by the officers of the *élections*, was forwarded to the Comptroller-General. At the same time he dispatched another memorandum, known as the Advice on Taxation (*l'avis sur l'imposition*), the first part of which contained a summary of the report on the crops and an estimate of the yield of the harvests, and the second, his opinion of the amount of tax his province could pay. These reports were next studied by the Council of

Finance (or rather by the Comptroller-General and his subordinates, the work of the Council being purely formal[2]), and rebates
were usually accorded to the more unfortunate *généralités*, the
amount being authorized in a writ known as an *arrêt du moins-
imposé*. In August, shortly before this writ was received, the
intendant, the subdelegates, and the officers of the *élection* made a
more thorough survey of the crops, paying particular attention
to stricken parishes. This task completed, the intendant allotted
the *taille* upon the parishes in the presence of the subdelegates,
the treasurers, and the officers of the *élections*, reductions being
granted to those communities that had suffered exceptional
misfortune. This process was known as the *département* or
repartition of the *taille*. Granted occasional injustices that were
not to be avoided under a system so difficult to work, the intendants arrived at an equitable distribution of taxation among
the parishes. The real iniquity of the assessments occurred in
the fourth and final allocation of the tax upon the peasants, which
was left mainly to parochial effort.

Turgot was plunged immediately on arrival into all this tedious
drudgery of the intendant's occupation. The man of ideas must
now cramp his mind with endless columns of figures, write
reports which would never be read, and transact paltry business
with those officious underlings of provincial bumbledom. He
had taken a glance at the crops scattered in small enclosures among
meadows and woods on the way from Paris. They were slightly
below the usual yield, that was always so niggardly. For four
consecutive years storms, frosts, and floods had reduced vast
regions almost to starvation, and as a consequence the payments
of taxation were greatly in arrears. But this was always so. What
was more unusual was that the richer peasantry were defiant:
they were flatly refusing to pay current taxation. And not without
reason, for the local financial courts, the *élections*, were declaring
assessments illegal and, as the news went round, work ceased in
the fields and a steady stream of men daily trudged their way to
the chief town of their *élection*. Here in a province was a local
skirmish between the courts and the Crown.[3]

We must go back to 1733, when Albert de Tourny was intendant
at Limoges. At the request of the Comptroller-General, Orry,
he had introduced as an experiment a new form of proportional
assessment known as the *taille tarifée*, the general lines of which
had been enunciated by the Abbé de Saint-Pierre.[4] Up to that
time a purely arbitrary assessment had been in force, the parochial
collector assessing his fellows as he pleased upon personal impression of the value of domains and products. Hence the tax
bore no exact relation to the acreage of land, its fertility, the costs of
production, or to the grain rents with which it was saddled. The

collector gave vent to old grudges, gave cause for new ones, and the only redress for his victim was a futile journey and a costly outlay to have his case heard in the *élection*. Almost invariably he lost more than he gained.

To replace this barbaric system, Saint-Pierre had advocated a regulated assessment. There was to be a land register : different kinds of land (arable, wood, meadow), and three different qualities of all these types were to be distinguished, valued, and assessed at fixed rates. Animals were to be taxed upon a predetermined scale, and money incomes according to yet another schedule.[5] Tourny followed closely the details of Saint-Pierre's project, and kept him informed of the progress of the undertaking. In 1733 he commanded all landowners and the tenants of the absentee landlords to be ready to declare within fourteen days, before a commissioner and in the hearing of the principal inhabitants of the parish, the value of their domains, the acreage of their meadows, arable, rough pastures, and woods, the amount of seed they planted each year, their dependants, their beasts of labour, cattle being reared for sale, grain rents and quit rents owed or received, details of contracts, mills and forges, and so forth, a separate declaration being necessary for every domain. The non-agricultural classes were to state their professions and incomes, the men they employed, and the amounts paid out in wages. For false declarations the penalty was 10 *livres*; for non-compliance an arbitrary assessment at twice the usual rate of tax.[6]

This reform was patently ambitious, and far too complex for a region where peasants kept no books and where rents were paid in kind. Seven years later over one-third of the parishes had done nothing at all ;[7] in the remainder the declarations had been so false that assessments were even more unjust than under the arbitrary system. Therefore, between 1738 and 1743 Orry and Tourny attempted to make an official survey, the costs being borne by the landowners. This they accomplished in only two-thirds of the parishes, which were known as the *paroisses abonnées*. In the remainder the original declarations were the basis of assessment, and these were known as the *paroisses tarifées*. But there was nothing to choose between the two : the surveys were hastily made by officials who ignored instructions and who preferred not to have their findings contested in an assembly of hostile and surly peasants. They made their measurements by eye, and even the weather did not check their haste, for they continued their activities when the snow was on the ground.[8] Ill-managed from the first, very little attempt was subsequently made to rectify assessments or to bring the taxation rolls up to date. Two commissioners only were retained to supervise nearly 1,000 parishes. The one—Du Tillet—was a rogue ; the other—La

Valette—being finical about his health, worked in the mornings only. The result was that one domain might be assessed at twice, three times, and even four times the rate of another.[9]

The nobility, the bishops and clergy, farmers of tithes and grain rents, the officers of the *élection*, the peasants themselves had all opposed the innovation. There were riots, defaults, and endless petitions to the *élections* and to the *Cours des aides* of Clermont and of Paris.[10] From the standpoint of these corporations the new system was illegal; for it had been introduced under the authority of an administrative ordinance.[11] Normally the magistrates would have annulled the assessments as rapidly as the peasants cared to present their complaints; and, posing as demagogues, they would have reaped a rich harvest in fees. But at the time, under the provision of an Edict of 1715, the courts were forbidden to judge assessments for the *taille*, this work now devolving upon the intendants. Hence Tourny and his successors ignored all protests, and used their authority to keep an unsettled peace. But in April 1761 the Ministry, under the appropriate pressure from vested interests and against the advice of the intendants, restored to these courts the cognizance of assessments. It was from that time that the peasants had besieged the *élections*, and it seemed as if the Abbé Saint-Pierre's ingenious method of taxation would have to go.[12]

Turgot knew all about this particular administrative problem before he went to Limoges. He had talked it over with Bertin, the Comptroller-General, and with d'Ormesson, one of the intendants of finance, who were Permanent Under-Secretaries for Financial Affairs. He also understood the *taille tarifée* which had been introduced in other parts of the kingdom, and he had probably studied Saint-Pierre's book. What is more, he believed in its general principles, the total tax fixed beforehand, divided in stages, and finally assessed upon a scientific estimate of clear profit as distinct from gross production. He disagreed on points of detail; and he was aware of the difficulties in administering the system; but he hoped to reform it, and was determined to prevent the restoration of the arbitrary, parochial assessments.[13]

But perhaps he was being unduly optimistic. Officialdom in Paris usually had its own way of dealing with these problems, and more often than not took a line of least resistance. It was most unlikely that the Ministry would suspend the Edict of April 1761 in the *généralité* of Limoges, and thus restore to the intendant the cognizance of disputes concerning the assessments. D'Ormesson was quietly trying to make peace with the *Cour des aides* of Clermont, and had probably reached the understanding with one of its presidents that the old method of taxation should be restored if the magistrates no longer made difficult the recovery of royal taxation. He had asked Turgot not to give any offence to the members of the courts.[14] It was probable that this official would carry Bertin with him. Hence Turgot, determined to frustrate such a surrender, himself opened negotiations with the courts. One of his personal friends, Malesherbes, a man inclined towards liberal ideas, was a president of the *Cour des aides* of Paris. To him he submitted a proposal which he hoped might do three things : satisfy the demands of the magistrates, secure the maintenance of proportional taxation, and commit the Government to a policy of reform. The courts were not to be deprived of their business of hearing disputed assessments : that was a principle, whether he liked it or not, Turgot must accept. But under the existing system of the *taille tarifée* there was no means of their doing this judicial work efficiently, for the *élections* had no copies of the evaluations of each landholder's property. Turgot proposed that he should furnish the courts with replicas of these *feuilles de relevé*, as they were called.[15] Then might they superintend the system. He himself undertook to reform the chaotic assessments. He asked in return that the superior courts should give a provisionary legal recognition of the *taille tarifée* : they would be able to judge of the progress of reform : and, if he failed to put the system in order, they would still be in a position to abolish it.[16] He went out of his way to admit that the indignation of the courts had been most righteous and, partly as an act of good faith, but mainly because the man deserved it, he dislodged the commissioner, Du Tillet, from his well-feathered nest.[17]

The *élections* of Brive, Tulle, and Limoges had already called a truce following upon d'Ormesson's advances to the *Cour des aides* of Clermont. Malesherbes advised the other two *élections*, Angoulême and Bourganeuf, likewise to desist while negotiations were pending. ' I will not hide it from you ', he wrote, ' that I know some of the ideas of your new intendant and I have the greatest hopes in him.' [18] Later he called together the principal members of the *Cour des aides* of Paris at his house and submitted to them Turgot's suggestions, which were cast in the form of a royal declaration for official registration. The magistrates, who always rendered administration an arduous diplomacy, objected to occasional phrases, legal niceties, which seemed disrespectful of their rights ; but they approved of the project subject to a time-limit of three years. They were prepared to trust Turgot ; but intendants changed, and a man of his ability might not remain long at Limoges.[19]

Turgot confronted Bertin and d'Ormesson with a *fait accompli*.[20] This was, perhaps, most imprudent conduct for a man new to his post. But he had solved a grave difficulty for the Government, and d'Ormesson, a stolid and unimaginative civil servant, though pressing for a while with his own solution, gave way finally and went on with routine. On 30 December, Turgot's measure received the King's sanction, was registered in the *Cour des aides* of Paris in January, and in the following May (the Court had been in vacation) was duly recorded in that of Clermont. He had committed the Government to reform.

(2)

His first move was to create a civil service. After Du Tillet's dismissal he had placed temporarily the *taille* rolls at Angoulême in the hands of one of his most trustworthy subdelegates, Boisbedeuil, who previously had gained great distinction as a steward on the domains of the Grand Duke of Tuscany. The other commissioner stationed at Limoges, La Valette, who was thoroughly honest, but who had found the work beyond him, was also dismissed, and for a short while Turgot took charge of the rolls himself. But by June 1762—we know neither the exact date nor the precise number of officials—a civil service had been created for the administration of the *taille*. Turgot's first circular to his newly-appointed agents gives some indication of the scale of this measure : ' I have taken the course of dividing all the parishes of the *généralité* among a large number of commissioners, so that each of them can verify annually the rolls of the parishes under his charge and . . . make assessments within a month or six weeks at the most. . . . I have divided each *élection* into a number of cantons and each of these into three subdivisions, and I have entrusted to each commissioner one or two whole subdivisions. . . .' [21] In 1778 the commissioners numbered fortyfive, and each was responsible on an average for just over twenty parishes.[22] But probably by that time fewer were needed, the initial inequalities in assessment having been remedied. On the assumption that they were fifty in number and received the two *deniers* in the *livre* paid to the old parochial collectors for making the yearly rolls, each earned on an average £12 to £14. All this is conjectural. The commissioners may have been more in number : Turgot may have supplemented their salaries from other sources. But the office was sufficiently attractive to gain for him the services of able subordinates—of men like Glori, Étienne, La Porte, all landowners of leisure and also of means. A number of subdelegates held the office ; it seems probable that they were given charge of smaller regions, perhaps of three or four parishes within easy reach of their dwellings.[23]

' I will not hide it from you ', Turgot informed these commissioners, ' that you must arm yourselves with courage if you are to surmount the obstacles that multiply in your path. The details into which you will be obliged to enter are perplexing. . . .'

They were not to regard themselves merely as fiscal agents. In words that express his own apostolic fervour in his calling he added : ' One of the most sacred duties of those who take part in administration is to succour the weak and feeble. . . . You ought never to miss the opportunity, by displaying patience in listening to them and by moderation in your actions, of promoting among the people the greatest confidence in your office. . . .[24] Do not neglect to inform yourselves of the condition of agriculture in each parish, the number of lands lying fallow, the ameliorations of which they are susceptible, the principal productions of the soil, the local industries of the inhabitants, those new industries it might be useful to suggest to them, the places where they sell their productions, the conditions of the roads, whether they can be traversed by vehicles or only by saddle-beasts. The location of each parish, the salubrity of the air, the most frequent epidemics among men and animals, and the causes to which they are attributed—all these also are worthy matters for inquiry. You might also hear complaints from individuals upon every topic . . . discover abuses of all kinds which afflict the parishioners— irregularities in the various branches of administration, vexatious exactions, popular prejudices which may disturb the well-being and contentment of the people. You might co-operate with the parish priests, from whom I have requested similar information, with nobles and gentlemen whom you have occasion to meet and with the principal members of the *bourgeoisie*. All these details I should like to have in writing, for it is the only way that I can get to know my province. I have asked my subdelegates to send me similar reports. . . . You should also gather accurate information of doctors and surgeons, of charitable persons who give their time to medicine or who distribute remedies to the sick and needy. . . . I should be glad also if you take note of the parishioners who, in the work of checking the taxation rolls, impress you by their intelligence and are honest and reliable. As you are aware, much of our success in reforming abuses in the rolls depends upon our discovery of intelligent parishioners. In fact, the com- missioners should regard themselves, so to speak, as itinerant subdelegates. Although these particular duties are not the immediate object of your journeys through the parishes, I am sure you will become more and more aware of their value . . .' [25]

Their immediate task was to make duplicates of and to rectify the evaluations of domains (the *feuilles de relevé*) from which the annual taxation rolls were made. These papers contained records of every field or plot for which a peasant paid taxation, no matter whether he was a proprietor, leaseholder, or *métayer*. All informa- tion was grouped under the names of taxpayers. When a morsel of land or a whole domain changed hands, it was a relatively simple task (or rather it ought to have been) to rectify these records. For every plot or field in a parish had a number, and often a name, and these were also entered in the *feuilles de relevé*. At the intendance was kept a primitive land register. Here again each field was recorded, named, and numbered, but this time under the headings of parishes. These two records should have tallied. But La Valette and Du Tillet had never been able to keep pace with the changes of owners and tenants. The permanent record had always been gravely defective : the *feuilles de relevé* from which the yearly assessments were made were utterly chaotic—much more so than Turgot had imagined when he promised to deposit copies at the *élections* within six months.[26] These, then, had to be checked hurriedly before the more important task of amending the land register was begun. But the difficulty did not end here. The land register contained no record of the *paroisses tarifées*, which had never been surveyed, and therefore one-third of the *feuilles de relevé* could not be rectified. To satisfy the *élections*, all that Turgot could do was to deposit in their archives the actual taxation rolls of the parishes concerned for the previous year.[27]

The new civil service set to work. The parish priest announced from the pulpit the day of the commissioner's visit, and exhorted his flock to speak the truth. He explained the nature of the work and how they could be helpful; he told them that the commissioner would be pleased to listen to complaints; he encouraged them to tell tales about their neighbours, and consoled them that they need not fear their landlords. And when the day arrived, he assembled the parishioners to the sound of the parish bell and again recalled to them their obligations to God and the Treasury. He produced in readiness certificates of death and baptism (there were rebates for large families), and also testaments and marriage contracts. Poor as he was himself, he often refused the customary fees for these small services. Then, after the commissioner had gone, on the last Sunday of September, after Mass, he himself made a record of the recent sales and changes in the ownership of land.[28]

Throughout the late summer of 1762 the commissioners toured the province. Already other little tasks had been thrust upon them. In law the parish was responsible for the *taille*, and all sums not collected one year were levied upon the whole community the next, the parochial collector bearing the immediate loss. Sometimes he never saw his money; more often he rewarded himself handsomely by over-charging the parish the following year. To put an end to such practices, the commissioners were commanded to obtain signed records in the parish assembly of all defaults.[29] Quite soon these same officials were holding informal courts to hear disputed assessments; there was no tedious journey for the peasant to the *élection*; there was no need to employ a battening lawyer; there were none of those terrors of formal pleading. All the peasant had to do was to visit the nearest commissioner.[30] Turgot was thus gradually regaining the concessions made to the courts.

(3)

There remained the greater undertaking of revising the land register. But meanwhile Turgot had reached the conclusion that it would be better in the long run to make a new one. In August 1762 he asked the Government for the sum of 60,000 *livres* for three or four years in order that he might begin this work. The letter in which he made this request is that in answer to the offer of the intendance of Lyon, a more leisurely and lucrative office for which his mother had suggested him to Bertin. A little earlier he had declined the intendance of Rouen. The second offer—that of Lyon—had surprised him: had, perhaps, disappointed him, since he believed that Bertin was interested in the reforms that were being undertaken at Limoges. For Bertin stood for enlightened government; he was developing a Board of Agriculture; he had plans for mitigating the *corvées*, and he was hoping to reform the *vingtième*. But perhaps he was too engrossed in his own schemes and in the routine of his office to appreciate the ardour of a young intendant.

Having complained of the utter chaos in assessments and the colossal task confronting him, Turgot announced to Bertin that he could abandon his undertaking only with regret. It would be a shameful waste of effort if, having made himself master of the bewildering situation, he went elsewhere. 'But', he ended, 'if it should happen that you are not in a position to afford me that (financial) support so necessary for my success, then I shall consider myself alone, and I should then be glad if you would ask the King to transfer me to Lyon.' [31] He remained at Limoges; yet financial support was not forthcoming, and he was left to his own resources, to the wearisome task of rectifying piecemeal the old land register.

To that work he and the commissioners devoted twelve whole years. Sections of the land register were hauled round the province on ox-wagons, and the more glaring anomalies were removed one by one. From time to time Turgot and his agents persuaded a number of parishes to defray the costs of accurate surveys.[32] And as all this work slowly progressed, he attempted to abolish the gross inequalities of taxation as between parish and parish. He asked his commissioners to collect information of prices of sales and leases, to make statements of the taxable land in each parish, and to include also details of privileges and exemptions. With all these figures at his disposal he hoped to allot taxation more equally among the parochial communities. But the information was not forthcoming in sufficient bulk. There was little leasehold; the peasants would not readily disclose their business, and the commissioners were too much occupied in checking the damage done to harvests in 1766 to coax it from them.[33] In 1767 he again asked the Government for a grant to make a new land register. Again a refusal.

And so there was little point in undertaking on a vast scale another reform that he had in mind. He had wanted to revise Saint-Pierre's graded scales of assessments, to tax in accordance with strict physiocrat doctrine true profits, and not mere production. But it was futile to attempt to apply a carefully graded scale to chaotic evaluations.[34] Yet in little ways, keeping within the letter of the law, he made many changes. In a long and technical circular to the commissioners he unfolded his plan, the outcome of which may be briefly stated. He exempted beasts of labour from taxation; he reduced the assessments upon cattle for sale; he decreased considerably the tax on industrial workers; and he suppressed entirely that on sheep. For he believed that the keep of beasts of labour was a cost of production, that, as the food of other animals had already been taxed, it should not be taxed again, and that, as impositions on industry must always be a charge upon land, it were better not to attempt to levy them upon the artisans and industrial masters.[35]

During 1765 the provisionary period of three years in which Turgot had promised to reform the proportional *taille* had come to an end. But the system neither received legal sanction nor, on the other hand, was it abolished. From time to time the courts, ever ready to gain fees and prestige, on the most preposterous evidence made attacks upon the commissioners. That the magistrates could trump up only ridiculous accusations is ample proof that the commissioners were doing their work with the greatest efficiency.[36] But there is more ample proof: it is the taxation rolls now to be found in the local archives. In them may be traced every sale, every bequest, every division of domains, every charge upon the land, the intake of the waste, the making of artificial meadows, the conversion of arable into pasture—so thoroughly did the commissioners do their work.[37]

(4)

Although the commissioners made the taxation rolls, it was still the unfortunate lot of the peasantry to take turns in collecting taxation. Every year at least 8,000 wretched parochial officials had to leave their fields to trudge the scattered parishes to squeeze from hostile neighbours ridiculously small instalments.[38] Doors were barred against them, and they were frequently assaulted.[39] To call in a money-grubbing crowd of bailiffs meant life-long revenge from other parishioners. 'A collector', Turgot told the Government, 'is one of the most unfortunate people one can imagine : he is likely at any moment to find himself in prison ; he is obliged continually to pay out of his own pocket sums of money which he can retrieve but slowly, and only by means of expensive and ruinous lawsuits, and he spends two or three years in running from door to door to the neglect of his own affairs. In the provinces of *la petite culture* a turn in office in an ordinary parish is reckoned at a loss of three to four hundred *livres*.' [40] What is more, the office tended to fall upon the poorer parishioners. The rotas, which were drawn up by the chief parochial officials, the *syndics*, were notoriously unjust. Turgot's predecessors had frequently vowed heavy penalties to those officials and to those who aided and abetted them in throwing the burden upon parochial outlaws. But merely to repeat the law was useless. Here, quite obviously, was yet another duty for the commissioners. To them was entrusted the task of making the rotas ; the parish was saved yet another lawyer's fee ; for it was no longer necessary for a notary to draw up an agreement of rotation.[41]

There was another scandalous abuse in the collection of taxation —one peculiar to Limousin. In this region the man who collected the *taille* also had to recover payments for the *vingtième*. This tax was less harsh ; it was levied almost entirely upon the landowners, and not on the *métayers* ; and, as the individual and not the parish was responsible, all that the collector had to do was to report defaulters to the receivers. But in Limousin, the *vingtième*, owing to its administration by the collectors of the *taille*, had acquired many of the characteristics of the more exacting imposition. Turgot separated the two and abolished the parochial collectors of the *vingtième*. In their place he created a body of overseers, each official taking charge of several parishes. For his trouble the overseer received 4 *deniers* in every *livre* collected. He also enjoyed the privileges usually accorded to the collectors in other regions—exemption from the office of collector of the *taille*, from forced labour on the roads, and, most desired of all, exemption for himself and one of his sons from service in the militia. The office was sufficiently lucrative to attract an able type of servant.[42]

Du Pont de Nemours maintains that Turgot extended this reform to the collection of the *taille*.[43] His statement is misleading. Turgot had, indeed, as early as 1762, and again in 1763, suggested this course to the Comptroller-General.[44] For where the *taille* was concerned he could not legally appoint overseers until he was authorized by a royal declaration registered

in the courts.   Nothing came of his proposals.   But he was quite
at liberty to conclude local agreements with groups of parishes.
In earlier times the parishioners used to elect one of their number
to the office of collector, and election was still the law, even though
in practice men were forced to take the burden.   There was no
reason, however, why a parish should not appoint a collector who
was ready to take office; and there was no reason why several
parishes should not choose the same man.   The difficulty was to
find a capable person who was prepared to accept the work.
Turgot promised to find him and, having found him, arranged for
his election in all the parishes concerned.   He inaugurated this
reform in 1764, but it was never easy to enlist men for these offices,
especially in those regions where the homesteads were more widely
scattered.   It was in the *élection* of Limoges that the reform met
with most success.   Here during the financial year 1765–66 one-
third of the imposition was collected by these new officials.[45]

(5)

Every reform depended upon, or was itself, an elaboration of the
civil service.   Yet neither the number of these new officials nor
the character of this bureaucracy was sufficient for Turgot's
purposes.   The deficiency he quickly remedied.   He sought the
co-operation of the parish priests; he took them entirely into his
confidence; and they responded to his call.   Their contribution
was twofold.   In the first place, they employed the moral force
of the pulpit and confessional for administrative ends.   Living
among the peasantry, sharing its suffering and privations, they
were able to break down little by little the barriers of prejudice,
hostility, and fear.[46]   Therefore Turgot kept them informed of
every administrative measure, entreating them to use their
influence to promote reform and to counteract the attempts of
influential landowners to frustrate the administration.   'Here,
gentlemen,' he would write, ' is yet another occasion for you to
show your goodwill.'   And those very priests who had often
encouraged a hostile peasantry to defy Tourny were soon collaborating in Turgot's noble efforts.   In the second place, these same
parish priests undertook numerous administrative duties; they
became unpaid officials—natural subdelegates, as Turgot called
them.   The ways in which they aided the commissioners have
already been described.   They were also called upon to compose
official reports on the crops and social conditions; to provide
useful instruction for the young; and to watch over and keep
accurate records of parochial business.   They managed much of
the detail of Turgot's reform of the *corvées*, and it was often they
who found men to take office as overseers for taxation.   They
collaborated in organizing schools of midwifery in the *généralité*,

the result being that in a very short time there was a large body of trained midwives who were sufficiently skilled to save a considerable loss of life among the peasant women. Then, again, the parish priests, at Turgot's request, advised their parishioners on points of law, and in many ways succeeded in keeping them from the clutches of the lawyers. They also assiduously collected receipts of all payments of feudal dues, telling their parishioners never to part with money or products without receiving acknowledgement. All these documents were sent to Turgot's clerical staff, which scrutinized them carefully, and woe to the bailiff who was found guilty of unlawful exactions. Sometimes the priests has curious duties to perform. When Turgot offered prizes for slaying wolves, the *curés* signed certificates and kept an ear of the wolf so that the same head should not be presented twice to receive a reward.[47]

There was one reform—that of the system of granting rebates on taxation to those who had suffered misfortune—which depended entirely upon the goodwill and the unremitting energy of the parochial clergy. The kindly priest had always assisted the peasants in drawing up petitions, and the number that annually reached the intendant was very considerable. But they were vague, incoherent, rambling tales of woe, referring to losses of long standing. Believing that his complaint would more readily be heard if he took it in person, the peasant would make the long journey to Limoges or to the town where Turgot might be staying. The new intendant was known to be kindly; and, for his kindness, he was condemned to listen to pitiful stories of poverty and hardships, of family histories, and of parochial quarrels. To avoid these wasted journeys, and also to save his own valuable time, Turgot appointed the priests as receivers and investigators of petitions. He supplied them with printed forms and prescribed definite rules which must be followed. On the first Sunday of every month, after Mass, the priests were to receive information of losses of crops and animals in the presence of the principal inhabitants of the parish. Every three months these records were to be sent to Limoges, where they were filed in readiness for the allocation of the *taille*. Then, just before the commissioner made the roll, the priest received a statement of all the individual rebates which had been granted.[48]

It was two or three years before this new machinery was running smoothly, for many minor adjustments had to be made where the civil and ecclesiastical parishes did not coincide. But when all this was done, Turgot thanked his helpers: ' The letters I have received from a great number of *curés* . . . have given me the most profound satisfaction and are a testimony to their zeal in devoting their energies to public welfare.' He was yet to make another call upon them : in 1769 there began the worst famine ever experienced within living memory.

(6)

By the year 1765 Turgot's essential financial reforms were in operation, and for the remainder of his intendance he was occupied in imparting to them greater perfection. But much as he might exert himself in reforming taxation, of more immediate importance was that he should convince the Ministry of the excessive fiscal burden borne by his province. Throughout this region it was a common opinion that taxes were appreciably heavier than elsewhere. The brief period of prosperity, when cattle sold well and wines were in great demand, had brought a large quota upon the *généralité* of Limoges.[49] The subsequent decline the central bureaucracy had failed to appreciate, and consequently the increase of impositions during the eighteenth century was a far greater burden here than in other provinces. But perhaps the most important cause of excessive taxation was that in regions of *la petite culture* the *taille* was always heavier than elsewhere. For one thing, land was assumed to be always productive, though in practice it often lay fallow. For another, either the owners of the *métairies* or the *métayers* themselves were assessed upon total production, no allowance being made for the landlords' advances or for the rents owed by the *métayers*. Indeed, it holds good for the whole of France that the poorer the region, the heavier the taxes.

Of this injustice the majority of intendants were well aware, and were for ever imploring the Council for reductions. Lacking actual figures (which would have been more impressive than exaggerated general statements), they did their best to paint in the darkest colours the conditions of poverty and wretchedness within their provinces. It was therefore no easy matter for the Comptroller-General to discriminate between these lurid catalogues of hardships which passed before his eyes. ' Looking at them all in the same light,' admitted Turgot, ' the Council leaves matters as they are. The evidence of the intendants is discredited because . . . they all plead with equal force.' For a while he himself merely stated his general impression that his province was bearing an excess of 600,000 *livres* in a total of about 2,200,000 *livres*. Later he endeavoured to prove his assertion, and he summarized his findings in his famous *Mémoire sur la surcharge*,[50] which he submitted to the Council in 1766, and part of which was published the next year in the *Éphémérides du citoyen*.[51]

The work of collecting statistics was no easy matter. Hoping to employ Du Pont upon this task, in August 1764 he had asked Bertin if he could pay for these services out of the funds allotted to the Society of Agriculture at Limoges. ' I have already arranged ', he concluded, ' for a number of landowners in different parts to place at his disposal their account-books, and he will therefore soon be able to establish for us the value and revenue of lands under a régime of *la petite culture*—a matter of which at present we have insufficient knowledge.' [52] Permission was granted.[53] But unfortunately Du Pont was fully occupied elsewhere. At one time he was doing statistical work for the intendant of Soissons; later he was in charge of the *Journal du commerce*; still later, having toured France with the Duc de Saint-Mégrin, in 1768 he succeeded Baudeau as editor of the *Éphémérides du citoyen*. While waiting for Du Pont, Turgot, utilizing mainly the information of leases and sales collected by the commissioners, began the work himself. For statistics of other regions he depended largely upon figures obtained for him by La Valette, whose principal domains were situated in the *généralité* of La Rochelle.[54] Yet more information he obtained from the border parishes, where the domains of many absentee landowners were assessed for taxation in other *généralités*.

The figures in the *Mémoire* are of great importance, for, in an age when statistics were frequently vague and picturesque illustrations, they represent an attempt to base figures upon a careful scrutiny of facts. They form perhaps the best contemporary estimate of the rate at which taxation was levied in a particular region. They may be summarized briefly. In several parishes in the *élection* of Tulle $56\frac{1}{2}$ per cent. of the landowners' profit went in taxes to the King. In yet another group of parishes in Tulle the figure was 54 per cent., and in Angoumois $48\frac{3}{4}$ per cent. But in Saintonge in the *généralité* of La Rochelle only 24 per cent. disappeared in impositions. La Valette's own calculations produced a similar result. His domains in Limoges paid 56 per cent. of the profits in royal taxation, but those in Saintonge paid only $19\frac{3}{4}$ per cent. It is not surprising, then, that the *cahiers* of 1789 in Angoumois demanded that the whole province should be separated from the *généralité* of Limoges, and should become, like Saintonge, part of La Rochelle.[55] All these conclusions Turgot checked by an elaborate comparison of the *taille* and *vingtième*.[56] He found that the average rate of impositions was at the least 48 to 50 per cent. of the total income of the land. On the domains of the *métayers* he believed the figure to be somewhere in the region of 80 per cent.

He petitioned the Council for a reduction of 700,000 *livres*. Every year he repeated his demands, and all to no avail. Every year he vividly described the wretched conditions in his province —the constant drain of agrarian capital, the loss of crops and cattle, the difficulty with which the peasants were able to with-

stand disasters arising from meagre harvests and epidemics among
the cattle.   Not until Turgot became Comptroller-General did
the province have its quota reduced, and then only while he
remained in power.   Montyon criticized him thus : ' A Minister,
who in order to make his loss felt in Limousin granted this province
a decrease in its assessment . . . and all this without any inquiry
to justify this rebate.' [57]   Montyon had never read the *Mémoire
sur la surcharge*.   But others had.   In 1789 the nobles, clergy, and
third estate of Tulle, Brive, and Uzerche joined in demanding that
there should be granted ' a diminution of impositions so ardently
requested by M. Turgot '.[58]

CHAPTER V

THE REFORM OF THE *CORVÉES* AND THE *MILICE*

(1)

' BRISTLING with mountains, the Limousin has no communication with her neighbours; the products of the soil are consumed locally owing to lack of means of transport, and the proprietors, content merely to pay their dues and feed themselves, cultivate only what is necessary to fulfil these aims.' Thus wrote Pajot de Marcheval to the Comptroller-General in 1760.[1] Yet for more than twenty-five years Turgot's predecessors had been endeavouring to reconstruct the great highways that traversed this region. With a view to facilitating the movements of the armies, the Ministry had begun that prodigious activity in road-building which continued to the Revolution. At the beginning of the period Orry was Comptroller-General; Daniel Trudaine was director of the *ponts et chaussées*. In collaboration with the chief engineers, each of whom was responsible on an average for four or five *généralités*, and with the assistance of the intendants and subdelegates, they planned a vast network of roads linking up all the important towns of France. These highways were to be 48 feet wide; a ditch and grass verge 6 feet wide were to run on either side, and trees were to be planted at regular intervals to overhang the road. The magnitude of this undertaking is obvious from a glance at the memoranda that passed between Tourny, then intendant at Limoges, and Orry and Trudaine.[2] Landowners had to be compensated; narrow streets in the towns had to be reconstructed; and every detail had to be submitted for official confirmation. At first the landowners were commanded to repair and reconstruct, if necessary, the highways that crossed or bordered their domains, it being intended that they should exercise to the full their seigneurial right to demand forced labour from their tenants.[3] But, owing to the apathy of the seigneurs, the instruction remained a dead letter, and consequently the intendants were commanded to impose the royal *corvées*.[4] In Limoges the appropriate ordinance was promulgated in September 1732: the *syndics* of the parishes were instructed to submit the names of the *corvéables*, and these, as soon as the harvest had been gathered, were to labour under the supervision of the subdelegates and engineers, taking with them their own implements and carts.[5] To an impoverished Government this device had much to recommend it. Orry was not anxious for a conflict with the sovereign courts which would have undoubtedly arisen had he attempted to increase taxation, while Trudaine preferred the *corvées* to a larger grant to his department, as he feared that funds allotted would continually be raided by Governments in need.[6]

Tourny first began operations upon the Paris–Toulouse and the Paris–Bordeaux roads, which branched at Limoges, the one in a southerly, the other in a south-westerly direction. Shortly afterwards he extended road-works to other important highways— to the Poitiers–Bordeaux road which ran through Angoulême, to the road from Angoulême to La Rochelle, and to the highways that radiated from Limoges to Clermont in the east, to Moulins in the north-east, to Angoulême in the west and to Poitiers in the north-west.[7] But during the time that Tourny was intendant little impression upon the work in hand was made. ' I have often heard it remarked ', Trudaine wrote to him, ' that you have merely traced out the roads in Limousin, that the greater part of them are still impassable, that the surfaces are badly constructed, and that adequate foundations have not been laid.'[8] When Turgot took up office at Limoges he found that, although the *corvées* had been exacted to the full, there was little to show for the energy expanded. ' I can assure you ', commented Turgot to Trudaine, ' that there is every reason to complain of the *corvées* in Limousin, where the administration has been conducted ruthlessly and negligently and where . . . the highways have remained as bad as ever.'[9] The road from Limoges to Clermont had been declared open in 1758, but was fit only for beasts with pack-saddles ; that running from Paris to Toulouse through Limoges, although reported to have been finished, was actually in a worse condition than before works were begun upon it.[10] Indeed, so little really concentrated effort had been organized that each stretch of road was ruined almost before it was completed. Small groups of men had been set to work at intervals along the highways under the entirely inadequate supervision of the parochial *syndics*, it being impossible for the subdelegates and engineers to do much more than glance at the works in progress as they journeyed rapidly from one district to another. ' You know ', wrote Turgot to the parochial clergy, ' that every parish situated near the highways has been allotted a distance of road to construct upon a reckoning of the number of inhabitants and their carts. They have been obliged to complete these tasks by *corvées* by a fixed date, and though many of the parishes have worked hard to fulfil their obligations, frequently the results of their labours have been washed away by storms.' The burden had fallen almost entirely upon the parishes near the high road, and where in the hilly regions of the province these parishes were small and few and far between, the *corvées* had been particularly exacting. The remedy had been worse than the original abuse : in sparsely populated regions it had been the practice to demand *corvées* from the peasants who lived as far as 10 to 15 miles from the scene of works, and to compel them to drive their lumbering carts up steep gradients from their villages tucked away in the highlands.

The organizer of this parochial labour on the roads, the *syndic* —an official in early times elected by his fellows, but later appointed, like the collectors, according to a rota—had a most unenviable task. Upon the receipt of an order from a subdelegate or an engineer, he must leave his harvest in the fields or his land un-ploughed and plod across the hills and moors to pass on instruc-tions to his neighbours. And as the homesteads in Limousin were sometimes widely scattered, or grouped in small villages in isolated valleys, he lacked that intimate knowledge of his fellows so vitally necessary for parochial government. Men died without his knowing, they feigned illness, or hid themselves ; the result being that the unfortunate official might spend weeks in collecting thirty or forty men to accompany him to work upon the roads.[11] Still more difficult was it for him to requisition animals and carts ; the peasants would plead that the oxen which but a day or so previously had ploughed the fields were now in the byre being fattened for the market ; hence it frequently happened that, when the work of the *corvéables* had been allotted and the time and place of meeting had been appointed, at the last moment all arrangements had to be cancelled owing to shortage of animals and carts. ' The *corvées*', explained Turgot to the Comptroller-General in July 1764, ' are perhaps practicable in those provinces where there are horses, where the parishes are close together, and where the *syndics* are intelligent farmers ; but I consider that it is impossible to make the roads in the *généralité* of Limoges without spending considerable time upon them and without crushing entirely the parishes that must bear the burden.' [12] Actually the loss of money occasioned by the *corvées* might easily amount to the sum the peasant paid in *taille*, and it might be infinitely greater if, as so often happened, a cart was damaged or an animal went lame.[13] According to Turgot's calculation, the total annual cost of the *corvées* in his *généralité* was no less than 200,000 *livres*.[14] It was therefore no exaggeration when Du Pont remarked that ' the *corvée* was one of the most pernicious inventions that ever emanated from the administrative mind '. [15]

In the environs of Limoges and Angoulême an exceptional difficulty had to be faced. From both towns, the inhabitants of which were exempt from the *corvées*, the highways radiated in all directions and, as a consequence, the burden of road-making and upkeep fell with added force upon the peasantry. Millière, who was intendant from 1751 to 1756, had issued ordinances requiring the inhabitants of Limoges and Angoulême to work upon the roads. But both towns could prove exemption granted in a charter by Charles V and confirmed by subsequent Kings of France, so that Millière was obliged to give up the attempt, and both he and his successor, Marcheval, were left to carry on the work upon these roads with the labour supplied from the parishes around. Turgot was in a quandary; he knew only too well that it would be futile to follow Millière's example in attempting again to impose a *corvée* on these towns; yet it was equally obvious that he could not with justice demand from the peasantry more time upon the roads.[16] Such was the immediate problem which faced Turgot in 1761. It was, in fact, but part of a greater difficulty which he must solve. To make the roads durable he must concentrate upon shorter stretches at a time, and that would mean a great injustice to a small number of parishes. On the other hand, to attempt to allot the burden more equally would mean another twenty years of futile effort, of work ill done and at the mercy of the weather. From the outset Turgot saw that some form of commutation, causing the whole *généralité* to contribute to the cost of the roads, must be devised. But there were serious obstacles. In the first place, the peasants had to be convinced that the intendant was not merely seeking to increase the burden of taxation, for, though eager to be rid of the *corvées*, they were always reluctant to part with ready cash. In the second place, the Central Government was not at all likely to favour commutation, for at the time it was particularly anxious to avoid a skirmish with the magistrates, who would certainly oppose the levy of a local imposition. Turgot therefore must do two things: first, he must win the confidence of the peasantry; secondly, he must somehow raise the money so that the imposition should not come before the courts for sanction. It is true that the magistrates might still make protests to the Central Government, but if he could by any good fortune achieve the first, he knew only too well that the judicial officers would be obliged to adopt a more moderate tone than when they had the backing of local opinion.

With these principles in mind, he set to work to devise a method for commuting the *corvées*. He first of all made a study of the reform introduced by Fontette, the intendant at Caen. In order to overcome the difficulty of imposing a tax upon his province, Fontette took advantage of an opening offered to him by an instruction which Orry when Comptroller-General had dispatched to all intendants.[17] With a view to expediting the construction of the highways, Orry had asked the intendants to allot to each parish a specific task: if it were accomplished within a given time, a small reward was to be made to the community by way of a rebate on the *taille*; but if, as so frequently happened, a parish failed to fulfil its obligations, then hired labour was to be employed and the parishioners assessed to meet the cost. The primary object of this instruction was to authorize the intendants to punish defaulting communities, but Fontette availed himself of its provisions to commute the *corvées*. He and his subdelegates, calling together the parochial assemblies, persuaded them ' to fail the tasks ' imposed upon them, convincing them that the cost of hired labour would be less exacting than actual work upon the roads. This innovation aroused considerable hostility. In the parochial assemblies the richer farmers and the *bourgeoisie* endeavoured to wreck the scheme. Their cause moreover found support among the members of the magistracy, who reminded the intendant that any additional imposition to the *taille* of more than 200 *livres* could not legally be levied without the authority of a law duly registered. Nevertheless Fontette persisted in his reform, and much headway was made in the construction of the roads.[18]

But Fontette's methods could not be followed at Limoges. For one thing, Turgot was determined to have greater security from magisterial opposition; and for another, it was impossible to allocate equal tasks, owing to variations of soil and contour. Then, again, in Limousin it was imperative that the actual work of road-making should fall upon a relatively small number of parishes situated near the highways and, if concentrated efforts were to be made upon short stretches, the burden would fall in any given year upon twenty, or perhaps thirty communities, which would be required to labour for several weeks on end. Obviously Turgot must so arrange matters that the parishes concerned should be adequately rewarded at the expense of the rest of the province.[19]

(2)

In December 1761 Turgot approached Daniel Trudaine. ' I know ', he wrote, 'that you were always disposed to regret the imposing of so great a burden as that of the *corvées* upon the people, and I have heard you remark that you would prefer the method of an imposition if it were not for the fear, which is no mere fancy, that the needs of the State might lead to the confiscation of such a fund.' [20] Trudaine's reply was most encouraging. He suggested that Turgot should submit a detailed memorandum, together with instructions and ordinances for the execution of his plan, whereupon the Ministry would be approached to give the measure a full consideration. But Trudaine's last words were a warning : ' Do not innovate ', he said, ' without being authorized by a letter from the Comptroller-General.' [21]   The following July, Turgot submitted his project to the Government, answering at the same time a number of technical difficulties which Trudaine raised in the previous December. The principle of his proposed reform was as follows. The obligation to perform the *corvées* was to be regarded as a parochial misfortune, and the parish was to receive compensation in the form of a *moins-imposé*. This device was ingenious. Utilizing machinery, it made for economy in administrative effort. More important still, the procedure kept within the letter of the law—at least, so far as the law had been defined [22]—for the allocation of the reductions in taxation had for generations come within the scope of the intendant's duty. But there was still an opening of which the magistrates might avail themselves : they might contest the right of the intendant to increase parochial assessments. In the ordinary way when the Council granted a rebate to a parish it reduced the *taille* imposed upon the *généralité* by a corresponding sum. Clearly Turgot could not ask the Council to decrease taxation in the *généralité* of Limoges in order to compensate the diminutions granted to the communities performing the *corvées*. Therefore, before awarding a *moins-imposé* to a parish community working on the roads, Turgot must increase the taxation in the *généralité* by an equivalent amount. Herein lay the difficulty : unless the increase were authorized by a law duly registered, the Courts might raise objections, and in their judicial decisions succeed in wrecking the project.[23]   To obviate this danger Turgot must take great pains to make his reform acceptable to the *corvéables* by proving to the suspicious peasant of Limousin that the promise of payment was sincere. The best way to convince him was to give him part of his earnings in ready cash. Turgot proposed, therefore, to give each *corvéable* 2 *sols* a day for his mere presence at a roll-call in the morning and in the evening upon the scene of work, even though he idled the remainder of his time away. This sum in ready money, which was the equivalent of two-fifths of a day's wage in winter, was not to be despised by the needy Limousins ; and if, as Turgot hoped, road-works were arranged for the slack season of the year, it was obviously worth a man's while to journey to the high road. Once there, no longer suspicious, he would join in with his neighbours to earn the remainder of the promised reward.

That acute understanding of the peasant's distrustful and greedy mind evinced in this particular detail is again displayed in the

provisions for assessing the wages of those who worked. There
were five different types of labour to be rewarded. For the first
two—the hewing of stone from the quarries and the loading of
carts for haulage to the roads—the *corvéables* were to be paid by
piece-rate, the subdelegates and engineers fixing the scale of
payment upon consideration of the customary wages of the
district. But the third type—that of building the foundations
and the surface of the roads—did not admit of such a method of
reward; individual effort could not be easily assessed; and it
was also inadvisable to provide an incentive to hasty work. Hence
a fixed wage of 3 *sols* in winter and 5 *sols* in summer was to be paid
in addition to the 2 *sols* for presence at the roll-call. The *corvéables*
were to be divided into gangs and, as an incentive, an additional
reward was to be made daily to the man who, in the opinion of
his fellows, had accomplished most. Such sums, unlike the 2
sols a day which were to be distributed in ready cash, were to be
paid in the form of a reduction in taxation, the subdelegates being
instructed to keep a register of each man's credit. A fourth
class of work was that performed by beasts of labour. The
earning capacity of an ox was greater than a man's. To hire two
oxen and a cart cost from 30 to 40 *sols* a day. No wonder, then,
that the peasants had in the past taken greater pains to save their
animals forced labour than themselves. Hence when Turgot
proposed to pay the owners of animals the local rate of hire and to
recompense them for any accident that occurred upon the scene
of work, not only was he bound to put an end to the shortage of
carts that had hindered operations in the past, but he was also
providing an opportunity for the peasants to increase their annual
earnings. The fifth and final class of work was that required for
the upkeep and repair of completed roads—a branch of road
administration which presented considerable difficulties in
Limousin, where even the best roads rapidly deteriorated.[24]
At first Turgot allotted stretches of the highways to the nearest
parishes, but later—it is not certain when the new method was
adopted—he engaged contractors, who, employing local labour,
made themselves responsible for the upkeep of long distances of
roads, their work being regularly inspected by the engineers.[25]
Such was the outline of Turgot's reform, which, he claimed,
would reduce the burden of the *corvée* by one-half, distribute the
remainder over the whole *généralité*, and provide the province
with communications. How, Trudaine had asked in the previous
December, did he propose to find the money for the payment to
each man of 2 *sols* a day, and how did he intend to reward *métayers*
whose masters sometimes paid the *taille*? Turgot had at his
disposal a sum of 10,000 *livres* annually, which had hitherto been
spent, part upon an experimental farm at Cordelas, and the

remainder upon a nursery for trees, both of which were under the incompetent supervision of the Society of Agriculture of Limoges. The leases of these two domains had been terminated in December, and the sum thus saved was ample for his purpose. Out of it he could defray the payments at the roll-call; he could reward the *métayers* whose masters paid the *taille*; and the remainder would defray the cost of trees for the roadsides. Another difficulty had been solved by Turgot's creation of a special body of commissioners for the making of assessments. There was no longer the danger, to which Trudaine had called attention, of fraudulent practices in allotting the *moins-imposé* as a reward for work upon the roads.

Trudaine's final objection had been that the proposed reform would tax too greatly the capabilities of the administration, since it contained little or no provision for utilizing the existing organs of parochial self-government. The omission was not the result of bureaucratic arrogance on Turgot's part; he was not unduly impatient of local co-operation in administration; but he refused to deceive himself that self-government existed when it certainly did not. In a passage which anticipates the famous *Mémoire sur les municipalités* he writes: ' Indeed, one could wish that in each community there existed a kind of municipal administration which could be put in charge of the details of general instructions. . . . Every day administration would then be infinitely more simple. I have heard it said that this municipal government is established in Alsace and in several other provinces; but no place is so far removed from this condition as Limousin.' If he discovered intelligent parochial officers, he would make use of their services and grant them rewards.[26]

In August, Trudaine gave the Government's reply. Bertin was not disposed to attempt reforms while the nation was still at war. When peace was signed he hoped to establish an administration of the roads similar to the Turnpike Trusts in England— a measure which would render Turgot's plans superfluous. Nevertheless, added Trudaine, probably no objection would be raised if the reform were inaugurated as a makeshift to expedite the construction of the Bordeaux road.[27] Thus advised, Turgot began road-works in Petit Angoumois. Allotting to each community a task, and convening the parochial assemblies, he asked the inhabitants which they preferred: to adopt his reform or to do the work under existing conditions. As the news went round, *bourgeois* and aristocratic landowners attempted to bring pressure upon their tenants, and in spite of Turgot's appeal to the *curés* to exert their influence in favour of reform, the vote in a number of parishes went against it.[28] But Turgot ignored the decisions of the dissentient communities, commanded the presence of the inhabitants upon the roads, and paid them for their work. If they accepted payment—and there was never any doubt about the issue—he counted such an action a reversal of their earlier decision. In following this 'little comedy of deliberation', as he terms it, he was endeavouring to observe at least the shadowy forms of law. He was asking the parishes to impose upon themselves a rate similar to that which was levied for the repair of a church or for any other parochial expenditure. As intendant Turgot would sanction the imposition ; he would then prepare an *arrêt du conseil* and submit it to the Council for official confirmation. In the normal way the writs for local rates were then sent to the Finances, and the sums indicated on them were added to the *taille* imposed upon the *généralité*. Strictly speaking, when the intendant allocated the *taille* upon the parishes, he would allot the local rates to the parishes concerned. But it was always open for him to grant a reduction to those communities that, in his opinion, had been obliged to levy upon themselves exceptionally heavy burdens.

For the first year Turgot confined his road-works to the relatively small sum of 39,991 *livres*. He must test his project in the light of actual experience ; he must train his subdelegates and engineers in his new administration ; and he must concentrate upon the worst stretches of the Paris–Bordeaux road.[29] So successful were his early ventures, that he wished to extend his reform to other parishes and obtain official recognition of his projects. To Trudaine he sent a scathing criticism of Bertin's timidity. ' Up to the present ', thus ran the letter, ' the magistrates have always sought to display themselves as the protectors of the people against the Crown ; but the Crown would do well to unmask these magistrates and to show them as they really are—as corporations little interested in the well-being of the masses. I doubt whether they will be eager to attack a measure which cannot be other than agreeable to the public. What is more, the fact that the magistrates have denounced the *corvées* should make them disposed to favour this innovation, for then it would seem that they are willing to be consistent in their opinions.'[30] But Bertin remained apathetic. He could find no precedent for Turgot's measures ; he let it be known that he would not face the enmity of the courts ; and he again made the half-hearted suggestion that it would be better to wait until peace had been signed, when he himself would consider the road administration as a whole. Trudaine, who had passed on these opinions, was now less sympathetic, and accused Turgot of being unduly prejudiced against the *corvées*. His advice was that, as Turgot had committed himself to a number of parishes, he should execute the reform on his own authority, but not extend it. Turgot replied : ' My position is such that I can change nothing and I cannot postpone my project. Besides, it would lead to the most serious consequences in all my administration if I were to break my word with the communities. . . . I agree that the instructions dispatched by M. Orry to my predecessors, in providing that all parishes which fail to fulfil their tasks within a certain time should be compelled to pay in money for the work, give sufficient authority to the intendants to assess the inhabitants at a money rate. . . . But you should not forget that although this authorization is valid in the eyes of the Central Government, it is not accepted by the courts. . . . I have had to consider two possible results : the first, the danger which falls on me alone, and of which the only remedy is that the Government should ask me to resign my office, my only consolation being that I have acted for the best ; the second, the danger—which is much more serious—of discrediting my administration in failing to carry out my undertakings.' [31]   But Turgot was not dismissed ; nor did he obtain immediately official sanction for his work.   It is probable that at this point he entered once more into negotiations with a number of leading magistrates who respected him and who were prepared to exercise a moderating influence on their fellows.[32] At any rate he felt secure enough to extend his reforms to other parishes.

Ultimately the Government recognized his reform   In November 1763 Bertin was dismissed, and his successor, L'Averdy, following the custom of all newly-appointed Comptrollers-General, asked the intendants for detailed accounts of the impositions levied in their *généralités*.   Turgot took the occasion to explain at length the nature of his reform and to ask again for recognition of his work.   He could now draw attention to the progress on the Bordeaux road, and he could also tell the Government that many other parishes were anxious to adopt the new administration.[33]   But L'Averdy, who paid respect to magisterial opinion, at first was reticent.   It is even doubtful whether he took the trouble to read Turgot's communication—at least, to judge from his confused reply.   However, the finer points he had failed to grasp, and in despair Turgot wrote once more to Trudaine and asked him to explain the situation to the Comptroller-General in all its detail.[34]

But the next year, in April 1765, an *arrêt du conseil* gave official sanction for the levy of 116,443 *livres* for 1766, while retrospective sanction was granted for the years 1762–5,[35] and each successive year an *arrêt du conseil* was accorded.   The following figures, taken from the *Extraits du Registre du Conseil*, illustrate the increase in the operations undertaken.[36]

Year.	Imposition in *livres*.	No. of parishes concerned.
1762	39,991	20
1763	not known	not known
1764	116,443	52
1765	116,443	51
1766	116,443	52
1767	116,443	53
1768	130,704	42
1769	150,500	56
1770	189,251	47
1771	181,133	80
1772	186,750	83
1773	197,125	81
1774	254,188	not known
1775	259,375	not known
1776	259,375	not known
1777	311,250	93
1778	311,898	125

The imposition continued to rise steadily until the Revolution; in 1782 it amounted to 324,555 *livres*,[37] and in 1789 to nearly 340,000 *livres*.[38]

When Turgot left Limoges in 1774, over 450 miles of highways had been constructed. Other roads had been planned; upkeep had been established at an annual cost of 3,000 *livres* in 1764, which figure had reached 75,000 *livres* in 1777.[39] To his successors, d'Aine and d'Arbois, he bequeathed this masterpiece in road administration, and these two intendants, along with Trésaguet, the chief engineer, maintained the existing communications of the *généralité*, reconstructed sections of the old highways, and continued the work of building lesser roads. By 1872, 287 leagues had been built,[40] and by 1783 over 300, of which nearly 100 had been constructed under the organization of the relief works (*ateliers de charité*) first opened by Turgot in the famine years of 1770–2, and continued after that time to provide work for casual labourers and for those whose small domains were insufficient to provide a livelihood.[41]

All these highways were among the finest in the kingdom. Built by Trésaguet, who, before Macadam, constructed roads with sound foundations and with cambered surfaces of chipping set in hardened mud,[42] these were the roads which Young described as being ' much more like the well-kept alleys of a garden than a common highway . . . without dust, sand, stones, or inequality, firm and level, of pounded granite '.[43] Others, too, were loud in their praise of both the roads and the system. When, in 1777, the Government invited the intendants to submit details of the administration of the *corvées* in their *généralités*, d'Aine of Limoges replied: 'Do not change the form of administration established here in 1763. The basis is an annual imposition of 300,000 *livres*, which is paid without reluctance . . . the works are done much more quickly and much more solidly than before. . . . The *corvées* in labour are impracticable here where for fifteen years the *corvéables* have worked for money . . . the deliberations are perfectly free. . . . Maintain the existing state of things.'[44] In 1783 Chaumont de la Millière, who made an official inspection of the roads, reported to the *ponts et chaussées* that all the highways, completed twelve to fourteen years previously, were in excellent condition, with the exception of the Paris–Bordeaux road. This particular route, built upon chalky soil with softer local stone, had been much used by heavy traffic, especially during the American War, when the regiments, their convoys, and artillery passed through Limoges and Angoulême before embarking at Bordeaux. Yet, in spite of this hard wear, its foundations were strong, and all it needed was concentrated effort on its surface.[45] But one more authority must suffice. 'Experience', writes a parish priest from Haut Limousin in 1776, 'has already convinced the public in the *généralité* of Limoges that this form of administration is the only means by which it is possible with the minimum of expenditure to carry the roads to that degree of perfection reached since this system was established. . . . The peasants are unanimously in favour of the method followed here, and are all grateful to this famous magistrate.' [46]

(3)

While engaged in mitigating the burden of forced labour on the roads, Turgot was also giving some attention to the older forms of *corvée* : the obligation of the *taillables* to assist in the transport of army equipment and to provide billets for the troops. These demands were exceptionally heavy in Limousin, where, owing to the plenty of the pastures, cavalry regiments were frequently quartered. While it is true that the inhabitants, finding in the requirements of the regiments a steady sale for agricultural products and even manufactured goods, derived considerable prosperity from the presence of the troops, the demand to transport equipment brought untold hardships upon the parishes lying near the highways. The amounts paid by the army for the hire of horses and oxen amounted only to one-quarter or one-fifth of the customary rates. The peasant, loth to leave his fields at harvest or at ploughing, and reluctant to have his cattle overworked and maltreated by the soldiers, resorted to every dissimulation to evade his obligations. The *syndics* spent countless hours in searching for defaulting confreres, and those who made a punctual appearance at the meeting-place appointed, idled the day away in waiting until the convoy was completed. And when finally the regiments were on the move, the peasants and the soldiers often came to blows. Men in the ranks, weary of walking, swarmed upon the ramshackle wagons already overloaded; and young and insolent army officers, impatient at the slowness of the cattle, goaded them fiercely with the point of the sword.[47]

The regiments were not expected in Limousin until after the conclusion of the Seven Years' War; but in 1762 Turgot had already begun collecting information with a view to planning a reform.[48] He also made a study of the systems established in Languedoc and Franche-Comté, where an imposition was levied to replace the *corvées*, the proceeds going to employ contractors.[49] Working from statistics supplied by the intendant of Franche-Comté and by the municipal officials in Limousin, he decided to levy an annual tax of 15,000 *livres*. At first difficulty was experienced in finding a contractor, but when the fund was increased in 1767 to 17,000 *livres*, a wealthy merchant, Henri Michel, undertook the work, Turgot's reform having received official sanction in the previous year.[50]

Shortly afterwards the rumour came to Turgot's ears that the Government was making arrangements for large contractors to take charge of military transport throughout the whole kingdom. Apprehensive lest local funds might become part of the central finances and at the mercy of Ministries in need, and fearing that yet another powerful corporation of contractors might come into existence, he wrote to the Comptroller-General, d'Invau, who had followed L'Averdy, begging him to leave the administration in the hands of the intendants, who had a knowledge of local rates of labour, and who could give the necessary attention to matters of detail. In that same letter he made two valuable proposals for reducing costs of transport: first, that the contractors should move all equipment not required *en route* to its final destination, the object being to save on the hire of animals; secondly, that for transporting the less bulky stores needed on the journey, the army should acquire its own carts and horses. No individual, Turgot explained in making this last suggestion, ever goes to the expense of hiring a horse to make a long journey: he invariably buys one, and sells it again upon his return.[51]

Turgot next reformed the system of billeting. One of its chief abuses was that small detachments of men descended without notice upon a town and, having made themselves thoroughly objectionable, decamped in the morning not having paid their bill. To remedy this and other irregularities Turgot negotiated separately with the towns, arranging that each community should contract with the inn-keepers for billeting soldiers.[52]   At Limoges he planned a more radical reform.   Having obtained the promise from Choiseul that one regiment at least would be sent to Limousin every year, he built barracks in the town, utilizing stone from the old walls and watch-towers, and thus reducing the cost to only 200,000 *livres*, a sum which was raised by taxation over a period of ten years.[53]

(4)

There remained yet another, perhaps the most detested burden which fell upon the peasantry of the *ancien régime*, and that was the obligation to serve in the militia.[54]   The provincial regiments or territorials commanded by officers drawn from the local nobility and the richer *bourgeoisie* had been created by Louvois in 1688, a law of that same year, along with subsequent legislation, regulating the mode of making the levies.   In theory every year (though in practice the writs were issued at irregular intervals) the King, on the advice of the Minister for War, commanded that a certain number of militia-men should be enrolled to complete the provincial regiments, and sometimes even those of the regulars. Each *généralité* had to provide a contingent, and it was left to the intendants and their subordinates to distribute the burden among the parishes.   The final levy was made by drawing lots ;   all those eligible for the militia were assembled by the subdelegates and *syndics*, and the unfortunate ones who drew black tickets were doomed to six or seven years of service.   The parish was responsible for its soldiers :   if a territorial died or fell ill, or from any other cause could no longer serve, then the community must find a substitute.

From this duty to serve in the provincial regiments there were many—nobles and their servants, clergy, lawyers, doctors and surgeons, schoolmasters and officials—exempted by law.   Others, too, escaped the obligation under the special regulations drawn up by intendants.   As a rule, the eldest sons of those paying over 35 *livres* annually in *capitation*, and also the only sons of aged peasants were allowed exemption.   In the main the burden fell upon bachelors and widowers between the ages of eighteen and forty, and more particularly upon those living in the countryside ; for in nearly all towns, which were also required to provide men for regiments, a method of recruiting volunteers prevailed. According to a contemporary, Bourgelat, compulsory service in the militia affected only one-fortieth of the whole population. Out of all those who might be conscripted, about one in every ten was actually taken, the proportion varying from parish to parish, from one out of seven in some to one out of twenty in others.

The chances of drawing a black ticket caused great fear among the young peasantry, and when the announcement of the *tirage* was made, there were many youths who fled in terror. Some found their way to Spain, some to the towns, and others, if they did not become lifelong vagabonds, might find casual employment in other provinces. Turgot mentions two parishes in Limousin from which no less than forty men fled never to return. He states also that it was not uncommon for the terrified youths to mutilate their hands in order to obtain exemption. In every parish in the province the announcement of the *tirage* was the occasion for parochial civil war. Those who had escaped before the drawing of lots could, if captured, be forced to serve. Therefore it was the custom for the youths who duly presented themselves in readiness for the *tirage*, calling on their friends and relatives, to organize a hunt for the fugitives hiding in the woods. Work ceased in the fields for days and even weeks on end, the battle, in which nearly every one joined, ending usually in serious casualties and sometimes murder.[55] And when finally a sufficient number of fugitives were caught, they were bound hand and foot, handed over to the *maréchaussée*, and taken off to serve in the regiments.

Turgot, full of pity for these youths, began by forbidding the hunt of the fugitives. He asked the *curés* to inform their parishioners that, while in future the police would continue to apprehend those who fled, no effort would be spared to mitigate the horrors of the drawing of lots. Towards this end he took it upon himself to suspend the law forbidding the practice known as the *mise au chapeau*, by which all those drawing lots formed a fund which went as a consolation prize for those unfortunate enough to receive black tickets. At the same time, availing himself of a loophole in the law of 1765, he permitted, and also encouraged, the peasantry to engage volunteers to discharge the parochial obligation to provide recruits. For usually there were to be found enough landless men who were only too glad to serve the six years in return for money, hoping at the end of their service to buy a field or two and set up on their own. Such practices were fairly common in other provinces, and where they had come into existence, the intendants were seldom so heartless as to execute the laws against them. Turgot's measures quickly produced a salutary effect: the parochial warfare came to an end, and no longer did the youths take flight to the woods. In informing Monteynard, then Minister for War, of what he had done, Turgot suggested that this volunteer system should be given legal standing throughout the kingdom. At the same time he proposed that, with a view to equalizing a burden which fell haphazardly upon

the parishes, unions should be formed and the volunteers enlisted
for longer terms of service. The existing system he believed
to be barbarous, and an unwarrantable curtailment of the rights of
the subject, seeing that, as experience had shown, sufficient
volunteers would always be forthcoming.[56]

Monteynard's successor, d'Aiguillon, took up in earnest the
reform of the militia, and early in 1774 called a conference of the
intendants who happened to be staying in Paris. Turgot and La
Galaisière, who together took the chief share in these deliberations,
were asked to draw up a plan of reform. This they did, but on
the very day they submitted their project, d'Aiguillon was dismissed. The new Minister for War, Du Muy, attached no
importance to their proposals, and for a while nothing further
was done. Upon becoming Comptroller-General, Turgot, having
first enlisted the sympathy of Louis XVI, made another attempt to
reform the militia. Du Muy, however, remained opposed and,
with the support of two military experts in the Committee of the
Council that discussed the problem, persuaded Louis to maintain
the existing system, their argument being that volunteers would
never be sufficient and that the quality of the provincial regiments
would necessarily deteriorate. As a consequence, an ordinance
was promulgated in December 1774 drawing attention to the law
as it stood, and forbidding the practices that had grown up in
contravention of it. Actually the ordinance was generally ignored.
The Abbé de Véri found that in Berry and Bourbonnais the *mise au
chapeau* continued as before, and the men who were awarded the
fund would then often find volunteers to serve in their places,
paying to their substitutes only a fraction of the money, and making
a profit which at times came to 265 *livres*. In Toulouse it was
quite common for those eligible for service to find the volunteers
beforehand and, observing the formality of the drawing of lots,
to arrange that their men were chosen. These facts the Abbé
de Véri passed on to Turgot, who immediately brought them to
the notice of the King, in the hope of persuading him that he might
as well regularize a voluntary system.[57] But it was not until after
Du Muy's death that the militia was reformed. In December
1775 Saint-Germain, the Minister for War, virtually abolished the
provincial levies, with the exception of a picked regiment known
as the Royal Grenadiers. From that time onwards, although
militia-men were still conscripted, they were not required to
train but only to report at appointed times.

CHAPTER VI

TURGOT AND THE SOCIETY OF AGRICULTURE

(1)

SHORTLY after 1750 the French Ministry, the administrative officials, and many private persons, under the influence of new economic thought and the necessity of improving the national finances, began an inquiry into, and drew up a number of suggestions for developing, the agrarian resources of the kingdom. To these efforts an additional stimulus was given when, in October 1759, Bertin was appointed to the *controle général*. During his tenure of office he created a Ministry of Agriculture, the operations of which he himself directed; and when, in December 1763, he was dismissed from the Finances, the King, in recognition of his services, left him in charge of the administration of agriculture.[1] Bertin was one of Quesnay's following and a protégé of Mme de Pompadour. It was to their influence that he owed not only his promotion to the *controle général*, but also the permission, after he had ceased to be Comptroller, to continue his work in his new department.

Turgot's stay at Limoges coincides with that period when the Central Government redoubled its activities to develop the agrarian resources of the country.[2] As intendant he was called upon to execute the measures that Bertin promoted, and also to furnish information upon the special conditions and requirements of his province. Of his work in this connexion abundant evidence exists;[3] and this shows quite clearly that while he welcomed Bertin's intentions of encouraging agriculture, he was frequently critical and sceptical of the means proposed. From the very beginning he refused to put much faith in the Societies of Agriculture which Bertin was hoping to develop, with the aid of the intendants, into a regular machinery for agrarian administration.[4]

Turgot's predecessor, Pajot de Marcheval, an enthusiastic agriculturalist, had already, between December 1759 and July 1760, organized a Society or School of Agriculture upon his own initiative. The object of this institution was that the members should conduct experiments in agricultural science, it being

79

hoped that their discoveries and agrarian ventures might prove
a shining example to the province as a whole. Some of these
experiments were to take place upon the members' own domains;
but the expenses entailed were to be met out of public funds.
Other researches were to be carried out upon a model farm.
The difficulty of financing these ambitious plans was finally
overcome : Marcheval closed down and utilized the funds of a
State-owned tree-nursery which had become a veritable wilder-
ness, and with part of the proceeds leased the two domains of
Cordelas, in the parish of Panazol, near Limoges. These he
placed under the supervision of his Society of Agriculture. On
the one a supply of trees for the roadsides was to be grown;
on the other, which possessed a variation of soils, agricultural
experiments were to be made, each member of the School taking
charge of a particular venture.[5] ' You see, gentlemen,' wrote
Marcheval to the landowners whose assistance he invited, ' that
the Society will devote itself entirely to agricultural practice.' [6]

Bertin, upon hearing of Marcheval's plans, was most enthusiastic. He informed the intendant that this was precisely the
type of institution he desired to establish throughout the country,
and later he suggested that the Society of Limoges should be
given official standing, its constitution being embodied in an
arrêt du conseil.[7] The outcome was that a number of changes
were made in the organization of Marcheval's original Society,
the chief of which was the creation of three branches or bureaux,
one at Limoges with twenty members, another at Brive, and a
third at Angoulême, each of which were to have ten full members.
All the bureaux were to have a fixed number of associates and
an unlimited number of correspondents. Meetings were to be
held once a week, and records were to be kept of membership,
regulations and decisions, letters written and received, books
and periodicals in possession of the bureaux, and papers on
agricultural topics read to the members.[8]

Turgot first attended the Society on 24 October 1761, and as
intendant he was the president all the time that he remained at
Limoges. But his first action was to close down the experimental farm at Cordelas. He came to this decision after a full
inspection of the domain; he had found everything in great
disorder, and he could not avoid the conclusion that the expense
of the venture greatly exceeded its utility.[9] The report to
Bertin justifying this move has not come down to us, but a year
later, in reply to a circular [10] to intendants expressing the Government's intention of establishing farms for all the Societies of
Agriculture, he obviously draws upon his experience and his
knowledge of that at Limoges. ' Experiments made in common ', he wrote, ' are always badly made, and the attempt to

give them publicity often emphasizes their failures, so that methods which in themselves are most desirable are frequently discredited.'[11] It cannot be denied that nearly all the early undertakings of the Society of Limoges had ended in lamentable failure.[12] Early in 1762 the Marquis de Mirabeau wrote to the Secretary congratulating the body on having closed down an institution which was a waste of public money. The sum in question was 10,000 *livres* annually. Out of the saving, Turgot devoted 2,500 *livres* to the purchase of trees for the highways, and the remainder he utilized, as we have seen, in reforming the *corvées*. To finance the Society's activities for the future—a mere matter of meeting costs of books, periodicals, meterological instruments, and printing—he obtained from Bertin a grant of 1,200 *livres*.[13] This little service to the Society he performed as a matter of course; funds were available, and it was merely a question of saying how much was necessary. It is fairly obvious, then, that from the beginning he never rated the usefulness of the Society very highly. He attended its sessions (which became more infrequent as time went on) with regularity, and always displayed an interest in its activities without deceiving himself as to their value. He was not in any way antagonistic to the institution: he merely accepted it for what it was worth.

Bertin, on the contrary, continued to show unbounded enthusiasm for his Societies of Agriculture. From them he demanded reports every three months, and on numerous occasions he would send for copies of the papers read to the members.[14] Above all, he came to look upon these bodies as consultative committees, and, when framing measures for the encouragement of agriculture, he would ask them to deliberate upon his suggestions. One of the reforms in which Bertin was particularly interested was that of promoting the cultivation of the wastes and perpetual fallows. In August 1761 he issued an *arrêt du conseil*, which was applicable to fifteen *généralités*, including Limoges, freeing all land newly brought under cultivation from the *taille* and other royal impositions for a period of ten years. The response was disappointing, and Bertin, being far from satisfied, approached the Societies of Agriculture in the hope of discovering other means of promoting his designs.[15]

Already a number of these bodies had studied the technical problems of clearing and ameliorating land. In its early meetings in 1768 the Society of Limoges had read and discussed the abridged edition of Turbilly's noted *Mémoire sur les défrichements*.[16] In 1762 Lenoir of Limoges read a paper advocating the exemption from the ecclesiastical tithe as well as from royal taxation those lands reclaimed from waste and fallow, the privilege to hold good for a period of ten years. A year later the

bureaux were invited by Parent of the Society at Lyon to sub-
scribe to a petition for legislation freeing intakes of lands from
all impositions, including feudal rents, for a period of twenty
years.[17] At Brive, Saint-Hilaire read a most interesting paper
on this topic. He had observed that, following upon the law
of August 1761 which exempted newly cultivated land from
royal taxation, many peasants had been encouraged to leave
fallow the fields they usually ploughed, in order to cultivate
wastes of inferior soil. In his opinion it was not the amount
of arable that was lacking throughout the kingdom, but the
amount of labour employed upon it, and no encouragement should
be given to the peasants and landowners to plough inferior soil
to the neglect of improving those already tilled. Saint-Hilaire
convinced his audience, and the bureau of Brive decided not to
support the petition.[18]

To such reasoning the Government paid no attention. In
1764 exemptions from royal taxation and tithes were granted for
fifteen years upon all land reclaimed from marsh and fen, and in
1766 this privilege was extended to all types of newly cultivated
land.[19] These measures gave a satisfactory result: between
1766 and 1769 nearly 260,000 *arpents* were reclaimed or taken
from the waste.[20] But this imposing figure failed to impress
Turgot, who commented as follows: ' The statement of the
newly cultivated lands submitted to M. d'Ormesson appear to
prove a considerable extension of the arable. . . . But at the most
these clearings are and always will be very few, and far less
important than the ameliorations of lands already productive. . . .
This last kind of improvement is subject to no official scrutiny:
its costs are appreciably less and the profits accruing from it
are much more assured than those derived from the cultivation
of the waste.' [21]

He adopted a similar attitude towards Bertin's attempt to
abolish *vaine pâture* and *droit de parcours*. According to the
former, as soon as the hay-meadows and the arable had been
harvested, the land became a common pasture. The latter,
droit de parcours, was the right of intercommoning—an extension
of *vaine pâture* implying the reciprocal rights of two or more
adjacent communes to graze the cattle upon neighbouring commons after the harvests.[22] Bertin had once again consulted the
agricultural societies. At the time official opinion upon the
question of the commons was hesitant; on the one hand there
was an urge to bring every inch of land under cultivation, and on
the other a great reluctance to snatch from the poorer peasantry
those rights which were certainly essential to their livelihood.[23]
The Societies of Agriculture, including that of Limoges, were
disposed to favour legislation abolishing the common rights.

In Limousin, however, as the bureau of Limoges went on to mention in its report, the scattered commons were inextensive and the *droit de parcours* was a relatively unimportant feature in agrarian economy.[24] Hence, when later Bertin abolished the common rights, he considered it quite unnecessary to make his legislation applicable to the *généralité* of Limoges.[25]

In these discussions Turgot had taken no part. When Bertin sent to him a projected *arrêt du conseil* legalizing the cultivation of the commons, he merely passed it on to L'Épine, the Secretary of the Society of Limoges.[26] Then, again, when Bertin dispatched a circular in July 1766 asking for information and advice upon the *droit de parcours*, once more he handed it on to the Society, and himself made no comment.[27] But when, in 1762 and again in 1764, Bertin consulted the Societies upon his proposed legislation establishing free trade in grain,[28] Turgot displayed unbounded enthusiasm. Here was a matter of supreme importance, and here, in his opinion, was an opportunity of going to the root of the agrarian problem. He fully realized that one of the conditions of a flourishing agriculture in France was the removal of obstacles impeding the sale of the products of the soil. Therefore he spared no effort to persuade the members of the Society of Agriculture to declare themselves wholeheartedly in favour of free trade. Again, in 1763 he took great trouble to expound for their benefit and to overcome their objections to the Declaration of 25 May establishing a large degree of freedom of internal commerce in grain.[29] A few months later, having raised the question once again, he distributed to the members copies of Du Pont's *De l'exportation et de l'importation des grains*, which the author had read to the Society of Agriculture of Soissons and which, dedicated to Mme de Pompadour, appeared in print early in 1764. A reading of this work seems to have convinced the members of the value of free trade.[30] Later in the year the bureau of Limoges addressed a *mémoire* to the Society of Paris stating the belief that an even greater freedom of trade would enable the province to sell its surplus grain which had accumulated during the past two years, and would also encourage landowners in the region to bring areas of waste and fallows under the plough.[31] Some time after the Edict of July 1764 had been promulgated establishing freedom of export, the Society again discussed the problem, and the Secretary was instructed to send a minute to the Council stating that the province was deriving considerable prosperity from the increased price of grain.[32]

It was obviously Turgot's policy to employ the Society of Agriculture to propagate the doctrine of free trade. He had hoped that the members would give Du Pont's book the greatest publicity, and that as they moved about they would convert other landowners to the views that it contained. And when, following the poor harvest of 1765, local opinion grew hostile to free commerce in grain, again he turned to the Society for assistance. In March 1766 he dispatched to all three bureaux printed exemplars of his instruction to the police officials of the towns [33] giving a reasoned command to them to execute the laws of 1763 and 1764, together with copies of Letrosne's book *La Liberté du commerce des grains toujours utile et jamais nuisible*. These he asked the members to distribute throughout the *généralité*.[34]

(2)

Meanwhile Turgot was encouraging the Society to undertake researches to discover adequate methods of storing grain. For if, as he hoped, freedom of commerce would lead to the formation of large supplies in years of plenty, it was necessary to ensure their immunity from deterioration and from the ravage of pests. In Limousin and Angoumois the problem of storing grain presented at that time especial difficulties. Almost every year the crops were attacked by pests, which either devoured the grain while it was growing, or so affected it that it rotted in the granaries.[35] Particularly devastating were the *charançon* or corn weevil, and the *alucite*, a species of grain moth. Turgot endeavoured to identify these pests. He studied Réaumur's *Histoire des insectes* (1736), which described the increase of the *charançon* in Poitou, whence, it was usually supposed, it had made its way into Angoumois in the 'thirties. At the same time he wrote to Blossac, intendant of Poitiers, asking for available information of its ravages.[36] Already his predecessor, Marcheval, had prevailed upon the Council to send two members of the *Académie des sciences*, Duhamel and Tillet, to study the pest in Angoumois. Their researches, lasting two years, were published under the title *Histoire d'un insecte qui dévore les grains* (1762). Their advice was that grain for storage should be heated to a temperature of about 60° (Réaumur), but never above 70° if it was to be used for seed. To this work Turgot gave considerable publicity. In a meeting of the Society of Agriculture he announced his intention of having essential passages translated into dialect, printed, and distributed.[37] Then again, early in 1762, he asked the priests to inform their parishioners of the means of destroying the *charançon* and, in order to make it possible for the peasants to adopt the devices advocated, he had stoves constructed and acquired the use of seigneurial ovens.[38]

The members of the Society of Agriculture undertook their own researches. L'Épine claimed that the pests might be destroyed if the grain were exposed to the vapour of boiling water to which a small quantity of mercury had been added. Feytiat advocated the placing of certain herbs in the granaries, and Chareau suggested that the grain should be ground immediately after the harvest, and that the subdelegates should ensure that all seed-grain harbouring the pest was destroyed. It was, however, Montalembert, the president at Brive, who devoted most attention to the problem, and it was his researches that Turgot had published in pamphlet form in 1763. Montalembert advised heating the grain to a temperature of between 80° and 90° for a period of 48 hours, adding that, should it be required for seed, it should be soaked in water over-night As the peasants had no thermometers, they were to put a lump of butter in the oven: if it melted while they said *un Pater et un Avé*, they might be sure that the temperature was that required.[39]

By the year 1766 the scourge of the *charançon* had almost ceased. The extinction of the pest Du Pont attributes to Turgot's policy;[40] but what is more likely is that the severe frosts of the winter of 1765–6 destroyed the *charançon*; or it may have been that the year 1766 marked the close of a cycle of exceptional propagation upon its part. After that date the Society gave greater attention to other problems of storing grain, and also to improving milling. A new type of rat-trap introduced by Turgot (for rats devoured huge quantities of grain), a contrivance for drying grain invented by Saint-Laurent, a grinding-machine for which Musnier received a prize of 300 *livres*, a winnower and thrasher—all these figure in the Society's records.[41] In Musnier's *moulins économiques* Turgot was especially interested, and one could wish to know more of his efforts in collaboration with the Comte de Broglie to establish these mills throughout the *généralité*, his intention being to save the peasants from *banalités* and from the extortions of the millers.[42]

Other improvements in agricultural implements were made by the Society from time to time. A coulter plough constructed by Perret and a large eight-ox cleaning plough invented by Saint-Laurent had been successfully demonstrated at Cordelas. Later Saint-Laurent constructed a rather lighter model, which proved extraordinarily effective. The members also studied descriptions and diagrams of ploughs invented in other parts of France, while in 1766 a whole session was devoted to the examination of Randall's plough, an account of which appeared in the *London Chronicle*. At Brive a turf-breaking implement was constructed on similar lines to one in use in Languedoc; a study was made of drills for sowing rye; and a demonstration was given of a plough which hoed between the rows of plants. At a later date a harrow for use across the furrows was introduced, and by 1786 was to be found on several domains. For all such novelties Turgot displayed the greatest enthusiasm. At his invitation Montaigne gave a demonstration of a clod-breaking machine to the bureau of Limoges. On another occasion he introduced from Normandy a collar-yoke for oxen. So numerous were the inventions that Turgot suggested building a permanent agricultural exhibition at Limoges. The Society, however, persuaded him to employ the money in purchasing a drill and in distributing to the peasantry samples of good seeds.[43]

Indeed, the problem of obtaining better strains of seed, together with the kindred researches into methods of sowing, rotations, and preparation of the soil, had always received their fair share of attention. The bureau at Angoulême issued a pamphlet advocating deep ploughing for thick soils and frequent, shallow ploughing for thin, friable loams ; a fallow every third year for poorer land ; and upon the better arable maize or grass as an ameliorating crop in rotation to wheat and barley.[44] But the members at Brive found that maize as an ameliorating crop was too exhausting and, unwilling to jump to conclusions, suggested experiments which should be carried out over a period of years.[45] Meanwhile, the bureau at Limoges debated the advisability of thin sowing by means of a drill to replace the usual method of sowing thickly broadcast.[46] To that same body Saint-Laurent described his experiment of working the soil deeply and finely and of adopting a threefold rotation of barley, spring wheat, and roots. He claimed that whereas his *métayers* farming a similar type of land received only a steady yield of four to one, his own return was on an average well over three times greater.[47]

In these attempts to discover and apply new agricultural methods Turgot was ready to assist. On several occasions he distributed strains of wheat and barley with pamphlets on their cultivation, requesting the members to test them and to pass on seed to other proprietors. One species of wheat, in particular, delighted the bureaux of Brive and Limoges, and soon became widely cultivated.[48] Again, he obtained from Bertin plentiful supplies of madder seed, together with copies of Duhamel's treatise on its cultivation, and he made an arrangement with La Forêt, the textile manufacturer at Limoges, for the purchase of the crops.[49] Much more ambitious was his attempt to promote the cultivation of silk-worms, which in Limousin had always proved a failure.[50] Turgot's method was to offer bounties, 175 *livres* to every person who planted 1,000 sound mulberry trees and 7s. 6d. on every pound of cocoons over twenty.[51] But these measures served to encourage only a few large landowners, the cost of the outlay and the care required in this branch of agriculture being much too great for the poor and indolent peasantry.[52]

More successful were his persistent efforts to introduce potatoes. In France, as in England, it was a long while—in fact, the peasants had to be starving—before they would adopt them as a food, and it was still longer before they came to prefer them to inferior grains like buckwheat or easily grown foods like chestnuts. Potatoes had long been cultivated in several parts of France, but they were used exclusively for feeding pigs and cattle. In Limousin none were grown until the 'sixties. Their first mention in the records of the bureau of Limoges is for December 1763, when Perret read a paper [53] on their culture, and, displaying specimens he had grown, recommended them for regions which had no chestnuts.[54] A short while afterwards Turgot gave the Society a large sack of seed-potatoes, some of which, along with Perret's pamphlet, were sent to Angoulême and Brive. In the discussion to which the gift gave rise at Brive, ' it was recalled that *patates* had been introduced by an Englishman, the Duke of Hamilton, who stayed for a long time in the town under the name of the Chevalier Binet and who used to eat them mixed with fish'. Treilhard, ' who had tasted this mixture' and who had ' polluted his vineyards by growing potatoes', had no good word to say for them.[55] His views were shared by others, Feytiat of Limoges going so far as to say that potatoes were as harmful to pigs as to human beings. And it was a general opinion that the common folk could never be induced to eat them.[56] But Turgot persevered. Every day he had potato bread served at his table.[57] In 1766 he distributed a whole load of seeds among the bureaux, and from that time onwards he would frequently send them to the *curés*, asking them to grow them and distribute the crop among their parishioners. Gradually potatoes became part of the diet of Limousin. In 1765 Turgot mentions them for the first time in his official statement of the crops.[58] Shortly afterwards a number of landowners began to produce large quantities, and in 1772 Puymarets stated to the Society of Limoges that in recent years the peasants had taken rapidly to their cultivation.[59] Undoubtedly it was the famine of 1770–2, when the peasants had been glad to get anything to eat, that had led to the general acceptance of potatoes. By 1780 they had become a regular food for the poorer classes in Limousin.[60] All this had happened long before Parmentier had popularized them in other parts of France.[61]

With this notable exception of potatoes, the introduction of new crops was confined to the domains of a few progressive landowners. Nothing much came, for example, of the spasmodic efforts to popularize various kinds of grasses or to improve the hay 'and grazing meadows. Actually in Limousin the natural pastures were sufficient to feed the cattle up to the middle of the autumn, at which time most of the beasts were sold. Hence there was really no incentive to increase supplies of fodder. A more pressing problem in the cattle-rearing regions was that of saving the herds from disastrous epidemics. In 1762 there was a serious outbreak of murrain.[62] Turgot consulted Bourgelat, the famous veterinary surgeon, with whom he had become acquainted when staying at Lyon, and from him he obtained an instruction on the prevention and treatment of the disease. This he had printed and distributed throughout the province, the curés being asked to explain the contents to the peasantry and to dole out the remedies that the administration provided. Even after the general outbreak had died down, Turgot and the Society continued to distribute Bourgelat's pamphlet, and also another treatise written by Barbaret.[63] But valuable as these methods were in checking epidemics, they alone were not sufficient; and Turgot was anxious to supplement them by establishing a regular service of veterinary surgeons. Collaborating with the Society of Agriculture and with Bertin, he arranged for pupils to be sent to Bourgelat's school at Lyon, which had been established in 1762. By 1765 he had founded a school at Limoges under the directorship of Mira, one of Bourgelat's pupils. But this institution, to which Du Pont gave great publicity in the *Journal du commerce*, was not a success. Although Turgot supported pupils out of public funds and gave them capital to establish practices, the recruits attracted to this new profession were far too few to justify expenses, and therefore he reverted to the original plan of sending students to study at Lyon.[64]

It is not at all likely that these beginnings of a veterinary service were sufficient to decrease considerably the mortality of cattle from epidemics, or even those losses of a more normal kind. Very few of the peasants could afford the fees, and nearly all persevered with their traditional remedies. Nor was there any widespread improvement in the care of the herds. A few gentlemen farmers did indeed begin to bed down their cattle, to build good stables and byres, and to provide enough hay and roots for winter-feeding.[65] Otherwise the practice of turning out the calves to face the rigours of the cold winters still continued, often with disastrous results, as for example during the years 1767–70, when the loss of young animals was so considerable as to produce ultimately a shortage of meat in the Paris market, the peasants being without the ready money to replace the one-and two-year-olds that had perished.[66]

Much the same is true—that is to say, some success upon the part of a few landowners, but none to speak of upon that of the peasant proprietors—of sheep-farming in the *généralité*, in spite of the encouragement given by Turgot and the Society of Agriculture. The hilly regions of Limousin were admirable for sheep, and the members of the Society agreed that the administration ought to finance new breeds, particularly the best from Holland and England, in the hope that the peasantry might be persuaded to adopt them.[67] Turgot did his best to meet this demand. He introduced new breeds from Spain and England, and during his intendance there were several fine flocks to be seen upon the domains of the larger landowners. Furthermore, he abolished taxation upon sheep and offered substantial rewards for the slaughter of wolves. But when all is told, little progress in sheep-farming was made: and even the new flocks were soon to perish from rot.[68]

(3)

Although the lone enthusiasts of the Society of Agriculture were chiefly interested in their own domains, nevertheless a few of them felt it was their duty to coax the small proprietors to renounce their old-fashioned methods. Several individuals offered prizes to their tenants. ' This means more impositions. It is a trick of the landowners in Brive to make us work harder,' grumbled the *métayers* upon Treilhard's domains, until, being shown a *louis d'or*, they began to toil from sunrise to sunset and even by moonlight to win the reward for the best-tilled plot. But in spite of proposals made from time to time to establish a regular system of prizes, nothing was done; the profits of Cordelas, out of which it was hoped to establish a prize-fund, never materialized, and a proposal that members should follow the English custom of contributing for this purpose met with no response.[69] It was Turgot who finally established yearly prizes, not, however, for a well-kept farm, but for dissertations on agricultural topics. One prize of 300 *livres*, provided out of the funds of the Society, was to be awarded for a treatise on agrarian practice; another similar award, for which Turgot himself found the money, was to be made for the best essay on economic theory.[70]

For the first year, 1767, the subject of the treatise on agricultural practice was the cheapest and least wasteful method of distilling wine, and the prize was carried off by the famous agriculturalist, the Abbé Rosier, whose work was later published at Turgot's instigation.[71] The title of the economic dissertation was *L'Effet de l'impôt indirect sur le revenu des propriétaires des biens-fonds*. Turgot's motive in setting this subject is obvious: he was hoping to stimulate the interest of the landowners in the problems of taxation. In the programme [72] that he drew up he explained briefly the terms he had employed in the title and added a concise account of physiocratic theory.

What in fact he wanted was an elaborate study based upon this doctrine with facts and figures bearing out each contention. The next year he chose a similar subject, and one which had a close bearing upon his financial reforms. Competitors were asked to describe *La Meilleure Manière d'estimer exactement les revenues des fonds dans les différents genres de culture*. His motive was two-fold : he wished to arouse interest in a *cadastre* for tax assessment ; he hoped also that a number of people might be induced to undertake that statistical work which was to have been done by Du Pont and on which he himself had made a beginning in his *Mémoire sur la surcharge*.[73] Again he took the trouble to explain the terms in the title : by *revenu* was to be understood the profit that remained when all expenses—costs of seed, labour, rents, tithes, improvements—had been deducted from gross income.

The prize for the treatise on the *impôt indirect* was given to Saint-Péravy, whose essay was later published at Turgot's request.[74] Among the ten other efforts submitted, Graslin's, actually upholding indirect taxation, received honourable mention.[75] Upon these two works Turgot composed long *critiques* which, no doubt, he read to the Society when adjudicating the awards. But Turgot's subject for 1768 attracted only one competitor, whose work was too inferior to merit a reward ; and even when the prize-money was doubled, no other candidate was forthcoming.[76] The subject, entailing a laborious study of the accounts of several domains, was far too exacting. When earlier Turgot had asked the members of the Society of Agriculture to undertake such a task upon their own estates, his request had met with no response.[77]

These attempts to interest the Society in economic theory found little favour with Bertin, who as early as 1764 had circularized the Societies requesting them not to discuss academic questions to the neglect of agricultural practice.[78] Upon receiving a copy of the notice of prizes offered at Limoges, he was much concerned. To L'Averdy, the Comptroller-General, he suggested that the Society should be compelled to draw up another programme. L'Averdy agreed, and authorized him to send a reprimand. To the Secretary he wrote, ' I believe—and the Comptroller agrees with me—that it is extremely dangerous to encourage the public to discuss administrative problems, and it is greatly to be regretted that the programme was ever published. It is the wish of the Government that similar subjects should not be announced in future.' [79] But when it was learned that Turgot was giving the prize-money out of his own pocket, the matter was allowed to drop,[80] though as a precaution the Secretary, L'Épine, was asked to forward to the government all *mémoires* on economic theory, the intention being to silence

possible attacks upon the administration.[81]   As it happened, no
treatise gave cause for Ministerial anxiety; Saint-Péravy's essay
was a plagiary of Mirabeau's *Philosophie rurale*; while Graslin's
work was a heavy academic treatise which could hardly give rise
to discussion outside the earnest readers of *Éphémérides*.   Turgot
continued to offer prizes for expositions of economic theory.[82]
Yet no further efforts were forthcoming; official disapprobation
was sufficient to cool the ardour of the agriculturalists of the
Society, nearly all of whom were in the habit of citing their
achievements when asking the Government for offices or even
for financial assistance.   To give one example: when Joyeuse
was applying for a post in the Marine at Marseilles, he gave as
his chief qualification his *L'Histoire du charançon*,[83] which had
earned him an award at Limoges in 1768.

By that time the Society was in decline, and even the prizes
for dissertations on practical subjects—yoking, horse-ploughing,
and care of vineyards—attracted no competitors.   The number
of yearly sessions had been slowly diminishing since 1761.   Turgot's attempt to revive the Society in 1769 at Bertin's request
met with no lasting result, and the efforts of his successor suffered
much the same fate.[84]   In 1782 the branch at Limoges became a
literary society, the members ironically declaring that ' they
would take as great an interest in agriculture as before '.   In this
form the institution dragged out its existence until 1790.[85]   While
the Society had been a novelty it had attracted much attention;
but, having discussed every topic there was to be discussed,
there was nothing to be done.   Even in the very early days
the members at Angoulême had told Bertin emphatically that
' the work of the Society is entirely useless while the husbandmen are unable to afford the introduction of new methods '.[86]
Nor were the achievements of individuals really of much importance.   Arthur Young, who undoubtedly was lavish in his
praise of a good farm when he met with one, was not enamoured
of the achievements of the more noted agriculturalists like Turbilly and Rosier, and he would certainly have been amused with
the activities of the less famous men at Brive, Limoges, and
Angoulême.   When his attention was drawn to the Society of
Agriculture of Limoges, he remarked: ' This society does like
other societies: they meet, converse, offer premiums, and publish
nonsense. . . . I asked particularly if the members of the Society
had lands in their own hands. . . . I was assured that they
had; but the conversation presently explained it; they had
métayers round their country seats, and this was considered as
farming their own lands. . . .'   Young went on to suggest that
the Society ought to have a model farm.[87]   He had evidently not
heard of that at Cordelas, which was, in fact, farmed by *métayers*.

CHAPTER VII

TURGOT AND FREE TRADE IN GRAIN, 1761–74

(1)

For centuries the Government of France and the authorities in the towns had subjected the grain trade to a bewildering mass of regulations, the little freedom allowed to other kinds of trade being denied entirely to that in corn. Most people would have agreed with the Abbé Galiani when he wrote: ' I am not an enemy of liberty of commerce; I welcome it when it is a matter of luxuries. But bread is another thing; it belongs to police and not to commerce.'[1] Export of grain to foreign countries was prohibited by law upon pain of a fine of 500 *livres*. There were, however, occasions when these restrictions were relaxed. In times of plenty permission was given either generally to all merchants, or to certain individuals, to export grain. General licences were granted in the form of an *arrêt du conseil*, in which were specified the grains which might be exported and also the duration of the privilege. Special permits issued to individuals were signed by a Secretary of State; these again prescribed the duration of the privilege, the quantity and kind of corn to be exported, and frequently its destination.[2] But far more vexatious than these impediments to export were the regulations to which the grain trade was subjected within the kingdom. Corn and flour could not be moved from one province to another without specific or general permits similar to those required for export. Before a licence was granted, all details of the enterprise had to be submitted to an intendant; and after the grain had been transported, a certificate must be produced showing that the consignment had actually reached the prescribed destination.

Within each province grain was subjected to further restrictions. An ordinance of 1727[3] stipulated that all wheat, flour, barley, oats, and other grains should not be bought, sold, or measured anywhere else than in the halls and markets or in the ports, towns, and boroughs of the kingdom. In all such places there obtained yet another series of regulations, drawn up by the police authorities, and executed much more rigorously than the general laws promulgated by the State. It was a common practice to allow the local inhabitants to make their own purchases of grain before the markets were thrown open to foreigners from other parishes and towns, or even to the bakers. In times of shortage, additional precautions were put into force. Merchants were compelled to bring their stores to the markets and to sell them at prices fixed by the local police; house-to-house searches were organized for secret hoards of grain; and every one—merchants, landowners, and even consumers—was instructed to relinquish their supplies.[4]

Needless to say, these measures increased the price of bread; not only did the costs of transport rise when cereals had to be carried to the towns, but also there were tolls levied upon the grain in transit, and upon its sale in the markets. But from these precautions, for which he paid so dearly, the consumer derived no real security. Instead of averting shortages of grain, the regulations served only to make local famines more frequent and a general dearth throughout a province much more serious. For they retarded the development of a corn trade sufficiently large in volume and extensive in organization to transfer the plenty of one region to make good the want of another. Throughout France there were wide fluctuations in corn prices from market to market, especially in the backward provinces like Limousin; therefore there should have been every incentive for merchants to transfer the grain from one district to another, in spite of the high costs of transport. That very variation in prices, however, only shows that a large volume of commerce in corn did not exist; and this condition must be attributed chiefly to the tolls and regulations that fettered the dealers and prevented them from developing their trade. Here was a vicious circle: the lack of a highly organized commerce in grain perpetuated the restrictive régime, which in turn impeded the growth of a corn trade. A few miles away from a region where the people were starving, there might be a seasonal abundance rotting in the granaries; in one province the farmers might be unable to sell their surplus harvest; in a neighbouring province the yield might be only half the average. In quite normal times there was hardly any movement of grain between Tulle and Brive, though prices at Tulle were usually only three-fifths of those at Brive. No wonder, then, that when both towns were short of grain there existed no adequate commercial organization to bring relief from outside the province.[5]

In the absence of a sufficiently large grain trade, the Government itself was obliged to assume responsibilities for the nation's food. Utilizing the intendants' reports upon the crops, the Ministry bought grain where the harvests were good for the relief of those regions where the yield was low. During the reign of Louis XIV an administration known as the *Grains du Roi* had been created to carry out this work, and large granaries had been established to house the purchases made by officials.[6] In the *généralité* of Limoges only one such depot had been maintained, in spite of the intendants' plea that others were necessary.[7] During the famine of 1699 the supplies of grain were entirely inadequate, and throughout the province the poorer inhabitants died like flies.[8] Such occurrences were fairly common, and the administration, in its unsuccessful efforts to feed the people, usually brought upon itself the abuse to which the mediaeval world had subjected the miller, the engrosser, and the baker. From the reign of Louis XIV onwards the dealings of officials were frequently suspect, and at different times the Marquis de Prie, the brothers Pâris, Henri, duc de Bourbon, Fleury, Machault, L'Averdy, Choiseul, the Abbé Terray, the Du Barry, even Louis XV and Louis XVI—all were accused of having amassed fortunes from grain monopolies. Outcries and demonstrations in the *faubourgs* of Paris and in the provincial towns were daily events; and almost invariably the magistracy, wishing to gain prestige by attributing famine to the reckoning of the Government, encouraged agitation, and sometimes engineered the riots.

When Turgot was at Limoges, the famous slogan, *pacte de famine*, had not then been coined, but the facts upon which it rested, or rather the fabrications of Le Prévôt de Beaumont, derive from this period. These alleged disclosures were written down by Thiery, and were entitled *Horrible conspiration, ligue ancienne entre le ministre, la police, le parlement de Paris, contre la France entière, décourverte en juillet, 1768, par Jean Charles Guillaume Prévôt de Beaumont.* It was the evidence from this source that became one of the charges against Louis XVI, and it was these disclosures also that led L'Averdy to the guillotine, it being alleged that he had caused stores of grain to be thrown into a pond in the park of his château.[9]

(2)

To understand the incidents leading to Beaumont's story of a *pacte de famine*, we must go back to August 1761, the month that Turgot took up residence at Limoges. On arrival he found a circular from Bertin asking the advice of the intendants upon a projected declaration allowing free trade in grain; and the first day of his intendance he spent in composing a reply, emphatically pronouncing for free trade, and citing the authority of his old friend and master, Vincent de Gournay.[10] The outcome of Bertin's inquiry was the Declaration of 25 May 1763, establishing internal free trade in grain, all subjects, whatever their rank, profession, or trade, being permitted to buy and sell corn at any time, at any place, and to transport it free from all tolls save those

levied in the markets. But further than this Bertin was not prepared to go. He was afraid lest free exportation might have
disastrous results, and his experience in his former office of
lieutenant of the police had convinced him that the corn supplies
of Paris must remain the concern of the royal administration.
As a consequence he exempted from the provisions of the declaration Paris and its environs, where the ancient regulations of both
the city and the State were to be executed as before.

Bertin's successor, L'Averdy, was at first less timid and, urged
on by a number of officials, economists, and even by a section of
the provincial magistracy, decided to increase the freedom of the
corn trade. The task of drawing up the edict was entrusted to
Trudaine, and he consulted Turgot, who in the summer of 1764
was paying his annual visit to Paris. In turn Turgot invited Du
Pont to take a hand in drafting the legislation, and in the end the
projected edict was the combined effort of four men—Daniel
Trudaine, his son, Trudaine de Montigny, Turgot, and Du Pont.
As Du Pont tells us, they all worked independently and later pooled
their efforts. Their final draft was rejected. ' M. L'Averdy ',
continues Du Pont, ' refused to adopt the project in the form that
we proposed it, and while the Ministers were revising the salutary
measure of which we were the authors, I composed, in anticipa-
tion of their efforts, a memoir entitled *L'Anti-restricteur*, in which
I criticized the modifications of the measure and exposed the
dangers that would arise from them.' [11]   The original draft has
not survived, but a reading of the preamble to the Edict of July
1764 will reveal signs of revision, and it is obvious at a glance
where L'Averdy, supported by Bertin, reduced its scope. The
first part, employing the language of the Physiocrats, decrees
complete free trade in grain: the second part adds: ' in order
that there shall be no anxiety . . . it has seemed necessary to us
to fix a price of grain above which all export shall be forbidden
. . . and as . . . we ought not to lose the occasion to encourage
industry, we have resolved to favour French Navigation in
granting to our vessels and our crews the exclusive right to carry
exported grains.' [12]

The price over which export was forbidden was 12½ *livres* per
quintal, or 30 *livres* the *setier*, Paris measure. This provision
restricted export for considerable periods and, in some parts of
France, rendered the law inoperative. At Marseilles, for example,
the price of grain remained from 1764 to 1771 at a figure always
above 12½ *livres*.[13]   Nevertheless, for the greater part of that time
there was a moderate export trade through some of the twenty-six
ports, and also through a large proportion of the 459 frontier towns
specified in the edict.[14]   Even Limoges, remote from sea and
devoid of really good land communications, derived some benefit

from the free-trade laws. From 1763 to 1765 there was a succession of good harvests, and yet prices, which formerly fell in times of plenty to a level ruinous to the producers, remained during 1764 and 1765 at a figure which brought relative prosperity to the province.[15] And at a later date, 1769, after a sequence of poor harvests, when normally there would have been an extraordinary rise in prices in the early winter, supplies from neighbouring regions found their way to the province, so that it was not until the month of December that prices attained a famine level.[16] 'In 1764', wrote Turgot to Condorcet, 'agriculture was in decline. Many farmers were ruined. Since then they have become solvent.' He was writing in 1772, a few months after free trade had been virtually abolished, and he adds: 'Perhaps in a few years husbandry will be in a worse plight than in 1764. I have just been investigating the difference in conditions to-day with those in 1764 in a small region of my province. It is gratifying to find that there yet remains proof of the prosperity produced by free trade.' [17]

But in spite of these results, there arose throughout the kingdom fierce opposition to the legislation of 1763 and 1764. In 1765 the harvest in many parts was much inferior to those of the preceding years, and prices began to rise from 6½ *livres* to 8 *livres* the quintal in the early winter. Everywhere there was alarm, even among those classes who had profited from the export of their surplus grain. It was soon forgotten that the good prices of previous years—6½ *livres* instead of 4½ *livres* the quintal—and also the sale of grain which would otherwise have been wasted resulted from free trade. Nor was it generally realized that export was decreasing automatically, that whereas from August 1764 to August 1765 about one million *setiers* had left the kingdom, during the early winter of 1765 in the majority of towns through which corn could be carried the export trade had entirely ceased even before prices reached the statutory figures of 12½ *livres* the quintal.[18]

Yet it was not so much the fear that home supplies might pass to the foreigners, as the movements of grain from one region to another, that caused mediaeval prejudice to assert itself once more. Apprehensive lest local stores might soon be exhausted, the townsmen clamoured for the restoration of the ancient laws, for the right to buy before the merchants and the bakers, and for organized searches for secret hoards. To these demands the municipal authorities lent an ear, and one by one, ignoring the laws of 1763 and 1764, they began to put in force the old regulations. Demonstrations took place in the towns where prices had begun to rise; angry grain-mobs made attacks upon the merchants who were buying corn, or upon individuals suspected of having secret hoards. During the three winters that followed, riots, assaults on merchants, and searches for engrossers continued; placards denouncing the King, his mistresses, and the chief Minister, Choiseul, were paraded through the streets; and the Parlements, once again hoping to steal a march on the Ministry, gave encouragement to the insurgents. At Bordeaux the Parlement, in defiance of the laws decreeing free trade, inflicted heavy fines upon a merchant who had bought from a farmer a crop of wheat still growing in the fields.[19]

With great dismay Turgot watched this triumph of mediaeval prejudice and the chances of economic regeneration disappear. From such a catastrophe he was determined to save his province. First of all he tried the way of persuasion. To this end he had printed and posted throughout the *généralité* exemplars of the laws of 1763 and 1764, of the precise nature of which the masses, and even the local police officials, were ignorant. To these last, and also to influential people, he dispatched copies of Letrosne's brochure, *La Liberté du commerce des grains toujours utile et jamais nuisible* (1765), which within the compass of 100 pages gave succinctly the arguments for free trade and a concise explanation of the laws of 1763 and 1764. To these same police officials he sent in February 1766 a circular in which he entreated them, having first of all convinced themselves from a reading of Letrosne's work, to endeavour to influence opinion in favour of free trade. ' And the way to do this ', he added, ' is to listen with sympathy to objections raised upon all sides; to overcome prejudice with quiet but impelling argument, by speaking the language of reason rather than that of authority; and to encourage the *curés*, gentlemen, and all persons who by virtue of their station and education are best qualified to mould opinion to study M. Letrosne's treatise . . . so that they may join with you in convincing others.' But if persuasion failed, then Turgot was prepared to avail himself of force. As he went on to tell the officials, ' those who are so unenlightened as to revive these police regulations are liable to severe punishment by the Government and by the superior courts. If alarm spreads among the people, if agitators inflame the populace, the magistrates must not remain inactive. . . . It is the King's intention, as shown in the Comptroller-General's letter to the Attorney-General of the Parlement of Paris, that proceedings shall be taken against persons causing impediment to the free transport of grains and that these shall follow the rigour of the law.' Turgot went on to call attention to a police order that he himself had issued forbidding all combination for the purpose of interfering with the transit of corn, and promising instant arrest to any one who should harangue a meeting with the intention of causing sedition and riot. Finally, he announced that he had ordered the subdelegates and the *maréchaussée* to maintain a constant watch and to keep him informed of all happenings in their districts, so that he might send police reinforcements should the occasion arise.

But in order to remove the cause of popular outcries, he approached the leading merchants in Limoges and other towns, and suggested to them that, as it was to their interest that free trade should continue, they should make themselves responsible for preventing a dearth of grain, even though this meant forgoing part of their profits. He impressed upon them that it was within their power to tide over a difficult period—perhaps of a few months only, until the harvests proved again abundant. Free trade was in its infancy, and it would be several years before it could create a vast organization based upon private enterprise. Local famines, though gradually mitigated of their worst effects, would still be frequent and disastrous enough to cause opinion to clamour for the ancient regulations. A setback of this nature had occurred during the winter of 1765–6; there was a danger that free trade might fail entirely; and if it failed, it might be a long while before the experiment was repeated.[20] Whether the merchants took this advice or not it is impossible to say. If they did, then their display of public spirit was not sufficient to bring a lull in the hostilities in the towns; nor did Turgot's appeal to public opinion meet with any appreciable success; and in the *généralité* of Limoges, as in France at large, the conflict continued unabated. And like that other struggle which disturbed eighteenth-century France—that between the Jansenists and Ultramontanes—it ended in a battle between the Crown and the Parlements.

(3)

Throughout the century it had been the usage to keep 40,000 *setiers* of grain for the relief of Paris. It is not surprising, then, that L'Averdy, knowing that he was ultimately responsible for these supplies, had been most anxious in 1764 to retain restrictions upon export. The next year, in collaboration with Courteille, an *intendant des finances*, he endeavoured to reorganize the grain administration. Instead of allowing officials to purchase the supplies for Paris, he made a contract with one named Malisset, who was to manage the King's Mill at Corbeil, to make the corn reserves into flour and to replenish the stores when occasion should arise. For his services Malisset was to receive a commission of 2 per cent. upon all purchases of grain, two officials of the Government, Chaumont and Rousseau, being asked to scrutinize all transactions. But these two men declined the responsibility; and the corn company or, as it was afterwards called, the *Société*

Malisset was allowed to carry on without real governmental supervision.

Late in 1767 Courteille died. His successor, Trudaine de Montigny, a scrupulous and meticulous young man, took the wise precaution of inquiring into Malisset's transactions over the two preceding years, and he discovered many irregularities, it transpiring also that Malisset himself was heavily in debt. The outcome was that the two Trudaines and L'Averdy brought the contract to an end and instituted an inquiry which dragged on and on until 1791.[21] The affair added to L'Averdy's many worries. For during the years 1765–7 the Paris merchants, unwilling to compete with Malisset's monopoly, had transferred much of their business to provincial towns, the result being that the amount of grain in Paris was greatly diminished. The Government again approached Chaumont and Rousseau, who finally agreed to purchase supplies which, in view of the shortage occasioned by the emigration of the merchants to the provinces, were to be increased to 113,000 *setiers*. These events in the capital had repercussions outside. Not that the governmental purchases could actually have caused a rise in prices and a shortage in the provinces : all told, the consignments of grain for Paris, which were acquired in small quantities, amounted to only a minute fraction of the grain in the kingdom. Nor did the officials make a profit for the Government, for they bought at high rates and sold at a loss. But the knowledge that agents were prowling round the markets augmented alarm, and the rise in prices and the dearth of grain were popularly attributed to the Government. To make matters worse, the transactions of the Paris merchants in the provinces—and it is a fact that a number of speculators, including Necker, made considerable fortunes—aroused further fury, the clamours for the abolition of free trade increasing in volume as time went on.[22]

In December 1767 the Parlement of Paris demanded that the King should remedy the lack of food. Louis, prompted in part by the free-traders and more so by a determination not to let the magistrates detract from the royal authority, replied bluntly that the shortage was not the outcome of free trade, but of a general failure of harvests. In March 1768 the Parlement repeated its demands and, upon receiving yet another unfavourable reply, instituted an inquiry. Quite soon the provincial parlements took up the cry in earnest. That of Normandy, in collaboration with the inferior courts within its jurisdiction, organized a search for secret hoards ; and in August 1768, in complete defiance of the Royal Council, suspended freedom of export. Other provincial chambers followed suit, and by the autumn of that year free trade in grain was non-existent in the greater part of France.

That same autumn the *Chambre des vacations* of the Parlement of Paris submitted further representations to the King: ' Instead of prosperity, of happiness, of an increase in the population, all of which were to have followed free trade in grain, this spectacle alone is seen—famine in all regions; the wretchedness of the people increases, their tears flow, and mothers of families fear and deplore their fecundity.' To which the Ministry replied much as before: ' The shortage has been occasioned by the inclemency of the seasons and has become more acute owing to popular alarm.' A few days later d'Invau, who had replaced L'Averdy, ironically ordered the Parlement to take proceedings against individuals who might be responsible for the shortage of grain, the Government being fully aware that the original inquiry instituted by the magistrates had brought nothing to light. To this challenge—for it was a challenge rather than a command—the Parlement could merely reiterate its vague and alarmist accusations: ' Monopolies are always carried on by the most elusive people who, in their secret dealings with others, form a tangle impossible to unravel, for no one can discover the first strand.' [23] No sooner had these words been uttered than the Parlement of Normandy announced that a vile conspiracy to rob the people of their bread had been discovered. Their informant was none other than Le Prévôt de Beaumont, who had told his story to the Prince de Conti, a councillor in the Parlement and for several years a leader of factions hostile to the Crown. Actually, Beaumont knew but very little; and unlike his Englsh counterpart, Titus Oates, his bow drawn at a venture failed to bring down a quarry. He had no knowledge of Malisset's malversations. All that he knew was that Malisset had made a few purchases of grain. For his indiscretion Le Prevôt was cast into the Bastille, where he remained until its fall.[24]

These startling events Turgot followed from Limoges, and discussed them in his correspondence with Du Pont. At the time Du Pont was editor of the *Journal de l'agriculture, du commerce et des finances*, a physiocratic publication enjoying the tolerance of the Government, and in this capacity he became a self-made Minister of Propaganda, displaying a greater activity than the Ministry itself, for apart from having thrown Beaumont into prison, it had done next to nothing to silence the opposition to free trade. With one of Du Pont's pamphlets, *Lettre de . . . conseiller au parlement de Rouen à M. de M. . . . premier président*, which answered the charges made by the magistrates, Turgot was particularly delighted; he had copies printed at Limoges and distributed throughout the *généralité*. The Parlement ordered the pamphlet to be burned, and at one time was for taking proceedings against the author. Turgot, fearing that the Ministry might not protect Du Pont, advised caution. 'I admire your courage,' he wrote, 'and I detest the barbarity of the *boeufs-tigres* (the magistrates). But most of all I despise the cowardice of those (Montigny, d'Invau, and Choiseul), who allow themselves to be trampled upon and gored by these stupid and ferocious animals.' Two days later Turgot added: 'You must give up fighting for these cowards. . . . Send me your papers and lie low.'

It is in these letters written to Du Pont during December 1768 and January 1769 [25] that Turgot expresses more forcibly than elsewhere his intense hatred of the Parlements and his utter disgust at the timidity of the Ministry. He believed that the Ministers ought to ignore the protests of the courts and execute rigorously the free-trade laws. Instead, the Government, hesitant and indecisive, had allowed the magistrates to become the leaders of the populace and unenlightened masses. 'The ministers', he comments to Du Pont, 'advise moderation. A happy policy, to be sure! Moderation is admirable in times of peaceful and tolerant discussion; but when these liars and impostors excite the hatred of the populace on any pretext, it is then the time to unmask them and reveal them as they really are.' Then almost in despair he adds: 'Let us weep for Jerusalem and console ourselves in writing for an age of enlightenment which we shall never see.'

It was about this time that Turgot asked d'Invau for his father's old office of *Prévot des marchands* at Paris.[26] The request is not surprising. When earlier he had refused the intendances of Rouen, Lyon, and Bordeaux, his ardour and his optimism were still sufficient to prompt him to remain at Limoges. But in 1768 he was tired of provincial office; his disappointments had been many; and now he feared that the battle for free trade was lost. His words of 1771 might well have been uttered in 1768: 'I believe that the labours of a leisured man in his study are perhaps much more useful than those of an intendant, rowing as hard as he is able amidst rocks and currents.' [27] He would have welcomed the opportunity to return to Paris, there to be near his friends and to write for the instruction of another generation. Yet he was destined to remain intendant of Limoges and to watch the victory of the interests opposed to free trade.

In November 1768 the Parlement of Paris, citing as its authority a law of 1577, established an extraordinary police tribunal to hold yet another inquiry into the grain supplies of Paris, and once again failing to discover the Government's dealings, issued a declaration forbidding free trade in grain. The Ministry remained hesitant: it neither silenced the magistrates, nor insisted upon the execution of the law. At the end of 1769 a court intrigue and the antagonism to his fiscal policy brought

about the fall of d'Invau ; on the choice of his successor depended
the issue of free trade. Turgot's name had been mentioned, but
not seriously considered ; for Choiseul was most averse to him in
view of his early anti-parliamentary record. In the end, after a
series of tortuous intrigues, Maupeou obtained the Finances for
his protégé, the Abbé Terray.[28] Terray was a reactionary.
Whereas L'Averdy was open to persuasion and d'Invau mildly
sympathetic to physiocratic doctrines, their successor had
neither their enlightenment nor their timidity, and in so far as he
had any convictions at all, was hostile to free trade, contending that
liberty increased the profits of the merchants, and hence the price
of grain. Immediately upon his appointment he placed Brochet
de Saint-Prest, an intendant of commerce, in charge of the royal
grains, and together they resumed governmental purchases on a
scale far larger than L'Averdy's. When in 1770 there was yet
another general failure of the harvests, he dispatched a letter to the
intendants suggesting that all export of corn should be prohibited
when its price had reached 8 *livres* the quintal.[29] The majority
of the intendants pronounced for the continuation of free trade.
The reply of the intendant of Auch is typical of many : ' Free
trade has given the greatest benefits . . . and it has led to a period
of prosperity not hitherto experienced in this province. Actually
we have not sold much abroad, but the steady export from other
regions has kept up prices.' [30]

Turgot was about to begin a tour of inspection of his famine-
stricken province with a view to organizing relief when he received
Terray's circular. In reply he wrote his famous seven *Lettres
sur le commerce des grains*, the first before his departure at the end
of October, the last upon his return at the beginning of December.[31]
The *Lettres* form a veritable treatise on economics, and the achievement was the more remarkable because five of the letters must
have been written piecemeal in the evenings after days of hard
riding in the heavy rains of November.[32] Their spontaneity and
exceptional fervour give them a character which is lacking in
Turgot's more leisurely compositions. They reflect the conditions under which they were written. Around him he saw the
peasantry starving ; yet, owing to the cessation of the grain trade,
only very scanty supplies were forthcoming from outside. But he
was thinking perhaps even more of the future. If free trade were
abolished, there could be no hope for his people ; in times of
good harvests prices would fall again, and the province would
continue in the poverty it had known for half a century.

Upon the Government's practice of buying grain for Paris
he was particularly outspoken. For it was to these purchases
that he attributed the outcry against free trade. He went on to
explain the paradox : ' I know well that the merchants who buy

grain in Poitou to transport to Limousin are called monopolists by the populace and the magistrates in the small towns.   But so are the agents whom you employ to make purchases for the depots . . . for provisioning Paris. . . . Above everything it is these outcries made in the provinces against such purchases . . . which carried from mouth to mouth as far as the capital itself, excite the hostility of the Parisian mob against these alleged monopolies.   That is what happened in 1768, and that is what is happening now.   You, without doubt, know this as well as I.'[33] But Turgot might have spared himself the trouble.   It is almost certain—at least Turgot surmised it, and his friend Albert was ready to swear to it—that Terray never read the letters.[34]   At any rate, on 23 December 1770 an *arrêt du conseil* was promulgated virtually abolishing external and internal freedom of trade. Article I audaciously declared in vague and general terms for freedom;   the remainder re-established a restrictive régime. Farmers and labourers were allowed to buy grain for sowing only ; all corn was to be sold in the public markets ; millers and bakers were forbidden to buy to sell again ; and no merchant was to purchase corn directly from the producers.[35]   To these anti-liberal measures others were added in 1773.   In order that the Government might make its purchases unhindered, all private traders were to obtain special licences, in which were stipulated the markets where they could buy.   When the Parlement of Toulouse ordered the execution of the laws of 1763 and 1764 which were not definitely rescinded, Terray replied by quashing their ruling by an *arrêt du conseil*.   To the intendants he sent orders commanding them to see that the ancient regulations were executed, and re-questing them to compose detailed statements of the harvest, so that he might know the needs of the provinces.   Against such measures a number of intendants again protested ;   but Terray was not to be persuaded, and was even prepared to argue that freedom of trade merely brought money to the agriculturalists who had little need for preferential treatment.[36]

But, as Turgot had prophesied, the outcries against monopolies increased.   Terray and his friend the Du Barry were commonly accused of making extortionate profits.   As we shall see, though for a time he was able to protect himself against his detractors, it was these calumnies which brought about his dismissal, and it fell to Turgot to reverse Terray's policy and also to liquidate his transactions.

CHAPTER VIII

THE FAMINE, 1769–72

Relief Works in the Généralité *of Limoges*

(1)

FROM 1765 to 1771 the provinces of Limousin and Angoumois experienced a sequence of poor harvests. In 1765 the hard frosts of early spring ruined the crops completely in 100 parishes, and summer thunder-storms beat down the ripening harvests in many that had escaped the earlier misfortune. The next year a protracted drought in early spring reduced the yield of rye and buckwheat to barely a quarter of the average, and caused wheat and maize in Angoumois to fail for the third time in succession. The year 1767, when harvests everywhere were light, brought further losses to Limousin, drought, frost, and then a July storm causing the yield to be the worst in the memory of man. 'All has failed at once', reports Turgot ' —rye, pastures, vines, and even chestnuts. Buckwheat alone provides food for the peasants, there being sufficient to prevent the price of rye from reaching a famine level.'

In 1768 the losses of the previous years were partially recovered, and prices during the winter were not unduly high, but the winter rains continued until the spring, and at sowing-time the land was waterlogged. ' In every part of the *généralité* ', Turgot informed the Government, ' the harvest . . . is hardly sufficient for feeding the cultivators ; none remains to supply the markets ; none remains to provide food for the industrial workers scattered throughout the countryside and centred in the towns.' Worse still, the chestnut yield was only one-third of the average, and it was this, as in the dreadful winter of 1739, that was the signal for alarm.[1] As early as October the price of rye at Limoges was over 5½ *livres* the *setier* (Limoges measure), as compared with 3 *livres* 5 *sous* in October 1768. It is true that an almost identical level had been reached during that same month in 1767 ; but that year prices had decreased throughout the winter, the more plentiful supply of chestnuts and buckwheat enabling the farmers to sell their rye, and the good sales at Limoges attracting grain from Auvergne and Bourbonnais. In 1769, however, the harvests were poor in neighbouring provinces ; the peasants everywhere needed all their rye themselves ; and therefore prices continued to rise, reaching nearly 7 *livres* in December, nearly 9 *livres* in March, and in June 12 *livres*.[2] In the lesser towns prices were higher still, for whereas a little grain trickled from the Montagne into Limoges, other markets depended entirely upon the meagre stores relinquished locally.[3]

The position of the wage-earners, who were always the first to suffer, was most unfortunate.   Rye at famine prices was far too costly for them, and inferior grains were not to be had.   What was more serious was that the peasants were rapidly exhausting their resources.   The cattle-breeders, it is true, had money for grain, but only because, the pastures being poor, they had sold their beasts early in the year.   Consequently their position, too, was unenviable, for they would be unable to buy young animals for the following year.[4]   Most unhappy of all was the plight of the *métayers*. ' Many of the landowners ', Turgot told the Abbé Terray, ' have had the inhumanity to turn their men adrift, for, as at this time of the year the land needs little labour, they hope to be able to engage new tenants a few months hence.   These unfortunate *métayers* swarm upon the roads from all directions, begging for employment from the contractors,[5] who at present have none to offer, the funds for road-building even in normal years being insufficient to absorb supplies of casual labour.' [6]

It was not long before a general lawlessness prevailed in the *généralité* of Limoges.   Robberies were committed on the high-ways in broad daylight ; houses were broken into in the night ; and in nearly all the towns there were riots, the merchants being attacked when they attempted to transport grain from one district to another.   At Saint-Léonard two or three hundred starving people rioted every evening, and threatened to set fire to houses of the town officials if bread were not forthcoming.   On one occasion they assaulted and robbed the bakers from Limoges who had bought rye there ; and on another they looted the house of a wretched woman who was reputed to have a secret hoard of flour. So alarming were these riots that Turgot quartered an attachment of the *Condé Cavalerie* upon the town.[7]

The late summer eased the situation just a little, but only temporarily, for the harvest of 1770 was wretched, and even in October the price of rye at Limoges reached 8 *livres* the *setier*. Turgot's inspection of his province revealed that its resources were more slender than in 1769 and, what was more forboding, that the rye crop in the Montagne, a region which had afforded relief to other areas in 1769, was barely half the average.   During the winter the peasants had been tempted to sell their seed-grain ; they had sown their fields sparsely in the spring and, having struggled through the summer, had reaped their crops too early. The tithe returns, which Turgot examined carefully, showed that the slightly better yield elsewhere was not enough to counter-balance the failure in the Montagne, still less to restore again to normal a province which was utterly exhausted. Much of the grain was poor, some of it so soft that it could not be ground ; and some so affected by fungi that those who consumed it endangered their health. People died in hundreds of gangrene, and those escaping death were left crippled for life.[8]

(2)

Nevertheless, Turgot was resolved to uphold free trade, even though at the beginning of 1770 it seemed likely that the courts and municipal bodies would succeed in restoring the ancient grain laws. On 17 January the Parlement of Bordeaux had issued an *arrêt* commanding producers, merchants, and farmers of tithes to take sufficient grain daily to the markets and forbidding them, on pain of heavy fines, to buy and sell elsewhere. Determined to stay the execution of this measure, Turgot first employed persuasion. He negotiated with Dudon, the Attorney-General in that court, who finally agreed to dissuade his colleagues from following up their ruling. In order to make Dudon's task the easier, he requested Du Pont to cease his literary attacks upon the magistrates.[9] ' In giving annoyance to these gentlemen ', he explained, ' you will be doing unwittingly great harm to my province and to me. . . . The Ministry has, I think, not the least desire to compromise itself in a struggle with the magistracy over such a trifling matter. You will see, then, that it is essential that you should hold your tongue and leave the *boeufs-tigres* to bellow at their ease, for fear they should devour us.' [10] With this request Du Pont willingly complied. But already the *arrêt* of 17 January had given the lead to the lesser magistrates ; and in almost all towns the restrictions on the grain trade and house-to-house searches were revived.[11] To all intents and purposes, free trade was at an end.

At that time Turgot was endeavouring to stimulate a trade in grain by offering bounties to the merchants, to whom he had also promised protection from the searches of local officials, for on no other terms would they have consented to continue their trade.[12] But although an intendant possessed the authority to overrule the findings of a *sénéchaussée* or of a *cour consulaire*, an *arrêt du conseil* was required to annul a decree of a superior court.[13] There seemed very little chance that the Council would quash the *arrêt* of the Parlement of Bordeaux. Shortly after it had been

issued, Turgot had received instructions from the Abbé Terray
to execute it immediately.[14]   These orders he ignored, and straight
way applied for the necessary *arrêt du conseil*. Strange to relate,
his request was granted. The Abbé Terray, it seems, gave way
to the more liberal members of the Ministry, in the hope of
provoking a struggle with the courts and, having done so, of being
able to force his colleagues ultimately to give way.[15]   At any rate,
Turgot received the authority to enforce the free-trade laws of
1763 and 1764, and on 1 March he issued an ordinance
accordingly.[16]

   But his commands were not everywhere obeyed. At Turenne
the *échevins*, under pressure from a grain mob, re-established the
old regulations, organized a search, and fixed prices in the market.
Turgot overruled these measures and quartered troops on the
town.[17]   A little while later he was called upon to meet a more
serious situation at Angoulême, where the lieutenant of the
police had ordered all grain except that required for immediate
consumption to be deposited in a public granary. Turgot was
expecting relief supplies at Angoulême, and he feared that, if the
police order remained in force, he would be unable to have them
distributed.[18]   He therefore annulled the lieutenant's ruling and,
having done so, applied immediately to the Council for retrospective sanction.[19]   In other parts of his province, too, he was
called upon to assert his authority. At Meynac, a small town in
the Montagne, at Brive, where he had made a depot for relief
supplies, at Tulle, where there were serious riots, he quartered
troops, and he asked the Government to see that similar precautions were taken in a number of small towns in neighbouring
généralités through which corn would be passing on its way to
Limoges.[20]

   But although Turgot took stern measures against those who
hindered the merchants, he could not rely upon complete free
trade to bring food to his province, and he was the first to admit
that while the merchants might import sufficient grain in a year
like 1767, when the shortage was less acute, they could hardly risk
their fortunes in a year like 1770. As he told the Government,
' the lack of transport in this mountainous country, where grain
can be carried only on the backs of mules, renders relief from other
provinces exceptionally expensive and very slow. Rye . . . will
not support a high cost of transport which, usually raising the
price of wheat by only one-third, increases that of rye by over one-
half.' [21]   The grain trade which had developed since 1763 and
1764 was still very local. The merchants of Limoges confined
their activities to Poitou, Auvergne, Berry, Quercy, and Bourbonnais, and only two or three trading-houses in Angoulême
imported supplies by sea. When in 1769 Turgot suggested to

the merchants that they might make a good profit if they boug ht
the cheap grain advertised at Dunkirk, the reply was that they had
insufficient capital for this undertaking. Obviously the administration must organize relief ; that was a conclusion it would have
been folly to ignore. But, as Turgot informed the Abbé Terray,
there were two methods of procuring grain. The one, which was
commonly employed [22] and which ought to be avoided, was that of
appointing officials and merchants to purchase corn regardless of
cost and sell it in the public markets at a heavy loss. In Turgot's
opinion there were three sound reasons against this practice :
first, it provoked popular outcries ; secondly, it led to losses by
frauds ; and finally, it meant the suspension of trade in grain,
for no private merchant would risk his capital in competing with
officials trading at a loss. A preferable course was to provide an
artificial stimulus to free trade by offering bounties to merchants
who imported grain. He proposed therefore to pay 30 *sols* the
setier on all wheat and 20 *sols* on all rye reaching Angoulême on the
Charente, Souillac on the Dordogne, and Saint-Léon on the
Vézère, and so that grain might reach remoter parts, an additional
bounty of 10 *sols* on all consignments arriving at specified towns.
Finally, with a view to ensuring speedy relief, he stipulated that
these bounties should be paid only when grain reached its destination before 1 June.

These measures, which Turgot adopted without waiting for
official sanction, found little favour with the Abbé Terray, who
as an alternative suggested that money should be lent to merchants
upon condition that it were repaid before the end of June. In
vain did Turgot insist that under such conditions no merchant in
Limoges would risk his fortune in buying grain in northern
Europe, that so considerable were the costs of transport first by
sea, and then by pack-animals, that the traders feared a loss
on every deal.[23] Weeks passed by ; and the situation was becoming worse and worse. All efforts upon Turgot's part to persuade
the lesser merchants to scour Limousin and neighbouring provinces for those small hoards of grain that undoubtedly existed
produced no appreciable effect ; and even when he sent a commissioner secretly to buy grain in the Montagne, he could obtain
only a paltry 400 *setiers* of rye.[24] The Government's delay in
sanctioning his plans was proving disastrous ; not a day went by
but he received pitiful reports from the *curés*. The cargoes that
he had ordered in 1769 had been delayed in the frozen Baltic
ports, and could not be expected until the end of May. Worse
still, the Charente and Dordogne were at low level : ships could
no longer reach Angoulême and Souillac ; and therefore there was
a danger lest other supplies expected from Dunkirk and Bristol
might be unable to enter the province.[25] Turgot grew more and

more impatient. 'There are times', thus he reproached the Abbé Terray, ' when the wisdom of those in the Central Government compels them to give entire freedom in matters of detail to those of the executive residing on the spot. Such a situation is, I think, to be found in this province, and I could have wished that I had merited your confidence. But this I can say : I shall do all in my power so that you may have no cause to regret your failure to support me.' [26] In his next letter he again defiantly told the Abbé Terray that he would go his own way.[27] This he did and, having done so, presented his bill, describing with justifiable pride the measures he had taken.

During the year 1770 the greater part of the grain supplies for the relief of the province were brought in by three wealthy merchants. One of them, Henri Michel, purchased corn to the value of 152,000 *livres* in Bordeaux and Nantes. The second, Pétinaud, obtained consignments from Amsterdam, his total outlay being 61,000 *livres*. But the merchant who afforded Turgot the greatest service was François Ardent of Limoges. His purchases were made in Dantzig, and amounted to nearly 193,000 *livres*. All told, the amount of grain imported by these merchants was 47,285 *setiers* (Limoges measure), their expenditure, including cost of transport, being over 383,000 *livres*. The next year Ardent was responsible for most of the supplies. He bought grain to the value of nearly 340,000 *livres*, all of which was brought up the Charente and distributed by carts and pack-animals. He also advanced money for financing other merchants—Malepeyre of Brive, the brothers Jauge of Bordeaux, and Dupuy of Sainte-Foy, who obtained consignments from the north of France and northern Europe, Turgot taking it upon himself to make good their personal losses and also to guarantee the capital advanced.

Needless to say, transactions of this kind led to a deficit. The interest upon the money lent by Ardent at $\frac{1}{2}$ per cent. per month amounted to 2,307 *livres*—a sum which, as Turgot told Abbé Terray, might have been saved had he been authorized to borrow from the receivers of the *taille*. Again, 8,000 *livres* were due as compensation to Malepeyre, Dupuy, and the brothers Jauge for the loss of a vessel and for the ' sweating ' of a cargo which had been foolishly seized by the police officials at Angoulême. To these same merchants Turgot owed another sum of nearly 17,500 *livres*, part being their commission in payment of their work, and part the compensation for loss on sales. A further deficit arose from a contract made with Joseph Touvenin, a wine merchant at Limoges. Wishing to break the monopoly of the bakers, who were demanding prices out of all proportion to the cost of grain, Turgot persuaded Touvenin to withdraw his capital from the wine trade and to invest it in building ovens, in buying stores of grain, and in making bread at a price below that asked by the bakers.[28] Touvenin's losses were not really heavy; upon the majority of his transactions he obtained a 5–6 per cent. return; in all he lost only 3,000 *livres*, most of which expense arose when, at Turgot's bidding, he bought grain at excessively high rates to prevent the bakers from cornering the market. This loss made the total deficit just under 40,000 *livres*.[29]

All things considered, this deficit was trivial. During the two famine years Turgot had brought grain to the value of 800,000 *livres* into his province; and a loss of only 5 per cent. upon all transactions, as compared with 30 per cent. on the grain supplies for Paris, was a remarkable achievement. Even more remarkable is that he had done nothing detrimental to free trade. He had been thinking not of the immediate crisis only, but also of the time when harvests would be plentiful again, and when his province, if it were to be prosperous, would need the services of the merchants.

Fortunately the harvest of 1771 proved more abundant and the chestnut crop was the best for years; but in the Montagne there was again a shortage, and once more Turgot was compelled to organize relief.[30] The details of his transactions during the winter of 1771–72 are not known, but it is certain his measures were speedy and effective. Setting out at the end of August in the sweltering heat, he made a thorough inspection of that region. Under the physical strain of this undertaking his health gave way; and yet another attack of gout compelled him to return, his task unfinished.[31] But already he had put his subdelegates in a position to relieve him of much of this wearying work. With that thoroughness so characteristic of everything he did, he had devised a system whereby he might learn quickly and accurately the food resources of his *généralité*. In the previous July he had instructed his subdelegates to study carefully representative groups of parishes in their districts and, utilizing the tithe records, to compile accurate reports of the yield of grain immediately after the harvest, expressing their estimates as a percentage of an average year.[32]

(3)

Except for small quantities distributed in Limoges and the Montagne, all of Turgot's grain supplies were sold in the markets at current prices. This achievement is astounding. Even in normal years the wage-earner bought only a dozen *setiers* (Limoges) of grain, costing in all just over 30 *livres*. To purchase that quantity during the early part of 1770 he must pay upwards of 100 *livres*, and his total earnings were usually less than this amount. Nor were the peasants any better off; for, having exhausted their supplies, obliged to commute their grain rents at the current price of corn,[33] having sold their cattle, and even their homes, they were utterly destitute, and had to tramp the roads.[34]

Usually the Council granted relief to a famine-stricken province, first by making an appreciable reduction in its taxation, secondly by distributing food among the poor, and finally by increasing the grant for public works. But on this occasion the Government gave very feeble support. Between December 1769 and November 1771 Turgot received only 180,000 *livres* as an outright gift, and a further sum of 200,000 *livres* upon the understanding that it should be employed for buying grain, and then returned.[35] Even the *moins-imposé* of 450,000 *livres* in 1770 was a concession less substantial than it appears at first sight, for in times of relatively good harvests rebates amounted to 200,000 *livres* ; and that of 270,000 *livres* in 1771 was farcical, for the greater part of the Montagne, usually paying 500,000 *livres* in taxation, could simply not be taxed.[36] In vain did Turgot point out that the *généralité* of Bordeaux, where prices were much lower, received more favourable treatment than his own ; and that, if justice were to be done, a *moins-imposé* of at least 900,000 *livres* ought to be accorded.[37]

Turgot and his province were thrown upon their own resources. His first thoughts were for the *métayers*, who, at all costs, must be kept upon their domains. Following Tourny's example,[38] he issued in February 1770 an ordinance compelling all masters to feed their *métayers* and domestics until the following October.[39] Next, in collaboration with Dudon, he attempted to put an end to the ruthless exactions of the seigneurial courts, which almost everywhere were compelling the *censitaires* to commute their grain rents at high prices. The outcome was that in March 1770 the Parlement of Bordeaux issued an *arrêt* ordering that all grain rents should be commuted at the average price of grain in August 1769, August being the month when these rents were due. This ruling did not apply to Angoumois, which was within the jurisdiction of the Parlement of Paris ; but shortly afterwards Turgot applied to Maupeou, the Chancellor, asking him to obtain a similar order from the Parlement of Paris, and explaining that, though such a course might seem at variance with absolutist doctrines, the measure was laudable in every way, and was indeed legal under the Royal Declaration of 8 October 1709.[40] The magistrates in Paris, flattered no doubt at this recognition of an ancient right, readily adopted the proposals. Judged by the standards of the best monarchical traditions, Turgot's action was indiscreet, but had he applied to Terray for an *arrêt du conseil* to achieve this result, weeks might have elapsed before sanction was forthcoming.[41]

Such measures, while easing the situation for the *métayers* and peasant proprietors, obviously gave no succour to the destitute, whose large numbers called for exceptional relief. In eighteenth-century France there was no poor law comparable to that evolved in Tudor England. Although the parish was responsible for the collection of taxation and for the supply of recruits for the army, it had, strictly speaking, no obligation to provide for paupers. The care of those in need was left mainly to religious houses, to the *curés*, and to other charitable persons, the State in times of exceptional poverty supplementing their efforts with grants of food and alms.[42] In some *généralités*, however, the intendants made regular provision for the impotent and levied a tax for that purpose.[43] Again, several intendants had attempted to reduce the numbers of vagrants. For example, Tourny of Limoges had issued an ordinance in 1736—a measure reminiscent of the Tudor Beggars' Act of 1531—forbidding all mendicants to solicit alms unless they first obtained a licence from the *curés*, all persons thus favoured displaying the letter M upon their shoulders.[44] But although there was much private charity in eighteenth-century France, and although the administration had assumed responsibilities, there was no regular organization to meet even in normal times the distressing needs of the poor.[45]

During the winter of 1769–70 Turgot established a system of poor relief in his *généralité*. Early in December he conferred with the Bishop of Limoges, and the two resolved to develop a parochial administration which would enable Church and State to co-operate. First, they called together distinguished people and issued an appeal, but there was little response, the nobility being particularly indifferent to the sufferings of the masses.[46] Once more Turgot conferred with Dudon and the Parlement of Bordeaux. The outcome was that on 17 January 1770 the magistrates issued an *arrêt* decreeing that in every parish an assembly should be convened to draw up schemes for providing the poor with money, food, and work. Each community was to submit its suggestions to the intendant for approval, whereupon it would be empowered to levy a tax upon all inhabitants to meet the cost.[47] The lead was given by Turgot and the Bishop. In Limoges they formed a poor-relief assembly, which, meeting for the first time in the large hall of the intendance on 11 February 1770, decided to raise money by voluntary contributions, and not to exercise for the time being the authority to raise a tax, unless— and this reads like the early poor-law statutes of Tudor England— people failed repeatedly to fulfil their moral obligations. A register was to be made of those ready to make monthly subscriptions until the end of June, Turgot and the Bishop each promising 500 *livres*. Subsidiary subscription lists were to be opened by the guilds, and also by the parish clergy, who were to exhort all people (those who had been unable to be present at the meeting, spinsters and widows who were not allowed to attend, and lesser tradesmen who had been reluctant to mingle with their betters) to make fitting contributions. For the distribution of relief a committee, composed of the Bishop, François Ardent, and representatives of the guilds and the clergy, was appointed, and, to enable this body to carry out its work, the *curés*, assisted by sub-committees, were to compose parochial reports giving detailed statements of poor persons, their age, their sex and degree of destitution, particulars of the respectable poor, and information concerning beggars and vagabonds.[48]

A little while later Turgot sent an account of these deliberations, and also an instruction upon the execution of the *arrêt* of the Parlement of Bordeaux, to all *curés*, notables, and magistrates in the *généralité*. ' The relief of the sufferings of men is the duty and concern of all,' he told them. And having drawn attention to the danger, waste, and futility of indiscriminate almsgiving, he added, ' It is, then, above all things indispensable that the richer and charitable persons in each town, parish, or community should unite to form *bureaux de charité*, all the members of which should agree to make subscriptions, giving their alms in common, in order that their gifts may be employed in a manner the most advantageous to the poor.' In organizing these committees, and also in administering relief, the clergy were to take the lead. To them Turgot gave special instructions. In dealing with vagrants they were to discriminate—so many were the *métayers* who had been turned adrift—between vagabonds by lifelong habit and those temporarily wandering from their parishes. These last were to be encouraged to return to their homes ; they were to be given licences to ask for food at specific parishes on their way ; and should they be unable through illness to make the journey immediately, they were to be admitted to the nearest hospital.[49] Equally humane were his orders concerning the *pauvres honteux*. ' It is not advisable ', he wrote, ' to include them in the statements of the poor ; all the same it is highly desirable that they should receive relief. There seems to be only one way of overcoming this difficulty—to set apart a proportion of the funds . . . and to allow the *curés*, assisted by one or two members of the bureaux, to distribute money confidentially.'[50]

To what degree this organization prevailed it is impossible to say with certainty. At Meynac a committee was instituted in February, and it was agreed that the wealthier inhabitants should provide the poor daily with hot soup. Within one month the committee had dispersed, the members having quarrelled over matters of rank and precedence.[51] In all probability very few parishes responded, and this conjecture seems to be borne out by Turgot's action in issuing on 1 March an ordinance instructing the police officers in the towns and the syndics in the parishes to convene assemblies within eight days. According to these new instructions, every parish must either establish an adequate system of voluntary subscriptions or, failing that, a definite tax. The motive was to throw the onus of calling the assemblies upon the syndics and police officials, who, unlike the *curés*, could apply compulsion.[52]

It was left to individuals to choose one of two ways of making contributions: either they could give a money payment, or they could promise to feed a number of poor persons till the harvest, in which event they could compel recipients to work, providing that, in addition to giving each a daily ration of $1\frac{1}{2}$ lb. of bread, they paid a wage of 3 *sols* a day. Turgot greatly favoured this last form of contribution, it being his intention to remove incentives to idleness. With that same motive, he appealed to landowners to undertake improvements of their land and buildings, pointing out to them that they would gain in availing themselves of cheap labour. He himself set an example. Many public works planned for the two or three ensuing years he began at once. On the highways there were already *ateliers* under the supervision of contractors and of the engineers of the *ponts et chaussées*, and these, the result of his reform of the *corvées*, were now to prove invaluable for absorbing casual labour. In February 1770, without waiting for the sanction of the *ponts et chaussées*, he opened new road works and engaged twice the usual number of labourers. As a rule, tasks requiring little skill—quarrying, levelling, and so forth—were undertaken, so that all might be employed. Upon the highways gangs 100 strong worked under the direction of the engineers and subdelegates. Upon the lesser roads smaller groups were employed, again under supervision, for Turgot obtained the assistance of the commissioners of *tailles*, of the parochial clergy, and even of a few of the nobility. Upon these by-roads specific tasks were allotted to families for completion within a given time. All wages were paid in the form of tokens,[53] which could be exchanged for food upon the scene of work. To every *atelier* an official baker was attached, and from him the workers could buy their bread at a reasonable price. Soup kitchens, too, were established, and it was from these that the peasants bought potatoes. There was much to recommend this method of payment by token: it saved the trouble of obtaining and distributing small sums of money, and it ensured that wages would not be dissipated in the taverns.[54]

So popular were the *ateliers* that men left their fields and even their trades to seek work upon the roads, and, as time went on, it became necessary not only to reduce wages to a figure a little lower than current rates, but also to inquire more carefully into the circumstances of those applying for employment. But it seems fairly certain that work was found for those really in need. For towards the end of February, in issuing a second series of instructions upon vagrancy, Turgot was prepared to punish idlers with all the severity advocated by the Council. Having recalled the leniency of his earlier commands, he adds: ' The measures that have been taken in all parishes . . . to provide food and work for the indigent leave no pretext for begging ' [55]—and Turgot was not the man to issue such an order prematurely. A reckoning of the sums expended and of the work completed points to the same conclusion. All told, he spent over 218,000 *livres* out of public funds, and a further sum of 12,000 *livres* which was the gift of the Prince de Soubise.[56] Much of the money subscribed to the *bureaux de charité* was utilized for road works, and to finance employment in the Montagne another loan was raised from Ardent. In all 300 miles of roadway were constructed.[57] Within the space of two years the mule-tracks of the Montagne became good highways.[58] A *curé* who supervised an *atelier* in this district tells us that so few were those who aimlessly tramped about, that any casual observer would have thought it a most prosperous region.[59]

It had also been Turgot's intention to undertake other public works, but the difficulty was one of finance, and it was in vain that he asked for an increased grant to the *ponts et chaussées*, or even for an advance payment of the next year's quota.[60] At Limoges, where there was no road-making to be done, he opened an *atelier* for the repair of the ancient ramparts.[61] But elsewhere he could only advise towns and parishes to seize the opportunity of executing local works at about half the normal cost, and, to encourage them, he offered to advance the money free of interest until prosperity was restored.[62] At the same time he held an inquiry into the petty dues payable by certain landowners for parochial expenses, but of his achievements no record survives.

Again, very little is known of his efforts to provide lighter kinds of employment. Although hundreds of women and children were occupied on the roads in sorting stones and levelling soil, the amount of work of this type must have been limited. It was Turgot's intention to provide facilities for spinning and lace-making, which had always found a place in the hospitals and poor-houses; [63] and in his instructions to the *bureaux de charité* he offered to provide instructresses to teach these arts to the peasant women. It is recorded that he sent spinning-wheels to his sub-delegates for distribution in those parishes where merchants had been unable to introduce them—a fact which suggests that he had previously asked the clothiers for assistance in this work.[64]

According to his *compte-rendu*, he spent 1,691 *livres* of Government money on wheels and materials, and probably of the 1,500 spinning-wheels which are known to have been distributed in the *généralité* from 1765 to 1775, the greater number were provided during the famine years. Such figures do not in themselves indicate a considerable development of textile occupations. But the wheels that he spoke of distributing were intended to serve as models; and the very fact that he spent such a moderate sum upon a form of relief which he considered so necessary, suggests that the merchants and the *bureaux de charité* had been able between them to provide a large amount of work.

On every possible occasion it was employment that he sought to offer. He recognized every man's right to work; but he could not tolerate an unqualified claim to alms, and he detested the degrading practice of assembling the poor like cattle to distribute food and money.[65] Yet to those who were impotent and infirm he gave ample assistance. The funds of the *bureaux de charité* were supplemented from other sources. The moneys available from local charities were methodically administered and applied where needs were greatest. A sum of 20,000 *livres* granted by the Council was spent on rice, on which also, impatient of waiting for official sanction, he expended a further 27,000 *livres*. The distribution of these supplies was entrusted to the *bureaux de charité*, to which bodies he sent a pamphlet containing eleven recipes and also a leaflet on potatoes.[66]

Yet another form of relief was necessary to complete the salvation of the province. All those who had been employed in public works must be restored to their domains and placed in a position to make a recovery from their failures. One reason for the disappointing harvest in 1770 had been the sowing of poor grain. To avoid a repetition of this disaster, Turgot organized a grain loan. Paying particular attention to the Montagne, and assisted by parochial committees, he collected elaborate statistics of the requirements of every parish in that region. All loans had to be refunded after the harvest, and, whether in money or in kind, the repayment had to be the equivalent not of the quantity, but of the value of grain advanced. The loans were to be the first charge upon the crops; and when *métayage* rents, tithes, seigneurial dues, and all other obligations were finally levied, they were to be assessed not upon the total yield, but only upon that which remained when the loans had been repaid.[67] Owing to these wise measures, the recovery of the province was as rapid as could be expected under a régime of restricted trade, and the Central Government continued to tax the *généralité* at its pre-famine rate, although the payments for the *taille* were nearly three millions in arrears.[68]

The facts of Turgot's administration during the famine speak for themselves. His noble work endeared him to the peasantry. All along he toiled with the barest minimum of support from the Comptroller-General, the Council, and the officials in the Central Government, all of whom failed to appreciate the gravity of the situation. But, as was his custom, he had not waited for official-dom's instructions; when necessary he had taken the law into his own hands; he had raised money by methods which were disapproved; he had risked his reputation in dealings in grain which might have incurred enormous losses; he had risked his private fortune in raising loans upon the security of his own estates; and he had embarrassed the Ministry in co-operating with the Parlement of Bordeaux. He finally presented his accounts: these, at least, he owed the Central Government, and it was not altogether without pride that he concluded: ' It is with much regret that I confront you with such a considerable deficit. I think, however, I ought to make a few remarks in justification of my actions: if instead of comparing this deficit with the total sum I have received (from the Government), you consider it in relation to the amount of my transactions, it will appear much less. In all, I have received 386,000 *livres* during the past two years. With this money and during this period I have brought into the *généralité* different kinds of grain to the value of 890,248 *livres*; I have executed public works costing 303,400 *livres*, and I have distributed 47,200 *livres* in relief. . . . I flatter myself to think that a deficit of 90,000 *livres* upon transactions to the value of 1,240,000 *livres* will astonish you less, and that you will think less unfavourably of my administration—perhaps that you will con-sider that I merit some approval. Such is the chief recompense that I desire for all my work.' [69]

CHAPTER IX

MINISTER OF STATE

(1)

DURING the early part of 1774 Turgot was paying his annual visit to Paris, enjoying a well-earned respite from the drudgery and isolation of the intendant's life. Little did he think that he would not return to Limoges; he had resigned himself to provincial office, and the most that he could hope for was promotion to some other *généralité*. Within a few days of his arrival he was discussing with Trésaguet the programme of public works in his province for the ensuing year; and he was taking the opportunity of talking over administrative details with other officials. Much of his time was spent in visiting his friends. But from his circle there was a notable absentee: Du Pont had gone to Poland as tutor to the children of Prince Czartoriski. He had promised to remain for a period of twelve years.[1]

On Thursday 28 April, while Turgot was still in Paris, Louis XV fell sick of smallpox. The capital anxiously listened for the latest news, and courtiers, politicians, place-hunters, and Ministers waited, some with hope and some with fear, for the long reign to end. There were whisperings and intrigues; old quarrels were now ending and new ones were beginning; and factions and parties were forming for a future most uncertain. The Foreign Ministers hastened to inform their Governments of the madly fluctuating scene which promised to disturb a nicely poised balance of power. Yet there was little to be said beyond hesitant conjecture. Lord Stormont, the English Ambassador, wrote to Lord Rochford: 'The French King's illness has opened a scene of constant cabal and intrigue. The enemies of the present Ministry and of the favourite lady (Mme Du Barry) who is its chief support have long been waiting for such an event . . . in a firm persuasion that the moment the King has a serious illness he would be greatly alarmed, and that *that* alarm would instantly bring back all his religious scruples.'[2] The old and ailing Archbishop of Paris had a most unenviable position. One faction prevailed upon him to go to Versailles to warn Louis of the grave danger to his soul; another persuaded him to return, his mission unfulfilled, impressing upon him the advice of the physicians that any unnecessary disturbance would prove fatal to the King.[3]

On 10 May, between two and three in the afternoon, Louis died, having received the last Sacrament. The courtiers, deserting the antechamber of the dead King, hurried to pay their timely respects to Louis XVI. ' What a burden ! ' he complained. ' I have learned nothing. It seems that the universe will fall upon me.' [4] Formerly Duc de Berry, third son of Louis the Dauphin and grandson of Louis XV, the new King was not yet twenty years of age. He was an earnest, awkward, and timid youth, sullen in looks and grousing in speech. He displayed few of the characteristics of the Bourbon line; he lacked their sharp intelligence, their proud bearing, their command and strength of will. Most of his traits, both mental and physical, he inherited from his mother, Marie-Josèphe of the House of Saxony. His eyes were a pale watery blue, his lips were thick and shapeless, his complexion was uncouthly ruddy. But, despite this sensuous appearance, his only excess was over-eating to satisfy an appetite whetted by vigorous hunting and, much to the disgust of a genteel Court, by profuse sweating occasioned by fierce turns of manual labour. He would toil for hours with the masons and the smiths, and he was for ever violently rearranging his apartments at Versailles. Such labours were a joy to him, yet he gave himself up to them with some misgiving. Fully aware of his ignorance (which was never so great as is sometimes supposed, for he spoke German, English, and Italian fluently, and had been well grounded in Latin), he had attempted to gain some acquaintance with military science, with history and affairs of State. Nevertheless they had really taught ' poor Berry ' nothing—nothing of people, of factions and intrigues, of foreign policy and administrative matters. All he knew was that mistresses and extravagances were the bane of States.[5] From the beginning of his reign he showed a keen desire, and also some aptitude, to learn. Stormont believed that ' his profession of inability and inexperience gives room to hope that he will endeavour to learn, as the first step to knowledge is to feel that want of it. . . . He puts a great variety of questions to his Ministers and minutes their answers.' Yet Stormont was too cautious to mistake intention for accomplished fact. ' The strongest and most decided features in this King's character ', he wrote, ' are a love of justice, a general desire of doing well, a passion for economy, and an abhorrence of all the excesses of the last reign. . . . He is eternally repeating the word economy, economy, and begins already to enter into the minutest details. Whether he will embrace such a large and liberal plan of economy as suits a great nation like this, or suffer this wise principle to waste itself in an intention to little, paultry domestic savings, time will show.' In fact, Stormont was inclined to believe that Louis would accomplish little unless he fell into the hands of an enterprising statesman.[6]

But Louis was not the one readily to place his regal powers at the disposal of a chief Minister. Though he sought instinctively for some one to lean upon, he was impatient of control, and though he felt the need for advice, he often resented it when given; and he abhorred being governed or having the appearances of being so. He desired always to show his power; but this came not so much from a mind which felt its strength, as from one that always strove to conceal its weakness. He was suspicious of all those around him: secret information and the tortuous means of obtaining it held for him an irresistible fascination, and he knew men by their failings rather than by their qualities. Of so vulnerable a nature the slanderous tongues of the Court were bound to take advantage; and much as he might genuinely hope to place himself out of the reach of intrigue, the more he tried the more he was likely to make himself the very centre of it.[7]

Louis's petulant determination to reserve to himself complete freedom in action, yet his inability to detach himself altogether from the factions, made the part of his Queen an exceedingly difficult one to play. Moreover, when the King had no mistress, but was a model of propriety and decency, his Queen became the focus of intrigue and took, as it were, the place of a Du Barry or a Pompadour. Yet the influence exercised by Marie-Antoinette was always an element in the politics of the time which is not easily determined, and still less generalized. For she was incapable of any protracted design, and hardly understood the interests for which parties at the Court contended. Lacking entirely a calculated purpose, she was quite incapable of giving Louis consistent counsel.[8] She had no desire for power—only for favours which she asked for friends and acquaintances. She was unprincipled in so far as she was unreflecting, thoughtless of larger issues, impulsive in kindness and in hatred. The Abbé de Vermond, her tutor, had failed, much to the disappointment of her pious mother, to discipline a nature best left uncontrolled. When the chance came, she revolted against her early upbringing and against the mode of life of the old-maidish Bourbon women at Versailles, and around her there gathered kindred spirits to form a coterie which in the eyes of many was extravagant, indecorous, and licentious.[9] From the beginning of the reign her household became a centre of those aspiring to honour and office, and also a backstairs of foreign diplomacy. Her impulsive generosity and her habit of forming opinions on persons rather than on issues rendered her easy game to intriguers.[10] Except for

Louis, who often voiced the precept of his woman-hating tutor, the Duc de Vauguyon, that women ought not to meddle with politics, every one took it for granted that the Queen should have influence. Even Turgot considered it both right and expedient to seek her sympathy and support, and even Véri, who believed her to be a menace to the good governance of the State, conceded that, had her head been as good as her heart, her intervention in affairs would have been most welcome.[11]

To a relatively detached observer like Lord Stormont, whose Government was anxious to learn the truth, fearing lest Vienna should dominate Versailles through Marie-Antoinette, the Queen's credit was always 'problematical'. On 8 June he summed up his observations: 'Tho' the King's intention is that she should not meddle with politics and tho' she would lose her credit were she openly to assert it there, yet with her insinuation and address she must often *influence*, tho' I think she will not rule. . . . Her credit and influence will probably not be constant, but shew itself by starts and not tend to any determined point.' As Stormont explained later, the anti-Austrian party were ever ready to play upon the King's abhorrence of being guided by Vienna, and they were prepared even to turn the Queen's early popularity against her, Louis being told that she was out to make herself the idol of the people. No wonder, then, that the Austrian Ambassador, the wily Mercy-Argentau, avoided 'all appearances of business with the Queen', and made use of the channel of the Abbé de Vermond, fearing lest all the Queen's enemies, Mme Adelaïde at their head, should make the King believe that while he listened to her he would 'only be Vice Roi to the Empress Queen'.[12]

The young King and Queen received a great welcome from all sides, for there was general hatred of the reign just ended.[13] Those many interests violated during its last few years were anxious for a timely change of fortune and for the overthrow of the triumvirate, d'Aiguillon, Maupeou, and the Abbé Terray. These Ministers, though constantly intriguing among themselves, had each maintained his power through the influence of Mme Du Barry. Foremost among their enemies was the Duc de Choiseul, who towards the end of 1770 had been banished to Chateloup, where, though devoting himself to agriculture and meriting the praise of Arthur Young, he was 'bored to death'.[14] When the new reign began he hoped to turn the tables upon his inveterate opponent, d'Aiguillon. Insignificant in appearance, short in stature, plain, and sandy, yet highly popular because of his elegant and vivacious manner and undoubtedly great courage, Choiseul gathered round him a pro-Austrian faction. When formerly chief Minister, he had arranged the Queen's marriage; his protégé, Vermond, was in an influential position; and several women of his following, including the Princesse de Beauvau and Mme de Brionne, were in favour at the Court. He could therefore look with hope upon the future. He enjoyed also the support of the 'patriots', a party composed of the aristocratic coteries centred round the houses of the Duc d'Orléans, the Prince de Conti, and the Duc de Chartres, comprising not only nobles of the sword, but also those of the robe, while outside the higher ranks of society he found an enthusiastic following among the lesser lawyers and the Jansenist *bourgeoisie*. ' The Duke of Choiseul's party ', Stormont told his Government, ' certainly look upon the King's death as a fortunate event. The most sanguine expect his return to favour and all the fullness of his former power.' [15] But they had not allowed for Louis's fanatical hatred of their leader ; it is just possible that the King believed the scandalous story that Choiseul had poisoned the Dauphin.[16]

Opposed to the Choiseulistes were the *dévots*. To this body belonged the majority of the higher clergy, who could never forgive Choiseul's expulsion of the Jesuits and the moral laxity of his supporters. The *dévots*, too, had influential intriguers at the Court, among them the austere Duc Louis de Noailles, the Aunts Adelaïde and Louise, and the Comtesse de Marsan, governess to the royal children. Among their ranks were also several bigoted aristocratic families, including the Rohans, all of whom, in the interests of religion, upheld the royal authority against the constitutional claims of the magistracy. In this opposition to the courts they found a ready ally in the Comte de Provence, who accused Choiseul of curtailing the royal prerogative in subscribing to the theory that in the absence of the States-General the Parlements were the depository of law, possessing the right to remonstrate against, and to refuse to register, the legislation of the King in Council. If the Choiseulistes placed high hopes in the Queen, the *dévots* had good reason to place theirs in the King, for Louis had been strictly and successfully educated in their mode of life by his father, the Dauphin, and by Vauguyon.

Such was the alignment of parties in May 1774. There was yet a third interest, which was hardly a party, and still less a faction—that of the *économistes* and *philosophes*, who over a decade earlier had enjoyed the patronage of Mme de Pompadour. For them the new reign promised very little indeed. Voltaire, of course, could congratulate Maupeou on his *coup d'état* against the assassins of Lally and La Barre, and at the same time compliment Choiseul on having banished the Jesuits ; but he could never forget that the *dévots* and the magistrates alike were the constant enemies of free opinion. In general subscribing to the principles of enlightened or legal despotism, as they called it, the *économistes* and the *philosophes* declaimed against both the *dévots* and the

patriots, the former because they made the monarchy unenlightened, and the latter because they detracted from its despotism.

Of these parties and connexions at Versailles, Louis was
completely ignorant and, needing counsel, took up the suggestion
made by Mme de Narbonne and Mme Adelaïde of inviting
Maurepas to return from exile at Pontchartrain.[17] Maurepas,
who took up residence in the gilded attics vacated by the Du Barry,
was seventy-three years of age. Perfectly happy in his retirement,
he had slept and lived well. Véri, who as a young man had been
his neighbour for three years, gives us a glimpse of this extraordinary person, whose knowledge of people and anecdote was
never surpassed. The two used to walk together daily, and then
it was that Maurepas would astound the young Véri with his
vast stores of information. Véri used him as a dictionary.
Every new name he came across in his reading, or any event, he
would mention to Maurepas with the certainty that he would
set flowing a flood of anecdote. His great regret was that in
those early days he had not begun his diary, so many were the
stories worth recording in all their detail as they poured from
Maurepas's prodigious memory. Maurepas knew everything,[18]
and even during his retreat he was as well informed of the happenings of the Court as if he had lived at Versailles itself and had
eavesdropped at every keyhole. Advancing years had not told
upon his faculties, but had increased his store of crafty, worldly
wisdom. His old self-assurance was still there, and on the very
day that he returned he strutted around officiously as though he
had been in office all his life. Yet his ease and indolence were
strong antidotes to ambition ; his vanity, like his wife's, was amply
satisfied by figuring at the Court. He was never prompted to
tower above his colleagues, for it was not in him to attempt a
bold design ; but he was ready always by devious and crooked
ways to lay them low should they assert their independence. He
could safely be counted on to shun innovation, to adjourn contentious problems, and, with his consummate gift for intrigue, to
steer his way among the factions.[19] To Turgot, who little appreciated gentlemanly chicanery, Maurepas was roguish in his weakness. ' Public opinion ', said Turgot to the King, meaning that
narrow public at the Court, ' has an incredible influence upon
him, who, having knowledge and intelligence, ought to have
opinions of his own.' [20] Turgot was writing upon the eve of his
dismissal. He forgets that he himself would never have attained
such influence had one more steadfastly reactionary and one
stronger than Maurepas been appointed mentor to the King.

It was Louis's intention that Maurepas should be an adviser
only, and not Prime Minister. ' I understand ', Maurepas had
replied at their first interview, ' Your Majesty wishes me to show

him how to do without one.' And he genuinely set about teaching the King his business.[21] To this end he arranged for the Council of State to meet twice a week, the Council of Dispatches once, and for numerous small committees to discuss important matters in Louis's presence. He was even prepared to allow the King to learn from his mistakes, and, as Véri tells us, he patiently waited for Louis to come slowly to decisions which he could more easily have thrust upon him.[22] This plan was admirable in theory; but the difficulty was that Louis was hardly the one to make up his mind even when put in possession of the facts, all the more because to him the facts themselves were invariably suspect. Nor was it really possible for Maurepas to tender information and advice without stating his own opinions more or less authoritatively. His desire to teach the King merely meant that he would grind his own axe more gently than he would otherwise have done; and he could remain detached only so long as others did not steal an unfair advantage. Maurepas had taken on an impossible task. Yet it was one much to his liking, for he would not have acted very differently had he become Prime Minister.[23]

Maurepas knew only too well that Ministerial changes were bound to be made, though he himself was without a definite plan. Realizing that the King and Queen were prejudiced against his nephew, d'Aiguillon, and being content merely to break his fall, he advised him to retire while he might do so with honour.[24] And when d'Aiguillon promptly accepted this advice as an *ordre masqué*, Maurepas sponsored Breteuil, a Choiseuliste, as Minister for Foreign Affairs. Stormont and Rochford, who had a secret understanding with d'Aiguillon, took great alarm.[25] But Véri dissuaded Maurepas from this course the very day that the appointment was to have been announced, and suggested for the office Vergennes, once his own rival for diplomatic advancement.[26] This ' calm, prudent, cautious man ', as Stormont calls him, was to prove a diplomat who was rarely ruffled and in whom more boisterous personalities were to meet their match. Yet at the time when he was recalled from Stockholm his capabilities were not highly rated. His mediocre reputation and lack of party connexion made him acceptable to Maurepas; he could be expected to follow tamely where he was led—a surmise which was fulfilled, at least for a while.[27]

Vergennes's appointment was the second blow to the Choiseulistes, for already Du Muy, an old friend of the Dauphin, had become Minister for War. But by way of compensation Choiseul was allowed to return from exile, an event undoubtedly due to the influence of the Queen.[28] His arrival, which was applauded by his following from the roof-tops, caused Rochford to set Keith at Vienna and Stormont in Paris to watch carefully for *rapproche-ments* between the French and Austrian Courts. But Stormont was able to give his Government a momentary reassurance in reporting the well-known story of Choiseul's cold reception from Louis at La Muette. Choiseul returned to Chanteloup, not, as is sometimes said, because of the King's rebuff, but as part of his plan to play a waiting game, not wishing to return to favour without the fullness of his former power.[29]

Other changes in the Ministry were anxiously awaited; the *dévots* were hoping to see the last of Abbé Terray, and the Choiseulistes the dismissal of the Chancellor, Maupeou. In June the irascible Baudeau mentions in his *Chronique secrète* [30] that Turgot was being considered for the Finances. 'Between ourselves', he adds, 'he is accused of being a Jesuit and a dissembler, and it is given out that he is hated in his province.' And after prematurely recording that Turgot was in office, he dejectedly records on learning the truth: 'The Abbé Terray has not yet departed.' And Baudeau thought he knew the reason: the financiers, while sparing no love for Terray, were more afraid of Turgot. But the fact was that Louis did not know his own intentions and could not make up his mind to part with Abbé Terray, 'who was pliable enough to take any shape'.[31] In the end it was Boynes who had to go, and on 19 July Turgot was appointed to the Marine with a place in the Royal Council. He was perhaps somewhat disappointed. Montyon has it that, upon hearing of his promotion, he remarked, 'At least I shall not be returning to Limoges.' [32]

Like Vergennes, he was indebted for his office to the Abbé de Véri, who, assisted by Mme d'Enville, played upon Maurepas's fear that the Queen might obtain office for d'Ennery, a Choiseuliste.[33] Early in July Véri had recommended Turgot for the Seals, but it was felt that, though he had the requisite legal training for this office, his gifts were obviously administrative and financial. The remainder of Véri's disjointed narrative is nevertheless best told in his own words. 'The Abbé Terray wished to warn the King against Turgot's opinions . . . "Your Majesty must guard yourself against these principles of liberty. They are dangerous." Yes, indeed. I hope Terray will be guarded from them when they reveal the malversations and corruption which his own have occasioned in the operations of his agents (in the grain administration). The indecision in the King's character begins to obtrude. He wished to dismiss M. de Boynes and yet never succeeded in doing it. M. de Maurepas pressed the matter on Tuesday 19 July: " Affairs of state ", he said to the King, " require decision. You do not want to keep M. de Boynes. . . . You have spoken to me well of M. Turgot; take

him for the Marine since you have not decided to part with
Abbé Terray." The King gave no reply to these words, but in
the evening upon returning from his stroll he wrote asking M. de
La Vrillière . . . to summon Turgot immediately to his presence.'[34] There was now great joy among the *philosophes*, Condorcet optimistically announcing that he slept and dreamt as
peacefully as though he were protected by all the laws of England.[35]
Outside their ranks, however, Turgot was little more than a name.
If he had a reputation at all, it was, as Marie-Antoinette told her
mother, that he was ' a very honest man ' of whose appointment
she strongly approved.[36]   But the news came as a great blow to
his province. From the pulpit the parish priests announced the
event to their humble congregations, masses were said for him,
and the peasants left their fields to pay respect to their intendant.
Du Pont makes them say, ' It is good of the King to take him,
but it is a great misfortune for us to lose him.'[37]

(2)

Turgot set to work with his customary application to gain a
grasp of the many problems that his new office presented. First,
he had to inquire into the finances and organization of the new
naval schools at Le Havre and to decide whether their existence
justified their expense.[38]   Secondly, it came to his notice that
the ship-builders at Brest had received no payments for eighteen
months. He promptly paid them their arrears.[39]   Again, he
rendered speedy justice to Poivre, intendant of the Îles de France
and de Bourbon. According to Véri, Poivre had invested in
plantations on the islands, hoping to create a company for the sale
of spices in Europe. Accused by the Governor, Des Roches, of
serious dishonesty, he had been unable to obtain his money. Not
only did Turgot reimburse him, but also persuaded the King to
decide against a monopoly for the sale of spices which others,
including Monsieur, had hoped to establish in place of Poivre's
company.[40]   Finally, at Condorcet's instigation, he inquired into
the administration of Bory, the Governor-General of Saint
Domingo, and, finding that he had been unjustly dismissed, reinstated him in his office.[41]

It was upon Condorcet's recommendation, too, that he arranged
for Euler's *Théorie complète de la construction et de la manœuvre des
vaisseaux*, formerly published at St. Petersburg in a poor French
translation, to be printed in France and distributed for use in the
Marine.[42]   Indeed, from the moment that Turgot became
Minister, Condorcet became prolific in his suggestions, some quite
valuable—as, for example, the introduction of naval instruments
invented by Magellan ; some quite trivial—as, for instance, the
awarding of the Croix de Saint-Louis to one Pinel ; and others

quite preposterous—that he should use his influence to impose a contribution upon farmers of Church lands, and therefore indirectly on the clergy to replace the *corvées*. Turgot answered: ' I cannot reply to all your follies.' Nevertheless he adopted the suggestion that experiments in apparatus for the distillation of sea-water should be encouraged. A machine was set up on the vessel, *La Pourvoyeuse*, under the direction of Lavoisier and d'Estelle, and later others, Montigny, Macquer, Leroy, and Desmarets, were invited to display their inventions.[43] Turgot also favoured the use of vessels for scientific exploration. He obtained the King's permission for Saint-Edmund, a famous botanist, to equip an expedition to the Indies to study natural history, to discover if various grains and other plants might profitably be introduced into France, and to acquire information for the improvement of saltpetre. To his great dismay, the vessel and all hands were lost. Another botanist whom he assisted, d'Ombey, returned from Peru with a valuable collection in 1785. Again, it was while at the Marine that he dispatched an old acquaintance, the Abbé Rosier, to introduce tea-growing in Corsica, to teach wine- and oil-making, and to establish a school of agriculture.[44]

But all these matters were of trivial concern when compared with the great task of economizing on, and yet of increasing the strength of the Navy.[45] Turgot began by inquiring into the finances and organization of other European fleets, and this work was still proceeding when, at the end of thirty-five days, he left the Marine. But one of the schemes he had prepared was original and daring. Ship-building was more costly in France than in England, more costly in England than in Sweden, where wood and iron were cheap and plentiful. He estimated that a man-o'-war could be built in Sweden at two-fifths the normal cost. ' He did not grudge to a friendly and allied Power the profit accruing from this industry, for he argued that in the long run employment would not be diminished in France, since the Swedes drank French wines, consumed coffee and sugar from her colonies, and wore clothes of French manufacture.'[46] The only danger was that the art of ship-building might be lost in France. To obviate this he proposed to reserve a number of contracts for the French ship-yards. This scheme was never taken up by his successors, but another of his projects—that of replacing naval officers of the ' pen ' by civil administrators—was carried into effect in 1776.[47]

(3)

While Turgot was at the Marine, Baudeau continued to insult the Abbé Terray privately in the pages of his Diary and to declaim against the financiers. Yet it was not their sinister influence that was keeping Turgot from his rightful calling, but once more the sheer bewilderment and inertia of the King. Stormont believed that Terray would keep going longer than was usually imagined. For, though the Comptroller made jokes about his impending dismissal and gave himself a month before he was 'sent a packing', he was doing all he could to prevent it. He became prolific in suggestions for economy and affected to admire the sagacity and penetration with which the King entered into complicated details.[49] Upon Louis he heaped a bewildering mass of paper, hoping by this quackery to convey the impression that he was an expert custodian of the finances; and Maurepas, fully aware that all was not going well, grew alarmed lest Terray's artifice should succeed in setting the King's mind at rest. Urged on by Turgot, Vergennes, and Véri, and ignoring Terray's indignant protests, he placed all contentious financial business under the control of a council which the King himself attended.[49]

Meanwhile Maurepas, ever 'making headway by sailing with a side wind', was gently intriguing against Maupeou, who also joked about his coming fall, yet spared no effort to defend himself.[50] For the Seals Maurepas favoured Miromesnil, though he was also prepared to speak for Malesherbes, the 'idol of the people'.[51] But Louis, suspicious of their republican sympathies, wanted neither. Against Malesherbes, who had directed the publication of the *Encyclopédie*, he was especially hostile. 'Do not speak to me of him for any office,' he had said to Maurepas early in July, 'he is an encyclopaedist, and very dangerous.' [52] The same charge might have been made against Turgot, but the *dévots* had been taken unawares. Soon they were attempting to retrieve their loss. They opened and made copies of d'Alembert's correspondence with Frederick the Great, whom Louis detested for his profanity. Turgot's name was mentioned in these letters, and this fact was now brought to the notice of the King.[53] 'The whole is so fluctuating', writes Stormont in describing the efforts of the *dévots* to convince Louis of Turgot's irreligion, 'that no Minister can one day to the next be sure of the ground he stands on.' [54]

Towards the end of July, Terray's position became suddenly precarious. Louis had received an anonymous letter stating that Terray and Sartine had renewed the grain monopoly and accusing the King himself of receiving a share of the profits. Actually there was no monopoly, but there was a scandalous grain administration under the control of Terray and his subordinate, Brochet de Saint-Prest, and indeed a number of Sartine's police officials were acting under their orders. The letter worried the King, who became exceedingly suspicious when Terray began to blame Sartine and to make himself unusually scarce. To Maurepas, who was preparing to move with the Court to Compiègne, he wrote: ' When you are in Paris, try to find out about the alleged grain monopoly; and find me a Comptroller-General.' [55] But it was not until 9 August that Louis made up his mind to part with Terray and Maupeou, and even then he could not decide upon their successors. [56] He was still reluctant to give the Seals to Malesherbes, and when Maurepas suggested Turgot for the Finances, he replied: ' He is very much a man of theory; and he has associations with the encyclopaedists.' On 20 August Maurepas again pressed Louis to come to a decision; old ground was gone over; names were discussed, but still the King refused to make up his mind. ' Next Tuesday ', he said, ' I will give you my answer.' On Tuesday 23 August, Louis postponed his appointment with Maurepas until the following day. But about noon he sent for Turgot to discuss a matter concerning the Marine. For some time the two talked together about affairs in general—economies, the grain administration, and commercial policy. Turgot mentioned no names, showed no hostility to any one, but calmly gave to the King his own opinions on the grain trade. He was also prepared to speak his mind about the financial reforms that he considered indispensable, but Louis gave no opening. The next day, Maurepas, taking a firm line, pressed for an answer. Louis, while admitting that he still wanted to dismiss Maupeou and Terray, spoke of postponing nominations until the following Saturday. ' No! Certainly not! ' retorted Maurepas with vivacity. ' That is not the way to govern a State. Time, I repeat, is not a thing that you can waste at your caprice! You must give your decision before I leave. . . .' And when Louis protested that he was only twenty years of age and overwhelmed with business, Maurepas replied, ' Leave details and State papers to your Ministers, and confine yourself to choosing good and honest men.'

At length Louis made his decision: Turgot should have the Finances. ' But ', said Maurepas, ' before he accepts he desires an audience of Your Majesty, for he will be making a great sacrifice, and you ought to know his wishes.' The King answered: ' Yesterday I sent for him to hear his explanations. . . . I conversed with him about many matters which concern the Comptroller-General, and I was waiting for him to broach the matter.' ' He was waiting, I believe,' returned Maurepas, ' even more than you for an opening which should only have come from you. I will go and find him and bring him to you immediately.' Two other decisions were given by the King—the Seals for Miromensil and the Marine for Sartine. Maurepas then hurriedly excused himself. He found Turgot in the Abbé de Véri's study, and with him the Abbé de Vermond. The three had been talking of public affairs, of the extravagance of the Court, the King's indecision, and the slender hopes there were of retrenchment and reform. They had gone on to discuss Turgot's chances of the *contrôle général* and the difficulties that would confront the holder of this office. Vermond proffered an opinion: ' I know only one way of counteracting the King's weakness and procrastination, and that is to obtain his word of honour. His sense of duty, and above all his promised word, are perhaps the only bonds that he respects. Therefore, M. Turgot, if you are called to the Finances, in all important matters provide yourself with his word of honour.' These conversations were cut short by the entry of Maurepas, who, having recounted his interview with Louis, went in search of the Abbé Terray. Turgot departed to see the King, Vermond's advice still fresh in his mind. Here is the gist of the interview as Véri had it from Turgot's own lips. ' All that I have told you is a little confused, said Turgot, because I am still not at my ease.—I know that you are nervous, but I know also that you are constant and honest and that I could not have made a better choice; I called you to the Marine for a little while to have the opportunity of knowing you.—It is necessary, Sire, that you should give me permission to put in writing my general opinions and, I may venture to add, my conditions, concerning the manner in which you ought to support me in this administration, for, I assure you, the superficial knowledge that I have of affairs causes in me some misgivings.—Yes, yes, said the King, just as you wish; but I give you my word of honour in advance, he added, taking Turgot's hands, to follow all your ideas and to uphold you always in the courageous course that you have taken.'[57]

Véri's account has not come down to us in its entirety. But Mlle de Lespinasse, who was in close touch with Turgot and his friends, no doubt completes the story when she writes to her lover, Guibert, as follows: '. . . He had some difficulty in accepting the Finances for which M. de Maurepas proposed him. When he went to thank the King, Louis said to him, " You do not wish, then, to become Comptroller-General ? " " Sire," answered M. Turgot, " I assure Your Majesty that I would have preferred the Marine because the office is less precarious and I am sure that I should do more good there; but at this moment it is not to the King I give myself: it is to an honest man." The King took Turgot's hands and said to him, " You will never be deceived." M. Turgot added: " Sire, I ought to mention to Your Majesty the necessity of economies, of which you must give the first example. All this, no doubt, the Abbé Terray has already told Your Majesty." " Yes," replied the King, " he has told me, but not as you have."'[58]

That same day Turgot put in writing—in his famous letter of

24 August—the general outline of his programme. It is a long letter, and it probably took him the remainder of the day to write; it is one mass of erasures and interpolations. When reading it— and this applies to all the letters that he wrote to Louis—one must remember the extreme youth of the King. Turgot was endeavouring to descend to his level, and his words have the ring of a kindly pedagogue. The language of reason is translated into sentiment, for no other appeal to Louis could have been effective. Yet it was not without some misgiving that he availed himself of the Abbé de Vermond's strategy. In later days he told the Abbé de Véri that, afraid of abusing the confidence of so young a monarch, he decided to confine innovation to a barest minimum, being content to wait until Louis could be convinced in a rational way of the necessity for radical reform.[59] And it was therefore with great difficulty that he wrote a letter which would appeal to Louis's conscience and yet satisfy his own.

' Having just left Your Majesty's room,' he began, ' still full of the anxiety produced by the immensity of the burden you place upon me, overcome by the touching kindness with which you have deigned to encourage me, I hasten to convey to you my respectful gratitude and the absolute devotion of my whole life.

' Your Majesty has been good enough to authorize me to put in writing the promise you have made to uphold me in the execution of those plans for economy that are at all times, and to-day more than ever, of an absolute necessity. . . . At this moment, Sire, I confine myself to recalling to you these three phrases :

' No bankruptcy ;

' No increase of impositions ;

' No borrowing.

' No bankruptcy either avowed or disguised by arbitrary reductions (of interest on public stock).

' No increase of impositions ; the reason for this lies in the plight of your subjects, and still more in Your Majesty's heart.

' No borrowing ; because every loan always diminishes the unanticipated revenue and necessitates, in the long run, either bankruptcy or an increase in taxes. In time of peace it is perhaps permissible to borrow, but only in order to liquidate old debts, or to redeem other loans contracted on less advantageous terms.

' There is only one way of fulfilling these three aims : that of reducing expenditure below receipts, and sufficiently below to ensure each year a saving of twenty millions (*livres*) with a view to the redemption of long-standing debts. Failing this, the first gunshot will drive the State to bankruptcy.

' It will be asked, " On what can we retrench ? " and all officials, speaking for their own departments, will maintain that every particular item of expenditure is indispensable. They will be able to put forward very good reasons ; but, since the impossible cannot be achieved, all these must yield to the absolute necessity of economy.

' It is, then, highly essential for Your Majesty to insist that the heads of all departments should act in concert with the Minister of Finance. It is imperative that he should discuss with them in the presence of Your Majesty the urgency of proposed expenses. Above all it is essential, Sire, that, as soon as you have decided what amount is strictly requisite for each department, you should forbid the officials concerned to order any new expenditure without first arranging with the Treasury the means of providing for it. Without this regulation each department will load itself with debts, which will always become Your Majesty's debts, and your Minister of Finances will be unable to answer for the discrepancy between income and expenditure.

' Your Majesty is aware that one of the greatest obstacles to economy is the multiplicity of demands by which you are constantly besieged, and which have unfortunately been sanctioned too indulgently by your predecessors.

' It is necessary, Sire, to arm yourself against your kindness by a greater kind-heartedness, by considering whence comes this money which you are able to distribute to your courtiers, and by comparing the wretchedness of those from whom it is extracted (sometimes by the most rigorous methods) with the condition of those people who have the greatest call upon your liberality.

' There are certain favours which, it is thought, you can readily grant, because they do not immediately bear upon the Royal Treasury.

' Of this kind are profit-sharing in revenue collections (*intérêts* and *croupes*) and privileges ; they are the most dangerous and the most open to abuse. Every profit made on impositions which is not strictly necessary for their collection should be devoted to the relief of the taxpayer and the needs of the State.

' Besides, these participations in the rewards of the tax-farmers are a source of corruption for the nobility and of vexation to the people, since they afford all such abuses secret and powerful protectors.

' It may be hoped that, following an improvement in husbandry and also the suppression of irregularities in the collection of taxation, and as a result of more equitable assessments, a substantial relief for the people may be obtained without diminishing greatly the public revenue ; but unless economy is the first step, no reform is possible, because every readjustment entails the risk of interrupting the collection of taxation, and because increasing difficulties, caused by the manoeuvres and protests of those interested in perpetuating abuses, are only to be expected, there being no abuse upon which someone does not thrive.

' So long as the finances are continually subject to the old expedients in order to provide for State services, Your Majesty will be at the mercy of the Financiers, who will always be able by their stratagems to frustrate reforms. No relief will be possible either by way of lightening the burden of the taxpayer or through legislation and changes in administration. The Government can never feel at ease, because it cannot ever win affection, and because the discontent and impatience of the masses are always the means utilized by intriguers and disaffected persons to excite disturbances. It is, then, upon economy that, above all, the prosperity of your reign depends ; upon it, too, hangs the tranquillity of your kingdom, its reputation among foreign Powers, the happiness of the nation and your own.

' I must impress upon Your Majesty that I take office at a serious time when disquietude is widely prevalent respecting the sustenance of the people—a disquietude aggravated in the public mind for several years by the want of uniformity in the principles of administrators, by a number of imprudent operations on their part, and above all, by a harvest below the average. On this matter, as upon others, I do not ask Your Majesty to adopt my principles without first having them thoroughly examined and discussed, as well by yourself as by your counsellors in your presence. But should you recognize the justice and the necessity of these principles, I implore you to maintain with firmness their application, showing no fear for the clamours which are absolutely certain to arise, no matter what system you adopt or policy you pursue.

' These are the matters that I have been permitted to recall to Your Majesty. You will not forget that in accepting the office of Comptroller-General, I have felt to the full the value of the confidence with which you favour me ; I have felt that you entrust to me the happiness of your people, and, if I may be permitted to say so, the mission of promoting among your people the love of your person and of your authority. But at the same time I am aware of all the dangers to which I expose myself. I foresee that I shall be alone in fighting against abuses of every kind, against those who profit by them, against the many prejudiced persons who, opposed to all reforms, are such powerful instruments in the hands of vested interests intent on perpetuating the existing disorder. I shall have to battle even against the natural goodness and generosity of Your Majesty and of persons who are most dear to you.[60] I shall be feared, hated even, by nearly all at Court, by all who solicit favours ; they will attribute refusals to me ; they will call me a hard man because I advise Your Majesty not to enrich even those you love at the loss of your people's sustenance. And these very subjects, for whom I shall sacrifice myself, are so easily deceived that perhaps I shall arouse their hatred of the very measures I take to save them from exactions. Appearances being against me, I shall be subject to calumny, the aim being to deprive me of Your Majesty's confidence. I shall never regret losing an office which I never expected. I am ready to resign it to Your Majesty as soon as I can no longer hope to be useful in it; but the esteem, the reputation for integrity, the desire to promote the common good, all of which have led you to favour me, are more dear to me than life, and I run the risk of losing my reputation even though meriting in my own eyes no reproach.

'Your Majesty will remember that it is my faith in your promises which leads me to shoulder a burden perhaps beyond my strength, and that it is to you personally, to an honest, just, and good man rather than to the King, that I give myself.

'I venture to repeat here what you have already been kind enough to hear and approve. The affecting kindness with which you condescended to press my hands within your own, as if accepting my devotion, will never be effaced from my memory. It will sustain my courage. It has for all time welded my personal happiness with the interests, the glory, and the welfare of Your Majesty.' [61]

Such was Turgot's plan. It contained the promise of the barest minimum of reform; it nowhere departed from the principles of sound business and common sense; and yet, as he himself was well aware, his was a colossal undertaking, in view of the difficulties that he would encounter—the bewilderment and timidity of his master, the sinister influences of those around him, the ease with which vested interests could turn popular disaffection against the Crown, making even a moderate reform the most hazardous of ventures.

Yet Turgot's following were more elated than ever [62] and the kingdom at large hoped for better times. Mlle de Lespinasse wrote to Guibert, 'Every one was intoxicated with joy, my friend . . . I repeat to you: you missed a great deal here.' Paris and the provinces celebrated vociferously the disgrace of Maupeou and the Abbé Terray, and the fishwives of Compiègne, under cover of a time-old custom of the day of Saint-Louis, congratulated the King upon his good 'bag'. 'Men of all ranks', declares Stormont, 'vie with each other in demonstrations of joy.' Bonfires were lighted, the streets were decorated, and the fallen Ministers were burned in effigy.[63] Terray was fortunate not to be personally assaulted. The crowd at the ferry at Choisy-le-Roi were for throwing him into the river, and only by bribing the watermen, who pulled him quickly from the bank, did he manage to escape from the grasp of his ferocious pursuers.[64]

Far away at Limoges a touching and most appropriate ceremony

was organized. The municipal assembly sent to Turgot a letter
of congratulations, and on 8 September held a public fête which
ended with a firework display, the final effect being the lighting of
a Catherine-wheel upon which were the words, *Vive Turgot*.[65]

At the Court Turgot's appointment caused very little stir.
Opinion had not changed much during the short period that he
had been at the Marine, and it was still the *dévots* who denounced
him because of his former associations with the encyclopaedists.
But, as the King had overlooked the indiscretions of his early
years, they must grudgingly forgive him also. They must be
thankful that he was not a Choiseuliste. On the other hand, the
Choiseulistes must console themselves that he was not a *dévot*.
Neither party was then fully aware that as a result of their struggles
they had advanced a common enemy. Disappointed though the
various factions were, they must remember that things might have
been much worse. The Queen's interest was most sanguine.
Was not Turgot the Abbé de Vermond's friend ? Might he not
use his influence to promote the Queen's favourite, Sartine, to
the Royal Household ? Might he not improve the Queen's
financial position ? Such were the arguments that Mercy unfolded to the Empress ; and Marie-Antoinette wrote once again
to tell her mother that Turgot was a very honest man.[66]

No less satisfactory was Turgot's reception from the magistracy.
There was, of course, a vague uneasiness among them, and Nicolaï,
who received him at the *Chambre des comptes* on 31 August, while
lavishing praise and fine words upon him, hinted that systems were
dangerous and implored him to ' avail himself of simple and
facile methods in his financial administration '. [67]   But this was
hardly the time to voice open discontent. Turgot and Miromesnil
were to be preferred to Terray and Maupeou. Indeed, the
Ministerial changes promised well for the magistracy, for it was
known that Turgot favoured the reversal of Maupeou's *coup
d'état*.[68] It mattered little for the moment that he also held other
ideas which the magistracy held in abhorrence. For the time
being he must be welcomed : old scores could wait for another
occasion.

CHAPTER X

TURGOT AND THE RECALL OF THE PARLEMENT

(1)

ENCOURAGED by their victory of 1754, the Parlements of France had increased their power and prestige.[1] The popular hatred of the heavy taxation for the Seven Years' War, a growing body of opinion which regarded the magistracy as the one remaining check upon despotic monarchy, and the occasional ascendancy of factions at the Court favourable to their cause, had led the Parlements to intervene not only more frequently but also more effectively in the affairs of the State, and more than ever before their censures had intimidated the Ministers of the Crown. Exile came to have less terror for these hardy republicans, who always knew, as did every one else, that the lack of confidence in the judges replacing them, and the refusal of the advocates and attorneys to plead before tribunals composed of monarchical partisans, would lead sooner or later to their recall; and they anticipated also that when they returned they would be acclaimed by the populace, as at Besançon in 1762 when thanksgivings were held in the churches, when the guilds organized banquets, and sixty gaily dressed maidens came forward to offer them wreaths of laurel.

The power of the magistracy, already grown to such dimensions, was enhanced still further by their share in expelling the Jesuits. The destruction of the Order in Portugal brought attacks upon it in other kingdoms. In France events played into the hands of the Gallican magistracy. When Father La Valette, the head of the Jesuits in Martinique, lost his factory and his ships in an English raid and became bankrupt, the Order refused to assist him, on the ground that his commercial activities were contrary to its Statutes. Among his creditors were merchants from Marseilles. When finally their case came before the Parlement of Paris, Father de Sacy, General of the Jesuits in France, was ordered to pay the debt, and the magistrates, not content to let the matter rest at this, declared Jesuit principles irreconcilable with the laws of the realm and destructive of the Christian Code. At the time a faction led by Choiseul and Mme de Pompadour was in the ascendant at the Court, and in 1764 Louis XV was persuaded to banish the Order, it being represented to him that the Jesuits had been implicated in attempts upon his life. This victory, vociferously applauded by Gallican France, was popularly accredited to the Parlements.

Closely bound up with these events was the famous quarrel between the Duc d'Aiguillon, *commandant* of Brittany, and La Chalotais, Attorney-General in the Parlement of Rennes. The latter, having gained credit in denouncing the Jesuits, aroused his fellow-magistrates, among whom were many of the old nobility, to attack Bertin's fiscal measures of 1763, and also to denounce as unbridled despotism d'Aiguillon's capable administration of the province, including his reform of the *corvées*. The King, calling Chalotais to Versailles, ordered the magistrates to desist from their antagonism to d'Aiguillon's rule. But they remained defiant, and when, in 1764, L'Averdy, against the advice of d'Aiguillon, imposed additional taxation upon Brittany without consulting the Estates, they retaliated by suspending their administration of justice. Chalotais, suspected of uttering libels against d'Aiguillon, was arrested together with a number of his supporters; but even from prison he pursued his enemy and accused him of having brought about, in conspiracy with the Jesuits, the arrest of the magistrates. When d'Aiguillon returned to Rennes in 1766 (he had been in the South and could have had no share in ordering the imprisonment of the refractory lawyers) he was further accused of attempting to murder La Chalotais while in prison.

D'Aiguillon insisted that his detractors should be accorded a trial and, as a consequence, a newly-constituted Parlement was instructed to hear the case; but when no judges could be found to serve on this tribunal, and when other Parlements, including that of Paris, protested against this procedure, Louis, acting on the advice of d'Aiguillon, restored the old Breton magistracy in July 1766 and evoked the suit to the Council. And shortly afterwards, when the magistrates at Paris renewed their objections, fearing lest the struggle might get out of hand, he put an end to the proceedings and exiled La Chalotais and others without a hearing. But those of the old magistracy remaining at Rennes continued the struggle; opening an inquiry, they hoped to find irregularities in d'Aiguillon's execution of the Act expelling the Jesuits, and they again accused him of attempting to poison La Chalotais. D'Aiguillon, paying no heed to the warnings of his friends, demanded that these sensational charges against him should be heard, and insisted on his right to be tried by peers

in the Parlement of Paris.[2] The trial began in April 1770; but
in June Louis XV, acting upon the advice of the Chancellor,
Maupeou, once more annulled proceedings. Matters now came
to a head. Choiseul, fearing that the intrigues of Maupeou,
Terray, and Mme Du Barry were undermining his position, threw
in his lot with the magistrates, whom he encouraged secretly in
their opposition to d'Aiguillon. But this bold bid, combined
with his adventurous design for making war with England and
his undisguised hostility to Mme Du Barry, proved his undoing,
and Terray was able to give a final thrust by exposing to Louis
the extravagance of his administration. Choiseul was banished
to Chanteloup. There were great scenes the day he left: his
partisans turned out in force to cheer him and the populace
bought his portrait in the streets. He was succeeded, as he had
feared, by d'Aiguillon, and so began the rule of the Triumvirate.

Undeterred, even emboldened by these events, the magistrates
continued to attack d'Aiguillon, and arranged a special session for
3 December to remonstrate against the denial of their right to
hear the charges against him. When the day came, Maupeou
confronted them with a royal edict forbidding them ever to suspend
justice, to reject and modify the King's decrees, or to employ
words (*unité, indivisibilité*) expressing their claim that the courts
formed a single corporation. This measure, which was calculated
to offend them, the magistrates refused to register and, even when
forced to do so in a *lit de justice*, renewed their remonstrances and
suspended judicial business. And that was precisely what
Maupeou had counted upon: he wished to provide a pretext for
taking sterner measures. On the night of 19 January 1771,
musketeers delivered *lettres de cachet* to the magistrates ordering
each to reply immediately whether he would continue to discharge
his duties. The majority refused, and the next night 130 of them
were exiled and deprived of their offices.

Maupeou had hoped that the *Grand' Chambre*, dissociating
itself from the *Enquêtes* and *Requêtes*, would continue its sittings,
but when this tribunal also declined to carry on, he established a
temporary court, which, like the *Chambre Royale* of 1753, was
composed of councillors of State and masters of requests. But
lawyers would not plead before it, and it idled its days away.
Maupeou was compelled, therefore, to organize immediately a
new system of judicial administration within the jurisdiction of
the Parlement of Paris. This he did in promulgating the Edict
of 23 February 1771. Denouncing in the preamble the abuse of
épices (the custom of making presents to judges), the slow and
costly justice dispensed in the large resort of Paris, and also the
venality of judicial office as being wasteful of talent, he went on
to establish Superior Councils at Blois, Châlons, Clermont, Lyon,

and Poitiers, and a sixth at Arras to replace the existing Provincial Council. Each court was given, within the area allotted to it, the judicial authority formerly exercised by the Parlement of Paris. This last institution was retained in name, the *Grand Conseil*, which was assembled on 13 April, consenting to act as a tribunal for the special affairs of the Crown, as a court of peers, and as a registry for the laws of State. To this body, known as the *Parlement Maupeou*, was given the right to make legitimate remonstrances. Composed of seventy-five members, it was divided into two chambers, the *Grand' Chambre* and the *Enquêtes*, judges from both these bodies serving in the criminal court of the *Tournelle*.

Against these innovations there were further remonstrances from the old magistracy of France, and it was not long before the *Cour des aides* and the *Châtelet* were also abolished for continuing to defy the Crown. Maupeou, who had at first intended to limit his reform to the large jurisdiction of Paris, was in favour of suppressing the provincial Parlements and of establishing Superior Councils throughout the country. To such steps the King and the Ministers were opposed, and in the end two Parlements only, Rouen and Douai, were abolished. Nevertheless several reforms were introduced; venality of office and the *épices* were suppressed, and the number of magistrates everywhere reduced. In some places—at Besançon, for example—the ancient judges accepted the new form of office; in others—at Rennes, for instance—the majority refused and were exiled, while in Provence every single magistrate declined to carry on and a completely new service had to be recruited.

Such in brief was Maupeou's *coup d'état*. As Bertin told the Duc de Croÿ, the antagonism of Crown and Parlement had come to such a pass that ' a revolt on one side or the other had become inevitable ', and, in his opinion, the move was a timely frustration of a republican plot to destroy the monarchy and transfer sovereignty to an aristocracy. De Croÿ agreed that the magistrates had for a long while exceeded their rightful place in the constitution, and he was glad that the King had reasserted his authority; yet he was not altogether happy, for he believed that the balance of government had been disturbed and that a monarchy which was too absolute provoked constant opposition. Others, too, while delighted at seeing the power of the Parlements curtailed, deplored the outcome of the victory. ' This new tribunal ', wrote Véri, ' . . . left Terray absolute master to carry out his operations by simple *arrêts du conseil* and to give edicts already registered an application in excess of their original intention.' [3] But there were many—perhaps the bulk of the nation—who deplored the fall of the ancient Parlement. Gallicans and

Jansenists could see in Maupeou's revolution only a clerical plot engineered by the Jesuits; a large section of the provincial nobility were uneasy lest their rights and privileges should next be singled out for attack; and, though indeed in some regions the new magistracy were well received by the masses,[4] on the whole Maupeou's policy was resented as an intrusion upon provincial liberties. Maupeou, himself, was highly unpopular, and was on several occasions threatened with assassination. Hundreds of libels, the *Maupeouana*, made their appearance, and for over three years a literary warfare proceeded, several incidents—that, for example, when Beaumarchais accused Goezmann, a Maupeou magistrate, of corruption—supplying the source of more spectacular conflicts. Yet, despite constant antagonism, Louis and Maupeou refused to surrender. Gradually the new system began to work more smoothly, the attorneys and advocates one by one resuming their legal business. Maupeou was never so vicious or so sadistic in crushing his enemies as is often said. Ready to mitigate the hardships experienced by the exiled magistrates, he was also prepared to provide employment for those who would accept it. And the new judges were never so mean, so despicable, and so untalented as they are portrayed in the writings of their enemies and of disappointed suitors.[5]

(2)

It may appear strange that Turgot should have counselled the restoration of the ancient magistracy, yet in doing this he remained thoroughly consistent with his principles. It is true that twenty years previously, when a young master of requests, he had served upon the *Chambre Royale*, a body which was of much the same character as the *Parlement Maupeou*; but on that occasion he was merely given the alternatives of serving or refusing to serve upon such a tribunal, and it was not for him to proffer other suggestions. But in 1774 he was the holder of high office; it was his duty to counsel the King; and, having considered all things carefully, he pronounced for the reversal of Maupeou's *coup d'état*.[6] While at Limoges he had made some interesting comments to Du Pont upon this event. Of the fall of the Choiseulistes he said: ' I do not like those who have gone; but those who succeeded make me tremble'. About a month later he adds: '. . . the world will never cease to be governed by rogues: after the rain we shall have the deluge.' Then on 1 February, after the magistrates had been exiled, he remarks: ' I do not take a great interest in the broken pitchers (the Parlements), and I do not really know to what extent they have reason on their side in pursuing the aim that has occasioned the rupture. Their resistance might be valuable, if it were enlightened and

disinterested ; but the power they claim to veto the acts of governments is not only absurd, but a condition under which no ministry
can continue or govern reasonably. The misfortune is that the
government " buys " the parlement when it is the interest of the
people at stake. The lions (the nobility) have always made their
peace at the expense of the sheep. The little farce that is being
played at Paris seems to me more comic than tragic, and will
terminate, like the two I have witnessed, in the restoration of the
pitchers of which all the pieces will join together again, like the
nose and ears of Saint George and Saint Denis in *La Pucelle,* for
the flesh of saints is so firm and plump. The return may or may
not lead to changes. Meanwhile',—he is warning Du Pont to lie
low—' I advise you to keep quiet. The flesh of journalists is not
as good as that of the saints in *La Pucelle,* and you must preserve
a few tissues at least which hold together.'

' What ', he asks Du Pont on 28 February, ' do the economists
think of the new edict ? . . . As for myself, in detesting the causes,
the motives, and the underhand dealing, I do not regret the fact
of the matter, and it seems to me that if this condition continues
the public will gain in the long run more than it will lose.' By
13 March he had revised his opinion : ' From all that I hear, I
see that the present Ministry has failed. We shall be delivered
from the ravenous wolves, and the *boeufs-tigres* will come back as
stupid or even more stupid than ever. From neither side can one
expect any good. These men (Maupeou, d'Aiguillon, and Terray)
have undertaken with the very worst intentions, a thing which,
even with the best motives, would have been difficult ; but the
obstacles that they have encountered will be for a long while
hindrances to progress and to all change for the good.' [7] Turgot's
language is obscure, but his attitude is fairly clear : little as he
loved the Parlements and their policy, he hated even more the
Triumvirate that was ruling the country through the influence of
Mme Du Barry. ' The defeat of the Parlement ', he had written
to Du Pont, ' is equivocal : in abandoning to the magistrates the
poor people, the Government has given these scoundrels a valuable
weapon.' [8]

The happenings of the three years following Maupeou's *coup
d'état,* when Terray ruled at the Finances, had confirmed his
opinions. Moreover, he was now fully convinced that nothing
was to be gained from perpetuating a régime which was so unpopular. On the other hand, he believed that if the Parlements
were to be restored, they should be subjected to strict conditions,
which were that they should always register laws before making
remonstrances, should never remonstrate more than once, never
interfere with religious matters, and never suspend justice upon
any pretext whatever.[9] He was not, of course, so artless as to

think that the magistrates would quietly remain within these
bounds; and he knew only too well that sooner or later they
would attempt to make good the ground that they had lost; but
he also believed that, if the Government, by enacting wise laws,
deprived the Parlements of their leadership of the oppressed
classes in the realm, they could never again display such power
or such audacity as in the past.   In short, if conditions were
imposed upon the magistracy, and if these were followed up by a
strong and enlightened policy, everything was to be gained by the
overthrow of Maupeou's régime.   On the other hand, if Maupeou's
system remained in force, Maupeou and Terray might also keep
going, or perhaps a Ministry composed of *dévots* might saddle
itself upon the kingdom.

From the beginning of the reign Louis had been subject to
bewildering counsel concerning the magisterial problem.   Many
had pressed him to give effect immediately to the resolution,
made by his grandfather upon the advice of d'Aiguillon, to restore
the ancient Parlement.[10]   In June the Princes of the Blood had
submitted to him a memorial which, paying deference in hollow
phrases to the royal authority and eulogizing the ancient constitution, proposed a plan for the reversal of Maupeou's *coup
d'état*.[11]   Upon Louis this work made a great impression.   On
the other hand, Maupeou had 'every secret engine at work', and
the Aunts Louise and Adelaïde, the Comte de Provence, Du Muy,
and other influential *dévots* were for ever warning him that if the
magistracy returned, the Church would be in danger.   Louis
was at a loss.   'It cannot, I think, be imagined,' wrote Stormont,
' that the young King is able to take a comprehensive view of so
extensive and intricate a subject, and to form a decisive opinion
upon a thorough examination of the whole.   He must therefore
lean upon the opinions and follow the wishes of others.' [12]

It must be admitted that Maurepas had a difficult task in
advising Louis upon this matter—all the more so because he
himself could come to no decision.   His sentiments certainly lay
with the magisterial party, with which he had family connexions,
but, fearing lest Louis should suddenly turn against him if he
appeared too eager, he refrained from declaring himself openly
in favour of the Parlement.   He played a crafty game.   He was
not intent upon any particular solution to the problem; what
interested him was that in finding a solution his own credit and
popularity should not diminish.[13]   He was quite happy in leaving
difficulties unsolved, in finding not a real compromise, but a
temporary way out, trusting in the future to his nimble wits to
save his face again.   He vaguely suggested that a middle way
might be followed, that Miromesnil or Joly de Fleury should be
appointed to the Seals, and that members of the old and new

Parlements should be asked to form a *Grand Conseil*.[14]   But he did not persist in this proposal, which he must have known the old magistracy would never accept, and he had put it forward with a view to gaining time, hoping that the King would, of his own, gradually come to look upon the return of the magistracy as inevitable.   He was waiting for other influences to counteract the advice that Louis received from the *dévots* and from the Comte de Provence, who foretold a weakening of the royal authority ; [15] he was prepared to stand by and let the stony silence that greeted Louis and his Queen everywhere they went produce the effect that his own argument might lack.[16]   And it was with this same caution that early in September he held conferences with the leading magistrates, hoping to find some formulae which would satisfy them and at the same time lead the King to believe that the royal authority was not endangered.   Other Ministers, too, were similarly waiting upon events, not wishing to prejudice their positions by giving counsel which might not be welcome at this stage.   As Stormont put it, ' The present Ministers see in *part* and act in *part*, and to extensive lasting evils apply partial temporary palliatives '—a course—' condemned by men of all parties who look upon it as a patch work which cannot last.' [17]

In such a situation there was every chance that Turgot's proposals might be adopted as an obvious compromise, and in all probability his opinions carried great weight in the small committee composed of Maurepas, Miromesnil, Sartine, and himself—which, shortly after the Ministerial changes in August, met secretly at frequent intervals with the King.[18]   Little is known of the discussions that took place.   Stormont was unable to report the existence of the committee until late in October, and even Véri, who was usually able to penetrate the deepest secrets at Versailles, failed to learn much about its activities.   Its object, he says, was to put the King in possession of facts and opinions by supplying him with an account of all that had been said, written, and debated upon the affair of the Parlement, it being hoped that he would arrive himself at a decision.   ' This method ', he adds, ' had the desired effect, which was to make Louis regard as his own the plan adopted.' [19]   Whose plan it was, and whose opinion really prevailed, Véri does not tell us.   But it is reasonable to suppose that it was Turgot who prevailed upon Louis to insist upon a number of the more important restrictions imposed upon the magistrates as the condition of their return.   If the truth were known, he took the lead over Maurepas, and succeeded in preventing Miromesnil from arranging more favourable terms for the ancient magistracy.

(3)

The Parlement of Rouen was restored in October; that of Paris, the *Grand Conseil* and the *Cour des aides* on 12 November, and before the end of the year all the provincial courts had likewise been recalled. Once again there followed great demonstrations. ' Paris was intoxicated with joy,' wrote Mme Campan, adding that not one person in a hundred foresaw that the old magistracy would renew their attacks upon the royal authority. ' The Paris mob rejoiced without knowing why,' wrote Baron de Frenilly. ' The French people have gone mad with enthusiasm,' wrote Beaumarchais to Sartine, ' and I am not in the least surprised.' Without a doubt the new magistrates, many of them upstarts, had been highly unpopular, and enjoyed a worse reputation than the facts of their administration warranted. But the prolonged demonstrations could hardly have been the spontaneous outburst of opinion, and were certainly organized by the old magisterial families. On 21 November, the day of the *Messe rouge*—so called because the lawyers attended in scarlet—the patriots overflowed the Palace of Justice. The magistrates entered in procession to the sound of fifes and tabors, especial greetings being accorded to those well known—Saint-Vincent, Montblin, Seguier, Saint-Fargeau, and the presidents Gourgues and Lamoignon. The *Domine salvum fac regem* was interrupted by loud acclamations; and at the end of the ceremony the women embraced the First President, gave him a bouquet, and placed upon his brow a laurel crown. At that same time precisely the *Grand Conseil* was entering the Louvre for a session. There, too, a crowd had gathered, and there, too, the magistrates received a frenzied welcome. Yet the provinces outshone Paris in their reception of the ancient courts. At Rennes Chalotais was given a royal entry; 200 gentlemen escorted him on horseback; and a long line of carriages of the aristocracy brought up the rear of the procession. Never before in Bretagne had so many nobles gathered together for a public event.[20] At Bordeaux the fishermen and fishwives assembled to welcome Le Berthon, the first president, who went among the people and embraced them.[21] At Rouen a great feast was held; lotteries were organized; firework displays were given, and money was freely distributed to the populace.

Nor were the *philosophes* and *économistes* at all dejected at the return of the magistrates. Voltaire could only regret that those directly responsible for the deaths of Lally and La Barre were not excluded, and d'Alembert's only comment in a letter to Frederick the Great was that he hoped that four years of exile had made the Parlement more reasonable and less disposed to obstruct governmental action. Even Condorcet did not take a very different line. To him Maupeou's Parlement was vile and despicable : the old was insolent and hateful ; and what was wanted was a third, which he hoped would soon be established. Their position was substantially that which Turgot had adopted. They favoured despotism unimpeded, provided it were enlightened ; but during the past few years they had seen absolutism directed by men like Maupeou and Terray, who, sheltered from the criticism of the courts, had made it the most perverse of governments. Like Turgot, they had wanted restrictions placed upon the magistracy. Condorcet had written to Turgot : ' I persist in thinking that there is no reason or pretext for restoring the Parlements without imposing conditions upon them.'

The edicts—the actual phrasing of which was the work of Miromesnil—were read to the assembled magistrates on Saturday 12 November. At eight in the morning Louis heard Mass at the Sainte-Chapelle. Later he and his entourage passed into the *Grand' Chambre*, where he took his place on the throne, surrounded by the Princes of the Blood, the Peers, Ministers, and Great Officers of State—in a word, all those who had the right to assist at a *lit de justice*, except the Parlement itself. In a short speech he acquainted this high nobility of his intentions, explained his motives, and ended by saying that he would restrain his Parlements within their proper limits. The Master of Ceremonies then went to command the presence of the magistrates who had been waiting in the chamber of Saint Louis. They filed in in order of precedence—the Presidents, the judges of the *Grand' Chambre*, the *Enquêtes*, and the *Requêtes*. Before the whole assembly Louis took the oath. Then, in a loud, firm voice and with great dignity (which must have surprised his audience),[22] he admonished them : they had provoked the righteous anger of his predecessor, and if when returned they failed to respect the wishes of the Crown, they would be sent again into exile. The edicts and ordinances—ten in all—were then read by Miromesnil. The effect of these was to restore the Parlement and the *Cour des aides* of Paris, the *Cour des aides* of Clermont, the judicial council of Artois, and the *Grand Conseil*. Hereditary office and security from dismissal were affirmed, and the *Parlement Maupeou* and the superior councils were suppressed. The fifth edict requires a special mention. In establishing the *Grand Conseil*, which was composed mainly of the new magistracy, it provides for this court to take over the administration of justice if ever the Parlement itself refused to carry on or was suspended from its work of dispensing justice. This edict should be read in conjunction with the ordinance of discipline, which imposed the following conditions upon the magistrates. No court was to meet outside its appointed hours; there was to be no interruption of justice upon pain of dismissal; and, though the magistrates might make remonstrances within the period of a month after the issue of a royal edict, they were to lose that right should they attempt to impede execution by issuing *arrêts de défense*.[23]

But all these provisions were illusory, because the Parlements would attempt to gain inch by inch the ground that they had lost, and because no Ministry could be counted upon to remain firm for all time in face of opposition. The magistrates, Stormont foretold, ' will no doubt be lavish of assurances of unbounded duty and fidelity, suffer some expression favourable to the royal authority to be asserted in the King's edict recalling them and let those expressions pass unnoticed, well knowing that such expressions signify but little and, when favourable circumstances arise, they may easily be explained away '.[24] The speech given by Seguier in the *Grand' Chambre* the very day the edicts were issued was a warning for the future. His words, full of respect and literally giving no offence, carried a double meaning. Speaking finally upon the ordinance of discipline he said: ' Pre-eminently full of the respect that the presence of Your Majesty inspires, we believe that at this moment we can have no other duty than to submit.' Such was the tenor of all his speeches—and he spoke on every edict. But it was the faces of the magistrates rather than the words of their spokesman which made plain their opinions. They were obviously not pleased at being treated as the conquered party. When Miromesnil, even, passed through their ranks, he was met with black looks and recriminating murmurs. They had failed to win the speedy and complete victory for which they had hoped. Yet the future was theirs if they could wait. ' The young King ', wrote Stormont, ' thinks that his authority is sufficiently secured by the regulations he has made. He may probably find himself deceived by the end of his reign. . . . (The magistrates) will wait for circumstances, avail themselves of circumstances as they arise and, whenever there are divisions in the Ministry, (these will) be an engine which one Minister will play off against another, and which an able and daring Minister might perhaps wield in such a manner as to establish his own power on the ruin of the King's.' [25] Within a month of their restoration the magistrates, taking heart at their tremendous reception from the country, renewed the conflict with the Crown. At the opening of the courts the Attorney-General made a speech on the subject of true and false glory, obviously making Maupeou an example of the latter. In Brittany a section of the old magistracy defiantly refused to work with those who had accepted office under Maupeou. On 2 December the Parlement of Paris protested against the November edicts, claiming that, as the

Parlements owed their existence to fundamental law, they had no need to be ' re-created '. Louis gave way; he accepted the remonstrance, and therefore admitted the claims of the magistracy. A week later the Parlement held a general assembly. In vain did Monsieur speak of the necessity of submission to the King's pleasure. But Conti, ' who always had the vanity of appearing one of the principal actors,' harangued the assembly for half an hour with great eloquence, and carried a motion by 120 votes to 10 that individual magistrates should submit their objections in writing to the First President, who should then make a summary of them for the approval of all chambers at the end of December.[26] At the beginning of January, after the President had given his résumé of the opinion of individual magistrates, Conti proposed that protests should be made against the following: the brevity of the time allowed to the Parlement in which to submit remonstrances; the provision for the *Grand Conseil* to replace the Parlement when suspended; the establishment of a *Cour Plénière* to judge of and pronounce forfeiture or suspension of the Parlement; the power given to the *Grand' Chambre* to determine whether an affair was or was not of the nature to be judged by the *chambres assemblées*; and finally the judicial powers delegated by the Crown to individuals in the provinces. That same session, with the avowed intention of acquiring further popularity for the magistracy, Conti urged the Parlement to make further remonstrances against a number of Terray's financial edicts. The King gave no immediate reply. On 7 January the *Châtelet* drew up protests of its own and submitted them to Louis. It was not until 20 January that the assembled chambers read the King's reply. Louis was non-committal; his answer, however, failed to satisfy the magistrates, who renewed their protests in an *arrêté* proposed by Conti.[27]

Such was the beginning of yet another conflict between the Crown and the magistracy—a conflict which, from the outset, produced conditions most unfavourable to reform. Moreover, as a result of his share in recalling the Parlement, Turgot himself had made bitter enemies upon all sides. The *dévots* looked upon him as one of the evil advisers who had prevailed upon Louis to betray the Church;[28] the patriots, on the other hand, regarded him as the author of the edict of discipline imposed upon the courts. His brother, the Marquis de Turgot, wrote to him showing great concern: ' You surely do not ignore the infernal intrigues directed against you and the rumours that are spreading. The priests, financiers, all connected with them and all those who fish in troubled waters are united.'[29] Nevertheless, in spite of the murmurs of the factions, Turgot was relatively secure. The King had given him a solemn pledge; Maurepas, now more than ever in Louis's confidence, was upon the best terms with him and was, in fact, greatly disturbed when his illness at the beginning of 1775—a severe attack of gout—seemed likely to compel him to retire after such a brief period at the Finances; and Marie-Antoinette continued to display for him the greatest esteem, which, in collaboration with Maurepas and the Abbé Vermond, he was taking every care to retain. To these political resources, slender though they really were, it was impossible for him to add, and it was very easy for him to lose them—impossible to add because a reforming Minister could never maintain the usual kind of connexion at the Court, easy to lose because others, too—the unscrupulous politicians at Versailles—could also appeal to Louis's conscience when it suited them to do so, because the Queen was bound sooner or later to become an instrument in the hands of factions, and because Maurepas was fickle and cautious. All things considered, what is surprising is not that Turgot fell from favour, but that he was able to maintain himself in office for twenty months.

CHAPTER XI

THE FINANCES

(1)

IN theory the Comptroller-General was nothing more than a chief clerk to the Government, and the initiative in finance, as indeed in all affairs, was supposed to derive from the King in his Councils.[1] These were six in number.[2] First there was the *Conseil d'en haut* or *Conseil secret*, composed of the King and Ministers of State [3]—a body which dealt with matters of supreme importance, peace and war, treaties, diplomatic relations, and at times with great affairs of domestic policy. This institution had become differentiated from the mediaeval council in 1547. Fifty years earlier the *Grand Conseil* had taken shape as a tribunal of magistrates over which the Chancellor presided and which, hearing cases deemed to be outside the competence of the Parlements, was a perpetual object of magisterial opposition. And so also was the *Conseil des dépêches*—an institution which acquired a separate existence in Janaury 1630. This council, composed in the later part of the eighteenth century of the King, the Keeper of the Seals, the Ministers and Secretaries of State, and also two Counsellors of State,[4] dealt with domestic affairs, both judicial and administrative, including those of the Church, the municipalities, and of the *pays d'états*.

The fourth council was the *Conseil privé (Conseil des parties)*—a much larger body, in which sat forty-two Councillors of State and also twelve out of the forty-eight Masters of Requests, these last reporting the findings of the commissions upon which they served, though after 1738 never actually voting in the council. This tribunal dispensed the King's privy justice as opposed to the common justice given in the Parlements. In reality it was a supreme appellate body, evoking cases from the common courts and quashing by means of *arrêts de cassation* the judicial and administrative rulings of those same bodies. It possessed also—in theory, at least—*la grande direction des finances*—that is to say, it gave a formal decision embodied in an *arrêt* upon matters of financial policy—the domain revenues, the contracts with

149

financiers, the *dons gratuits* of the clergy and provincial estates. But in actual practice such decisions were really made elsewhere, by a number of commissions, some of which were permanent and others of which were created as the need arose. These same commissions sometimes reported not to the Privy Council, but to the fifth council, the *Conseil des finances*, an institution dating from 1630 (perhaps more strictly from 1661), or even to the sixth council, the *Conseil du commerce*, a body which first came into existence during the reign of Henry IV.[5] Between the *Conseil des finances* and the *Conseil des dépêches* it is often impossible to distinguish. Not only their composition but also their business was very much alike; their decisions took the same final form, the *arrêt du conseil*, and it was probably the custom to convene them simultaneously. Then again, as we shall see, these councils often never actually met, and an *arrêt du conseil* supposed to emanate from them was frequently nothing more than a single Minister's, or even a single official's decision ratified by the King at any odd moment of the day.[6]

No one made more rulings of this kind than the Comptroller-General, though it must be allowed that quite often he was merely passing on for the royal assent decisions really arrived at by other officials who could not approach the King directly. Ever since the day when Colbert received his special commission in 1665—for this was the real origin of the *contrôle général* of the *ancien régime*—the Comptroller had come to play an increasing part in the administration of the country, and by the eighteenth century there was hardly a branch of government with which he was not in some way or other closely associated.[7] Yet this development of business passing through the offices of the *contrôle général* tended in some degree to diminish the personal influence of the Comptroller himself. Having a multiplicity of affairs to attend to, many of them matters of sheer routine and others requiring much attention even though only trivial issues were involved, he was apt to lose his grip upon administration and become not a master, but a figurehead. The more he was called upon to decide, the more he had to leave decisions to his subordinates, who, keeping a tight hand upon their papers, defended themselves against the busy-body and the innovator and often succeeded in imposing their will upon their fleeting superiors.[8] Terray, for instance, had allowed his underlings—especially the more unscrupulous amongst them—a degree of freedom that amounted to negligence, and these officials had determined to a considerable extent the financial and economic policy of the kingdom.[9] A man of greater ability could, of course, by indefatigable industry do much to restore the Comptroller's personal influence. Turgot was obviously the man to do so; but if he meant to reverse his predecessor's methods and policy, he must first get rid of his unruly henchmen, and ensure that those in key positions were men whom he could trust.

The *contrôle général* [10] was divided into a number of sub-departments, nearly all of which were housed in the *palais Mazarin* in what is now part of the *Bibliothèque Nationale*. The most important of these was under a man named Leclerc, who among his many responsible duties was concerned with the payments made by the Treasury to the departments of State. If Turgot was to insist upon his own control of public spending as intimated in his letter of 24 August, he must above all things have a chief clerk whose views were in harmony with his own. Leclerc, it is certain, was corrupt; out of his position he had made a fortune, which he was gambling away or spending in extravagant living. Turgot dismissed him, and to the vacancy appointed Vaines, formerly Director of Domains at Limoges. According to Mlle de Lespinasse, to whose circle he belonged, he was a man after Turgot's own heart; he lived simply and worked hard—so hard, indeed, that he impaired his eyesight. Turgot's choice was an excellent one. Vaines retained his employment under all the Comptrollers-General of Louis XVI's reign, and became a veritable Under-Secretary of State.

Another department which was domiciled at Versailles, since among its functions was that of keeping the register of the Council of Finance, was left under the control of Mesnard de Conichard, and a third bureau, the *dépêches*, where official correspondence was sorted and dispatched to the appropriate governmental departments, remained under the supervision of an official named Broë. The *dépêches* worked in close contact with the Comptroller, and it was here that Turgot placed two of his friends; he appointed Morellet an official receiver of pleas and petitions, and he gave Du Pont, who returned from Poland (though it meant a loss to him of 380,000 *livres*), a nominal post in order to act as his private secretary.[11] In two other departments he dismissed the chief officials; he could not leave the administration of the life-annuities to Dupuy, who was one of Terray's nominees, and he could not trust Destouches, who had been employed by his predecessor as a right-hand man. These two he replaced by Leseur and Delacroix, the latter of whom was formerly his private secretary at Limoges. The remaining chief officials, Villiers and Barbey, he saw no reason to remove, and he made no changes in a number of the lesser departments. He was quite content merely to dismiss the more important officials who had played the chief part under Terray's régime.

But the *contrôle général* was not the only organ of government through which the Comptroller worked. The real business of

civil administration took place in the offices of the intendants of
finance and commerce, who had charge of the detail of financial
and commercial affairs.   In theory these officials took their orders
from the Councils of Finance and Commerce : in practice they
acted upon instructions from the Comptroller, or sometimes
upon their own initiative, for the properly constituted sessions
of the Councils were few and far between.   During the last few
weeks of Terray's term of office the Council of Finance had
indeed, at the instigation of Maurepas, Turgot, and Vergennes,
been stirred to greater activity ; but normally conciliar government was incompatible with the expedition of business ; for the
members of the councils, having other duties to perform, could
give very little time to meetings ; and the King tended to postpone
financial business, which was far too dreary and too uninteresting.
The description of these councils given in the remonstrances of
the *Cour des aides* drawn up by Malesherbes is strictly accurate
when they are said to be composed of only the Comptroller and
an intendant of finance and sometimes, when the Comptroller
was pressed for time, of an intendant alone.[12]   Seven in number,
the intendants of finance were really permanent Under-Secretaries
of State, and each was entrusted with a variety of affairs, there
being no really logical distribution of business among them.
D'Ormesson, for instance, had charge, among many other matters,
of direct taxation, the *don gratuit* of the clergy, public assistance,
rations, stores, and military convoys ; and Daniel Trudaine, who,
like d'Ormesson, was assisted by his son, was responsible for the
gabelles, the *cinq grosses fermes*, the *ponts et chaussées*, the tree
nurseries, royal manufactures, and for numerous other branches
of administration.   All these officials had no special building in
which they discharged their duties ; instead each had his head-
office at his own house, while with one exception all the sub-
offices under the control of assistants were to be found scattered
throughout Paris in private domiciles.

Turgot made no attempt, nor was there really any need, to
distribute the duties of these intendants in a less haphazard
fashion.[13]   All he did was to bring under the men in whom he
confided those branches of administration he hoped to reform,
and to dismiss from employment those officials who were inefficient
and corrupt.   The d'Ormessons, father and son, were meticulous, painstaking, unimaginative and docile civil servants.
Trudaine was overworked.   To him Turgot gave a very able
assistant, Fourqueux, who prepared that vast correspondence for
Turgot's signature dealing with the cattle plague of 1775 and with
the detail of commerce and manufactures.   But a third intendant,
Foullon, who had a particularly bad reputation, was replaced by
Boutin.   ' Foullon ', wrote Baudeau, ' is without conscience,

without pity, without shame. . . . He bought the office of commissioner of war. . . . Choiseul, who loved adventures, took a great liking to him and made him intendant for war. After Choiseul's fall the Abbé Terray put his nose into the War Ministry to grab a few millions. Foullon obliged and in return received the office of intendant of finances.' And Cochin, a despicable and mercenary little *bourgeois*, also had to go, though Turgot was forced to accept in his stead Amelot, Maurepas' nephew, who, even if honest, was most incapable. But from Amelot's department many important concerns were taken away, and these, along with those also withheld from Boutin's, were entrusted to Beaumont and Boullongne, both of whom were capable officials.

Subordinate to one of the intendants of finance, Daniel Trudaine, were the intendants of commerce, who were five in number. They, too, had their offices in their houses. In commercial affairs each was responsible for a region ; in industrial administration for a particular type of manufacture or industry. If anything, this distribution of business was a little more logical than that in the finances. Again Turgot made no drastic changes in the forms of administration. He was content merely to remove men whom he could not trust. Quincy and Montaran, although staunch upholders of mercantilist opinions, he left in office, and Cotte, successor to the famous Vincent de Gournay, was an able official. But Vilevaut, who was one of Terray's nominees, was replaced by Fargès ; [14] and Brochet de Saint-Prest, who, collaborating with Terray in the scandalous administration of the grain supplies, had made a fortune, was compelled to return his office to the economist Albert, who several years earlier had been dismissed by Terray to make room for his notorious protégé.[15]

Such were the changes that Turgot made in the personnel of the administration. Other appointments are also worthy of mention. His friend the Comte d'Angevillers became Director of Public Buildings.[16] Condorcet was given charge of the *Hôtel des monnaies*. Suard—another of his friends—was appointed official histographer ; and Baudeau, who was perhaps disappointed at not receiving an important governmental office, was nevertheless made editor of the *Nouvelles Éphémérides du citoyen* when that publication, which had been suppressed towards the end of Louis XV's reign, was again published at Turgot's instigation.

(2)

' Your Majesty's obedient servant ', wrote the repentant Terray when, shortly before his fall, he renounced in words though not in deeds his four years' policy of extortion, ' cannot look without alarm upon this situation ; while receipt and expenditure remain unbalanced, or even until income is made greater than expenses by the reduction of the latter, I shall never cease to give you warning.' He would economize upon the Household, the Army and the Navy; he promised creditors a speedy payment of interests on loans; he would mitigate the burden of taxation and, as a gesture, he persuaded Louis to forgo the customary gift made at the accession.[17] But the truth was that he was at the end of his tether; he could not drive harder bargains with the financiers, since all the important contracts had been made; and he could not increase further the burden of taxation, which by crooked means he had already augmented to the extent of 60,000,000 *livres*.[18]

The exact extent of the deficit when Terray left office and of his contribution to it are problems not easily solved or even stated. For there was no system of unified accounts; numerous bodies and individuals were handling money entirely independently of one another, and the work of the *Chambre des comptes* was of a formal character, the officials submitting only the most perfunctory of balance-sheets, which were anything from six to twelve years out of date.[19] Throughout the century the national debt had been piling up, and successive wars, continual chicanery, and the strength of vested interest had always defeated in the long run the more careful stewards whose administration might temporarily repair the damage. The Seven Years' War placed an enormous strain upon the finances; borrowings, anticipations of revenue, the mortgaging of resources all assumed larger proportions, so that other expenses which in themselves were not calamitous— those in particular for the upkeep of the Court—began to burden the finances with an accumulative effect.[20] The peace of 1763 averted an immediate collapse, but the deficit continued to grow. Bertin, hoping to touch the pockets of the privileged classes, was defeated by the courtiers and magistrates. A similar misfortune befell d'Invau. ' Your Majesty's finances ', he had told Louis XV in 1769, ' are in the most alarming confusion. To-day 50 millions are needed to make annual income balance expenditure. . . . Each year a new debt accumulates upon the deficits of previous years. The most urgent debts amount to nearly 80 millions. . . . the revenues for one whole year have been consumed in advance.' When Terray followed d'Invau, the condition of the finances, it must be admitted, had become even more critical. Terray's first report to the King not only confirmed what d'Invau had said, but also showed that matters were becoming rapidly worse.[21]

Towards the end of 1770 Terray announced his policy. Taxa-tion was to be kept at the existing level, and reduced when the position had improved; borrowing was to cease until credit was restored; and it was to economy, above all in the Household, that he looked to restore the finances. In spite of these professions, he soon became convinced that shorter ways were needed. Yet his policy was not that of Machault, Bertin, and d'Invau, which involved an attack upon the privileged classes, but one of bankruptcy in stages. He suspended payments upon what were really Treasury bonds (*billets des fermes générales* and *rescriptions sur les recettes générales*) [22] to the value of 200 millions ; he converted the *tontines* into annuities on single lives, and thus made for the State a profit of 150 millions ; he reduced by one-half the arrears payable to holders of *rentes* on the posts, the leathers, the lottery, and tax-farms, by which means he wrote off 11 millions of debt ; he postponed the repayment of capital where loans had expired ; finally, he suspended debt redemption and made an immediate profit of 17 millions. In all he reduced the annual cost of the debt by 39 millions.

Many argued at the time that it was folly to dismiss this extortioner who caused the financiers and *rentiers* to disgorge their ample profits, and no one can deny that he gave the moneyed classes an uncommonly bad deal,[23] but the effect of his administration was to retard the return of prosperity and to impair the credit of the State. For, having defaulted at the expense of the creditors, he had attempted to increase receipts to the chagrin of the taxpayer. He had levied an additional two *sols* per *livre* upon a number of taxes, and even upon numerous tolls, not all of which were actually the property of the State, but of towns and corporations. He had also borrowed lavishly by creating further life annuities and perpetual annuities. No effort had been made to economize : instead he had squandered money freely among the entourage of Mme Du Barry in order to maintain himself in office. For over four years he had supplied the needs of the Court, and had convinced the King that he was an able Minister. He was not a man of words, and therefore rarely gave himself away. He was able to deceive by his silences and by his confident and cynical ejaculations. Tall and stooping, haggard and shifty, uncouth and ungracious, sinister in every movement, he gave the impression of strength and ability. Yet really he knew very little about finance, and he never set himself the task of learning his business.[24] The claim put forward by his partisans after his disgrace, that he had left the finances in a more favourable position than he found them [25] was utterly fantastic, and conflicted with the statements he himself drew up in 1772 and 1773—and even these failed to reveal the whole damage he had done to the nation's credit. 'Turgot found things very different from what his predecessor represented them,' commented Stormont ; 'Abbé Terray's tableau was by no means exact.' [26]

Having first commanded all people with paper signed by his predecessor to state its value without delay, Turgot composed an

account of the financial situation, and this revealed, among other
irregularities, the heavy liabilities to be met after August upon
which Terray had been silent. According to Turgot's reckoning,
the annual deficit was 37,000,000 *livres*, and the total debt
235,000,000 *livres*. A little later he composed another statement,
which was not so much a record of the finances as he found them
as his budget for 1775. In this he reduced the estimated revenue
by 7,000,000 *livres*, it being his intention to diminish the *sous pour
livre* levied on the *octrois* of the towns, the duties on consumable
commodities in Paris, the *revenus casuels*,[27] and the impositions
levied upon Provence and Béarn. Again, for some reason which
has never been explained, he omitted an item of 3,000,000 *livres*
which was the annual *don gratuit* of the clergy of France.[28] In
that same budget he announced a number of economies—nearly
1,000,000 on the Civil Household, 1,000,000 on the *ponts et
chaussées*, just over 1,000,000 all told on the Artillery, the Police,
the Foreign Office, and the Navy, and more than 12,000,000 on
the *dépenses générales* which included stipends of councillors and
magistrates, pensions for princes, costs of poor relief, and a
multiplicity of lesser expenses. In all he proposed economies
amounting to over 23,000,000 *livres*, in spite of his intention to
pay immediately numerous smaller pensions which were in arrears.
Finally, he planned to save upon costs of collection of revenue.
All told he aimed at a real saving of over 34,000,000 *livres*.[29]

To carry out his programme he must have complete control of
public spending. Therefore he obtained from Louis the ruling
that *ordonnances de comptant*, or writs permitting expenditure of
public money, should never be issued without his knowledge,
and he also attempted to control the spending of all the chief
departments of government. But Du Muy refused to accept his
whole programme of economy,[30] and, though indeed he met with
greater success in controlling Sartine's expenditure at the Marine,[31]
when all is told he made no spectacular achievements in this
direction. He was compelled, therefore, to fall back for the time
being upon paltry savings here and there. He reduced his own
stipend and refused to accept expenses for his installation;[32]
he suppressed the treasurers of the *caisse d'amortissement*[33] and
the *parties casuelles*;[34] and he saved a little by using the old
inscription for the new coinage. Again, by establishing freedom
of trade in money, he deprived the court banker of his lucrative
commission upon Government transactions.[35] These were his
economies in 1774. Next year he abolished the lucrative office
of General Receiver of the *vingtième* in Paris, which Terray had
created for his nephew, Lenormand. With the money saved he
organized a less costly administration, to which later he entrusted
also the collection of the *capitation* from the Court, Council, and

Royal Households, having first of all abolished the special commission which formerly fulfilled this task in a corrupt and wasteful fashion. His new officials, much to the anger of the courtiers, increased the annual yield of revenue from this source and secured for the Treasury considerable arrears of tax.[36] There were two other important measures of a similar kind. First, he suppressed a multiplicity of office-holders who, in carrying out distraints, robbed the creditors of their rightful damages, and, where the recovery of taxation was concerned, the State of its revenue.[37] Secondly, he abolished the alternative receivers of the *taille*, leaving only one for each fiscal area. This measure caused an outcry: twenty thousand men, it was complained, had been deprived of employment.[38]

Relatively trivial though they were, Turgot's economies must sooner or later bring him into conflict with the courtiers. But he never recklessly attempted to reform abuses in this quarter, and on more than one occasion he realized it was policy to give way. He did not press, for instance, his plan to abolish the office of *premier écuyer* which Louis weakly gave to the Duc de Coigny.[39] He did, of course, attempt to prevent Maurepas from meeting the Queen's demand that the office of *surintendante de la maison de la reine*, carrying a salary of 150,000 *livres*, should be revived for her favourite, Mme Lamballe.[40] On the other hand, he was the first to appreciate the Queen's personal poverty when his attention was drawn to the fact by Mercy-Argenteau, and obtained for her substantial increases for the upkeep of her household. Some time later, when Marie-Antoinette, probably at the instigation of Mme Lamballe, agreed to give a dowry of 50,000 *livres* to Mlle de Guébriant, it was Turgot who enabled her to keep a promise which otherwise she must have broken. He was willing to assist the Queen, providing that it could be done without establishing a precedent. Mercy found a way out of the difficulty. He proposed, and Turgot agreed, that the increase in the Queen's privy purse should be made retrospective as from July 1774.[41] It cannot, of course, be denied that the Queen found Turgot's economies irksome at times, especially as she was inclined to excessive generosity. Yet there was never an irreconcilable conflict between her and Turgot, and on one occasion, in June 1775, she collaborated with him to postpone indefinitely a costly fête at Marly.[42] It is indeed remarkable that she displayed so little antagonism towards him, seeing that it became the policy of the enemies of the Ministry to provoke it.

(3)

While engaged in effecting these economies, Turgot was also attempting to save on the collection of indirect taxation. As we have seen, the task of levying impositions of this kind was entrusted, not to State officials working for a salary, but to tax-farmers working for profit. Foremost among these financiers were the Farmers-General. Their profession had become respectable; they married their children into the great aristocratic families of the sword and the robe, and they lived in fashionable quarters: the rue Grenelle, the rue du Bouloi, and the rue Saint-Honoré. Granted the fiscal habits of the age, theirs was not an unduly sinister occupation. Most of them, in fact, enjoyed reputations for honesty, benevolence, enlightenment, and culture. Fleury had described them as the 'pillars of the State', and Marshal Souré's retort that they held up the State as a rope holds its victim might perhaps apply to them as a body, but certainly not as individuals. Helvétius, for instance, was a *fermier général*; he had an impeccable character and, it is said, he recompensed those who suffered from the malpractices of his subordinates. The majority were in every way able administrators and had better ways of doing business than most Comptrollers-General. And if sometimes they were still the objects of ridicule, then it was because it was a literary tradition to make of them low comedy long after those with taste had ceased to laugh.[43] Indeed, attacks upon them during the second half of the eighteenth century came mainly from the *économistes* who condemned them not as upstarts, but as the figure-heads of a financial system they hoped to reform.[44]

The *ferme générale* formed a state within the State. It was a company of sixty contractors-in-chief who every six years made an agreement (*bail*) with the Comptroller-General to farm the *gabelles, aides, tabac, octrois de Paris, huiles, savons, marque des fers,* and certain *droits domaniaux*.[45] The contract was named after the financier who signed the agreement for the company. Thus in 1762 we have the *bail Prévôt*, in 1768 the *bail Alaterre*, and in 1774 the *bail David*, which had been arranged by Terray on 1 January to take effect in the following October. According to Terray's partisans the *bail David* had been concluded on terms more favourable to the national finances than its predecessor. It was claimed that whereas they had paid only 132,000,000 *livres* for the *bail Alaterre* in 1768, the Farmers-General had been compelled to advance 152,000,000 *livres* in 1774.[46] But the truth was, as a financier admitted to Stormont, that Terray had been squeezing the taxpayer by means of the tax-farmer.[47] What he had done was to give the financiers the right to levy three additional impositions which Lavoisier, himself a Farmer-General, reckoned at over 25,000,000 *livres*.[48] He had thus given away much more than he received. On the other hand, he had based the contract with the Farm upon an estimated yield of taxation favourable to the State; he had imposed upon the financiers a scale of profit-sharing with the Treasury which was also advantageous; and finally he had obliged the financiers to submit to numerous *croupes* and pensions by which persons of all degrees, who had no actual part in the administration of taxation, shared the profits of the Farm.[49] Nearly 2,000,000, or one-third of those profits, disappeared in *croupes* and pensions. In a list of pensioners and *croupiers* the ' family of the Abbé Terray ' and also the names of his protégés are frequently mentioned. In all, the family received 28,000 *livres* in pensions and two quarter-shares or *croupes*, his natural child, Mme d'Amerval, and his niece, Mme Thoynet, each receiving pensions of 3,000 *livres*. The royal family also enjoyed similar privileges. Marie-Antoinette, Madame, Mme Adelaïde, Mme Sophie, and Mme de Provence all received pensions valued at 6,000 *livres* each, while the protégés of Mme Louise profited to the extent of 15,000 *livres*, and those of Mme Victoire to the amount of 6,000 *livres*. Louis XV himself had two *croupes* of one-quarter and one of one-half, and his mistresses, Mme de Pompadour, Mme Du Barry, and Mlle de Romans, received further sums for their families and favourites. Among other names mentioned in the list we read those of nobles and magistrates, and also those of officials like Destouches, Dupuy, Bertin, and Sénac de Meilhan.[50]

These abuses in the tax-farm Turgot had mentioned to the King upon taking office, and he again called Louis's attention to them in a *mémoire* which he submitted on 11 September. Yet he proposed no radical reform. ' The considerable sums arising from this contract, forming as they do the greater part of the revenue of the State, and also the immensity of the funds which it would be necessary to return if the contract were broken, are two weighty considerations which must convince the Government of the necessity of maintaining this agreement and of also removing disorders, so that justice may be rendered to the financiers. . . . It would be an attack upon property and a danger to the nation's credit . . . if other Farmers-General and other partners . . . were appointed.' Even existing *croupes* he was prepared to tolerate, including not only those which were a matter of free contract, but also those which, against the wishes of the Farmers, had been imposed by bribery and intrigue. ' This last kind of *croupe* ', he wrote, ' excites universal hostility, and if the King could afford the ten millions necessary to refund the money advanced by the *croupiers*, it would be quite a simple matter to abolish them and to obtain the profits for the Royal Treasury.' But this sum was not to be found, and therefore the *croupes* must remain. And so also must the pensions; for it was highly impolitic to make a thorough investigation ' of the manoeuvres made to obtain them and of the circumstances of those receiving them '. Turgot was not prepared to make enemies by raking up the past. ' But ', he went on, ' if it is perhaps dangerous to remove summarily these abuses, it is most essential at least to prevent them from multiplying. The King, no doubt, will judge it necessary to take steps immediately to ensure equity, efficiency, and decency in the future. In order that this may be so, the Comptroller-General begs His Majesty to give him a ruling on the plan which he takes the liberty to propose.'

Three of Turgot's suggestions had as their object the prevention of unsuitable persons from obtaining employment in the *ferme générale*. No financier was to become a Farmer-General unless his ability and character were of high order. No son of a Farmer-General was to share the office with his father until the age of twenty-five, and then only if he had proved himself competent in other employments ; and no subordinate was to be appointed without first being examined by a committee composed of Farmers-General. Turgot's remaining proposals dealt with *croupes*. In future no covert-partnerships were to be allowed. The existing *croupes* falling vacant while the *bail David* remained in force were to be distributed among the Farmers and their acting partners. Again, all *croupiers* who failed to produce their capital on 1 October —the day when such payments were due—were to be deprived of shares proportionate to their default. Turgot's final suggestion was that the King himself should set a good example and forego the *croupes* he had inherited from his grandfather. This Louis did, and on 13 September sanctioned also the other proposals.[51]

Yet another abuse which Turgot reformed was that of the *pot de vin*, originally an outright gift of 300,000 *livres* made to the Comptroller-General by the Farmers when the *bail* was concluded, but later an annual gratuity of 50,000 *livres*. One version is that Terray had acquired 450,000 *livres* in all, having appropriated in addition to the yearly present to which he was entitled a sum of 300,000 *livres* in respect of the *bail David*. Not only did Turgot forego his annual perquisite, but he obtained the support of the King in compelling the Abbé Terray to disgorge the money he had pocketed. Such, indeed, is the story told by Mlle de Lespinasse, by Métra and repeated by Du Pont.[52] But Véri maintains that Terray had failed to gain possession of the 300,000 *livres* from the *bail David*, and that he was trying to seize this money as his rightful prize from Turgot, who had obtained it from the financiers. All are agreed, however, that Turgot prevented the Abbé Terray from appropriating the money and that he devoted it to the relief of the poor in Paris. The sum in question was distributed among the *curés* with the instructions to provide wool and cotton yarn for those without employment, and to devote the profits derived from the sale of products to the relief of the indigent.[53]

Other reforms of the tax-farm for which Turgot was responsible were aimed at abuses perpetrated not by the Government and the Court, but by the Farmers themselves. For instance, he set himself the task of ending a practice known as *extension* or, in other words, the interpretation of a variety of obscure fiscal laws in favour of the Farmers. The financiers, it appears, often took proceedings against fictitious persons, or against individuals whom they knew would not be defended, the verdict being embodied in a writ which was given a general application. ' The law of the tax-farm ', so run the Remonstrances that Malesherbes drew up for the *Cour des aides* in May 1775, ' is vast and remains uncodified. It is an occult science which no person, the financiers excepted, has studied or can study. It happens that an individual against whom action is taken neither knows himself the law under which he has been assessed, nor can he consult whom he wishes. . . . What is more, the laws of the Farm are not only obscure, but sometimes arbitrary. . . . Is there no check that can be given to the despotism of the financiers ? . . . There is one, Sire ; you can order the Farmers henceforward to publish exact rules of assessment, to state their authority for the levy of all impositions, and to compose a clear and methodical statement of regulations which concern the public.' [54] But to have carried out these suggestions would have meant a radical reform of indirect taxation, and Turgot was not prepared to begin such a task during his first few months of office. Instead he merely adopted the principle that in disputes between the collectors and the taxpayers, the latter were to be presumed free from imposition unless the financiers could furnish absolute proof to the contrary. Fourqueux and Trudaine were detailed to watch all litigation between the taxpayers and the Farmers, and they were to see that all cases were heard before the intendants, the lieutenant of the police of Paris or, where appeals were concerned, before the Council itself. Unfortunately Trudaine fell ill and had to travel for a change of air, but Fourqueux devoted considerable attention to the matter, and Turgot himself found time to give him some assistance. Against this practice the financiers protested, foretold the increase of fraud, and followed a policy of obstruction. But actually there was no increase of fraud ; commerce improved ; consumption increased, and also the profits of the Farm.[55]

Meanwhile Turgot was engaged in mitigating yet another abuse in the administration of the tax-farm. As we have seen, the Farmers-General collected the *gabelles* which, along with the *aides*, constituted the greater part of indirect taxation. The *gabelles* were a particularly irksome tax, since they were levied under the form of a monopoly. The Farmers and their officials had the exclusive right to purchase salt from the producers; they themselves paid the duty upon it, and then made good their advances, and also a substantial profit when they sold this commodity to the consumers. The regulations concerning the *gabelle* varied throughout the country; in some provinces and districts the consumers had to buy a fixed amount, the quota being divided among the parishes, and finally among the households in proportion to their size; some regions were free; some were privileged; while others, having compounded, paid instead of the *gabelle* an increase on the *taille*. These last were known as the *provinces rédimées*,[56] and it is here that the abuse had arisen, the Abbé Terray having attempted to deprive a province of its immunity so dearly bought. By an *arrêt du conseil* of 3 October 1773, which had been demanded by the Farmers, he gave to the tax-farm the monopoly of supplying salt to the depots of Riom and Aubusson, to the detriment of the rights of Auvergne, which was a *province rédimée*. The intendants and the towns had protested to the Council, but had been ignored; the *Cour des aides* had forbidden the execution of the measure, but its *arrêt* had been quashed by the Council of Finance in July 1774. Against the Abbé Terray's measure Beaumont, Trudaine, and Maupeou had made feeble protests, but had ultimately let the matter pass.[57] When Turgot became Comptroller-General, the towns and intendants renewed their petitions and the Farmers-General submitted memoirs in defence, claiming that they could provide a better grade of salt at cheaper rates than those engaged locally in the trade. Turgot's sympathies were obviously with the provincials.[58] On 14 October he rescinded the *arrêt* of 3 October, the financiers being recompensed for their expenditure upon the hire of depots and upon purchases of salt.[59]

Another of the Abbé Terray's fiscal expedients Turgot rescinded before it was fully executed. It concerned the administration of the royal domain.[60] Formerly, when the King wished to resume possession of lands which might be proved to belong to the Crown, it being assumed under feudal law that the King could not alienate them, the Farmers-General used to take possession and levy the appropriate dues which the Crown claimed in respect of its *domaine direct*. But in the *bail David*, Terray had deprived the Farmers-General of these functions, and in their place he proposed to establish in each *généralité* a *sous-ferme* with a contract for three years to take effect from 1 January 1775. These new tax-farmers, all of whom were nominees of Terray and Cochin, the intendant of finance, were to pay in advance on 1 October 1774 an annual sum of 1,564,000 *livres*. Actually the *sous-ferme* had already been established in the *généralités* of Caen, Rouen, and

Alençon, and also in Brittany. Terray proposed to extend this measure to the whole of France, hoping thereby to make a slight profit for the Treasury. What in effect he was about to do was to let loose again upon the provinces a crowd of officials who, in order to recoup themselves for the annual sum which they advanced and to reward themselves for their exertions, would strain the law to the very utmost. For he had granted to these agents, in addition to the right to levy the sum of 1,116,164 *livres* which normally accrued from royal lands leased to tenants, the power to appropriate profits from dues on other properties which they might claim in the name of the King, from wastes which they might bring under cultivation, and from more favourable leases which they might make as the usual six- and nine-year leases expired. No wonder that Baudeau roundly denounced the proposed administration. 'There are some men who are hiding in this business of the King's domains. It is all an intrigue upon the part of little Cochin to find profitable positions for his own and the Abbé Terray's nominees and to give *croupes* to clerks and wenches.' [61] Already an outcry had been raised in the provinces. The *engagistes*, or those farming royal lands, feared the extortions of the agents; many were being menaced with ruinous litigation in their efforts to prove their ownership of land; while the parishes feared the loss of their prescriptive rights on the lands *vaines et vagues* which the financiers might appropriate and lease to a tenant. 'The Abbé Terray and the Intendant Cochin', writes Véri, '. . . renewed an active research into alienated domains. Obscure agents overran the provinces; everywhere where they found traces of rights of domains, they caused them to be declared by making offers (of feudal rents) slightly above those paid by those in possession. . . . They gained the lease of lands reputed to be uncultivated and, by inquiring into the ancient rights of the royal domain, alarmed the small proprietors who had obtained by bequest a few acres which they had cultivated. A general outcry had led to the suspension of activities in Dauphiné, but elsewhere the possessors of lands reputed to belong to the royal domain were dispossessed, especially on the alluvia and land reclaimed bordering the rivers and the sea. . . . There was one family in Normandy (which was dispossessed) that could prove ownership by deeds for four centuries.' [62]

To reform this particular abuse to the best advantage was a matter requiring thought. Turgot might, of course, have given back the collection of these revenues to the Farmers-General, but, upon consideration, he found that their organization, to judge from past records, was hardly suitable. He had also contemplated entrusting this work to the receivers of domains and woods; indeed, these officials were actually approached; but it was found that the majority were not wealthy enough to make the advances required. What is more, their administration was not sufficiently unified : each official ran his department upon lines best suited to himself; and, though a few of them were undoubtedly competent, the majority were hardly capable of assuming fresh responsibilities. Hence there was only one course left to follow—to create a special administration. This was the decision embodied in an *arrêt du conseil* of 25 September, which also gave due compensation to the financiers who had already made advances. The new administration, composed of twenty-four persons, some of whom were chosen from among the directors of domains, was established for a period of nine years, the members being called upon to provide a sum of 6,000,000 *livres* which was to be repayable at the rate of 1,000,000 during the last six years of the lease—an arrangement, it will be noticed, quite unlike that of the tax-farms, under which the financiers paid a sum to the Treasury and collected sufficient income to cover this advance and to make a handsome profit. Under the new administration (a *régie* as opposed to a *ferme*) the members were awarded $5\frac{1}{4}$ per cent. commission upon revenue collected and $5\frac{1}{2}$ per cent. interest on the money they advanced. It was estimated that they would collect for the Treasury an annual sum ranging between 4,100,000 and 4,340,000 *livres*, and that the cost of collection would consequently amount only to 16 *deniers* the *livre*. In this way Turgot secured for the national income a sum well over twice that which Terray had hoped to obtain ; future resources were not imperilled, and the Treasury would gain as the value of leases rose ; more important still, the agents of the new administration had no incentive towards sharp practice by reviving claims where tenants had enjoyed a prescriptive ownership for many generations.[63]

With a view to improving the national revenues, Turgot created two other *régies*. The first, which was organized in November 1774, replaced the *régie Rouselle*, established by the Abbé Terray for the collection in the provinces of duties on mortgages (*hypothèques*), registration (*greffes*), and upon the sale of immovables.[64] Terray had required the *régisseurs* to advance 8,000,000 *livres* in instalments, the last of which was to fall due in July 1781. The interest upon advances was fixed at 6 per cent. But the *régisseurs* were also to receive 6 per cent. upon their first instalment and a further sum of 480,000 *livres*. This was a bad bargain for the Treasury. In the new *régie* that Turgot established the advance required was 4,000,000 *livres* greater ; the number of revenues to be collected were increased; and the interest allowed to the *régisseurs* was to diminish as the Government returned the capital.[65]

The other *régie* that he organized was for the supply of saltpetre and gunpowder to the State. Formerly these supplies had been obtained from a company which enjoyed a monopoly, its contract having been renewed in 1772 for a period of six years. One of the provisions of the agreement was that the Government should receive its powder at a price considerably less than the price to the public—at a figure less, in fact, than the costs of production. In time of peace this arrangement was not a heavy burden upon the company; and even in time of war the contractors were not really hard pressed, for they increased only slightly their production, the Government being compelled to obtain supplies elsewhere. Abuses, however, did not end here: the company was under the obligation to obtain saltpetre from the *salpêtriers du Roi*, who had a monopoly in Paris, and, in time of war, additional supplies from the provincial saltpetre-makers. These purchases were originally fixed at 7 *sols* per *livre*. Later, prices having risen since these arrangements were made, the company demanded an indemnity of 2 *sols* per *livre*, but, having received this concession from the Government, failed to pass on the 2 *sols* to the saltpetre-makers. In turn the saltpetre-makers oppressed the public. Moving from place to place in order to obtain rubbish from demolished buildings (for their trade was extraordinarily primitive), they exercised the right to be billeted where they were working, and to draw from the communities free supplies of wood. They enjoyed hospitality for protracted periods, and as in turn each village compounded in order to get rid of these unbidden guests, they moved to another district, where they again lived on the public. Furthermore, they possessed the right to supply at lucrative rates quantities of salt to the Farmers-General. At the time it was calculated that each pound of saltpetre supplied to the gunpowder company at about 7 *sols* cost the public more than 12 *sols*. And even the conditions of these unfavourable contracts were never kept, for the commissioner of powders, usually one of the company, connived at irregularities. The result was that the company and its underlings enjoyed enormous dividends, and the Treasury reaped no benefit from the monopoly it had granted.

Towards the end of 1774 the Abbé Satti de Bruges approached the French Government with an offer to form a new company and to employ the new processes for making powder in use in Prussia and Sweden. Turgot discussed the matter with Montigny of the Academy of Science.[66] About six months later—actually in May 1775—he revoked the contract of the old company, promising to pay back its capital in four years and to grant an indemnity of 800,000 *livres*. There arose an outcry against this operation. But Turgot carried on and established a *régie* to replace the old company. The members of the new administration were to advance 4,000,000 *livres* for the repayment of the old, and were to receive only 10 per cent. upon their money, it being stipulated that accounts were to be inspected every month. At the same time he abolished the *corvées* for providing transport of materials and plant for making saltpetre, and also the obligation of the public to provide free wood and billets for the saltpetre-makers, who were recompensed by an increase of price in their commodity. Furthermore, he prohibited as from 1 January 1778 their entry into all buildings without the permission of the owners. Finally, he approached the Academy of Science, asking its members to carry out researches into the making of saltpetre, to offer a prize of 4,000 *livres*, and to provide a course of instruction upon new processes.[67] Lavoisier was placed in charge of the new administration, and he has left a record of its achievements. French gunpowder, he wrote in 1789, 'has become the best in Europe. . . . One can say with truth that to it North America owes its liberty.' From 1 July 1775, when the system came into operation, to 31 December 1778 the value of productions was 14,000,000 *livres*, of which 5,000,000 were sent to the Royal Treasury; powder to the value of nearly 1,300,000 *livres* went to the magazines of the Navy and Army at 6 *sols* the *livre*; 1,200,000 *livres* were spent on capital improvements; and emergency stores were provided. The new system was a saving of 2,400,000 *livres* annually.[68]

(4)

The influence of the financier upon politics is always assumed, and yet unfortunately never fully revealed by contemporaries. Nevertheless all accounts speak of the opposition of the financiers to Turgot in terms which, though vague and general, suggest that they were a body to be feared. But it was not until the early part of 1776 that they adopted a definite plan of withholding the advance of capital upon which to a large extent the Government depended. The reforms that Turgot had introduced were not so revolutionary as to call forth such a policy of retaliation: indeed, he gave the moneyed classes a fairer deal than they often received from other Comptrollers-General.[69] But what was always feared was that as the credit of the State improved, Turgot might be tempted to carry out more radical reforms. In February 1775 the rumour, which had first circulated upon his appointment to the Finances, again went round that he would suppress the Farmers-General.[70] The rumour was not without foundation. Turgot was certainly contemplating a radical reform, and was probably engaged in collecting the necessary information and planning the detail. But we have no record of his projects. According to Véri, the matter was still ' secret ' in November

1775, by which he means that no definite announcement had been made.[71] Véri was alarmed, and so were Maurepas, Malesherbes, and Trudaine, for to abolish the *ferme général* necessitated a sum of 93,000,000 *livres* to pay back the annual advance made by the financiers to the Treasury. Véri endeavoured to persuade Turgot to renounce the plan. He called attention to the possibility of a European war in which France might find herself involved; he foretold a loss of revenue of 15,000,000 to 20,000,000 *livres*, explaining that salaried officials were less exacting than the Farmers and their agents, who, in working to make a profit for themselves, increased the national income; and he gave the warning that the financiers would render reform impossible by holding back their capital and that, allying with the vested interests at the Court, they would raise such an outcry that Maurepas and the King would take alarm. Turgot refused to listen.[72] In December he was still intent upon his reform. And when Véri argued that if he carried out his projects he would be breaking a fundamental contract, his reply was that it was enough for him that the tax-farm was a crushing burden to the people, and he went on to say that he feared no loss of revenue other than that which could be met by further economies.[73] Yet nothing came of Turgot's plans because, no doubt, Maurepas and the other Ministers were strongly opposed, and because Louis was not to be convinced of their utility. For already other rumours, which the financiers did their best to circulate, were discrediting Turgot, and many people, even those who might have been disposed to look favourably upon his stewardship of the finances, began to question his abilities.[74] The financiers had begun already their attack upon the Minister they feared. Their first campaigns were simple indeed. All they did, and all they had need to do, was to convince that narrow public at the Court that Turgot was a charlatan, a 'man of system', and a danger to the nation.[75] But in the spring of 1776, adopting bolder tactics, they attempted to discredit Turgot by undermining the credit of the State. They gave orders to their receivers to retard the payments to the Treasury and, keeping the monthly returns at a very low figure indeed, they gave it out that this fall in revenue was the result of Turgot's failure to give them adequate support. The outcome was that the smaller capitalists began to withdraw their funds; money grew scarce; and the larger capitalists began to reap a higher rate of interest.[76]

Just before Turgot fell from power he was talking of taking steps to suppress the *gabelles* and other forms of indirect taxation. But he never hoped to give his ideas immediate application; he intimated that this reform should be executed by the Provincial Assemblies, and we know for certain that it was not his intention

to prevail upon Louis hastily to establish these bodies.[77]   Moreover, the plan involved an increase of direct taxation, and he had
obviously no desire to add to the burden of these impositions while
they remained for the most part unreformed.   And that task—the
reform of the *taille*, the *capitation*, and the *vingtième*—he had hardly
yet begun.

(5)

Turgot had learned from the experience of his predecessors,
Machault, Bertin, and d'Invau, that any attempt to subject the
privileged classes to a greater share of direct taxation must
certainly arouse their animosity, and he saw the necessity of
moving cautiously.   But again his opponents, in order to discredit
him, adopted a policy of attributing to him the intention of carrying out immediately the full extent of his ideas.[78]   It was said
that he would straightway apply physiocratic doctrine and replace
the *taille* and *vingtième* by a *subvention territoriale* levied upon the
proprietors of real estate.   It would, of course, be futile to deny
that he contemplated reforms of direct taxation.   In the Letters
Patent of 1 January 1775 which approved certain financial reforms
in the *généralité* of Paris, he caused the following words to be
inserted : ' We hope soon to be able to explain ourselves more
definitely concerning assessments for impositions—a matter
worthy of all our attention, and one of essential interest for the
welfare and tranquillity of our people.'[79]   But the words do not
necessarily promise drastic changes.   At the most he contemplated
the abolition of the two *vingtièmes* and the additional 4 *sols* per
livre, and the substitution of a *subvention territoriale* levied upon
all landowners irrespective of their class.   Of the actual details
of the scheme no record has survived ; but Du Pont assures us
that Turgot had spent much time in making the necessary calculations for determining the rate at which the new tax must be
levied if the Treasury were to reap from it a sum equal to that
derived formerly from the *vingtièmes*.   Needless to say these
preliminary investigations must have been an exacting work, for
it was necessary to arrive at a knowledge of the value of those
properties which should, but actually did not, pay their rightful
tax.   By the time that Turgot fell from power he had, it seems,
acquired sufficient information, and he had drafted his plan in
sufficient detail for consideration by the Ministers of the King.[80]
But, pending this work that he had undertaken, he took steps by
means of instructions to intendants to mitigate the burden of the
vingtième.   On 18 October 1775, for example, he wrote to the
intendant of Bordeaux outlining the policy to be followed in the
making of assessments for the ensuing year.   ' The rolls ', he
explained, ' must not contain any alteration of assessment which

is not the outcome of a survey carried out with exactitude. . . . Every arbitrary increase is reprehensible in the eyes of His Majesty, and he disapproves of those who make it a practice of increasing the revenue from the *vingtième*. . . . It is necessary to take appropriate measures so that, in the coming year, the assessment for the *vingtième* shall be divided among parishes and among the taxpayers in such a manner that, in the parishes which will have been verified, the proprietors can regard their impositions as stable and safe from all augmentation. . . . Do, I implore you, on your part, all that you can to let the inhabitants of your *généralité* know the true intentions of the King. . . .' [81]

The more iniquitous tax, the *taille*, also called for Turgot's attention. On 3 January 1775 he submitted to the King a long *mémoire* in which he described the abuses in taxation, singling out the *contrainte solidaire* for special condemnation and advocating its immediate abolition. ' Sire,' he wrote, ' I believe it to be my duty to propose to Your Majesty the abrogation of a law which to me has always appeared cruel and, if I may say so, unjust to the inhabitants of the countryside, the rigorous execution of which I have seen on more than one occasion prove the ruin of the husbandmen. I speak of the law that authorizes the receivers of the *taille* to choose a number of inhabitants among the highest taxed in a community in order to compel them to make good, on threat of imprisonment, the amount that the parish, owing to its failure to appoint a collector or to the insolvency of the collector appointed, has failed to pay. . . . I ought to tell you that, during the course of my administration in one of your provinces, I was on many occasions a witness to the ruin of honest citizens resulting from the *contrainte solidaire.*' Happily the remedy for this abuse was very simple : it was merely a question of demanding straightway from the parish that money which sooner or later fell upon it ; for the principal inhabitants, who made good the default, had the right to demand that the intendant should levy the sums concerned upon the whole of the parish during the next financial year. ' Why, then,' asked Turgot, ' not suppress this odious intermediary distraint against a few of the inhabitants when (ultimately) all the parishioners are conjointly responsible ? Why not attack directly all the parish ? The receivers of taxation will perhaps say that, as they are obliged to advance to the King the total sum of the *taille*, it would be unjust to cause them to wait one or two years for the collection of the " re-imposition ". In justice one must recognize these advances made by the receivers ; but it is merely a matter of levying upon the " re-imposition " their legitimate expenses and the amount of interest accruing to them up to the moment when the debt is collected and reimbursed to them.' Such clemency, however, Turgot did not propose to extend to rebellious parishes which defiantly refused to contribute to the *taille* or to appoint collectors. But, when parochial machinery had temporarily broken down, or where the collectors had been negligent or insolvent, he was anxious to mitigate the severity of the law, for, as he says in his preamble, ' these rigorous measures, which render the principal inhabitants likely to lose their fortunes and their liberty, cause great fear in the country-side, discourage agriculture—the object the most worthy of our protection and our cares—and involve the receivers of the *taille* in considerable expenses . . . which it is their duty and interest to avoid as much as possible.' [82] To these proposals Louis gave approval, and he signed immediately the royal declaration that Turgot had submitted with the *mémoire*.

Turgot's provincial experience of the feebleness of parochial government had also impressed upon him the necessity of intro-ducing officials for making assessments for taxation. But he realized that it would have been a waste of effort to organize, as he himself had done at Limoges, a body of commissioners for those *généralités* where the *taille tarifée* had not been established. Nor, in his opinion, was it worth a struggle with the courts to replace the *taille arbitraire* by the *taille tarifée*. It were better to wait until such time as he could effect the more radical reform of replacing the *taille* by a *subvention territoriale*. Yet he was ready to give every encouragement to intendants who were prepared to act upon their own. While he himself was at Limoges, Berthier de Sauvigny, the intendant of Paris, had begun a most important reform of the *taille* in the large *généralité* of Paris. Like Turgot, he had established a body of commissioners with the intention of composing a land register. Berthier's work, which was making great progress, had not received official sanction. Turgot, who knew the difficulties of serving an apathetic Government, was anxious to give the intendant due recognition of an achievement which was as great as his own. Accordingly, on 1 January 1775 he issued letters patent giving authority to Berthier's instructions to his commissioners and granting a retrospective sanction for the years 1772, 1773, and 1774.[83]

Such were Turgot's reforms of direct taxation. Far more imposing—though again, when all is said, they were relatively trivial—were the adjustments he made in indirect taxation. While at Limoges he had endeavoured to persuade the Abbé Terray to reform the *octrois*,[84] or duties upon articles of consump-tion entering the towns. ' Nothing is more irregular than the *octrois*,' he complained. ' Some of them are levied under claims which not only lack legal forms . . . but which also have the defect of being stated in vague and uncertain terms. . . . The result is a multiplicity of lawsuits which are vexatious to individuals and also to the corporations.' An even graver defect was that nearly everywhere the foodstuffs that the poor consumed had been singled out for taxation. 'If, for example,' he continues, ' a levy has been made upon wine, care has been taken to place it upon that consumed in the inns and to exempt that which the *bourgeoisie* acquire for home consumption; similarly, the food-stuffs that the *bourgeoisie* bring in from their domains in the country have also been exempted; so that those who profit most from the communal expenses of the towns are precisely those who contribute practically nothing.' Ideally, he concluded, the *octrois* ought to be abolished altogether, but, as opinion was not favourable to such a measure, the best course to follow was to place the administration of these taxes under the control of the intendants, who should be asked to draft schemes or reform appropriate to their *généralités*. He himself offered to set the example by beginning work at once.[85] But he was not allowed to do so; for the Abbé Terray displayed no enthusiasm for such an undertaking.

Shortly after Turgot became Comptroller-General he dis-patched to the intendants a long circular, portions of which repeated word for word his letter to the Abbé Terray. His object was to obtain detailed reports upon all the *octrois* levied in every single town, distinguishing those which fell to the Treasury, those which were levied in place of the municipal *dons gratuits*, those which benefited charitable institutions, and those which were utilized to meet local expenses. All this information he required in order to draft the general principles of a reform applicable to the kingdom at large.[86] But he was asking too much of his harassed subordinates, and he failed to obtain the knowledge he wanted. He therefore confined his activities to the town of Paris. Here he reorganized the office for recording privileges of exemption from the *octrois*. He never attempted to abolish in entirety the immunities enjoyed by the wealthier citizens, but he did succeed in keeping the abuse within definite limits.[87] A little later he attacked the coach-riding classes, who had been accustomed to drive at a furious rate through the city gates to avoid payment of duties, the clerks being obliged to draw away for fear of being crushed. In an ordinance of 15 February 1775 he commanded that all postillions, coachmen, and drivers, even the equipages of the King, the Queen, the Princes of the Blood and of ecclesiastics, should stop at the barriers at the first request, and that all trunks, boxes, valises, and so forth should be examined. The penalties threatened for the disregard of this order were confiscation of merchandise, a fine of 500 *livres*, and imprisonment for offenders who persisted.[88]

Little by little Turgot lightened the burden of the *octrois*. In December 1774 he suppressed the tax levied on meat sold during Lent by the fraudulent overseers of the *Hôtel de Dieu*, which had the monopoly of supplying the sick and the feeble. A month later, hoping to provide cheaper food for the poor and to encourage the fishing industry, he freed from duty all salt fish entering Paris during Lent, and he diminished by one-half that which was levied upon fresh fish. So successful was this measure (for consumption of fresh fish had increased threefold) that in April he made it applicable to the whole of the year. Already he had exempted dried cod, a food within the reach of the poorer classes, from all duties throughout the kingdom; and, as its price remained relatively high during Lent 1775 on account of the increased demand, he contracted with a merchant to bring in larger supplies from November onwards in readiness for the following year.[89] It was about this same time, too, that he suppressed a number of vexatious charges which the Abbé Terray had arbitrarily reimposed upon the citizens of Paris. Here the town officials had compounded for various dues known as the *droits réservés*,[90] and in so doing they had been able to free fats, leathers, and rice-flour from these taxes. But the contract was due to expire at the end of 1774, and Terray had made arrangements for a tax-farmer named Bossuat, who along with his partners already collected the *droits réservés* in the provinces, to take over the administration of these duties in Paris. The arrangement came into force as a matter of routine on 1 January 1775. Later, an outcry arose. Turgot, who was ill at the time and fully occupied with other matters, was much grieved that such a thing should have happened when he was in power. Hence in March he prevailed upon the King to remove the *droits réservés* upon those commodities that the town had freed, due compensation being paid to Bossuat and his colleagues.[91] The Abbé Terray had also imposed additional taxation, 8 *sols* per *livre*, on merchandise circulating within the kingdom. This, too, Turgot rescinded because—so runs his preamble—'all these aforesaid dues fall for the most part upon His Majesty's poorest subjects'. [92]

Numerous other taxes were also abolished. In order to facilitate agreements between the owners of the tithes and the parochial clergy, he exempted their contracts from the *droit d'amortissement*. From that same tax he freed also religious buildings when sold or leased for secular purposes. Then, hoping to facilitate the commuting of *rentes foncières*, he suppressed the *centième denier* upon contracts between the proprietors of these dues and those who owed them. More important still, he exempted all leases of rural property from the *droits d'insinuation, centième denier,* and *franc-fief*, his object being to encourage the wealthier peasants to take long leases of land. A similar benefit he bestowed upon industry : all contracts relative to mastership he exempted from the *droits d'enregistrement*. And even the army classes received an important concession when military offices were freed from the *marc d'or* to which they had been subjected in 1770.[93]

Just before he fell, Turgot was planning further financial reforms—the simplification of the *droits de contrôle*, the reorganization of feudal dues, the abolition of the tax on playing-cards, and many adjustments in the *droits domaniaux*, not to mention other fiscal changes designed to give a greater freedom of trade.[94] These projected reforms, like those he had executed, involved no sweeping changes. Here and there a mitigation of abuses in taxation, occasional economies in collection, the conclusion of contracts with the financiers more favourable to the Treasury— these were his moderate achievements and the niggardly reward of piecemeal reform. But he was doing what he had promised : he was balancing the national budget.

(6)

Turgot had proposed to make a real saving of over 34,000,000 *livres*. He had also budgeted for a deficit of 37,000,000 *livres*, of which, 15,000,000 were destined for meeting arrears of debt payable on demand. Throughout the year 1775 he had been called upon to meet much exceptional expenditure—the costs of the Coronation, of the Princesse Clotilde's marriage, of a household for the newly-born Duc d'Angoulême, of the grain riots, and finally of the cattle plague. Nevertheless the annual deficit was not beyond his estimate. But his achievements did not end here : he had diminished the debt payable on demand by 14,600,000 *livres* ; he had reduced anticipations of revenue from 78,000,000 *livres* to just over 50,000,000 ; and he had made further reductions on the debt to the extent of nearly 24,000,000 *livres*. Out of these savings, which, all told, amounted to 66,200,000 *livres*, just over 50,000,000 *livres* represented a diminution of the cost of what were in reality forms of loans. The figure is impressive. Yet, strange as it may at first appear, it is an economy of the relatively trivial figure of 5,600,000 *livres* that really gave the greatest hopes of financial recovery. That particular figure indicates the reduction of interest upon loans pure and simple—from 8,700,000 *livres* (the average for the previous eleven years) to just over 3,000,000.[95] The efforts to pay off arrears of debt and to reduce anticipations were gradually restoring the Government's credit, and towards the end of 1775 money was to be had at 4 per cent. The Treasury could now begin to borrow freely in order to refund the expensive loans that had told so heavily upon the finances.[96] Therefore a more spectacular recovery could justly be expected for the year 1776. Turgot had kept strictly to his three points : there had been no bankruptcy of any kind ; there had been no increase of taxation ; and, if indeed money had been borrowed and further borrowing was being contemplated, such loans were in reality a debt conversion from 7 to 4 per cent. And it was not only the State, but also other bodies in the kingdom that reaped a benefit from the recovery in the national finances : the clergy, the provincial estates, and also many towns were able to adopt a policy of debt redemption.[97]

Turgot was already planning his financial policy for 1776. In the summer of 1775 he began negotiations for a loan of 60,000,000 *livres* from the Dutch bankers, his object being to reduce still further the national debt, both capital and interest, to finance further reforms, and to render the Treasury more independent of the French financiers. This loan could not possibly have been raised in Paris ; the financiers, fully aware of Turgot's motives, would have engineered a shortage of money. Such, at least, was Turgot's own opinion. Nor was it easy to raise the money abroad ; not until Malesherbes entered the Ministry did the Dutch display any confidence ; even then the chief banker, Grand of Amsterdam, demanded the additional security of the Spanish Court ; and it was not until 1776 that the negotiations were completed.[98]

Turgot was also counting upon another loan which he intended to raise directly from the French public, and not through the intermediary of the financiers. The investing classes, it seems, were withholding their money from the financial houses, and were only too glad to invest elsewhere, for as Véri tells us, ' to leave it in their coffers was not to sow their fields '.[99] In order to obtain this cheap money, Turgot established the *caisse d'escompte*, which was a kind of bank similar in some ways to the early Bank of England, though it was not given the right to issue notes. Like those who originated the Bank of England, Turgot was really floating a loan, and this he proposed to guarantee on the security of the profits from the Posts. There were to be 5,000 shares of 3,000 *livres* each. Out of the total sum subscribed, 10,000,000 *livres* were to be deposited in the Treasury, and were to be repaid in twenty-six half-yearly instalments at 4 per cent. The chief banker was Mory ; he was to be assisted by seven directors chosen by the shareholders, provision being made for a general assembly to determine policy. This company was given no monopoly of banking. On the other hand, it was given obligations—to discount bills and commercial paper, to keep deposit accounts without cost, and to abstain from ordinary forms of trade.[100] The project caused an outcry, especially among the clergy who adhered to the canonist doctrines of usury. But it was never carried into execution, Turgot having fallen before the date announced for its inauguration. By that time the Government's credit had decreased. Rumours of Turgot's dismissal had brought a fall of 3 per cent. in Government bills, and his disgrace a further 8 or 9 per cent.[101]

With these schemes in mind, Turgot had reckoned in his budget for 1776 upon an annual deficit of only 24,000,000 *livres*.[102] But this figure many people questioned, and some went so far as to challenge all his achievements, contending that the gains effected were really the outcome of Terray's operations, and citing, for instance, a trivial sum from the sale of grain after the corn company was liquidated. Maurepas was certainly bewildered by the conflicting opinions that came to his ears.[103] Therefore he submitted the budget for 1776 to two men of different opinions— to Necker and Baudeau, the one an avowed and ignorant opponent, the other a disappointed and light-hearted supporter. Both reported unfavourably. Necker, knowing nothing, or affecting to know nothing, of Turgot's intentions, and making no allowance for the Dutch loan, the *caisse d'escompte*, or for various economies which were being planned in the King's Household, estimated the deficit at 37,000,000 *livres*. Du Pont, allowing for all these, calculated that the budget would have been balanced by the end of 1777, even supposing that no considerable retrenchments in the Household materialized. And later Necker himself, in his famous *Compte-rendu* of 1781, virtually admitted that Turgot's estimate was right and his own in error : ' The last statement placed before Your Majesty by M. de Clugny (at the end of 1776) announced a deficit of 24,000,000 *livres*.' That is the very figure Turgot had forecast, Clugny during his short period of office having made only a few minor alterations. Necker continued : ' At a glance I saw that it would not be difficult to make good this deficit . . . and also I discovered . . . means to assure a balance . . . but I could not for long entertain such great hopes, for I soon learned that the political situation obliged Your Majesty to improve the Navy.' That political situation had arisen when the Ministry decided to aid the English colonies. Turgot had advised against intervention, his chief argument being that war would impair the finances.[104]

Neither the King nor Maurepas studied closely the details of fiscal policy. Dry figures did not appeal to a busy intriguer like Maurepas : financial statistics never excited the kind heart of Louis XVI ; and Turgot never bothered them with his dull arithmetic. The little knowledge Maurepas had of the finances was thrust upon him by Véri, who was for ever telling Turgot that he also ought to make Louis and Maurepas listen. But he preferred to regard himself as a trusted custodian of the Treasury, little thinking that enemies were attacking his management as well as his reforms, little realizing that busy tongues were telling Louis and Maurepas that he was not really restoring the finances, but that, being a man of theory, he was merely attempting to reform the social order. Once when Véri implored him to show his worth in facts and figures, he replied: 'I should be trying to flaunt my value and that is not my method.'[105] It was here that Terray, and later Necker, had the advantage of him.

CHAPTER XII

FREE TRADE IN GRAIN
AND THE GRAIN RIOTS OF MAY, 1775

(1)

SHORTLY after Turgot had written the seven letters on the grains, the Abbé Terray, having virtually rescinded free trade, renewed Chaumont's commission to purchase corn supplies for Paris. About the same time he organized a grain administration, which he placed under the charge of Sorin de Bonne and Doumerck, it being arranged that these two men should receive a commission of 2 per cent. upon all transactions and also interest upon their advances. Under their supervision were placed also the King's mills at Corbeil, and later other mills at Lamothe and Chiessat, both of which were Terray's own property. Against these measures Albert, the intendant of commerce, whose department supervised commerce in grain, vigorously protested; but he was dismissed from office, and in his place Terray installed the notorious Brochet de Saint-Prest. And, even when a governmental commission reported unfavourably upon this new administration, the Abbé Terray refused to mend his ways and defiantly continued his sinister operations.[1] Actually the purchases of grain made in the provinces were never considerable; but Sorin and Doumerck, working first in one locality and then in another, caused rapid fluctuations in prices, which invariably resulted in much speculation. An outcry arose, and the shortage of bread that was really the result of failing harvests was usually ascribed to the manoeuvres of Terray's agents.[2] Véri, who toured the provinces in 1773, found that every one was convinced that a monopoly existed and that enormous profits went to enrich the King, the Du Barry, and the Abbé Terray. Riots broke out in several places. But Terray, having persuaded the Ministers that these were engineered by his political enemies, ordered the intendants to seek out disaffected persons and to take criminal proceedings against them. He never succeeded, however, in imposing silence upon his detractors, and when, at the accession of Louis XVI, the mediocre harvest was becoming slowly exhausted, it was openly said, though there was no truth in the statement, that the corn company was meeting at Brochet's house. And Louis XVI, in spite of his gesture of distributing corn freely at the beginning of his reign, was now accused of stealing his people's sustenance; and Sartine, who as lieutenant of the police had been universally respected, suddenly became the subject of the vilest calumnies.[3]

Louis, thus taken by surprise, was most anxious indeed to remove the cause of popular suspicion. Marie-Antoinette, with whom he discussed the matter, was also, as Mercy has revealed, of a like opinion; and Maurepas, called upon to shield his charge from such base accusations, could not remain indifferent.[4] All three were disposed, therefore, to listen to Turgot's economic doctrines. On 13 September he submitted to the King an *arrêt du conseil*, which received immediately the royal sanction. But the measure gave rise to Ministerial wranglings; for the preamble had not only denounced previous governmental policy, but it had also departed from the usual forms.[5] In it Turgot had appealed to public opinion. 'You will find it platitudinous and long-winded,' he told Véri with a laugh, 'but I wished to make it so clear that every village lawyer can explain it to the peasants.'[6] In other words, he wanted to avoid a repetition of those misconceptions that prevailed in 1763, when no one seemed to grasp the real intention of the law. In the end he had his way, and the legislation was promulgated in the form that he had cast it.

But the measure itself, which re-enacted the Declaration of May 1763, was certainly moderate. It established the freedom of the grain trade within the kingdom only, and it left in their entirety the restrictions obtaining in Paris. Upon second thoughts after consideration of Bertin's words of warning, Turgot had abandoned his original intention to establish complete freedom of export, and he contented himself with reserving to the King the right to declare such freedom when times were more propitious.[7] At the moment little was to be gained from facilitating export. As he told Stormont at Compiègne, if it were a matter of setting an example, then it was England which ought to take the lead.[8] What France needed at the time was an import of grain to supplement her dwindling supplies. To meet this requirement Turgot was even prepared to offer bounties upon incoming corn,[9] and, as yet another precaution until such time as a flourishing trade would render the measure superfluous, he retained a corn depot at Corbeil, which he placed under the control of the lieutenant of the police. Here, having recourse to the expedient that had proved successful at Limoges, he provided for the making of bread, which was to be sold at a price determined strictly by costs of production.[10] So cautious, indeed, was Turgot's corn policy that Galiani, the author of the *Dialogues sur le commerce des blés* and an accomplished critic of the *économistes*, received congratulations from all parts of Europe on having gained such a convert.[11]

But it was only in thus restricting his programme that Turgot was able to obtain sufficient ministerial support to reverse the Abbé Terray's régime; and it was that same moderation of his legislation that led that Parlement of Paris to accept it with very little comment. Turgot, as Stormont discovered, thought it advisable to wait until the magistrates returned before actually promulgating his measure in the form of letters patent. At first sight this must appear a concession which asked for trouble, for the last act of the old Parlement before its exile had been the registration of Terray's decrees destroying the liberty of the grain trade. But it seems that Turgot was well aware that during their exile in the provinces the magistrates had learned that a growing body of opinion favoured the removal of restrictions. His information proved to be correct. Although in registering his legislation the Parlement added a *retentum* (which had no legal force), that the King should take all steps within his power to see that the markets were well supplied with grain, the motive, as Stormont learned from conversation with a number of magistrates, was primarily to satisfy the more disgruntled members, who claimed that the provisions for feeding Paris were most inadequate.[12] Perhaps, moreover, the magistrates as a body wished to keep a door open in the event of a skirmish with the Crown; and no doubt it was policy to pay lip-service at least to the popular prejudices that they had voiced so long. In contrast, however, to those of Paris, the magistrates of Rouen were staunchly opposed to Turgot's legislation and, upheld by Miromesnil, who had once been their colleague, issued a ruling which violated its very principles. But in the end Turgot carried the day and quashed the ruling in an *arrêt de cassation*.[13]

Turgot was now free to liquidate Terray's administration of the King's grains. Already a very strange incident had made a full inquiry an urgent necessity. On 17 September fishermen at Boulogne had found in the River Seine a number of sacks full of documents, and these, when taken to the *contrôle général*, were found to be the records of the dealings of Terray's agents. A judicial inquiry, which was opened on 29 September and the findings of which Turgot summed up in a *Mémoire* to the King, resulted in a damning case against Sorin and Doumerck. These two agents, instead of employing the 12,000,000 *livres* advanced to them from the Treasury to reward the merchants whose services they engaged, had kept the money for their private use; they had purchased grain on credit: to pay one merchant they had borrowed from another, to pay him they had borrowed from a third, to pay the third they had borrowed from a fourth, and so on. They had also drawn interest upon fictitious advances, and they had fraudulently obtained commission upon sales and purchases of supplies, many of which they had exported to America and some of which were not composed of grain but of sugar and other commodities. These men were not alone in perpetuating such frauds, but had been aided and abetted by the officials Brochet and Leclerc. The former had received a large share of the spoils. A poor man before he acquired his office, he had built a palatial dwelling, where he entertained lavishly and gambled adventurously. When he was dismissed, a wit chalked on the wall of his house *L'Hôtel de la Farine*.[14] For long Brochet protested his innocence in vague and general terms; but he never succeeded in answering the specific charges of dishonesty that Turgot brought against him.[15]

Sorin and Doumerck were ordered to refund the money advanced by the Treasury. But at the time no further action was taken against them, and it was not until the days that followed the corn riots of 1775, when the Government was attempting to discover the organizers, that Sorin and Doumerck were cast into the Bastille and subjected to a cross-examination by Albert, who had become the lieutenant of the police. The further inquiry merely confirmed Turgot's original indictment; but there was no evidence forthcoming that they had been subsequently engaged in stirring up sedition, and they were given their freedom on 20 June 1775. Both had been extremely fortunate, for the original charges might have led to heavy penalties. But Turgot, probably wishing to avoid a sensational law-case which would undoubtedly have given rise to a bitter conflict, was content to ask for their dismissal, and did not probe the matter further. Métra, who makes a running commentary on these events, and Du Pont, in his correspondence with the Margrave of Baden, both aver that Terray was implicated; but Véri, who was usually well informed, contends that the fallen Comptroller-General was not so much a rogue as a fool and the dupe of his prodigal and intriguing hirelings.[16] At any rate, Turgot was not disposed to rake up Terray's past: once begun, there was simply no knowing where the affair might end.

(2)

The legislation freeing the grain trade was well received. The industrial interests for the most part pronounced in its favour, the merchants of Bordeaux going so far as to address to Turgot a congratulatory message,[17] and the grain-producers, too, looked forward once more to times of prosperity. Turgot therefore had every hope that in time other interests would come to recognize the value of free trade in grain.[18] Nevertheless, his measures soon gave rise to a renewal of the pamphlet war between the mercantilist and the free-trade schools, Turgot's own supporters tending to cast caution aside in a literary onslaught against their enemies. It was Véri's opinion that the physiocrat journalists only succeeded in making the grain trade the subject of quite unnecessary controversy.[19] What is more, they created the impression that the Comptroller would systematically carry into effect the whole range of his doctrines within a short space of time, with the result that many people who were prepared to tolerate a small measure of reform now became unduly alarmed. Opponents were quick to seize upon the opening thus afforded and, if it was invective that won over opinion, the Physiocrats were fighting a losing battle. In Linguet, the most scurrilous and most poisonous of all the pamphlet-writers of the age, they certainly met their match. But of even greater concern than the literary attacks upon free trade were the popular outcries that arose towards the end of the winter. The harvest of 1774 had been mediocre, and prices soon began to rise. There was a repetition of the events that had followed the free-trade laws of 1763 and 1764. The police officials of the towns, ignoring Turgot's edict, began to revive the old regulations, in La Rochelle, for example, a house-to-house search being organized in March 1775. Turgot acted as he had done at Limoges: he quashed the rulings of the local officials and reissued printed copies of his edict ; he ordered the intendant of Caen to have troops in readiness and to arrest the ringleaders of a grain mob at Cherbourg ; and he advised other intendants to offer bounties to merchants who undertook to bring in supplies by sea.[20] On 24 April he gave this last measure application throughout the kingdom. ' All merchants, French and foreigners alike, who bring in grain between 15 May and 1 August ', so runs his preamble, ' shall be paid 18 *sols* on every quintal of wheat and 12 *sols* on every quintal of rye . . . and to those who during this same period transport grain to Paris and Lyon shall be paid, over and above the bounties awarded at the ports, at Paris 20 *sols* on every quintal of wheat and 12 *sols* on every quintal of rye ; at Lyon 25 *sols* on every quintal of wheat and 15 *sols* on every quintal of rye.' [21] Nor was this all. As at Limoges, so now at Paris, he persuaded a number of merchants that it was in the long run to their advantage to uphold the cause of free trade by tiding over the period of shortage.[22] Finally, where the dearth was exceptional—for example, at Dijon, Beaunne, Saint-Jean-de-Losne, Montbard, and Pontoise—he abolished various local duties on grain which caused supplies to ' avoid the markets '.[23] Upon all these measures Maurepas commented flippantly to Véri: 'It is the high price of bread that occupies us now, or to put it better, causes us anxiety without wasting our time; for we have no remedy to suggest when even M. Turgot changes his principles.'[24]

The situation was becoming really serious. In March revolts had taken place at Évry and Metz, and early in April there was a riot at Rheims. On 18 April an ugly demonstration took place at Dijon. Here the insurgents, 400 to 500 strong, drawn mainly from the countryside around, plundered houses, demolished a mill, and tore up the streets. Then, attacking the house of one of the Maupeou magistrates, whom they accused of causing the shortage of grain, they drank dry his wine-cellar and, becoming extremely violent, next went off to find the Governor to put him to death. It was not until the Bishop, who, risking his life, remonstrated with them that they finally dispersed. This 'little Bartholomew of Dijon', as Voltaire termed the riot, was merely a prelude to what was to follow. It was not the spontaneous violence of hungry wretches, or a natural reaction to rising prices which were only 30 per cent. above the normal, but an organized looting, the insurgents destroying the grain whenever they found it.[25] Turgot was quick to realize that political enemies were at work. It had been reported to him that more peasants than usual were loitering round the markets in the towns north of Paris, their general demeanour showing that they meant no good. In Brie, Soissonais, Vexin, and Haute Normandie bands of disaffected persons were exciting the poorer classes to rebel. There were occasional lootings in the markets, and the merchants, taking alarm, sometimes sold their grains at a loss. Granaries and farmhouses, and vessels on their way to Paris were being pillaged, and on 29 April two whole boatloads of grain at Pontoise were thrown into the river.[26]

Turgot's plans for bringing relief to Paris were seriously jeopardized. He had already planned *bureaux de charité* somewhat similar to those he had established at Limoges, in order to furnish the poor with money with which to buy the incoming flour and bread; and among the indigent for whom no work could be found he had arranged to distribute alms.[27] But now there was the danger that supplies would be destroyed in transit. No sooner had he sent out the circulars to the *curés* organizing relief than further riots broke out at Beaumont-sur-Oise. The revolt spread like wildfire southwards.[28] On 30 April the depots at Brie, Meaux, Saint-Maur, and Saint-Germain were raided, and on 1 May the army of Jean Farine reached Versailles. It was late in the evening when they arrived. Next morning they stormed the flour-stores and the market, and later they invaded the courts of the palace, demanding loudly a reduction of the price of bread and displaying specimens of a green and mouldy aliment upon which they claimed to be subsisting.

Turgot was in Paris at the time, making ready for the defence of the capital; for Versailles was safe enough, there being 10,000 troops in attendance on the King. Louis, in his own obstinate way, remained quite firm; he had refused to listen to the courtiers who advised him to abolish free trade, and in the morning he had ordered the Prince de Beauvau to protect the markets. To Turgot he hastily penned two letters—one at 11 a.m., the other at 2 p.m. In the first he wrote: ' Versailles is being assailed, and they are the same men of Saint-Germain. I am going to confer with M. du Muy and M. d'Affy (Colonel of the Swiss Guards) to see what can be done; you can count upon my firmness. I have just ordered a guard for the market. I am very pleased with the precautions you have taken in Paris; it was for there I was most afraid. . . . You will be doing the right thing in arresting those people of whom you speak; but remember when you have got them—no haste and many questions. . . .' [29] Three hours later Louis wrote his second letter, which refutes the often-repeated story (taken from Métra [30]) that, having failed to harangue the crowd from the balcony, and being full of pity and fear, he commanded the police to sell bread at 2 *sols* the *livre*. Actually it was the Prince de Beauvau who gave this order. While guarding the market he had been covered from head to foot in flour; he had weakly asked the rioters what they wanted; and, on being told, had granted their demand. Louis heard of this as he was writing to Turgot. Having first of all described the further precautions he had taken to defend the markets and the highways, Louis went on to say: ' I am not going out to-day—not from fear, but just to let everything settle down. M. de Beauvau interrupts me to tell me of the foolish manoeuvre that was made, which was to let the insurgents have bread at 2 *sols*. He contends that there is no middle course between this and obliging them at the point of the sword to buy it at its present price. This particular bargain is an accomplished fact; but it must not be repeated, and precautions must be taken to prevent their coming back to dictate the law; let me know what these measures should be, for this situation is very awkward.' [31] Such was Louis's letter. It is somewhat strange that an apocryphal version from the *Mémoires de l'Abbé Terray* [32] was the only one to be known until the original was found. At the time Véri knew the truth; but, then, there was little which he did not know.[33] And it is interesting to note that St. Paul, who was deputizing for Lord Stormont, also knew, for he had acquired a copy of the King's letter, and this he sent to England on 10 May. St. Paul had watched the riot at Versailles (he had gone there to discuss the debts of the

French East India Company), and his account agrees substantially with Louis's own. The apocryphal version maintains
that Louis confessed to an 'error of policy', which he was 'anxious
to repair', and that he summoned Turgot to return 'without
delay'. As a fact Turgot did return (as a normal course) that
very day. But in Foncin's somewhat vague suggestion that he
tried without success to persuade Louis to command the troops
to fire upon the mob there is no truth.[34] Actually the insurgents
had already gone. Véri tells us that they had been led away
'like a flock of sheep'. Neither Louis nor Turgot, who seem to
have planned carefully all their moves, was anxious merely to
disperse the rabble. They wanted to find out the organizers.
'Remember,' Louis had said, 'no haste and many questions.'

All night the troops patrolled Paris and the countryside around.
Next morning the rioters, 400 to 500 strong, and armed with
batons, drew near Paris. The bakers outside the gates were
emptying their ovens and arranging their loaves for sale. A
police ordinance posted by Lenoir after consultation with Turgot
on the previous day required them to carry on their business and
to sell bread at current rates, compensation being promised to
those whose shops were looted. But a number of the bakers,
considering the risk too great, had hidden their bread in neighbouring houses. These were the first to have their supplies stolen.
About seven o'clock the insurgents rushed through the gates on
the northern boundary. The populace locked their doors and
gazed from the windows calmly as upon a procession, watching
the rioters systematically demolish the bakers' shops. By
midday not a loaf was to be bought. All this while the troops
did nothing. The *Gardes françaises* were attending Notre Dame
for the blessing of their banners, the Duc de Biron, acting upon
Maurepas's advice, having refused to postpone the ceremony.[35]
Some of the other troops fraternized with the rioters, and even
when the Musketeers arrested a dozen rebels, the police released
them, saying their orders were merely to disperse, and not to
apprehend those who got out of hand. But, if these were really
the orders, the police had not obeyed them. The Chief, Lenoir,
making the excuse that he was waiting for a written command,
did nothing at all. Turgot, upon hearing of the fiasco, made
haste from Versailles, and arrived in Paris at ten o'clock to find
that the mob, having pillaged the Abbaye Saint-Victor and having
first contemplated an attack on the Bastille, were swarming round
the *contrôle général*, displaying their specimens of mouldy barley
bread and shouting, 'This is what we have to eat.' While
Turgot was talking to Lenoir, the mob moved off to the Halls
and Markets, and again destroyed supplies. About eleven
o'clock the rioters calmed down from sheer exhaustion, while

the huge crowds of citizens, who later in the morning had un-
locked their doors and ventured into the streets, gradually dispersed to take a midday meal. Throughout the afternoon all was
relatively quiet. Biron had now posted his men at all important
places, and the Dragoons and the Suisses patrolled the streets.

Turgot returned to Versailles in the evening and prevailed
upon Louis to call a Council, which sat until the early hours of
the morning of 4 May. Maurepas was not consulted. According to the *Relation historique*, he went that night to the opera,
but Véri holds that he had gone on the previous evening—the
day of the revolt at Versailles. At all events, he kept constantly
clear of the whole business and, when reprimanded by the Abbé
de Véri for this neglect, his only excuse was that as he had found
Turgot giving orders to everybody, he therefore let him carry on.
But he could not explain—and this was his real folly—his advice
to Biron to take the troops to Notre Dame. If he was at the
Council he took a back seat and said nothing at all. Turgot did
all the talking. He spoke vehemently against Lenoir, and had
him dismissed along with two of his commissioners and the
commandant of the watch. Véri seems to think that Lenoir's
insubordination was due not to design (not, as was rumoured, to
a plan concerted with his friend Sartine), but to lack of experience
in a new office.[36] And that seems to have been Turgot's own
opinion: he could ' not risk a second day like yesterday '—these
were his words in informing Lenoir of his master's wishes.[37]

Another result of the Council was that Turgot was given a
blanc-seing to employ the military authority as he thought best.
The generalissimo, as he was called, drew up immediately a plan
of campaign. An army of 25,000 was organized. Biron took
charge of Paris; the Marquis de Poyanne, the Haute Seine;
the Comte de Vaux, the Basse Seine; and the Musketeers patrolled
the Marne. Throughout the morning of 4 May, Paris was relatively calm. Two or three men were posted at each bakery;
the markets and public squares were guarded; and pickets
continually went the rounds. There were a few instances of
disorder. One or two people were robbed; sentinels were
occasionally insulted; here and there insurgents began to tear
up the streets; and the bolder spirits posted placards with the
words: ' If the price of bread does not diminish we shall exterminate the King and all the race of Bourbons.' Later the cry
went up for an attack on the Bicêtre to free the prisoners; but
the soldiers intervened and arrested nearly 200.

(3)

By this time the Parlement of Paris had begun to interfere.
Louis had kept the magistrates informed of his actions and he

had warned them that they were not in any circumstances to take a line different from his own. These instructions had been received in silence. But on 4 May the Parlement assembled to discuss the events of the previous day. The outcome was a ruling which, while forbidding the populace to assemble, affirmed that the King ought ' to take measures . . . to reduce the price of bread to a rate proportionate to the needs of the people '. The next day the magistrates protested against the *commission prévôtale* that had been set up to try the insurgents who had been arrested, a function which they claimed for the *Grand' Chambre*. Already the magisterial ruling of 4 May was being posted in the streets. At Turgot's instigation the Musketeers were ordered to smash the printing-blocks and to cover over the notices with the King's ordinance of 3 May forbidding crowds to gather or to demand grain and bread below the current prices. This done, Turgot hurried back to Versailles, wakened the King at midnight, and persuaded him to hold a *lit de justice* for the registration of the letters patent establishing the extraordinary tribunal. Next morning the magistrates were ordered to present themselves at Versailles wearing their black robes. But before they set out they defiantly demanded that bread should be sold in Paris at 2 *sols* the *livre*.

At the Palace the magistrates were sumptuously entertained. Later Miromesnil spoke on behalf of the King. He described briefly the disorders that had taken place, and ascribed them to a foul conspiracy : ' It seemed that a plot was hatched to lay desolate the countryside, to impede navigation, to hinder the transport of grain on the highways, and to starve the large towns, above all Paris.' And he went on to explain the necessity of taking summary proceedings against the malefactors in an extraordinary tribunal, thus avoiding the serious delays of the usual legal procedure. Neither d'Aligre, the First President, nor Seguier, the *avocat général*, opposed the King and, among the peers only the Prince de Conti voiced a dissenting opinion. Then Louis himself, with force and firmness, closed the session : ' Sirs, you have heard my intentions. I forbid you to make remonstrances which will impede the execution of my commands.' [38] Afterwards he wrote to Turgot : ' I have just carried out that upon which we agreed. . . . A few demanded the restoration of the old regulations, but the majority had modified its impertinent tone and was in great fear. I hope all this will give tranquillity. . . .' Later he wrote again and, having described the instructions he had given to the military, added : ' It will be seen from all this that I am not so feeble as is believed, and that I know how to carry out that upon which I am resolved. . . . The truth is that I am more afraid of one man alone than of fifty. . . . The news from Paris is good. . . . All is quiet here.' [39] Louis was revelling in his strength. As Véri says, he showed a spirit of courage and a *sang-froid* which could hardly be expected at his age and with his peaceful frame of mind. After the Council at Versailles he had said to Turgot: ' We ourselves have a good conscience, and in this we are very strong.' [40]

In his second letter of 6 May he had gone on to refer vaguely to the sinister organization behind the revolt. All sources are agreed that the rioters had moved with military precision, and that much time and money had been spent in planning their movements. None of them was hungry; they were not pitiful specimens of humanity, not winged raggedness, as Carlyle calls them, crying out for bread, but healthy ruffians singing as they marched. The mouldy bread they carried had been specially prepared: plenty of corn was obtainable, but none of them seemed to want it except to destroy it.[41] They all had money in their pockets; the rank and file received twelve francs a day and the leaders of each band a golden *louis*. One man who was arrested (he was probably a paymaster) had 500 *louis*. When Poumeuze, a magistrate, offered a woman rioter a coin, she threw it away and jingling her pockets said she had money enough. What is more, they carried printed copies of a false *arrêt du conseil* purporting to authorize the pillage and the sale of grain at 12 *livres* the *setier*. All this Louis knew, and from the beginning had his own suspicions of the master-hand behind the scenes. But already bewildering and conflicting rumours were reaching his ears. The factions had begun the attempt to reap where others had sown. Louis wrote to Turgot: ' It is a very dreadful thing—the suspicions that we have already and the embarrassing course it will be necessary to take; unfortunately these are not the only ones who are spoken of; I hope for my good name that these rumours are only the work of calumniators. . . .'

There were few people of importance who were not at some time or other accused of having engineered the flour war. The Prince de Conti, the Abbé Terray and his grain officials, the clergy, Maupeou and his magistrates, the Choiseulistes, Sartine and Lenoir, the Queen, Maurepas, the English, even Turgot himself—all in turn were said to have been behind the plot. Du Pont holds that Louis finally penetrated the secrets of the conspiracy, but took no action and destroyed the evidence. Weber, a brother of Marie-Antoinette's nurse, suggests that the King, being afraid to strike at some high personage, decided that clemency was the best means of restoring tranquillity. Conclusive proof as to the origin of the plot will never be forthcoming. All the same, there is much evidence, vague and circumstantial though it is, which makes it possible to narrow down the issue. What is more, in itself the evidence is interesting. It gives a glimpse of those tortuous political manoeuvres of the age.

The charge against Turgot (it is not known who made it) was that he organized the revolt so that he could put it down, and thus make himself indispensable to the King. A slightly different version of this calumny, one which was held by Mirabeau and later by Maurepas, was that there had been no plot at all, but that Turgot had misrepresented to Louis a trivial grain riot for the same political reasons.[42] Such wild accusations require no comment. Nor do the vague rumours that English agents were behind the affair. And as for the fantastic suggestion—again a base calumny—that Maurepas was the culprit, there is not a scrap of evidence. The revolt, as Véri shows, took him by surprise. At the time, though far from happy about the outcome of free trade, he had simply no motive, and certainly no wish to bring about, the Comptroller's dismissal. It was the flour war itself that produced their estrangement, for, in giving Turgot the complete confidence of the King and in leading to intrigues against the Ministry, it excited in Maurepas a jealous resentment for his colleague. Turgot wrote on 13 May to Véri, who was then at Toulouse: '. . . Never has your presence been more necessary for me. The King is as firm as I am . . . but . . . the dismissal of M. Lenoir is not approved by one of your friends (Maurepas). He does not appreciate the services I have rendered him. If M. Lenoir had remained, I could have answered for nothing. I would have been dismissed and, in consequence, M. de Maurepas. Come without delay. I have courage, but come and help me.' Véri loved the fields of early summer far too dearly to take alarm at the Ministerial crisis. He replied: ' Be steadfast in your measures and, above all, keep your master firm.' [43]

Upon the eve of the grain riots the Queen, too, was perfectly satisfied with Turgot. She had, of course, begun to visit the *salon* Guéménée, the meeting-place of the young Choiseulistes, and the intrigue to employ her to dislodge Maurepas had already begun. But Mercy still wrote hopefully to Vienna that her interest was really in the keeping of Turgot and the Abbé Vermond. She was much affected, says Mercy, by the troubles; and Métra has it that during the days of the riots she would not eat her food. She, too, had her own suspicions, as she told her mother without mentioning names, and Marie-Thérèse agreed that there was ' something underneath '. Any suggestion that the Queen knew of the plot is patently absurd. The rumour, like so many other calumnies, was spread by her enemies. Nor is it even likely that the party with which she was associated had any share in preparing the revolt. Mme du Deffand, the hostess to the chief Choiseulistes, writing to Mme de Choiseul on 13 May, seems to be a bewildered yet delighted spectator.[44] No doubt the party hoped that the events would lead to the dismissal of Turgot and Maurepas, and that the Queen would then be able to bring about the return of Choiseul. But there is nothing to suggest that the Choiseulistes themselves prepared the riot.

Nevertheless Sartine, a friend of the Queen and an associate of the Choiseulistes, was later accused of being the culprit by Baudeau, who, however, disclaimed ability to produce absolute proof owing to the death of his witness. Mairobert [45] and Métra contend that Turgot subsequently compelled Baudeau to retract his remarks and to make apologies to Sartine. ' I abandon the economist to you '—so runs Métra's version of Turgot's reply to Sartine—' and if he is culpable may he be put in the Bastille.' A sensational lawsuit was daily expected, but for some reason or other Sartine decided not to take action against the querulous Baudeau. But Baudeau was not the only one to accuse Sartine. Turgot's friend, Saint-Sauveur, also denounced him and pointed to Lenoir as his accomplice. Certainly Lenoir took his cue from his friend and predecessor when he disobeyed instructions on 3 May. But it is most unlikely that Sartine had a hand in preparing the mischief. In all probability he, like Maurepas, welcomed the embarrassment that the affair gave Turgot, yet strongly resented the difficulties created for the Ministry and also the credit that the Comptroller obtained.[46]

What, then, of the clergy ? Of the thirty-one persons thrown into the Bastille, eight were parish priests.[47] Several others had been arrested, but were finally acquitted. Their offence was that they had exhorted their parishioners to join the revolt and to demand bread below the market price. But as a body the clergy had restrained their parishioners, and Turgot later commended them for their behaviour, in some instances giving them considerable rewards. And what is true of the clergy— that a number of wilder spirits joined in when the trouble had begun—holds good of the lawyers, who were little men chiefly without a reputation to stake. There were simply no signs of concerted activity upon the part of Maupeou's fallen magistrates, or, for that matter, upon the part of those who had recently returned to power.[48]

There remain the Prince de Conti and Terray's monopolists. Gustave Bord has maintained that the riot was the work of the corn speculators, whose calculations had been upset when Turgot, in liquidating Terray's administration, flooded the market with grain to the value of 6,400,000 *livres*.[49] If that is so, then their motive was to create a shortage in order that they might get rid of their stocks at a good price before the next harvest, and also to prevent the influx of corn brought in by bounties. That corn speculators sometimes adopted such tactics is evident from a letter which Turgot wrote to Condorcet in 1771 describing an organized riot at Clermont.[50] It is highly significant that the Government promptly arrested Sorin de Bonne and his partner Doumerck. But nothing, as we have seen, was proved against them. It is possible, of course, that other speculators organized the riot in a frantic attempt to raise the price of corn. Yet at the time suspicions of people usually well informed fell almost without exception upon the Prince de Conti. Véri (who on this point is somewhat vague, though he may have dealt more fully with it in the parts of his diary which are lost),[51] Turgot himself (though the assertion rests on the unreliable word of Marmontel), and also Louis—all seem to have believed that it was Conti's that was the master-mind of the plot. Du Pont, in his correspondence with the Margrave of Baden, states that Conti, Cardinal Laroche-Aymon (the Grand Almoner), and Souche (the Grand Provost) were incensed with Turgot because they believed that he was about to abolish the guilds, from which they drew considerable revenues, Morellet and Baudeau having imprudently announced that an edict suppressing the communities had been prepared. Du Pont adds that these conspirators were joined by members of the clergy and magistracy, by courtiers and financiers, and (he hints) also by grain speculators.[52]

No man was more capable than Conti of carrying out such a bold adventure. Possessed of much courage of a wild and romantic kind, of good looks and fine bearing, all of which gained him many daring friends, yet he was arrogant, intolerant, and quick to take revenge on those who crossed his path; and a staunch upholder of feudal privilege, he was greatly attached to his high prerogatives. He had quarrelled, for instance, with Marie-Antoinette on the occasion of the Archduke Maximilian's stay in France, his complaint being that the Austrian prince had not visited him. For years he had nursed other grievances against the Court. Falling from favour in 1757, he had formed the Court of the Temple, and from there had directed a constant opposition to the King and Ministers. It was from the Temple Press that the *Correspondance secrète de Maupeou et de Sorhouet* had been issued, while the *Mémoires de Beaumarchais* had been paid for with his money. From first to last he was a *frondeur*. He had now conceived a hatred for Turgot and his policy. It is therefore possible that it was he who organized the riots, and all the more likely because the insurgents first began to move in the region of his estate, L'Isle d'Adam. By what means did he recruit his army? It may be (though this is highly conjectural) that he utilized the services of the *Illuminés*, a freemasonry organization founded in 1762, or perhaps the Order of the Grand Orient, which had been established in 1772 with the future Philip Égalité as Grand Master. Danican's *Le Fléau des Tyrans* (1797) definitely attributes the corn riots of 1775 to the Templar Jacobins.[53]

But if Louis had any evidence against the Prince de Conti, he never acted upon it. Perhaps he thought that Conti's waiting grave would soon render punishment superfluous ; or perhaps he feared to stir into greater activity Conti's subversive movement. Neither Louis nor Turgot struck boldly. Two wretches were hanged, as Carlyle tells us three times over, on ' a new gallows forty feet high ',[54] one a master wig-maker, the other a gauze-maker, and they cried that they were dying for the people. The assassins of Lally, Calas, and La Barre protested. Turgot and Louis, it appears, had no share in this butchery, which was simply a matter of police routine. On that same day, 11 May, they issued an amnesty to those who would return peacefully to their homes, and they threatened to treat as vagabonds all people wandering without a licence.[55] As the news of the flour war had gone round, the peasants, led by agitators who said that they brought instructions from the King, began to riot and to burn the barns. But order was restored by the intendants employing the troops, and the amnesty soon produced a salutary effect. The situation was well in hand (though the precaution of guarding the markets was continued in Paris throughout the summer [56]) and Turgot began the laborious and costly task of granting the indemnities that he had promised.

He now proceeded to increase the liberty of the grain trade, issuing in all no less than twenty-three separate regulations towards this end, some of general application and some designed to meet local circumstances. On 2 June, as a result of numerous petitions from the towns, he abolished the *octrois* on grain, flour, and bread in all parts of the kingdom excepting Paris and Marseilles. That same month he suppressed the privileged companies of porters and grain merchants at Rouen, who, enjoying also a monopoly in neighbouring towns of Normandy, impeded the movement of corn to Paris. Later, in conjunction with the Minister for War, he attempted, and in part succeeded in, reducing the monopolist purchases of the army contractors. Again, in col-laboration with Vergennes he was planning reciprocity treaties with European Powers. In October 1775 he permitted a coastal trade in corn and flour so that supplies might more easily pass by water from one region to another. Next year he drew up a project for the suppression of feudal dues on grain. Already the provincial Estates of Burgundy had abolished these charges and had provided indemnities for the owners ; but elsewhere there had been an increasing number of sheer defaults, and in

July 1775 he found it necessary to make it known that the grain rents had not been abolished by the King. The next month he caused all owners of these dues to present within half a year their titles to these rights and he established a commission to hold an inquiry. It was as a result of the information thus collected that he drew up the project of suppression. But he fell from power before executing this reform, having previously failed to persuade the Estates of Languedoc to undertake a similar reform.[57] He had also hoped to abolish the *banalités* (or restrictions and levies upon milling) throughout the kingdom; but he allowed his project to remain a dead letter, finding that the burden of indemnities would be greater than the existing obligations. More serious actually than the *banalités* were the monopolies of the guilds of bakers. Hence he encouraged the intendants to establish a just ratio between the price of grain and that of bread—in fact, to do what he himself had done while at Limoges. ' If the Guilds of Bakers ', he wrote, ' are an obstruction to the fixing of a just proportion, then there will be another reason for hastening the day when this profession will be thrown open to all. . . .' Yet, except for establishing freedom of the bread trade in Lyon, he did not follow up this threat—not until he abolished the guilds of Paris.[58]

(4)

The grain riots, while increasing Turgot's credit with the King,[59] led to many attempts to undermine his power. Libels poured forth in great profusion. One caricature, which was widely distributed, depicted Turgot driving with Mme d'Enville in a coach drawn by Baudeau, Roubaud, Vaines, Du Pont and other economists. One of the scenes showed the coach capsized by a heap of grain, with Turgot and the Duchess in a most indecent posture and the words ' Freedom, freedom, complete freedom '.[60]

But of all the writings that appeared none caused greater stir than Necker's *La Legislation et le commerce des grains*. In some measure the *Nechromanie* of later years was now anticipated. Taciturn, cold, silent, and aloof, Necker loved humanity in the mass rather than as individuals. His life had been spent in an impersonal and narrow world of commercial speculation; he had that arrogance that comes from success in early ventures, and all the assurance of men of little minds. He was one of those people whose ideas were so shallow that he was practised, and even eloquent, in what he had to say. His glib patter brought him many friends among an aristocracy which never thoroughly despised wealth of plebeian origin; and that same confidence and ease of manner were to captivate and deceive even Louis himself. For Necker, Geneva's hell was sufficiently real, and commercial prudence such an adequate buttress to conscience, that he was disarmingly honest; he had come by money fairly, even as a corn speculator; and he quickly acquired an influential following. His wife had opened her own *salon*, but this, dedicated not to culture, but to Necker himself, was merely the door through which he passed from the counting-house to the world of letters; and Necker won admirers not because he defended mercantilist theories with any degree of skill, but merely because he, a successful man from the world of finance, had chosen to defend them.

About the time that Turgot was preparing the free-trade law of September 1774, Necker was writing a defence of Galiani. According to Morellet, a mutual friend, Necker offered to read Turgot his work in manuscript so that it might be decided whether it was suitable for publication. Turgot replied drily and hastily that, speaking for himself, Necker might publish what he pleased and the public would judge his work upon its merits. Bachaumont's legend that Turgot tried to suppress the book is entirely without foundation. He could easily have done so, but, as Morellet shows, he upheld always the freedom of the Press, providing opinions were honestly and academically expressed. As a matter of course the royal censor examined Necker's work and deleted several passages, but Turgot insisted that it should be published as it stood.

It was not until 19 April 1775 that Necker applied for a licence to sell his book. Sales began on 20 April, and the first edition was soon sold out. On 23 April Turgot was presented with a copy. He wrote to Necker: '. . . I should have waited for a more peaceful moment, when the matter would have interested only those people who can judge it without passion.' Necker replied that he had sent his book to the printers on 12 March, when there was no shortage of grain, and that he would gladly have withheld its publication had he been asked to do so. Morellet holds that Necker was in the right, and there is no obvious cause to disagree with this opinion. But some of Turgot's partisans accused Necker of being one of Conti's agents. If he were, then it is reasonable to suppose that, in view of his career and character, he was the dupe rather than an active accomplice. Necker was a vain man. Did Conti, then, and his agents lay their plans so deeply that they provided an 'independent authority' to justify the revolt in the eyes of the world? It is possible. Necker's work was completed in September 1774. Publication was delayed for over six months; and there is no evidence that Necker revised his work or that any opponent obstructed him. It is obvious that Turgot himself suspected some design. Yet he remained always true to his principles. According to Sénac de Meilhan, he frustrated the attempt of the Ministers to imprison

Necker in the Bastille, and—this is from Marmontel—he also refused to use his influence to have his antagonist recalled to Geneva. Du Pont probably knew something about this affair. He had a letter from M. de Bear, secretary to the Swedish Ambassador, which he never made public. All that he told the Margrave of Baden, to whom he mentioned this letter, was that the rioters when pillaging the market of the Place du Palais Royal were shouting : ' Long live Necker, the saviour of the people.' [61] What is certain is that from this day onwards attempts were made to bring Necker to the Finances. The chief agent of the intrigue was a disappointed and inferior poet, the Marquis de Pezay, who since the beginning of the reign had maintained a secret correspondence with the King, somewhat on the same lines as the Chevalier d'Éon's to Louis XV. At one time Pezay had flirted with the economists, and had denounced the Abbé Terray, but, upon being snubbed, he had turned against them and had begun to criticize Turgot's economic policy. He now began to write encomiums of Necker, from whose purse, it seems, flowed an ample reward.[62]

Necker's book was a flimsy apology for popular prejudices. It had none of the distinction and subtlety of Galiani's *Dialogues*. The argument was simple enough : neither complete liberty nor protection was for the public good, and even internal freedom had many disadvantages. What was needed was a thorough revision of the old grain laws. No single system could meet the situation. So far, so good. But Necker had really no practical suggestions to offer ; the whole work is a collection of utopist detail, a jumble of pious hopes and of sentimental effusions. Necker looked to a man of genius (presumably himself) to reform the grain administration—a Platonic economist who, inflexible and impassionate, would devote his energies to the public good, who would harmonize conflicting interests, who would lead rather than command, administer by instinct rather than by reason. But only quotation can convey a true impression of Necker's puerile remarks : ' So long as corn does not reach the price to which it can be raised without causing inconvenience, there should be the most complete liberty of sale and purchase. . . . But as soon as it shall have advanced to a high price, I would prevent all further increases caused by the intervention of merchants. I would bring the sellers direct to the consumers by ordaining that, beyond a certain price, corn should not be sold in the market.' No wonder the journalists took up the challenge— Morellet in his *Analyse*, Condorcet in his *Lettre d'un laboureur de Picardie à M. N* . . .—and Baudeau once again entered the fray with 300 academic pages called *Éclaircissements demandés à M. N* . . . *sur les projets de législation*.

CHAPTER XIII

THE CATTLE PLAGUE: PUBLIC ASSISTANCE:
AGRICULTURE AND INDUSTRY: THE MESSAGERIES

(1)

WHILE Turgot was at the *contrôle général* there occurred one
of the worst outbreaks of *épizootie* or murrain ever experienced
in eighteenth-century France. During the 'sixties the cattle-
plague had visited several provinces, and Turgot, when intendant,
had been called upon to take steps to prevent it from spreading
in Limousin. More alarming outbreaks occurred in the southern
provinces in 1770. In January 1771 Bertin ordered the intendants
to prevent the movement of cattle and to encourage the farmers
to destroy affected animals. This epidemic gradually died down;
but in 1774 murrain broke out again in the *généralité* of Bayonne
and spread rapidly to the *généralités* of Pau, Auch, Bordeaux,
Montauban, Roussillon, La Rochelle and to Languedoc. By
January 1775 the plague was causing such prodigious havoc
that Stormont described it as a ' great national calamity '.[1] Not
only were thousands of cattle-rearers ruined, but in many provinces the winter ploughing could not be done owing to the
heavy mortality among the beasts of labour.

As the epidemic spread, Turgot's correspondence with the
intendants increased in volume, and as time went on he took over
from the easy-going Bertin the task of stamping out the plague.
At first the intendants were left to their own devices, it being
recommended to them that they should enforce the existing
regulations prohibiting movement of cattle. In a number of
généralités insufficient effort was made to execute this ruling.
But Esmangard of Bordeaux displayed great capabilities: he
employed the troops and the *maréchaussée* to police the roads;
and he also called in veterinary surgeons from Bourgelat's schools
at Alfort and Lyon. This same intendant, having experimented
with various remedies, came to the conclusion that the only way
to combat the epidemic was to segregate animals showing signs
of disease and to destroy those proved to be affected. Turgot
accepted Esmangard's opinions and passed them on in the form

of an instruction to the intendants of Languedoc and Montauban, to whom he gave authority to offer indemnities for the first ten cattle slaughtered in any one parish.[2]   In December 1774 he gave these measures wider application, having previously consulted a special commission composed of Condorcet, Malesherbes, Trudaine de Montigny; two scientists, Duhamel and Tenon; and a co-opted member, Vicq d'Azir, professor of medicine in the University of Paris, who had already been called in by Turgot to make a report upon the *généralités* of Bayonne and Auch.[3]

From this time onward he devoted all his energies to stamping out the epidemic.   His achievement was all the more remarkable because on 3 January he fell sick of gout and for a while there was great anxiety for his life.   Most of the next four months he spent in bed.   From his sick-room he carried on the administration of the Finances and bravely continued the additional work that the cattle-plague had thrust upon him, interviewing daily his colleagues and subordinates and dictating that vast correspondence which belongs to this period of his Ministry. Or sometimes he was carried in a chair to the King's study, where he would work with Louis for three hours on end.[4]   On 8 January he issued an *arrêt du conseil* offering bounties of twenty-four and thirty *livres* respectively on every horse and mule imported into and sold in specified markets in the stricken provinces, his intention being to remedy the serious shortage of beasts of labour.   That same month he took steps to isolate, by calling upon the troops to guard the roads, regions as yet unaffected, and he also established an intelligence system so that he might learn quickly the progress of the epidemic.   In yet another order he forbade the Parlements to issue regulations conflicting with his own, or to interfere with the administration of the intendants, to whom he now gave authority to act as they thought best,[5] promising to sanction any further indemnities they might consider advisable to offer.[6]

In spite of the presence of troops guarding the highways, the peasants disregarded orders, and many succeeded in moving cattle.   Again, very few could bring themselves to slaughter their animals; instead they persevered with quack remedies for which there was a ready sale; and when their animals died they often sold the hides.   Hoping to ensure a more thorough execution of his orders, Turgot issued on 4 February a long *Mémoire instructif sur l'épizootie* to the intendants.[7]   This instruction reads like a campaign of battle.   It provides for cordons of troops to encircle the plague-ridden areas and to guard the Spanish frontier, and for small companies to isolate the parishes that had escaped the epidemic.   Each detachment was to be accompanied by a veterinary surgeon, or a medical practitioner, or, failing these, a person competent to recognize the symptoms of the disease and to carry out the directions, drawn up by Vicq d'Azir, for disinfecting the byres and stables. Furthermore, to each corps was to be attached a representative of the intendant, who was to pay immediately an indemnity of one-third of the value of every beast slain, providing its carcass, including the hide, were buried in lime.

During the next few weeks, Turgot, keeping himself daily informed of the situation, issued orders to the military commanders. One day he reinforces the military patrolling the canton of Saintonge; another, he orders a greater concentration upon the Spanish frontier at Guipuscoa; still later he throws a cordon round Limousin; or sometimes he sends detachments to the northern provinces of France where occasional outbreaks are reported.[8] By the end of May the situation was in hand. Yet the measures responsible for this achievement had been somewhat belated. Turgot himself was perhaps a little slow (though certainly he was quicker than others would have been) to appreciate fully the seriousness of the early outbreaks and to realize the necessity of employing a concentration of troops and police to enforce the regulations. Again, he was reluctant to order a wholesale slaughter of cattle; for, since indemnities must be paid, there were the finances to consider. But once he had exhausted the slender means that science could offer, and once he had realized that half-measures were of no value at all, he was prepared to establish martial law. But the epidemic was not completely at an end. Throughout the summer fresh outbreaks occurred in places which had been free for a little time, and also in Dauphiné, Toulouse, and the Landes du Marensin.[9] Hence, Turgot restored in full force the military precautions, especially in Toulouse, where the Parlement and municipal magistrates had, in sanctioning remedies, encouraged the peasantry to attempt to cure their animals.[10]

At the end of October he also found it necessary to recall temporarily Journet intendant of Auch, pending inquiries into his administration. For a long while Turgot had been dissatisfied with this official, who, undoubtedly not of the calibre of the best intendants, weakly gave way to local influence. In the early days of the epidemic Journet had executed a number of regulations of the Parlements of Pau and Toulouse which conflicted with those issued from the *contrôle général*. A further cause for complaint was that indemnities promised were not being paid, with the result that the peasants were refusing to destroy affected animals. At the beginning of October other irregularities came to Turgot's notice. In paying indemnities Journet had established officials whose remuneration amounted to half the fund he proposed to disemburse. These subordinates were thoroughly corrupt; they made false estimates of the value of cattle slain and granted indemnities for animals which had never been destroyed. Again, he had made no attempt to scrutinize claims sent in by the peasants, who were often drawing indemnities for cattle they had tried to cure, and he had paid without question numerous sums demanded by the military officers to defray their expenses.[11] The result was that he had distributed 2,000,000 *livres* in indemnities and had promised another 5,000,000—a sum which exceeded by many times that required for the large *généralité* of Bordeaux, where at one period 1,000 beasts perished every single day.[12] Journet's personal honesty was never suspect.[13] But he lost his courage, and on 28 November, a day or so before he should have appeared in Council, cut his throat. The Government very foolishly committed his servant to the Bastille and gave it out that he had been murdered. In this ridiculous police work Turgot had no share. Yet needless to say his enemies—for the affair was no longer secret—made much of the scandal and accused him of brutality.[14]

The *généralité* of Auch was now placed under Clugny of Bordeaux, who had, as a normal promotion, succeeded Esmangard. The new intendant reported that even in Bordeaux the regulations had been recently relaxed. Turgot again concentrated troops, and threatened heavy penalties to local magistrates who encouraged the peasantry to break the law. Later, acting upon Clugny's advice, he attempted to evacuate all cattle in a zone on the right bank of the Garonne to which the epidemic was quickly spreading. The plan was to slaughter a proportion of the animals for salting and to buy the meat for the navy, and at the same time to encourage the peasantry to sell the remainder to farmers on the left bank of the river.[15] Nothing, however, came of the scheme, and Turgot was compelled to persevere with the methods he had already devised. By April 1776 the epidemic was near an end, timely action having prevented the scourge from gaining a hold in Flanders and Hainault.[16]

The next problem was to expedite the recovery of those regions where losses had been heavy. The policy of offering bounties on imports of horses and mules was maintained throughout the epidemic, and in some regions continued for some time afterwards, the measure producing excellent results, particularly in the *généralité* of Auch, where horse-ploughing became more common than it had ever been before. Again, loans were organized to enable the peasants to buy new stock, and in order to increase credit facilities Turgot attempted, though without success, to obtain a revision of usury laws.[17] Most important of all, however, apart from the granting of *moins-imposés* to the afflicted parishes, was that the indemnities not yet paid should be given at once to those whose needs were greatest. At Auch a commission was established to liquidate Journet's finances, and the indemnities actually paid were reduced to 500,000 *livres*, legal action being taken against those who had made fraudulent claims—a course which was followed also in other *généralités*.[18]

When the danger of the epidemic had passed, Turgot turned his thoughts to the future. In April 1776 he established a commission composed of Lassonne, Vicq d'Azir, and six other specialists to inquire into the problem of epidemics in general. It was this body which later became the Royal Society of Medicine.[19] Indeed, throughout the whole period that he was in office he gave constant encouragement to medical studies. It was he who was largely responsible for the building of the School of Surgeons at Paris, and also for developing hospitals for the poor at this and other medical institutions. On several occasions he distributed literature on medical topics, chief among which were pamphlets on the treatment of venereal disease, on the Swiss treatment of toenia, and also on artificial respiration. At the same time he increased the governmental spending upon medicines which were sent to the intendants for distribution, and he also arranged to have a number of remedies tested by members of the Faculty of Medicine in the University of Paris.[20]

(2)

The cattle plague, combined with the relatively poor harvest of 1774, demanded that Turgot should pay some attention to the serious problem of poverty. As intendant of Limoges, so now as Comptroller-General he kept in mind three main principles : first, to make assistance more systematic ; secondly, to reduce indiscriminate charity which was wasteful of funds and productive of bad social effects ; and thirdly, to provide work where possible instead of alms. In the *arrêt* of April 1776, in which he had offered bounties for imports of corn, he had also announced his intention of extending relief works, spinning, lace-making, and road-making, which were already established in the poorer quarters of Paris. To all intendants who had applied for relief for their provinces he advocated *ateliers de charité* similar to those he himself had organized at Limoges. For example, in September 1775 he granted 45,000 *livres* to the intendant of Caen on the understanding that relief works should be opened for those whose crops had failed or who suffered loss of cattle, and he promised also that if the intendant would establish *bureaux de charité*, he would supplement subscriptions with an additional grant to the *ponts et chaussées* and a substantial loan which might be repaid when times were better. Again, to the intendant of Champagne he made a similar grant, chiefly with the object of relieving the town of Rheims, and on this occasion the total sum that he granted exceeded the figure of 100,000 *livres*. In May 1775, having first discussed the matter with the King, he issued an instruction this time to all intendants requesting them to open *ateliers* on the roads and to provide also textile occupations in or near the towns. In this circular he went on to suggest the details of the proposed organization—the methods of supervising road-works, the planning and distribution of specific tasks, the grading of work, registers and accounts, rewards, the methods of selecting applicants—in fact, all those measures that he had introduced at Limoges. Shortly afterwards he asked the intendants to col-laborate with the bishops and clergy with a view to bringing a multiplicity of local charities into the system. In all this work considerable progress was made, and had Turgot remained in office longer, an adequate organization for the relief of the poor might have been evolved, especially as his reform of the *corvées* would have reduced the amount of poverty by enabling the road contractors to employ regularly a large supply of casual labour.[21]

Having provided work for the able-bodied, Turgot next planned to reduce the appalling *dépôts de mendicité*, most of which had been established by L'Averdy at the cost of 1,000,000 *livres* a year. In the autumn of 1775 a committee composed of Turgot, Malesherbes, Brienne, Trudaine de Montigny, and Albert met frequently at Trudaine's house to discuss plans for reform. What these were is not known for certain; but it seems that Turgot was acting upon them in the orders that he gave to Fontette of Caen. To this official (and probably to others besides) he sent the instruction that all men who were not dangerous to Society were to be set free in order to find employment, and that those too old to work regularly were to receive outdoor relief to the value of 50 *livres* annually. Even suspects were to be given a chance, and only those who proved to be dangerous were to be imprisoned in one of the five depots retained at Saint-Denis, Tours, Bor-deaux, Bourg-en-Bresse, and Châlons. The young men who persistently begged and refused to work were to be segregated in a special house of correction at Roule near Paris, to be subjected to military discipline in labour corps and hired out to work, for which they were to receive 10 *sols* a day, and also one-fifth of the profits of their labour.[22]

(3)

Since Turgot had little faith in fostering agriculture and industry by direct means, we cannot expect of him an elaborate

programme of agrarian improvements or of industrial development. All the same, in many small ways he was prepared to
encourage husbandry and to promote new processes and manufactures which he believed to be useful. Of his efforts in this
direction, and also of numerous minor measures promoting
freedom of trade, brief mention must be made, if only to make
complete our survey of his Ministry.[23]

On several occasions he gave financial assistance to the intendants
who were endeavouring to introduce new cultures into their
provinces; and in those regions which were known to be suitable
he stimulated by bounties the cultivation of silkworms. Again,
with the object of fostering the growing of madder he freed its
sale from internal restrictions and protected it with a high duty
of 25 *sous* the quintal. He was even prepared to continue the
policy, originated by Bertin and d'Ormesson, of encouraging the
cultivation of the waste. Bertin's legislation according freedom
from taxation in respect of newly-cultivated land had led to many
disputes which were discouraging the farmers from taking advantage of the offer. Turgot therefore decreed that no exemption
was to be questioned after a lapse of six months from the time
that the owner or the tenant announced his intention of reclaiming
the land. But as intendant, so now as Comptroller, he attached
much more importance to the introduction of new agricultural
implements than to the intake of poor soil. Hence he offered
encouragement to inventors. For example, he provided the
money for a demonstration of Vélye's machine for watering
meadows, and he gave a sum of 10,000 *livres* to one named Cotte
to establish a pumping system for irrigation. Of greater interest,
however, are the agricultural reforms that he had designed just
before he fell from power. First, he had prepared, as we have
seen, legislation for the suppression of feudal dues on grain;
next, he had planned to abolish duties which restricted the
consolidation of domains; and finally, he had created a fund for
the abolition of royal tolls, it being his intention that this project
should come into force in 1777 and lead ultimately to the suppression of similar rights enjoyed by the siegneurs.

Far vaster than his correspondence dealing with agriculture
(for, after all, it was Bertin who was primarily responsible for
this branch of administration) was that concerning trade and
commerce, much of it consisting of answers to petitions from
individual merchants and industrialists and from the Chambers of
Commerce in the more important towns. To the porcelain
manufacture at Limoges he made a loan to tide it over a financial
crisis, and to La Forêt, who owned the textile industry in that
same town, he made a grant to enable him to extend his business.
The establishment of a nail factory at Givet; assistance in setting

up a lead-rolling machine at Rouen; permission to an Englishman to introduce a pump manufacture; the authorization of a
new tannery at Caen; the granting of a bounty for new types of
textiles at Lyon; the abolition of a monopoly of spangles in that
same town; the introduction of a biscuit manufacture at Saint-
Cyr; the encouragement of a new drapery at Marseilles; efforts
to bring back the artisans who had left Saint-Gobain to take up
work in Lancashire; permission to the town of Rochefort to
take part in the colonial trade; an indemnity to a textile trader
whose buildings had been burned: all these—to take at random
a few examples, and to say nothing of his collaboration with
Vergennes to bring about a modification of foreign tariffs—give
some idea of his administration of commerce and industry.

Sometimes he met requests and petitions, especially those
which sought to establish or to perpetuate monopolies, with
downright refusals. For instance, he would not allow a company
at Marseilles to gain the exclusive right to cart goods from the
town into the surrounding country; nor would he sanction
the demand made by several individuals for the privilege of
levying duties on coal. Then again, when considering applica-
tions for the permission to establish fairs and markets, for the
renewals of grants of local tolls or for the imposition of tariffs
against the foreigner, he invariably remained true to his economic
principles, and refrained from sanctioning measures which
reduced the freedom of trade. In fact, whenever the opportunity
arose, he removed restrictions upon commerce and industry.
At Rouen, for example, he granted complete liberty to the wood
trade, which the Parlement was attemping to subject to even
more stringent regulations than those which had hitherto prevailed.
In this town the magistrates were also endeavouring to control
commerce in window-panes; but once again he overruled them,
and this time established complete freedom of sale and also
permitted free import and export. Other measures are worthy
of mention: he suspended an old law forbidding the sale of sea-
wrack; he permitted the export of chestnuts from the *généralité*
of Caen; and he allowed the sale of oil made from field poppies,
which hitherto, though prohibited by law, had been carried on
in secret. More important were his revision of the duties on tin
and sheet iron and the reduction of the customs on foreign
copper, his object being to reduce the costs of raw materials.
With that same motive, he allowed various kinds of English yarn
and wool to enter the kingdom freely. Again, he relaxed the
gabelles in favour of the fish-curers, and allowed them to buy
salt freely in Portugal and Spain. In a ruling which he gave
in a dispute between the *ferme générale* and the merchants of
Marseilles he reduced a number of duties, and a little while later

he suppressed the tax levied on silk of French origin entering Lyon. This town was engaged in a long technical dispute with the Chamber of Commerce of Lille concerning internal customs barriers and levies on silk. Turgot took the occasion to write for the King a *mémoire* on the subject, hoping to prepare him for a thorough reform of the *douanes* which would render French commerce freer than that of England. But he fell before achieving this object. Two other measures—that suppressing the *marque des cuirs* and the reform of the *marque des fers*—similarly remained mere projects at the time of his dismissal.

As in agriculture, so in industry, he encouraged inventions. He subsidized Duhamel, who was engaged in researches in the making of steel, and he later appointed this scientist as an instructor in the process discovered. Then, again, he gave substantial grants to other individuals for the investigation of the use of coal in England, for the study of sugar-refining, wine- and brandy-making, and also for the improvement of textile machinery. It was he, too, who adopted Desparcieux's idea of a barrage for breaking the ice-floes at the confluence of the Marne and the Seine, though the *machine Turgot*, as it was called, proved a failure and cost the town of Paris 20,000 *livres*. Before he fell from power he was considering plans for saving rivers from pollution and for improving the navigability of the Garonne, having already sanctioned Trésaguet's project, which he had sponsored as intendant, for making the Charente navigable from Civray to Angoulême. Finally, he appointed d'Alembert, Bossut, and Condorcet inspectors of interior navigation, it being their duty to examine thoroughly all the many schemes that had been submitted. Before their offices were suppressed by Clugny, these three devoted their chief attention to the Picardy Canal, and finally pronounced against this costly undertaking. Indeed, the shortage of money meant the postponement of all canal schemes; but it is significant that when Turgot fell from power he had accumulated a fund of 800,000 *livres*. Moreover, he had established a chair in hydraulics at the Pères de l'Oratoire, and in November 1775, Bossut, the first to hold it, began a course of lectures for the engineers.

The advancement of knowledge in all its branches was one of Turgot's main preoccupations. During his Ministry he subsidised many publications, including Morellet's *Dictionnaire du commerce* and Roubaud's *Histoire des finances*. In April 1775 he suppressed the customs duties upon books, and just before his disgrace he was planning legislation to establish a freedom of the Press greater even than that which existed in England. Of all kinds of knowledge, he believed that none was more important than that of the economic conditions of the kingdom. Towards the end of his Ministry he had begun to make more regular the methods by which the Government obtained its statistical information. From the closing years of the seventeenth century throughout the eighteenth there had been many advocates, including Fénelon, Boulainvilliers, Vauban, Boisguillebert and Saint-Pierre, of a system for making accurate surveys of population, taxation, agricultural yield, and industrial production, and many experiments in method had been made. But it was Turgot who first developed a truly elaborate statistical survey of the population. Many of the *états par paroisses* composed at his instigation have survived, and are valuable social documents. It is noteworthy that Necker made use of them for *L'Administration des finances* (1784), though actually the survey was never completed.

(4)

One of Turgot's most famous reforms was that of the *messageries* and *postes*. These institutions had their origin in the Middle Ages, having been organized by the University to enable students to visit and to maintain connexion with their families in the provinces. Gradually the university messengers came to carry letters and parcels for other classes in society, and the system that grew up obviously suggested the establishment of the Royal Posts that came into existence in 1464. A further administration for public conveyances was created during the reign of Charles IX and elaborated during the course of the seventeenth century, part of the profits going to the University. In 1719 the *messageries* and the *postes* were united,[24] but up to the time of Turgot's Ministry they were not so much a service for which the State made itself responsible, as a multiplicity of monopolies from which the Treasury derived only a very small income. There was nothing to be said in favour of this archaic system. Petty restrictions as to the length of journeys and to the weight of goods which might be carried, the high costs of transport, the lack of an adequate number of vehicles, and the frequent recourse to litigation, all impeded the transit of goods. Journeys were slow: from Paris to Dieppe took at least four days, and to Bordeaux as long as a fortnight.[25]

In June 1775, having transferred all outstanding litigation to the intendants and the lieutenant of the police, and having ordered those enjoying monopolies to produce their titles, Turgot began a thorough inquiry into the *messageries*. He would have liked to abolish all restrictions and to proclaim complete liberty to all to run public vehicles on the roads. But fully aware that under such a régime it might be a long while before private enterprise would establish a sufficiency of diligences to meet the demand, and knowing that the Treasury could not afford to lose even the meagre income derived from the monopolies, he decided for the time being to replace the existing organizations in Paris, Versailles, and Saint-Germain by a *régie* controlled by the Government. This he accomplished in an *arrêt* of 7 August 1775 and in a number of supplementary edicts, having previously established committees to adjudicate indemnities. The new system of public conveyances was placed under the direction of Bergaut and a body of officials who each received a salary of 6,000 *livres* annually and commission. Further legislation reduced the costs of fares and freightage, established a tariff of charges, prevented the delays occasioned by the inquisitions of the customs officials, announced the services, and also the time-table. The new vehicles were to be well sprung and much lighter than the old, and were to be drawn by horses provided by the post-masters, who were also to select competent drivers. In executing all these details, Turgot relied upon the intendants and special commissioners who had already provided him with the figures showing the travelling facilities needed for their districts.[26] The organization was financed by a loan of 4,000,000 *livres* raised in Geneva, it being arranged that the revenue should be devoted to paying off both interest and principal.[27]

By the end of the year 1775 the new service was fully in operation, and Turgot had already begun a somewhat similar reform on the waterways of the Marne, Seine, Oise, and other rivers and canals.[28] Within a few weeks he had revolutionized public transport, and the system that he established, though growing yearly to meet new requirements, remained fundamentally unchanged until the age of steam. The journey from Paris to Bordeaux was reduced to just over five days; people began to travel; and merchants soon began to extend their business activities. Even in the early years of the new system the State made a profit of 1,500,000 *livres* rising to 2,000,000 in the time of Necker. And so successful was it that Frederick the Great appointed the Frenchman Bernard to organize a similar service throughout his kingdom.[29]

But the *Turgotines* (as the new diligences came to be called) excited much hostility and, until they proved their value, brought upon their originator much censure and ridicule.[30] The monopolists, although adequately compensated, were furious, alleging that 20,000 persons had been thrown out of work, and refusing to recognize that those formerly employed and many more besides were quickly absorbed by the new administration.[31] The clergy complained that the *Turgotines* would increase irreligion, that passengers would acquire the habit, which Turgot had already acquired, of absenting themselves from Mass.[32] The Queen, too, was for a little while particularly hostile. In July 1775

Turgot had obtained for himself, partly for administrative reasons, but mainly perhaps to keep the office from a courtier, the appointment of *surintendant général des postes* which the Queen had hoped to secure for the Chevalier de Montmorency. This office, which had been vacant since Choiseul's dismissal, was by custom under the control of the Minister of Foreign Affairs, it being argued that it enabled him to keep diplomatic correspondence secret and to obtain useful information by opening letters. When Turgot joined it to the *contrôle général*, although he refused to draw its substantial emoluments, he was accused of greed, and also of an inordinate lust for power. The Court was in uproar against him, and everything was done to play upon the Queen's feelings arising from her disappointment. Maurepas, too, had begun to complain; he was grieved that the reform of the *messageries* had brought discredit upon the Ministry, and, as St. Paul reports, he would 'never forget nor forgive the march M. de Turgot stole upon him '.[33]

But although Turgot had brought the Posts under the *contrôle général*, a measure which enabled him to operate more easily his new administration of the *messageries*, he never succeeded in dismissing Rigoley d'Oigny, who, enjoying the King's confidence, continued to direct the infamous *cabinet noir* where letters were opened. Nor did he succeed in inducing Louis, or for that matter Maurepas, to put an end to this despicable espionage. Véri believed that if Maurepas had only supported Turgot in this matter, Louis might have been prevailed upon to forgo his sinister delight in discovering bad reputations.[34] But Maurepas came even to take a morbid pleasure in obtaining news from such a polluted source, and, as a result, d'Oigny, whose enmity against Turgot had increased as a result of the subordination of the Posts to the Finances, remained in a position which, as we shall see, enabled him to intrigue for his enemy's dismissal.

CHAPTER XIV

THE GROWING OPPOSITION
JANUARY 1775–DECEMBER 1775

(1)

In December 1774 Choiseul for a second time had met with a cold reception from the King, and during the next three months his chief followers lay low at the *salon* of Mme du Deffand and waited upon events, hoping, as Stormont put it, that old Maurepas 'might drop or grow tired'.[1] But Maurepas showed no sign of dying. On 8 February Stormont wrote to St. James's more optimistically than usual: ' The public has at present no expectation of Choiseul's coming again into play, and I think his warmest friends are much less sanguine than they were. Their language is now very cautious, so is his conduct. He affects having bid adieu to ambitions, lives chiefly with his friends, and particularly and professedly avoids all intercourse with the foreign ministers. . . .' By the beginning of March, however, the Choiseulistes, and especially the young men of the party centred round the *salon Guéménée*, renewed their efforts to make Marie-Antoinette their Queen,[2] and in April Mme de Brionne, Choiseul's mistress, presented to her a *mémoire* depicting the unhappy condition of the country, denouncing the Ministry in power, and suggesting that she should use her influence to bring back Choiseul.[3] Véri, who shared Stormont's fears that Maurepas might not keep going long, was amazed at their audacity. He advised Maurepas, whom he still credited with the genuine intention of teaching the King to form his own opinions, to renounce this futile task and to employ his undoubtedly great credit to build a strong unified Ministry which would make the future much more certain.[4] But the old Minister thought little of the morrow, and laughed at death like a young man of twenty, though at the least sign of danger from the factions he prepared for his own immediate safety, fully convinced that he was acting for the good of the realm.

By the end of May Maurepas had real cause for uneasiness. During the corn riots and the days that followed he had watched,

as we have seen, not without irritation and remorse, Turgot's
rise as Louis's right-hand man ; and what was even more disturb-
ing was that the Choiseulistes were following a subtle line of
attack. They were representing d'Aiguillon and his following as
the authors of the writings and verses that libelled Marie-
Antoinette,[5] exciting in her, to use Mercy's words, ' the sentiments
of hatred and vengeance not characteristic of this young princess '.[6]
They calculated that Maurepas would be prompted to defend
d'Aiguillon if, as they hoped, Marie-Antoinette pressed Louis for
his banishment, and they surmised that, in defending his
nephew, Maurepas would incur the enmity of the Queen. The
moment for an intrigue of this kind was most opportune, for
d'Aiguillon's partisans and the Choiseulistes had taken sides in
the famous lawsuit between the Comte de Guines and his dis-
reputable secretary, Tort de la Sonde. The story is a long one.
Guines, who owed his advancement to Choiseul, was ambassador
in London. During the years 1770 and 1771, when there was a
chance of war between England and Spain following upon a clash
of interests in the Falkland Islands, Tort had speculated in the
London money-market, which was violently fluctuating. Although
he utilized his diplomatic knowledge in these ventures, his losses
were heavy, and his creditors claimed payment. He did not deny
his liabilities, but gave it out he was acting not for himself, but
for Guines. In turn Guines denounced his secretary as an
impostor, and had him sent to the Bastille, where he remained
from April 1771 to January 1772. Some time after his release
Tort again accused Guines, and the parties went to law. Meanwhile d'Aiguillon, upon succeeding to the Ministry of Foreign
Affairs, attempted to recall the Ambassador, who now alleged
that the new Minister was conspiring with Tort to discredit
Choiseul. It was not until June 1775 that the case was given a
hearing. Throughout the early part of the year the parties had
been preparing their evidence.[7] Guines and d'Aiguillon, whose
reputation was also at stake, both wished to publish their diplomatic correspondence, and at one time Louis, prompted by
Marie-Antoinette on the one side and by Maurepas on the other,
was prepared to grant them their request. But Vergennes was
opposed, and argued quite rightly that no nation would confide in
France if State secrets were thus made public. Hence Louis
read the relevant papers himself and instructed Vergennes to
write two letters, the first expressing satisfaction that d'Aiguillon
had been impartial in his dealings with the Ambassador, and the
second to Guines [8] ordering him to refrain from publishing his
papers. Resenting this treatment of their protégé, and further
embittered when in April d'Aiguillon's correspondence appeared
in print, the Choiseulistes prevailed upon Marie-Antoinette to

obtain from Louis the permission for Guines to make public portions of his papers which were necessary for his defence. This she succeeded in doing, and Guines again attacked d'Aiguillon and also La Vrillière.   On 16 May, however, Louis, probably at the instigation of Maurepas and Vergennes, suppressed Guines's *mémoire* by an *arrêt du conseil*.   Nevertheless the Ambassador won his lawsuit, and on 6 June returned to London.[9]

It was an anxious time for Maurepas, who was accused of conducting a dirty intrigue to protect his relatives.   He became the subject of scurrilous libels.   Most disconcerting of all was that he had incurred the displeasure of the Queen, who was beginning to exert a greater influence with the King.   Not only had she intervened on behalf of Guines, but she had also secured for the Duc de Fitz-James the office of Marshal in face of the opposition of Du Muy and the Council, the King having gone back upon his word to follow the wishes of the Ministers.[10] Sometime in April Maurepas had established a contact with the Abbé Vermond in the hopes of coming to an understanding with the Queen.[11]   But he had met with no success, so strong was the Queen's hatred for d'Aiguillon, whom Maurepas was endeavouring to restore to favour.   When Véri arrived in Paris, having, as was his custom, spent the springtime rusticating on one of his livings, he found that Maurepas was still out of favour.   He advised him to come quickly to an agreement with Marie-Antoinette, whom he believed to be at bottom the most well-meaning person in the world and who deserved a better fate than to be advised by the scheming Choiseulistes.[12]   Maurepas saw the Queen on 6 June.   She told him that her patience was at an end, and she demanded that he should execute immediately the King's order, which she had already made public, exiling d'Aiguillon to Angenois.   She then assured him of her support and said that after the Coronation the King would devote his attention to his authority, economy, and public order, implying that she would give her full assistance.[13]   D'Aiguillon was elaborately preparing for the Coronation ; he was given a week to quit the Court and to take up residence on his estates.[14]   Once, again, then, Maurepas had been forced to sacrifice his nephew ; and once again the English diplomats feared the return of Choiseul.[15]   Just before the Court moved to Rheims, the Duke himself arrived at Versailles, ' extremely radiant, his nose in the air, so characteristic of his audacious genius. . . . The odds are ', continues Bachaumont, ' that he will have constant access to the Royal Council.' [16]

The dexterity with which Maurepas scuttled to make peace with the Queen and his absolute disinclination to form a Ministry which would take Louis in hand were ominous signs for Turgot, for at any moment Maurepas might intrigue against the Comptroller to save himself. Even for a colleague to stand on his own might, in certain circumstances, encourage Maurepas to undermine him. For the time being, however, much as he secretly resented Turgot's credit, he saw their common danger, and unable to lead, he could, at least, be sometimes led. It fell to Turgot to take direction of affairs. It was he who was probably responsible for Véri's suggestion—which was not altogether without danger—that Maurepas should come to an understanding with Marie-Antoinette. It was he again who prompted Véri's entreaty that a strong Ministry should be formed and that the fate of the nation should not be left to caprice. Moreover, in the belief that the Queen might keep Louis firm, he endeavoured to interest her in his work. Availing himself of the Abbé de Vermond's influence, he obtained the promise that after the Coronation she would promote his reforms and plans of economy. An even greater achievement was that he persuaded her to support Malesherbes's nomination for the Household. After the Coronation the dissolute and dilatory La Vrillière, a pleasant enough man in himself, was to retire after fifty years of office. The Civil Household, which alone consumed a greater revenue than the King of Prussia received annually during the first ten years of his reign, had become a matter of grave concern for Turgot. While La Vrillière dragged out his Ministerial old age, no substantial economies had been possible, and his corrupt underlings, in conspiracy with his vile and avaricious mistress, had squandered money to their hearts' content. Upon hearing that the Queen favoured Sartine for the Household and either d'Ennery or d'Estaing for the Marine, and wishing to bring Malesherbes into the Ministry, he had considered it advisable to act before the Court moved to Rheims. Maurepas, however, declined to press for Malesherbes's appointment, contending that the King's prejudices against it were as strong as they had been the year before. That was the situation when, on 9 June, the cavalcade took the road to Rheims, and Maurepas retired for a well-earned rest to his estate at Pontchartrain, there to reflect upon the bewildering scene, his own precarious position, the Choiseuliste menace to the peace of Europe, and the Abbé de Véri's words of warning. He must tighten his grip—or, what was more in keeping with his character, gather deftly together the strings of policy. Quick to appreciate the gravity of his situation, he soon arrived at a decision: for his own safety he must throw in his lot with Turgot, scotch the designs of the Choiseulistes, and support Malesherbes for the Household.[17]

But during the crowded week at Rheims, Marie-Antoinette had changed her mind. Sensitive to the gaiety of one hour and the awful solemnity of the next, thoroughly elated, and thankful that those very people who had cried for bread should cheer the royal progress, entering into festivities with unbounded enthusiasm, yet weeping when from her tribune she saw the doors of the cathedral flung open and heard the populace acclaim their Sovereign,[18] the Queen was more than ever a prey to the wiles of crafty politicians. Foremost among these was Baron de Besenval, a major in the Swiss Guards, who had climbed to favour by teaching Marie-Antoinette the game of *tric-trac*; it was he who had won her sympathies for the Comte de Guines, and it was he who now persuaded her to see Choiseul.[19] Employing what she thought was her womanly charm, but which others might say was a childish ruse, she arranged the meeting that she boasted of in a letter to the Comte de Rosenburg: ' You have probably heard of the audience that I gave to the Duc de Choiseul at Rheims. It has been so much talked about . . . that old Maurepas was afraid to go to bed. You know well that I could not see him without speaking to the King, but you would hardly guess the way in which I approached him so as to make it seem that I was not asking for permission. I told him that I wanted to see M. Choiseul and that my only difficulty was fixing the hour. I carried it off so well that the poor man himself arranged the most convenient time. I think that I made a good enough use of my rights as a woman on that occasion.' [20] This audience lasted three-quarters of an hour. Choiseul thanked her for all she had done on behalf of Guines and asked for him the *cordon bleu*. He begged nothing for himself, but he spoke of his grievances—his dismissal, his exile, the loss of his rank as Colonel of the Swiss Guards. He then spoke flippantly and disparagingly of the Ministry in power; he tried to detach the Queen from Mercy and Vermond ; and his parting words were that she should follow one of two courses in ruling the King—to persuade him gently or to play upon his fears.[21] Marie-Thérèse was horrified ; it was no longer—probably it had never been—Austrian policy to bring back Choiseul ; [22] ' She is taking great strides towards her ruin. . . . If Choiseul becomes Minister, she is lost.' Choiseul, however, did not return. This audacious move to restore him, prompted by the failure to dislodge Maurepas by attacking d'Aiguillon, came to nothing. Louis, keeping the promise he had made to Turgot before the Court left Versailles,[23] flatly refused to admit him to the Council,[24] snubbed his brother, the Comte d'Artois, who had imprudently pleaded the cause of the Choiseulistes, and, when receiving the Knights of the *Saint-Esprit* at Rheims, for the third time displayed in public his distaste for Choiseul. To Pontchartrain he sent news daily by special courier, the result being that Maurepas returned in the best of spirits and the rumours of his dismissal for a while died down.[25]

But even though Maurepas had regained temporarily his equanimity, the Ministers—Turgot, Vergennes, and Du Muy, and along with them Véri—were not content to let matters drift. The Queen was still surrounded by the Choiseulistes, who talked of gaining power during the course of the year. They had now changed their tactics. Instead of openly vilifying Maurepas, they had taken the more subtle and yet perhaps the easier line of discrediting Turgot, choosing for special condemnation his free-trade policy, and attributing to him the most fantastic projects. His personal integrity they dared not assail; so they praised him for his good intentions and denounced his plans as dangerous systems. Upon Marie-Antoinette, to whom they represented the voice of vested interest as the moans of the people, they undoubtedly made a deep impression. She came back from Rheims with her mind poisoned against the Comptroller-General and fully determined to frustrate the nomination of Malesherbes to the Ministry.[26] It was then that Turgot, leading Vergennes, Du Muy, and even Miromesnil, and availing himself of Véri's gifts of persuasion, pressed Maurepas, who was much too complaisant, to secure immediately Malesherbes's appointment. Véri himself was astounded at the rapidity with which these Ministers, who had so long been at sixes and sevens, united to face the common danger.[27] On 26 June they decided, with great perspicacity, to make Maurepas their leader and to push him from behind. Next day Maurepas went to the King and asked him to give Malesherbes the Household. At first Louis would not hear of this proposal, presumably because the Queen had been insisting on Sartine, but in the end he gave way, and Maurepas returned with the good news to Paris.

The task of informing Malesherbes of the King's decision was entrusted to the Abbé de Véri, who, knowing that he was reluctant to assume responsibility and fearing lest any procrastination on his part might afford Louis the excuse for changing his mind, invited Turgot and also Francès, the brother of Mme Blondel and formerly Ambassador in England, to take part in this mission. All three spent several hours in endeavouring to overcome Malesherbes's objections; they pictured to him the consequences should Choiseul return—the chaos in administration, the revival of magisterial agitation, a costly and disastrous war with England. All these Malesherbes would not deny, but he was loath to take office; as usual, he belittled his own capabilities and stressed his weaknesses, maintaining that though he might be fruitful in ideas, he was totally incapable of arranging for their execution. Yet he did not give a downright refusal, and asked for twenty-four hours in which to answer. The next day, however, he handed to Turgot and Véri a letter for Maurepas declining the appointment. They took it to Versailles, arriving there at nine o'clock in the evening. Maurepas was agitated. He had just finished an interview with Marie-Antoinette.[28] Though professing a desire to come to an understanding with the Ministers for the good of the King and the State, she had insisted on conditions, and had affected bewilderment that Turgot, in particular, should be opposed to Sartine for the Household. After all, she had asked, if these were not two honest men, then who was the rogue? Such was the news with which Maurepas greeted his visitors. After a long discussion the two Ministers resolved to go the next morning for a talk with Louis. Before returning to Paris, Turgot and Véri went to see the Abbé de Vermond. They told him what had happened, and he was astonished to hear of the attitude the Queen had adopted; that morning he had found her very reasonable; and he concluded that in the course of the day some one must have caused her to change her mind. But he gave them some advice: they must continue with their plans; he himself would have a word with her; and they could rest assured that in two or three weeks she would no longer be resentful of what they had done. That same night Turgot sent a courier to Malesherbes telling him of these events and imploring him to come to their aid. Next morning at eight o'clock Malesherbes sent a reply—again a refusal. Turgot and Véri set out for Versailles to take it to Maurepas. On the journey they clutched at last straws and probably arranged the plan which they certainly followed—to impress upon Maurepas what Vermond had told them. At ten o'clock Turgot and Maurepas waited on the King. The Queen was present, and expressed her views strongly. At length Louis replied: ' These, then, are your wishes, Madame: I am acquainted with them, and that suffices: it is for me to make the decision.' Half an hour later Turgot came away bearing a letter from Louis to Malesherbes: ' M. Turgot has told me ', so it ran ' of your reluctance to accept the place that I have offered you. I think that your love of the public good ought to overcome it. You can hardly believe the pleasure you will give me by accepting office, at least for a while if you do not wish to make it your resolution for all time. I believe that this is absolutely necessary for the good of the State.' Malesherbes was overcome. ' With the exception of mortal illness ', he said, ' nothing worse could have happened to me. But one cannot resist a wish which is much more impelling than an order.' He asked for time to compose his reply, which the next day Véri carried to Versailles. Malesherbes accepted, but reserved the right to ask for an early retirement, and once again expressed his incompetence for the office. Maurepas went straightway to congratulate the King. ' He is a man I give you to replace myself, and you will do well to put your confidence in him. He has the enlightenment to see all the great issues in government. The details, for which he is less capable, are in the hands of others. . . . My age will soon remove me from you, but more likely it will be the disposition of the Queen. . . . If I perceive that I continue to be distasteful to her, I must consider an early retirement.' ' No ! no ! Not that,' replied Louis, shaking his hand. ' No, you will not leave me quite so soon.' Louis, in fact, thought the world of Maurepas. A day or so previously he had said to his aunt : ' The more I see of him, the more I like him.' [29]

For a while the Queen openly expressed her loathing for Turgot and Maurepas,[30] but in the end the latter succeeded in consoling her by obtaining for Sartine a place in Council. Mercy, writing on 17 July, told Marie-Thérèse : ' In spite of what has happened, the Comte de Maurepas and Malesherbes . . . and also the Comptroller-General are all three decided to omit no proper means to obtain the support and the goodwill of the Queen. They explained all this to me in the clearest and frankest terms. They asked me to help them in achieving their aim, and therefore, if the Queen wishes to lend herself, my own position would become one singularly favourable for fulfilling all that the service of this august princess demands and at the same time that required by Your Majesty's.' [31]

Turgot, as Besenval admits—though he erroneously attributes the victory to the Queen's dallying—had won the day. But in Malesherbes he did not gain a colleague of the finest Ministerial calibre. Of short stature, and undistinguished in appearance, except for his bright and kindly eyes, simple in habits and slovenly in dress, the most charming of lawyers, Lamoignon de Malesherbes was eloquent and persuasive in the cause of reform, yet timid and pessimistic when action was called for. Condorcet once said of him, ' He discovered reasons without number to defend the *pro* and the *contra* and found not one to make him decide '; and Véri told Maurepas, ' If you want to know his weaknesses ask the man himself; no one is more eloquent or more ingenuous about his own failings.' [32] And yet no man entered the French Ministry with a greater reputation. Son of a former Chancellor and the brilliant offspring of an old magisterial family, he was a judge respected for his tolerance and generosity, while to the liberals of the age he represented enlightenment which was all too rare in his profession. He subscribed to none of the extravagances of magisterial republicanism, and, at the time when the claims of the old and the new magistracy were being debated, had occupied a neutral position, thus incurring the hatred of many of his colleagues. He had a fervent belief in the rule of law on the one hand, yet on the other was desirous of preserving the executive and even the legislative authority of the Crown. He would not abolish *lettres de cachet*, for these were essential for the execution of the royal will, but he would limit their use and subject them to conditions. His views concerning the liberty of the subject and his proposals for mitigating the abuses of despotism he had brought to the King's notice in a number of speeches delivered in his capacity as president of the *Cour des aides*.[33] On 6 May 1775 he had led the *Cour des aides* in drawing up remonstrances advocating religious liberty, the establishment of provincial assemblies, and reforms of taxation, prisons, *lettres de cachet*, and ecclesiastical discipline. These remonstrances had been printed and read avidly throughout France and Europe. Maurepas and Miromesnil were for ignoring them, but Turgot—and the rumour[34] that he had had a hand in their preparation seems not at all unlikely—prevailed upon Louis to receive them and to establish a commission to examine them. Louis replied that he would devote his attention to the reforms suggested; they were not the work of a moment, but would guide his endeavours for all his reign.[35]

Malesherbes's appointment was hailed in the liberal camp as yet another victory for reason. As Du Pont put it to the Margrave of Baden, the King, having turned his back on chattering scoundrels and ferocious faces, had ranged himself upon the side of humanity. Yet in reality, though defeat had been avoided, the battle had not been won and, indeed, it was the crudest optimism to judge the issue on the opening skirmish. It was something to have secured Malesherbes's services; it was something to have scotched the Choiseuliste intrigue; but it was quite another thing to carry through reforms in face of the opposition that was bound to arise. Malesherbes's entry into the Ministry made it possible to consider seriously the reorganization of the Household and the mitigation of countless abuses. But his very presence there, still more the reforms it encouraged Turgot to undertake, intensified the conflict with the gathering forces of vested interest. D'Alembert, writing enthusiastically to Frederick the Great, had nevertheless taken a glance at the danger: ' Great is the alarm in the camp of the scoundrels,' he says. ' . . . All the nation shouts in chorus " A better day dawns upon us ". . . . The priests alone make sound apart, murmuring softly, not daring to boast too much; but the King knows the priests for what they are, if it's only for the education they gave him.'[36] True, the scoundrels were alarmed and the priests were murmuring.[37]

(2)

No spectacle of the *ancien régime* was more imposing than the *Sacre*. For centuries the Kings of France, adorned in gold and crimson robes, had been anointed from the sacred phial of Clovis and had been crowned at Saint-Remi with the gold crown of Charlemagne. The splendid Court, the higher clergy, and noble families moved to Rheims; merchants transferred their capital to that city; and hundreds of poor wretches trudged all the way for the touching for King's Evil. A relatively small and quiet town overflowed with the glories and the miseries of old-world France.[38]

There were many—and among them Turgot—who believed that the time had come to transfer the *Sacre* from Rheims to Paris. His motive was twofold: first he hoped, in view of the grave financial straits of the kingdom, to reduce unnecessary costs, particularly those for transport; secondly, he believed that to hold the ceremonies in Paris would contribute greatly to the popularity of a reforming king.[39] Yet such changes would have met with opposition from the clergy and the *dévots*, and it was a foregone conclusion that Louis would give them no consideration. Turgot therefore was content merely to press for minor economies. First of all he established complete free trade in grain and other commodities for a fortnight in the town of Rheims, the provisioning of which was always a difficult and costly task when the Court descended upon it. Here, he thought, an object-lesson in free trade might be given to all those attending—to the aristocracy, the lawyers, the clergy, the merchants, and also the representatives of the European Powers. The measure proved a great success: there was an abundance of food at moderate prices.[40] To other plans for economies Louis gave his support. 'We must, if possible,' he wrote to La Vrillière, 'reduce the expenses of my Coronation. I wish to curtail the fêtes that have been planned for this ceremony. . . . Moreover, I shall make a stay of a few days only at Compiègne, and the sums allotted for these objects will be utilized to pay for that protection and relief which I owe to those among my people who have been the victims of recent sedition. I ask you to inform immediately the Comptroller-General and the Masters of Ceremonies of those expenses which must not be incurred. You will also express my wish to the Provost of the Guilds of Paris that there should be no festivities in that town, and that the money set aside for them should be employed for the benefit and relief of the inhabitants.'[41]

Of greater moment, however, than these minor economies were the principles that the Coronation raised. The higher clergy wished to take advantage of the occasion to impress upon the monarchy and the nation the claims of the Church; they hoped that pomp and ceremonial would supply an antidote to the impieties and profanities of the last reign.[42]   Many of the prelates were determined to abolish heresy root and branch.   In January 1775 the fanatical Beaumont of Paris had endeavoured to stir Maurepas and Miromesnil to launch an attack upon the Protestant communities.[43]   The extent to which the reactionary clergy were prepared to go finds admirable expression in the remonstrances that, shortly after the Coronation, they submitted to the King: 'We beseech you, Sire . . . to complete the work which Louis the Great began and which Louis the Well-Beloved continued.   It is reserved for you to give the death-blow to Calvinism in your Kingdom.   Order the suppression of the schismatic assemblies of the Protestants. . . . Exclude the sectaries without distinction from all branches of public administration.   Your Majesty will thus assure the unity of the Catholic cult among your subjects.' [44]   Against such outbursts of fanaticism and this desire to revive the Dragonnades, liberal opinion had frequently protested.   Some believed that the Coronation Oath, containing the King's promise to exterminate the heretic condemned by the Church, should be drastically revised.   Others favoured the abolition of the *Sacre* altogether, which they considered a relic of Gothic and unenlightened ages; but Turgot himself was content merely to press for a modification of the ceremony and for a degree of religious toleration.   Ever since March he had been planning to relieve the disabilities of the Protestants.   He had collected statistics to demonstrate the disastrous economic consequences of the revocation of the Edict of Nantes,[45] and he had also studied carefully the *mémoire* that the Protestants themselves had submitted to the Council, in which it was contended that, if toleration were proclaimed, hundreds of refugee families in England and Saxony, including those of wealthy industrialists and merchants, would soon become repatriated.[46]

Fully aware that among the lesser clergy there were many who favoured toleration, but who, owing to the attitude of the prelates, dared not say so publicly, Turgot decided to give the lead.   Véri warned him of the dangers—Louis's prejudices, the outcry from the higher clergy, Du Muy's fanaticism, and the certainty that Maurepas, while himself indifferently tolerant, would never make toleration a matter of principle.[47]   Impatient of this advice, Turgot submitted a *mémoire* to Louis suggesting that the Coronation Oath should run as follows: ' I promise God and my people to govern my Kingdom with justice according to the Laws; never to wage war except in a just and indisputable cause; to employ all my authority to maintain the rights of each of my subjects; and to work all my life to render them as happy as is in my power.'   With this *mémoire* he submitted a letter—a very touching and forceful one, according to Du Pont—which, most unfortunately, has not survived. Somewhat surprisingly, it convinced Louis, who for a while was ready to uphold Turgot against the other Ministers. But Du Muy was resolute against the changes; and Maurepas, hoping to regain direction of affairs and fearing to make the clergy and the *dévots* more hostile to his Ministry, took infinite pains to dissuade Louis from adopting Turgot's proposals, his main argument being that the existing oaths were mere words and placed the King under no obligation to persecute.[48] These counsels prevailed; and at Rheims Louis took the vow to extirpate heresy, though it was said he was plainly embarrassed and mumbled the words.[49] On 10 June Louis wrote to Turgot as follows: ' I think the proposals you have made are those of a very honest man who is strongly attached to me. I am most grateful to you, and I shall always be obliged to you for such frank expression of your views. I do not wish, however, at this present moment to follow your counsel: I discussed it with several persons, and I think it will be for the best if nothing is changed. I thank you nevertheless for your advice; you can be sure that it will remain secret, and I ask you also to treat this letter confidentially.'[50] But the secret was out. Maurepas had seen to that: he had announced his triumph to the public, and Choiseulistes, magistrates, clergy, and *dévots*—all the enemies of Turgot had joined in the applause.[51]

Turgot took the King at his word. Shortly after the Coronation, he presented to Louis a *mémoire* on toleration, encouraging him to treat the formulae to which he had subscribed as empty forms. Of this *mémoire* only part has come down to us—that which deals with the rights of conscience.[52] It is a plea full of simple eloquence, condescending, perhaps, at times, like all those *mémoires* which he prepared for the instruction of a young, well-meaning King. For there were times, indeed, when a few telling words were worth hours of intrigue.—Cast your eye over a map of Europe, Turgot argued, and observe how few countries there are whose sovereigns uphold the Catholic Faith. How can it possibly be that God has given Princes the right to decide which beliefs are true? And if you look further into the matter, you will find that religion, as proved by its own principles, is the private concern of the individual, who, having a soul to save, brings to this life-long task reason, intuition, and his conscience. Not even on the pretext of being the servant of the Church may the Prince interfere with men's beliefs. For religion concerns him only as a private person who also has a soul to save. In his public capacity he is required to toil only for the happiness of men on earth, and he who accomplishes this great work may die content, and need never fear to render his account to God.—Few Catholic Princes had ever heard the like of this.[53]   And it is little to be wondered that the prelates, suspecting that Louis now more than ever would be subjected to insidious influence, made ready to uphold the Altar and the Throne.   It was thought that at any moment Turgot, and with him Malesherbes, whose department was concerned with the affairs of the reformed religion, would straightway remove the disabilities of the Protestant communities.   Yet for a while Turgot worked behind the scenes and endeavoured to avoid an open conflict with the prelates.   Within the Assembly of the Clergy there was a liberal group led by the deist Loménie de Brienne, Archbishop of Toulouse, and it was to this body that Turgot looked for assistance.

The Assembly of the Clergy met on 3 July at the convent of the Grands-Augustins, under the presidency of the aged Cardinal Laroche-Aymon.[54]   The clergy formed a state within the State : they had their own administration, their own system of justice, and a financial organization entirely independent from that of the secular Government.   Every ten years they assembled at Paris to vote the *don gratuit*, which was in reality their only contribution to the expenses of the State.   They were now intent upon following up their victory of the previous month.   On 9 July they appointed a deputation to harangue the King on the condition of the country and, drawing attention to the recent riots, to plead for gentle government and for the mitigation of stern measures.   On 11 July the representatives of the Government—La Vriilière, Marville, the d'Ormessons, and Turgot—bearing the King's reply were received by the Assembly.   The response was not without irony : the Clergy should lead back those who had blindly been led astray ; then might they obviate the rigorous execution of the law.   Two days later those same representatives again visited the Assembly, this time to negotiate the *don gratuit*.   La Vrillière asked for the gift of 16,000,000 *livres*—a sum much greater than ever previously granted.   The ' King's Speech ' to the Clergy, in the composition of which Turgot no doubt had a share, went on to appeal to the more liberal-minded to co-operate in restoring the credit of the nation.   It emphasized the necessity of retrenchment and reform ; it mentioned the economies already achieved ; and it explained that the Clergy, the greatest landholding body in the kingdom, would undoubtedly be the first to benefit materially from free trade in grain.   Protesting their poverty and declaring that already their debts amounted to 97,000,000 *livres*, yet maintaining their willingness to sacrifice worldly goods for the sake of the kingdom, the Clergy voted the gift demanded by the King.   That sum was proportionately six times less than the direct taxation paid by the nobles, and infinitely less than the impositions falling upon the *tiers état*.   Even under normal circumstances the *don gratuit* of 1775 was no great hardship ; at that time it was a trivial burden,

for the Clergy were able to raise a loan at 4 per cent.[55]   No wonder,
then, that as a body the Clergy approved of Turgot's financial
administration, much as they denounced him for his impiety.[56]
Those who served both God and Mammon found it no easy matter
to decide whether they preferred Turgot ' who never went to
Mass ' or the Abbé Terray ' who went every day '.[57]

Financial business concluded, Turgot and Malesherbes launched
their campaign to secure toleration.   To the liberal section of the
Clergy they suggested that Protestant marriages should be made
valid, lay education established, the financial privileges of the clergy
reduced, and, in the interests of hygiene, that burials in churches
should be discouraged.   Only the last proposal met with general
acceptance ; the others alarmed the Ultramontane Clergy ; and it
was Maurepas again who encouraged them to take the offensive.[58]
Their fears were further increased by the appearance of Voltaire's
Diatribe à l'auteur des Éphémérides, which early in August was being
sold in the streets of Paris and extracts of which were published by
Laharpe in the *Mercure*.   For this work, upholding Turgot's free-
trade policy and denouncing religious intolerance, accused the
priests of having encouraged sedition.   ' When we approached
Pontoise ', wrote Voltaire, ' we were all astonished to see twelve to
fifteen thousand peasants rushing about like maniacs and shouting
" Corn, the markets, the markets, corn ! " . . . I saw a little priest
who, in a stentorian voice shouted to them, " Loot everything, my
friends : God wishes it.   Destroy all the flour so that we may have
food." . . .'[59]   Voltaire could never praise Turgot without cursing
the Church.   When the Clergy had opposed ' free meat ' in Lent,
he had asked sarcastically what harm was there for the poor to
nibble a little lard when the priests regaled themselves with soles
and turbot.   But such invective was embarrassing to Turgot, who
preferred to work calmly and unobtrusively.   It was now given out
that he and Malesherbes had commissioned Voltaire to write the
Diatribe.   Against this work the Clergy protested to the King,
declaring it to be ' disrespectful to the Holy Scriptures '.   The
Ministry gave way weakly and suppressed the offending pamphlet,[60]
and, thus encouraged, the Clergy began to attack other impious
writings.   ' Monstrous atheism is becoming the dominant opinion,'
they complained to Louis, citing for special condemnation the Abbé
Raynal's *Histoire philosophique des deux Indes* which had been well
received by the public.[61]   Turgot was much concerned at this
revival of fanaticism.   He obtained an interview with Louis, and
they are probably his words which the King delivered on 25
September to the deputation from the Clergy that had declaimed
against irreligion.   ' I will uphold always the religion of my kingdom ; but you ought not to leave everything to be fulfilled by
authority ; your example is the true support of the Faith, and your

conduct, your ways of life, and your virtues are the most efficacious weapons to combat those who dare to attack it.' [62]

Throughout the remainder of the year Turgot strove continuously to defeat the fanatics. In Council he spoke frequently for toleration, and in private entreated Louis to restore the Edict of Nantes.[63] The Clergy, remaining in constant fear that he would have his way, prolonged their Assembly, apprehensive lest, as soon as they had returned to the provinces, he would introduce an edict legalizing Protestant marriage.[64] The conflict had come to no conclusion when at the end of the year the Assembly dispersed. But the political situation that arose during these six months was of great importance. In the first place, the Clergy had made common cause with their age-long enemies, the magistrates. That union, though long in preparing, was finally sealed when the Parlement, at the instigation of Seguier, also condemned to the flames Voltaire's *Diatribe* and took punitory measures against Laharpe. Seguier's speech on that occasion evoked great applause among the Clergy : he spoke of the respect due to the Holy Scripture, to the sacred dogmas and mysteries of religion, and solemnly declared the Church in danger. A day or so afterwards he received a visit from the Archbishop of Rouen, who conveyed to him the congratulations of the Assembly of the Clergy.[65] Such was the first change in the political situation. The second was that Maurepas had again become uneasy.

(3)

In an entry for 2 July Véri records one of the many admonitions that he gave to Turgot. On this occasion he had warned him that his colleagues were accusing him of speaking disparagingly to the King of their administration. ' I see you are surprised at this reproach,' Véri had continued ; ' you do not believe it to be true even, for certainly you have no intention to be domineering. But you have a bad habit of never seeing a thing in itself. . . . Without regard to persons . . . you pronounce drily your judgement, yes, your judgement ; for you never utter a word with the least hesitation. . . . Yesterday morning . . . you recounted to me with the greatest elation what you had said in M. de Maurepas's presence of the claims of M. Francès to the Marine. Hardly had you left than the King remarked, " You heard that. Only his friends have merit and only his own ideas are good." . . . I wanted to tell you this in order to acquaint you with the King's opinion which you imagine to be entirely in your favour.' Hearing these words, Turgot was still half incredulous, but half repentant, and Véri took yet another opportunity of driving home the lesson that Turgot ought not to be so rigid, but ought to give way with better grace and pay some deference to the opinions of Maurepas.

There was, in fact, constant friction between the two. They wrangled over small matters. For instance, Maurepas wished to give Longchamp, whose office of treasurer of the *caisse d'amortissement* had been suppressed, another sinecure—a course to which Turgot was resolutely opposed. But the trouble really lay much deeper. Maurepas was more jealous than ever of Turgot's influence with the King and more and more resentful of the attacks that his reforms were bringing upon the Ministry; and he was coming to suspect, or at least he could not discredit entirely, the libels making the accusation that Turgot had designs to promote Malesherbes to the position of chief Minister. On his side, Turgot grew impatient of Maurepas's delays, his petty intrigues, and his readiness to retreat inch by inch before the vested interests. As time went on, Véri, while never ceasing to upbraid the one for his domineering habits, came to recognize that the real fault lay with the other. Maurepas, he wrote, 'preaches economy in public: he preaches it in his private interviews with the King; but all these vague sermons do not carry the weight of vigorous resistance upon a given point. These sermons result in a thousand resolutions for the future—but always for the future. . . . Maurepas will say that the King is too easy-going and that Turgot does not hurry himself enough to present projects ready for execution. I shall tell him that he is the one to blame, or, at least, that nature has not endowed him with the vigour that his position requires. . . .'

It fell to Véri, who had become their political confessor, to keep the peace between the two, and he enjoyed the privilege of admonishing both without losing their friendship. He never claimed to be able to correct their faults, but only to supply the '*goutte d'huile*' that reduced the friction to a minimum; and no sooner did he leave them than they came to loggerheads, and each would send for him to reason with the other. In August he set out to spend the late summer on one of his livings. Hardly had he gone away than he received two letters, the one from Mme Maurepas and the other from Turgot. 'You are peaceful among your fields,' wrote the former, 'but we are hardly so here. Never had we more need of you: you are the only man who can make one of your friends see reason.' Turgot also entreated Véri to return: Malesherbes was doing his best, but was unable to remove the obstacles that Maurepas was raising. Véri saw that he was needed, yet was most reluctant to leave the country that he dearly loved. So he sent to Turgot one of his 'sermons', and a few days later he heard from Mme de Maurepas that the altercation was at an end, and that Turgot, quite ungraciously, had given way. Friends had asked Véri why he left them to wrangle. It was then that he complained of the misfortunes of the confidant: 'What a fine part to play, this of *raccommodeur perpétuel*! and to give myself the air of intrigue in entering continually the studies of the Ministers, without having any business at all to be at the Court ! ' He went on to explain his reluctance more fully. He loved better the rustic occupations of the lowly proprietor ; he resented those intruders who besieged him daily to press for favours ; and he had hated to be hearing always complaints against his friends. But he was fully appreciative of the responsibilities that had thrust themselves upon him, and went so far as to prophesy that upon these quarrels between Turgot and Maurepas hung the fate of over 20,000,000 people. At times he thought that if they would only thrash their differences out and say to each other what they said to him in private, all would go well. Yet what puzzled him most was that Maurepas, of all people, who was famed for his powers as a mediator, should have found Turgot so difficult to manage.[66] The fact was, however, that Maurepas was always, and now more than ever, compelled to employ his art in another quarter.

For towards the end of July he again sensed danger. The magistrates and the Church were in alliance ; the Financiers were uneasy; and there were bewildering intrigues at the Court. Frederick the Great, who kept himself admirably informed of the affairs of Versailles, expressed the fear that Louis might commit some stupid blunder. The *philosophes*, who a little while before had been so sanguine, now expected at any moment to hear of the fall of the Ministry.[67] At first it was the *dévots* who were endeavouring to bring this about, the Choiseulistes for a brief time being unusually inactive. Mercy expressed the fear that Monsieur might become the King's adviser, adding that, although the Queen's interest was at that moment still in the keeping of Maurepas, Malesherbes, and Turgot, her position was nevertheless being prejudiced by the factions at Versailles.[68] To Baron Neny he wrote on 16 August, concluding as follows : ' in short, the Ministers of France are working together in relative harmony. There is little intrigue among them, but on the other hand there is a great deal among the courtiers and this always frustrates the endeavours of the Ministers.' [69] It was probably Monsieur's party which, employing the services of Guimard, one of the servants of the Household, had placed before Louis a pamphlet entitled *Le Roi de ses peuples* declaring that no king could be loved while bread was costly.[70]

Maurepas was quick to realize the need of obtaining the support of Marie-Antoinette and of cementing the alliance that the appointment of Malesherbes to the Household had temporarily broken.[71] There were many favours for which she was asking : she wanted the Government of Languedoc for the Duc de Chartres, although the King had promised the office to another ; she was clamouring for the recall of Tort de la Sonde ; [72] and she wished to reward the Princesse de Lamballe with the office of *surintendante* of her household, a course to which Louis and Turgot in the interests of economy were strongly opposed.[73]   Moreover, much to the uneasiness of Mercy and the Austrian Court, she had made another circle of friends, the Polignacs.   The Comtesse Jules she wanted to make Governess to the royal children; for the uncle she wanted the Embassy in Switzerland; and for the Comte de Polignac a dukedom and the office of *Premier Écuyer*.   Needless to say, the new favourites were the sworn enemies of Turgot, who firmly refused to renounce his plans for economy.   But what was more foreboding was that Baron de Besenval, having spent the summer with Choiseul at Chanteloup, returned to Versailles and was received with open arms in the *salon Polignac*.   It seems that his task was to promote an alliance between the Polignacs and the Choiseulistes, and to attempt once more to reconcile the Queen and Maurepas.[74]

At the beginning of September, Maurepas received a visit from Besenval, who told him that the Queen, while complaining that he had acted contrary to her wishes, was really much attached to him, and that a word or two would put matters right.   It was the Comptroller, whose foolish systems were ruining the country, that displeased her most; and it was to him she really attributed the opposition to her wishes over the choice of the Ministers.   If Maurepas could only see that he was being deceived and that Turgot was gaining for himself all the King's confidence, then it would be an easy matter for him to come to an understanding with the Queen.   Maurepas admitted that it would be advantageous for him, for the King, and for the country if he could act in concert with the Queen.   He had learned too late of the Queen's wishes respecting La Vrillière's successor, and, even had he known earlier, he was not in a position to make them prevail; moreover he had no grudge against the Comptroller-General, who must necessarily have the principal influence in the King's affairs.   But he did believe, and had advised the King accordingly, that the Queen should decide upon domestic details at the Court and should be in a position to grant favours to her friends.   A short while afterwards the Queen herself sent for Maurepas.   At first she showed some resentment, but hardly had she spoken a few words than Louis entered the room, and she turned to the discussion of details concerning her household.   Then she spoke to Louis: she had been mistaken in her opinion of Maurepas; all difficulties had disappeared, and they were now in perfect agreement upon all matters.   Louis was overwhelmed; he kissed the Queen tenderly and shook Maurepas's hand.   The Queen's emissaries were soon following up the opening. They told Maurepas that he ought to call in the Queen to aid the King in his work.   Maurepas was embarrassed; but he replied that if they meant that there were matters in which the Queen was interested, he would certainly be glad to know of them and to give them his consideration. He was soon called upon to keep his promise, and he readily agreed that the Princesse de Lamballe should become *surintendante* of the Queen's household.[75] 'The Comte de Maurepas', wrote Mercy, '. . . . undertook to find and get the King to accept the means by which the wishes of the Princesse de Lamballe might be gratified. The result is that the old Minister is at present very much in favour with the Queen; Her Majesty is equally satisfied with Malesherbes . . . who has entered willingly into these arrangements. There is only the Comptroller-General who may still be treated coldly by the Queen, but I hope that, during the season at Fontainebleau, there will be a way of leading Her Majesty back to the Minister of whose conduct she has nothing to complain and who, on all occasions, has shown her a zealous and respectful attachment.' [76]

To Véri, who had returned from the 'fields' at the end of September, Maurepas pretended that he offered resistance. But Véri was not easily convinced. He accused Maurepas to his face of having prejudiced Turgot's position. Maurepas replied that he had protested, and asked what else he could do but give way when the Queen had said in the presence of the King that the happiness of her life depended upon this matter.[77] Turgot was working under great difficulties. Here was Maurepas, who always hastened to save himself, even though his position was not seriously menaced. Here was Malesherbes, who was always ready to compromise. And here was Louis, who at any moment might give way to the Queen. Writing at the beginning of October, St. Paul believed that Turgot's fall was imminent. For Maurepas had been saying in public that he had been deceived when he advised Louis to call Turgot to the Ministry.[78]

Throughout October the Choiseulistes continued to gain favour with the Queen. Monsieur's party, on the other hand, which was hoping to restore the Jesuits, received a setback, for one of its influential members, Mme de Marsan, was obliged, at the instigation of Marie-Antoinette, to retire without a pension.[79] The Queen was now especially friendly with Princesse de Guéménée, whose *salon* she visited frequently. It was here that she extended her favour to the Duc de Lauzun, the protégé of Mme de Gramont, who had kept in touch with Chanteloup after Choiseul's fall. Lauzun, whose philanderings called forth the stern and puritan censure of Sainte-Beuve as being symptomatic of a degenerate society, who was in turn the lover of Mme de Stainville, of Lady Sarah Bunbury, and of the beautiful and tragic Princess Czartoriska, and who was a seducer of women in almost every country, had been recalled by Vergennes from Warsaw, where he had mingled love and free-lance diplomacy. He had reached Paris in March 1775, and within the space of two months had become a 'sort of favourite', having met the Queen at the *salon Guéménée*. He began to ride daily with Marie-Antoinette, and he unfolded to her his fantastic schemes for a secret treaty between the Queen of France and the Empress of Russia. The corn riots cut short his progress, for, much to the distress of Marie-Antoinette, he was obliged to join his regiment. Returning to Paris in the early autumn, he was soon in favour more than ever, particularly when his horse won the first *Newmarket français*, and he continued to expound his diplomatic extravagances, to which the Queen listened without showing astonishment. The Choiseulistes hoped to profit from Lauzun's favour ; but, if his own story can be believed, this very man who was trying to persuade the Queen to make a treaty with the Empress of Russia, was too deeply attached to her to encourage her to interfere with the Ministers ! Mme de Gramont, to whom he expressed this opinion, was angry, and later joined the Duc de Coigny, the Comtesse Jules de Polignac, and Baron de Besenval in the hope of depriving Lauzun of his favour.[80]

All these happenings gave rise to the opinion that Choiseul would soon return to power. The diplomats again grew anxious when the Duke himself arrived in Paris on 3 October. St. Paul had him watched. When Choiseul postponed his departure, then more than ever it was believed that trouble was brewing ; and, though Louis remained firm in support of his Ministers, it was felt that at any moment he might give way.[81] Such was the position when on 9 October the Court moved to Fontainebleau. The next day Du Muy died a painful and courageous death after an operation for stone lasting thirty-five minutes. This event gave rise to further intrigues. The Choiseulistes, acting through Besenval, who was still in favour, were hoping that Du Muy's successor would be either Castries or the Comte de Guines, both of whom the Queen was thought to favour. But Maurepas forestalled them, for the Queen was still extremely grateful to him for securing office for the Princesse de Lamballe.[82] She kept the Court in ignorance of her understanding with Maurepas, and Besenval, it seems, owed his subsequent fall from favour to his persistence and effrontery on this occasion in pressing the claims of the Choiseulistes.[83] Maurepas, Turgot, and Malesherbes were agreed upon their choice. According to Véri, at the moment when Du Muy died the Ministers had been taking a rest, Turgot being at Tremblay staying with his sister. Hearing the news, he left for Paris to see Maurepas and meeting with him said : ' I have an idea which you will think ridiculous. . . . I thought of Saint-Germain.' ' If your thoughts are ridiculous', replied Maurepas, ' then mine are also, for I was just about to go to Fontainebleau to propose him to the King.' Later Maurepas, Turgot, and Malesherbes met at Fontainebleau. They reflected that none of them really knew the man. Maurepas said that he had a means of judging, and he went to fetch a *mémoire* which Saint-Germain had submitted when he acknowledged his pension.   A perusal of this little treatise upon military economy confirmed what they had heard of him, and it was decided to propose him to the King.[84] According to Besenval, they showed the *mémoire* to the Queen, who, being highly flattered, readily fell in with the arrangement.[85]

In his youth a Jesuit, Saint-Germain deserted the Order to enter the French army.   During his career he saw service under many flags : he served in the Palatinate, the Austrian and the Bavarian armies ; and he had acquired a great reputation, above all upon the field of Rosbach.   Later, he returned to France, but Broglie and Belle-Isle engineered his resignation, and the end of his military service was spent in Denmark, where he reformed the Danish army. This task done, he retired to Alsace to live ' upon a small pension in an obscure retreat in which he probably expected to end his days '. The Abbé Dubois, who went to Alsace to summon him to Fontainebleau, found the new Cincinnatus pruning the trees in his garden ; he ' had neither wardrobe nor carriage ' ; [86] and when he arrived at Fontainebleau he could obtain only a miserable room, all the rest having been taken by the sightseers who came to watch his arrival.[87]   It was Turgot who received him and presented him to Louis and the Queen, and some say he took the opportunity of arranging for a preliminary examination of the finances of the War Office and some measure of control for the future.[88]

Turgot now hoped to reform, in collaboration with Malesherbes and Saint-Germain, both the Civil and the Military Households. But difficulties arose.   Malesherbes made little headway ;   he loathed his work ;   and whereas formerly he had looked forward to his daily tasks, now he could hardly drag himself from his bed to face hours of discussion of endless details with which his philosophic mind was bored.   When the *ordonnateurs* presented to him their accounts, he was bewildered and, much to the delight of Maurepas, contended that nothing could be done.[89]   It was left for Turgot alone to take a stand against continued waste of public money, and in doing this he incurred the hatred of the Court.   Six hundred *louis* went to pay the Comte d'Esterhazy's debts, and a widow's pension was given to the Comtesse de Lamarche, who was separated from her husband.   The Comtesse de Polignac received a pension that Turgot had opposed ; she thanked him for his kindness and, when he replied that the favour was not his doing, Marie-Antoinette composed a scathing reply.   The same thing happened again when yet another pension was awarded to Mme d'Andau, the aunt of Jules de Polignac.[90]

Saint-Germain, on the other hand, promised to be more energetic. ' He appears indeed ', wrote Stormont, ' to be a man who has the good of the service much at heart. . . . His great aim is to abolish

. . . the *corps privilégiés* . . . and to put the whole army upon a
footing of equality, as it is in the Prussian and still more in the
Austrian Service.' What, moreover, he hoped to do was to raise
40,000 additional troops without increasing costs. He proposed to
abolish almost entirely the *maison militaire*, which was an expensive
and really useless force ; he hoped to reduce by one-quarter the
Guards and the *Suisses* ; and he planned to retain only a sufficiency
of *gendarmes* and cavalry for the purpose of parades.[91] Turgot
was anxious to collaborate with him in effecting further reforms.
In two *mémoires* to Saint-Germain [92] he proposed the establishment
of fixed garrisons, improved methods of provisioning, a reform of
the fortresses, the reorganization of the military school, and
economies upon the offices of military governors of the provinces.
He also encouraged Parmentier to improve the soldiers' food at the
Invalides ; he arranged matters so that the purchase of army
supplies should not impede free trade in grain ; he freed buildings
leased to the army from the *droit d'amortissement* ; and he mitigated
the punishments for desertion. Had Turgot's and Saint-Germain's
co-operation continued, much might have been achieved, in spite
of the opposition that was aroused. But Saint-Germain came to
oppose Turgot's interference in army finance ; above all, he resented
the searching criticism to which his budget for 1776 was subjected ;
and he ended by asserting the independence of his department.[93]
Turgot appealed to Maurepas ; but Maurepas looked on and,
welcoming the quarrel between them, did much to foment it.
Whether the fault lay in Turgot's domineering habits or in Saint-
Germain's growing pride, it is impossible to say ; but the fact
remains that together they played into Maurepas's hand and greatly
prejudiced the cause of reform. Their real interests were identical :
they both required the support of the King against the vested
interests at the Court, they both should have fortified Malesherbes's
waning courage, and they ought to have taken together a decided
line with Maurepas. They did separately what they should have
done in concert. Saint-Germain, for instance, was telling Louis
exactly what Turgot had been saying always : that economies would
become impossible unless His Majesty ' shut his ears to all solicita-
tions, how pressing, how respectable soever '. Saint-Germain
had no easy task. As Stormont put it, ' he continues to meet with
many obstacles, and has already his full share of that indiscriminate
censure which is so liberally bestowed upon all those who sacrifice
the interests of individuals to plans of general utility.' Foremost
among his opponents were Monsieur and Marie-Antoinette. The
Queen, while willing to see d'Aiguillon's light cavalry reduced,
was set against the reduction of regiments in which her friends held
office. Maurepas, on the other hand, persuaded the King not to
curtail drastically his nephew's regiment.[94] When charged by

Véri with being responsible for frustrating the army reforms, Maurepas feebly blamed Louis, and, when pressed further, could provide no satisfactory answer to the accusation.[95]

Saint-Germain's reforms increased the unpopularity of a Ministry which was now a house divided against itself. The Court intrigues continued and, perhaps, it was only a question of time for them to produce some effect. Monsieur's party resumed its activities. Monsieur, himself, presented to Louis one Cromot, *surintendant* of his own household and formerly an official in the *contrôle général*, who was said to have plans for improving the finances and for mitigating the burden of taxation.[96] The Choiseulistes, too, despite occasional setbacks, continued their efforts to win the Queen. At the end of the year Besenval had fallen completely from favour. Lauzun, too, was losing his privileged position. For with this would-be Potemkin, Marie-Antoinette was bored; and she was now heart and soul for the Polignacs and for Mme de Gramont, who, according to design, had caught the Queen's fancy by bringing another young courtier, the ambitious Duc de Coigny, to her notice. These were now the Choiseuliste vanguard, whose activities disturbed the peace of mind of Maurepas and also that of the English diplomats. For Choiseul, himself, was loudly criticizing the Government's inactive foreign policy. England's difficulties in America had presented a vital diplomatic problem for France to solve. There were some who hoped, but hardly expected, that the colonies would be forced into submission, for they feared that otherwise England might be prompted to make good her losses by seizing part of the French colonial empire, which, owing to the disastrous state of the finances and the decline of the navy, could not be adequately protected. But there were others who saw an opportunity for a war of revenge. This was Choiseul's plan. 'The sentiments of the Duke of Choiseul and consequently of his party', wrote Stormont, 'are indeed well known. He says openly . . . that the Ministers are idiots for missing this golden opportunity.'[97]

Such, then, was the position at the end of 1775 within the Court and the Ministry. Outside, among the vested interests at large, the cries of an opposition were growing still louder, adding force and authority to that form of public opinion which trickled in insidious whispers to the King. Numerous libels made their appearance. One, called *La Seconde lettre de M. l'Abbé Terray à M. Turgot*, a scurrilous composition and a tissue of lies, attributed to Turgot the increased cost of bread. Another, entitled *Lettre d'un profane à M. l'Abbé Baudeau, très vénérable de la scientifique et sublime loge de la Franche Économie*, and composed by a lawyer named Blondel, singled out Vaines for attack, portraying him as a scoundrel who abused Turgot's confidence. Turgot, who usually took no action against libels against himself, showed his contempt for the author by persuading the King to bestow the office of *lecteur de la chambre* upon Vaines and by giving publicity to a letter which he wrote to his subordinate. 'You have no need for justification,' he said, 'but having seen that the author and those who are voicing this libel imagine they can prevail upon me to credit their accusations by sending me a multitude of anonymous letters, I owe it to myself to show authentically my disdain for their atrocious calumnies. . . . We must say to ourselves what the King said to me the day of the riot at Versailles : " We ourselves have a good conscience ; and in this we are very strong." ' [98]   Vaines was not left long in peace ; in November a second libel made its appearance, and Vaines had Blondel sent to the Bastille.   That same month numerous other scurrilous attacks were made upon Turgot's administration.[99] Very few of these libels made any pretence to criticize specific measures, except perhaps those which denounced the reform of the *messageries*.[100]   The more usual method was to present him as a visionary who would ruin the State rather than relinquish one single idea. 'What a nation !' says Métra. 'Even the men least interested in maintaining abuses echo the accusations of these scoundrels, and the unhappy honest men are too few in number to lift their voices and to make themselves heard in a nation which is lighthearted and which mixes inconsequence and unreasonableness in its pleasures, its projects, and its government.'[101]

But Turgot's partisans were certainly not idle at this time when freedom of the Press and freedom of speech were greater perhaps than at any time during the *ancien régime*.   Boncerf had already published his *Inconvenients des droits féodaux*.   Condorcet (and not Voltaire as was supposed) had written his *Lettre d'un laboureur de Picardie à M. Necker, prohibitif* and also a pamphlet *Sur l'abolition des corvées*.   Moreover, in the *Gazette de l'agriculture* edited by Abbé Roubaud and also in the *Nouvelles Éphémérides* numerous articles were published in support of Turgot's measures.   But all these writings played into the hands of opponents, for in their enthusiasm the authors often announced reforms which were certainly not in preparation.   A glance at the table of contents of any issue of Baudeau's publication will illustrate the point.   Turgot endeavoured upon numerous occasions to hold back the eager journalists, but usually the harm had been done before their publications came to his notice ; and he, who believed in freedom, could not honestly have censored these writings before they were published.   Mercy, writing on 17 December, remarks : 'The great changes which are being prepared in the administration of the State give much anger to those who have an interest in maintaining abuses ; this fermentation excites much scandalous licence in conversation and in writings.'[102]   The storm was gathering.   The vested interests were preparing to resist Turgot's famous Six Edicts.

CHAPTER XV

THE SIX EDICTS

(1)

On 8 November 1775 Stormont sent to Rochford a most interesting dispatch, having taken great pains while with the Court at Fontainebleau to ascertain the political situation. He had undoubtedly heard from every one he met that the Comptroller was a rigid, dictatorial, and speculative man. He himself was not disposed to sympathize with ' systematic visionaries ' ; yet his sound commonsense compelled him to admit that Turgot's proposed reforms were most laudable projects, although he believed the chances were that they would be frustrated by the vested interests ; and it was with rare insight that he went on to describe the obstacles that confronted Turgot and to indicate the means by which his opponents would attempt to remove him. ' He certainly stands upon slippery ground and has powerful enemies to contend with. These enemies derive no small advantage from the opinion the public has that the Queen is by no means favourable to him ; from the difficulties that must always attend such changes as he wishes to introduce, and from such general prejudices conceived against him, which he is not sufficiently solicitous to remove. . . . He is an absolute novice in all court intrigues, is by no means calculated to form an interest there or extend his connections beyond a few select friends. He has a coldness of manner which is naturally construed into haughtiness by those who are not particularly acquainted with him. He does not know how to soften or qualify a refusal, and is, besides, not only very tenacious of his opinions, but impatient of the least contradiction. . . . All this, my Lord, joined to the opposition that every attempt to correct inveterate abuses and rapine must meet with from those who live by plunder and have so strong an interest to defend their spoils, must throw numberless obstacles in his way. But his greatest danger, in my opinion, is the disposition of the Parliament of Paris and the keen opposition he will certainly meet with from that quarter. They are, I am told, determined to remonstrate strongly against the edict for suppressing the *corvées*. . . . They will ground their remonstrances chiefly upon two points

231

—the injustice of laying part of the tax of twelve millions, which is to be substituted in the place of the *corvées*, upon the gentlemen of the country who were not subject to the former burden.[1] This argument, tho' I hear great stress will be laid upon it, is specious at most, as there can be nothing so clear as that good roads are a general benefit of which men of property have their full share. The next ground of opposition is the danger of this tax being diverted hereafter to a different purpose from that which it was given. . . . There is another project of Mr de Turgot which the Parliament will likewise oppose when it comes before them. This project, which is not yet quite ripe for execution, is to abolish all the *corps de métiers* throughout the kingdom and to have all trades quite free as they are in our towns as have no corporations. The flourishing state of these towns is no bad argument for the general wisdom of such a plan, but still, my Lord, as it thwarts the interests of so many individuals, it will necessarily create great murmurings and, as I am assured, be strongly opposed by the Parliament, who, like all bodies of men, have leaning in favour of old establishments and who have, besides, a personal interest in supporting the *communautés*, which find them such constant employment and open so large a field for chicane. . . . It is very probable that Mr de Turgot's enemies will take a handle from this opposition of the Parliament to alarm the French King with an apprehension of a return of all these contests which disturbed the last reign, and which his present Majesty made such sacrifices to remove. Much will depend upon Mr de Maurepas's conduct. If he warmly supports the Controller, the King will, I think, be steady ; but it is very possible that Mr de Maurepas, who wishes to avoid everything that tends to clog the wheels of government, may abandon Mr Turgot in the struggle. He has that same love for the public good that the Controller has, but he has not the same stiffness of opinion, nor the same warmth of zeal. This natural character, joined to long experience, makes him afraid of innovations, studious to avoid all violent struggles, and contented to drive the nail that will go with ease, to lessen the abuses that he cannot reform, and to apply palliatives to evils of which he thinks it too hazardous to attempt a radical cure.' [2]

The two projected measures of which Stormont was speaking were the major items of a programme of reform which later became known as the Six Edicts. These measures, owing to their nature, had been long in preparation, and they had been noisily announced and impatiently awaited by Turgot's radical following. What is frequently forgotten is that they were not the result of haste upon Turgot's part, but the result of his decision, in view of the lack of support from Maurepas and Malesherbes, to move more slowly and, while the King was still young and really incapable of thinking for himself, to renounce more radical and difficult measures. This resolution earned for him the greatest praise from Véri, who had always advised him to take in hand immediately a short programme of reform so that he might proclaim to the world his true value as an administrator and impress upon Louis his worth as a minister. Indeed, Véri later ventured the opinion that the suppression of the *corvées* could easily have been accomplished twelve months earlier.[3] Turgot's well-known words, ' In my family we die at fifty ', are misleading if taken out of their context.   He was not suggesting a reckless speeding-up before he died, but was flippantly answering Malesherbes, who had made the preposterous and defeatist suggestion that, in view of the opposition of the magistrates, the execution of the Six Edicts should be spread over a period of several years.[4]

Although for a long while Turgot had discussed his projects with the King, it was not until January 1776 that the Edicts were submitted at intervals to the Council, where they were debated in Louis's presence.   Anticipating the numerous objections that the Ministers and others round the King would raise, and fearing that every effort would be made to misrepresent his proposals, he took the wise precaution of composing for Louis a *mémoire* [5] outlining their scope and explaining in simple language their necessity and justification.   He was following his wonted method and, indeed, the only one that was possible, for again it was a question of appealing to the King in the name of humanity and of justice, of overcoming his timidity, of making him resolute, and of counteracting the intrigues and insinuations of other advisers.

(2)

One of the Six Edicts,[6] in the form of a Declaration dated 5 February, suppressed all dues levied upon grain, cereals, and pulses in Paris with the exception of a number of relatively trivial impositions upon inferior grains, which were left as perquisites for the porters and measurers.   Earlier legislation, as we have seen, had not applied to Paris, the letters patent of 2 November 1774 having merely reserved to the King the right to declare the grain trade free in this city when circumstances permitted.   The surviving restrictions upon commerce in grain and flour in Paris and its environs detracted from the freedom accorded elsewhere. For one thing, Paris was the centre of the road-system of the kingdom, and also of the waterways formed by the rivers, Seine, Yonne, Marne, Oise, and Loire and the canals of Briare and Orleans ; for another, the grain merchants had tended to transfer their capital and their activities to the free towns of Rouen, Bordeaux, and Lyon, with the result that prices in Paris were always a little above the average, even in times of general abundance.   Again, the governmental purchases of corn for

Paris, which had necessarily to be continued to supplement the dwindling supplies brought in by the merchants, continued to cause outcries in the provinces, for sometimes the traders employed by the officials bought at high prices in districts where a shortage prevailed. These were Turgot's economic reasons for completing the legislation establishing free commerce in grain. But he had also a political motive, which he stressed in his *mémoire* to the King ; he wished to take away the opportunity for the magistrates to make ' a parade of their paternal solicitude and to pose as the protectors of the people in searching the houses of masters and merchants '.[7]

Another edict was complementary to the Declaration of 5 February. It suppressed a multiplicity of officials of the ports, quays, halls, and markets of Paris, many of whom were notoriously corrupt. On several occasions these office-holders had been deprived of their benefices, only to be reinstated a short while afterwards, the Government as usual making a little profit in employing this habitual fiscal expedient. The offices in question had been abolished once again in 1759, but had been restored provisionally the next year until the holders could be compensated. Turgot's edict really executes that of 1759 which had fixed the indemnity. In doing this it provides that taxes formerly levied by these officials should in future be collected by the *ferme général*, the proceeds being devoted to the compensation of those who had lost their employments. Turgot thus arranged matters so that this particular reform occasioned no loss to the Treasury. The other measure, however—that suppressing the dues on grain —meant a diminution in revenue of 52,000 *livres* annually ; but this deficit he had already made good as a result of the reform of the levy of impositions in Paris.[8]

A third edict abolished the *Caisse de Poissy*. This institution, purporting to facilitate the cattle and the meat trade, was really nothing more than a means of levying an imposition, very little of which found its way to the Treasury. Originally established in 1690, and re-established in 1707 to meet the rising expenses of the War of the Spanish Succession, suppressed again after the Peace of Utrecht, and finally restored in 1743, the *Caisse de Poissy* was supposed to advance money to the butchers to enable them to pay the dealers, and the dealers in turn to pay the farmers, who normally were compelled to wait a long time for their money. But all that the financiers of the *Caisse* did in practice was to advance money to the wealthier butchers who had no need for credit and, in doing this, to levy a commission which increased the price of each beast by 15 *livres*. Upon all advances they received a profit of 92 per cent. per year, their total earnings (there were 100 of them) being 1,500,000 *livres* annually.[9] There was really no justification for the *Caisse* : numerous petitions had

denounced it, and very few people had the effrontery to defend
it.[10]   Turgot himself had heard it universally condemned by the
farmers of Limousin, by the butchers in Paris, and most loudly
of all by the consumers.   Consequently this institution was a
vested interest sufficiently isolated as to be easy to attack.   The
difficulty was that if the owners were to be compensated its suppression promised to be exceedingly costly.   To make good the
loss to the Treasury, Turgot was compelled to increase other
dues which were levied on cattle and on meat, a new scale of
charges being incorporated in the Edict; but he was hopeful
that his reform would lead to increased consumption and that,
as a consequence, he would be able in the near future to diminish
these taxes.[11]

The suppression of the *Caisse de Poissy* was at once a small
instalment of free trade and an economy in the collection of
taxation.   And this is true again of the last of the lesser Edicts
which, issued in the form of letters patent, reorganized the
administration of impositions upon suet.   These, dating from
the sixteenth century, were heavy in themselves and onerous in
the method of collection, the Guild of Chandlers, a body which
had the right to buy all suet produced by the butchers, being
entrusted with the levy in return for an annual contribution to
the Treasury.   If, however, Turgot succeeded in abolishing the
guilds, then the impositions upon suet could no longer be levied
in this way.   He would, of course, have liked to forfeit altogether
the sums accruing from this source; but again the Treasury
was not in a position to stand the loss of revenue.   Therefore he
imposed a small additional tax upon live cattle which could be
levied economically along with the existing levies.   At the same
time he reduced the heavy duty upon suet brought in from outside
Paris from 7 *livres* 13 *sous* to 50 *sous* the quintal, the former rate
being prohibitive, and therefore unproductive of revenue.[12]

Such were the four lesser Edicts.   They were relatively trivial
measures designed to reduce slightly the cost of living for the
wage-earners in Paris, to promote a little more the freedom of
trade, and, in doing these things, to provide, if all went well, a
small gain to the Treasury.   Substantially of the same nature as
numerous other reforms for which Turgot was responsible, they
were not in any way an outrageous attack upon property.   For
all the owners of offices concerned were adequately compensated,
and the lesser financiers received much more lenient treatment than
they might have expected, for example, from the Abbé Terray.

(3)

'Your Majesty', wrote Turgot in 1776, 'has known for a long
while my thoughts concerning the guilds. . . .'   Already he had

attacked restrictions upon labour, and also the monopolies enjoyed by the commercial and industrial communities. In November 1774 he had freed the citizens of twenty-three imperial towns from the *droit d'aubaine*, under which the property of certain deceased aliens escheated either to the Crown or to the seigneur. For he believed that this archaic survival ' debarred from settling in France a great number of skilled men, industrious artisans, capitalists, and useful merchants who desired nothing more than to make France the centre of their activities '.[13] Again, in February 1775 he had refused the request of the Master Cutlers of Rheims that the administration should curtail, in the interest of good workmanship, its issue of licences to artisans outside the communities; he had told the guildsmen on this occasion that the public was quite capable of protecting itself from any attempt of the free artisans to foist upon it inferior goods. In the following June, with a view to encouraging the discovery and adoption of technical improvements, he freed the trade of steel-polishing entirely from the control of the guilds. Of much wider scope was the instruction which he dispatched to the inspectors of manufacturers in April 1775. ' Nothing is more urgent ', he wrote, ' than to provide for the protection of the labouring classes. . . . You are not to seize any material or merchandise belonging to them on the pretext of its faultiness. You are to confine yourselves to exhorting these poor artificers to make better articles and to telling them the way to do so.' This instruction produced some effect; at least it called forth a vigorous protest from the Six Companies of Paris. In other ways, too, he reduced the guild monopolies. On numerous occasions he caused disputes between the guildsmen and interlopers to be settled to the disadvantage of the masters, and he frequently remitted the penalties that were imposed upon ' free-traders '. He granted licences freely to non-guildsmen, and forbade the industrial communities to take legal action against any individual without first obtaining the permission of the intendants, to whom also he had sent his instruction of April 1775.[14]

Towards the end of June 1775 he persuaded Louis to establish a commission, ostensibly to hear the complaints submitted by the *six corps des marchands*, but more particularly to consider the answers he himself had composed refuting the demands for industrial restrictions.[15] About the same time, in collaboration with Albert, he began the long and tedious task of drawing up his case against the guilds and of arranging the details of the Edict for their suppression. Albert summarized his findings in a *mémoire*, and it was this work that Turgot recommended to Louis in his own condemnation of the guilds.[16] That the choice of an assistant should have fallen upon Albert is not at all surprising: he had a thorough knowledge of industrial matters, acquired when holding office as intendant of commerce; and now that he was in charge of the police, it would fall upon him to execute the projected Edict. Nor is it surprising that Turgot took possession of a sum of 800,000 *livres* lying in the coffers of the guilds; for it was not his intention that these assets should vanish when the real attack began.[17]

By the beginning of 1776 he had completed his case. His *mémoire* to the King and his preamble to the Edict discuss the industrial communities from every point of view. First, he examines with great powers of analysis the place of the guilds in mediaeval economy, and with even greater insight the legislation of 1581, 1597, and 1673 by which the State, in order to increase momentarily its revenue, had sold a multiplicity of monopolist rights, thus giving a new lease of life to archaic institutions. Then, bringing to bear upon the subject his own economic doctrines, he denounces the tyranny of monopolies and exposes their ill effects upon the industrial life of the nation. He singles out for special condemnation the masterpiece which, along with other exactions levied to prevent the poorer artisans from setting up as masters, gave rise to a stream of emigrants taking their skill and their capital to other kingdoms. France could hardly afford to lose so many of her enterprising subjects. Rather than drive her artificers to seek employment in other countries, France ought to make every effort to retain them, and at the same time to attract industrial skill and capital from outside her frontiers. For this last policy the moment was singularly opportune; in England there were hundreds of textile workers who had lost employment owing to the cessation of commerce between the mother country and the American colonies, and these idle artificers might be induced to settle in France.

There were other pressing reasons for abolishing the guilds. In the first place, the majority of them were saddled with debts, some the result of loans raised to meet the demands of the Treasury, and others the outcome of ill-managed corporate transactions. Fortunately the communities in Paris possessed sufficient assets to meet their liabilities, but outside Paris the situation was not such a happy one, and, as Turgot told the King, a thorough examination of the finances of the provincial guilds must be made before the Treasury could take over responsibility without incurring heavy losses. In the second place, the guilds increased the price of food. In times of normal grain prices, for example, the people of Paris ought to have been able to buy bread at 2 *sous* 2 *deniers* the *livre*: as it was they were called upon to pay 2 *sous* 9 *deniers*, or well over 10 per cent. too much. Finally, the guilds were constantly involved in litigation, and this not only conduced indirectly to high prices, but also involved numerous individuals outside the communities in heavy and ruinous legal costs. In this particular abuse one vested interest was linked with another; as Turgot warned the King, the *gens du palais* were sure to defend those institutions that provided them with steady employment and a lucrative reward; [18] and, as usual, they would aver that they were protecting the masses, this time from the sharp practice of traders and merchants, who, if left uncontrolled, would flood the markets with inferior commodities at outrageous prices. Such arguments Turgot thought it advisable to answer in advance. Above all, he wanted Louis to realize that the most flourishing industry was to be found in the faubourgs and in the countryside where the guild régime had never existed.[19] ' Liberty ', he explained in the preamble, ' has never produced . . . ill effects in those places where it has been established for a long while. The workers in the faubourgs and in other fortunate places do not work less well than those living in Paris. All the world knows that the police system of the *jurandes* purporting to ensure competent work is entirely illusory. . . .' Such, in brief, was his arraignment of the guilds. ' I regard the destruction of the *jurandes*, Sire,' he wrote in his *mémoire*, ' . . . as one of the greatest benefits that you can bestow upon your people; after liberty of commerce in grain it is one of the best moves that the administration may make towards . . . the regeneration of the kingdom. This second measure will be for industry what the first will be for agriculture.' [20]

The Edict itself contains twenty-three clauses. The first declares that all subjects and foreigners residing in the kingdom shall be free to follow any trade or trades. Of the remainder, a number provide for the suppression of the guilds of Paris, and others for various limitations to the scope of the Edict. These last make it clear that Turgot had no desire to establish an entirely unregulated and anarchical freedom of trade. All merchants and artisans were to register their occupations with the police, and all employers were to keep a record of their servants. The pharmacists, goldsmiths, printers, and booksellers were exempted from the provisions of the Edict, the intention being to reform in the future rather than to abolish immediately a number of regulations which were, in principle at least, essential to the safety of the public and the State, and which must necessarily be considered in relation to the laws governing the sale of drugs, the currency, and freedom of speech.[21] Again, the barbers and wigmakers were also exempted from the Edict because, holding what was really a kind of office, they must be compensated at a cost which at the time the Treasury could not meet. Another clause was a wise precaution: the bakers and butchers were prohibited for one whole year, upon pain of forfeit of 500 *livres*, from changing or abandoning their trades.

Further provisions of the Edict concerned new duties devolving upon the police—the hearing of law proceedings still in progress, the liquidation of the finances of the guilds of Paris, the transfer of charitable endowments to the Church, and the provision of machinery to deal with breaches of commercial contracts. All these measures deserve a passing mention because they show how thoroughly the reform was planned.[22] Clause xiv requires fuller comment. ' It is similarly forbidden ', so it runs, ' to all masters, journeymen, workmen, and apprentices of the aforesaid guilds and companies to form any association among themselves under any pretext whatsoever.' These words have frequently been misunderstood, it being contended that Turgot's motive was to prevent the rise of industrial combinations. Nothing was further from his mind. His real motive was to prevent the re-establishment of the guilds under different forms. He was legislating not for the nineteenth century, but for the times that he knew. In clause x he provides for unions of merchants and artisans composed not according to trades, but to districts ; and these bodies, it would seem, were to be administrative assemblies for facilitating the work of government in industrial affairs.[23]

(4)

Of all Turgot's reforms, the most eagerly awaited was that suppressing the *corvées*. ' The provinces ', Condorcet wrote to him as early as September 1774, ' are expecting the same good work that you accomplished at Limoges.' [24] Less than one month later Turgot was studying the ways and means of such a measure.[25] In collaboration with the younger Trudaine, who was eager to assist, he was investigating the numerous *mémoires* which Daniel Trudaine had collected for submission to the Abbé Terray.[26] By December he was ready to raise the question in the Council, and Louis, on being shown the information that had been collected, was quick to feel the grave injustice of the *corvées*.[27] Probably this was the occasion when he presented to the King the memorandum to which he refers in 1776. ' When I had the honour more than a year ago to read to Your Majesty a first *mémoire* on the suppression of the *corvées*, your heart seemed to decide the matter immediately. Your resolution soon became common knowledge ; the provinces came to hear of it ; and from that moment it became impossible not to abolish this imposition.' But the only decision taken in the Council was that of asking the intendants for their opinions.[28] In the following February Turgot drafted a circular to these officials, yet, for some unknown reason, it was never dispatched.[29] In all probability he thought it advisable to wait until he was ready to place before them a scheme for discussion. This was not done until the end of July. But by that time, actually on 6 May, during the days of the corn riots, he suspended the *corvées* temporarily throughout the kingdom, instructed the intendants to concentrate only upon the upkeep of the roads, and for this purpose established, as we have seen, the *ateliers de charité*.[30] Needless to say, these measures were much criticized at the time, and it was later contended that he had allowed the road administration to fall into utter confusion.[31] But from that time onward it was perfectly obvious that reform could no longer be delayed, and it seems likely—though there is no document to bear out the contention—that his real motive in summarily suspending the *corvées* was to put an end to the dilatory tactics of his fellow-Ministers.

His projected reform of July 1775 was based upon three general principles : first, the intendants, in consultation with the engineers, were to compose annual budgets for public works in the *généralités*, and these, having been sanctioned by the Council, were to be registered in the *Cours des aides* ; secondly, the sums thus approved were to be levied on all landowners, no matter what their status, in proportion to their incomes ; finally, all such taxation was under no circumstances to be paid to the Treasury, but was to remain in the hands of the local officials of the *ponts et chaussées*. In this way Turgot hoped to obviate the danger that an imposition to replace the *corvées* might be diverted to other needs.[32] The project in general was approved by the intendants, several of whom had interesting comments to make. Corée of Franche-Comté and Fontette of Caen, while favouring the measure for the regions where the unreformed *corvées* prevailed, preferred the systems they had introduced themselves. Journet of Auch feared that the imposition might prove unjust, but only for the reason that the *cadastre* in his *généralité* was highly defective. A number of replies expressed the fear that the privileged classes, with the connivance of the *Cours des aides*, might quickly gain exemptions from the tax, with the result that a heavy burden would fall upon the *taillables*. Calonne of Metz and Esmangard of Bordeaux went so far as to suggest that the *Cours des aides* should not be given cognizance of the imposition, which should be levied solely upon the royal authority.[33]

Not until the replies from the intendants had been received was it possible to draft the actual Edict. At a later stage each separate detail gave rise to interminable discussions between Turgot, the Ministers, Trudaine, and the officials of the *ponts et chaussées*. At one time Turgot was occupied in devising an alternative scheme to avoid the registration of the road tax in the *Cours des aides*, for he had always been appreciative of the difficulty that the intendants had raised. Then, again, Trudaine firmly contended that the real problem of preventing the misappropriation of funds had not been solved, and he was ever pointing out that the imposition would assume a proportion considerably higher than Turgot was prepared to admit.[34] It would be interesting to know more of the wranglings which went on during the early winter of 1775, and even more interesting to know why Turgot took so much trouble to argue each detail with Trudaine. For this he certainly did, and the usual charge against him that he always brushed aside objections raised by his colleagues cannot possibly be substantiated in this instance. As far as one can gather, Trudaine voiced the official opinion of the *ponts et chaussées*, which was certainly hostile ; and Turgot, it seems, was not altogether happy in ignoring the prejudices of the departmental experts, for he was fully aware that in Council the Ministers would make much of official opinion in their constant endeavours to frustrate his plans. Every delay made Turgot's path more difficult ; the opposition from the Court and the magistracy was growing daily, and the Ministers and officials, taking alarm, became more determined than ever to oppose the Edict. Trudaine, for all his liberal opinions, was extraordinarily sensitive to the rumours and calumnies that reached his ears. One moment he was ready to go forward ; another he was all for drawing back. After a conversation with Malesherbes's cousin, Lamoignon, who probably told him that the magistrates would give way in the long run, he wanted to draft the Edict without delay, and was greatly disappointed upon learning that Turgot's sciatica meant postponing this work for another day. But a little later, hearing at the house of Fleury, another magistrate, that Conti would lead the opposition to the Edict, he lost his nerve. Fleury had told him that ' it was precisely the despotic system of Constantinople that protected the people against the aristocracy ', and all that Trudaine could say in reply was that, being himself a civil servant, he could only ' wait patiently for some one to provide the money with which to work '. ' It is always important ', he wrote to Turgot telling him of this conversation, ' to know with whom one has to deal.' Later still, however, after the Edict had been placed before the Council, he was most eager to expedite its execution, and in reply to Malesherbes's suggestion for modifying it, he composed one of the most eloquent pleas for enlightened despotism ever written.[35]

It was on 6 January that Turgot presented the Edict to the King, who immediately gave it his approval.[36] The preamble contains a summary of all his earlier writings denouncing the inveterate abuses and injustice of the *corvées*. It goes on to draw attention to the success of reforms inaugurated by a number of

the intendants. Then, answering in advance all those who might
repeat the objections raised by Trudaine, it carefully explains
that funds were to remain within the provinces, that all accounts
were to be audited by the *bureaux des finances* and *chambres des
comptes*, and that the imposition to be levied upon the *pays
d'élections* was under no circumstances to exceed 10,000,000 *livres*.
Finally—and this is true also of the accompanying *mémoire* submitted to the King—the preamble contains a thorough condemnation of privilege in general, as being destructive not only of
justice, but also of the fundamental principles of political economy.
It was the landowners who derived the material benefits from good
roads, and therefore it was they, and they alone, who ought to
advance the capital required.[37]

(5)

Throughout the remainder of January the Six Edicts were
debated in a committee of the Council, and, although the detailed
provisions do not seem to have been known to the public until
the second week in February,[38] the general principles aroused
considerable discussion throughout the kingdom. The magistrates began their offensive before receiving the texts for official
registration ; they took no trouble to ascertain the scope of the
Edicts ; and even when finally they were given this knowledge,
they simply ignored it, preferring to misrepresent the measures
and the ideas of the man responsible for them.[39] Although it
was the Edict abolishing the guilds that more than any other
infringed their professional interests, they concentrated their
attack upon the legislation suppressing the *corvées*, for the simple
reason that they could enlist the support of the clergy and the
nobility. Both Malesherbes and Véri frequently warned Turgot
of the danger he was running. Yet neither of these sympathizers
went so far as to advise him to withdraw. Véri, in fact, gave
him constant encouragement, endeavouring at the same time to
convince Maurepas of the necessity of a firm policy at this juncture
in the interests of the royal authority.[40]

Turgot first tried to reason with the Parlement. Early in
January he arranged an interview with d'Aligre, the premier
president, hoping to convince him of the utility and justice of
the Edicts. D'Aligre was unbending ; a warm conversation
ensued, ending with the threat of unflinching opposition on the
one side and of the determination to prevail upon Louis to hold
a *lit de justice* upon the other.[41] For Turgot to have given way
would have meant an end to all reform. Then again, as a King's
Minister he considered it his duty to uphold the monarchical
prerogative against the attacks of the Magistracy ; for, from the
very beginning, it was not exclusively a question of his Edicts,

but of the nature of sovereignty.   That was a point which
Maurepas failed to grasp firmly.   While on the one hand he knew
that it was expected of him to promote Louis's authority, yet on
the other he was prone to listen too carefully to those who were
for ever telling him that he was the one to protect the throne from
the wild designs of visionary reformers.

It was Conti who came forward to lead the magisterial opposition.   Standing to lose 50,000 *livres* annually if the guilds were
abolished, and welcoming always any opportunity to weaken the
royal power, he adopted an uncompromising attitude.   On
29 January, paying no heed to ' the signs of death that could be
read upon his face ', and braving the bitter cold that prevailed,
he took his place in the Parlement to arouse the magistrates
against a pamphlet on the *corvées* written by Condorcet.   This
particular work, *Bénissons le ministre* . . ., had been published by
Laharpe in the *Mercure*.   Like Voltaire's *Diatribe*, it was most
inopportune,[42] and Turgot had taken some pains to prevent its
circulation.   A few of the magistrates were for ignoring it,
and among them Seguier ; but the majority condemned it as a
seditious libel, and some were for having it publicly burned by
the common hangman.   The debate displayed clearly the temper
of the Parlement.   ' Mr. de Turgot ', reports Stormont, ' was
more than once reflected upon by name, and ranked among those
innovators who in a wild enthusiasm for their own chimerical
opinions would beat down every barrier, and to whom no property
is sacred.'   It was d'Esprémesnil, a young, headstrong, and
excitable magistrate, who proposed the vote of censure and who
gained a passing fame in denouncing the economists as ' an
absurd, fanatical, dangerous sect, the more dangerous as they
now had one of the King's Ministers at their head '.   He compared
them to the Jesuits, and held up Necker for admiration as an
orthodox economist.   Conti expressed his agreement with these
opinions, and before leaving asked to be informed when the Edicts
were to be laid before the Parlement, adding that if he were unable
to come in his carriage, he would be brought on a litter.[43]

The magistrates had been encouraged by the knowledge that
matters were not moving smoothly in the committee of the
Council.   It was Miromesnil, *normand et rusé*, who was at once
their informer, their accessary, and yet to some extent their
instrument.   A man of little talent and of little mind, and by
nature a petty Machiavellian, he became in spite of his mediocrities
the mouthpiece of the privileged classes.   Mistaking in the first
instance the feebleness of Maurepas and of the other Ministers
for a spirited opposition to Turgot's Edicts, oblivious of the
real issues at stake, and having his own magisterial reputation to
regain, he did everything to encourage the opposition of the

Parlements. Here was a vicious circle: Maurepas and the
Ministers grew ever more alarmed, and Miromesnil ever more
convinced that he was acting for the best. The Ministers hardly
knew which way to turn. They resented the attack that Turgot's
measures had brought upon the Government, and yet were
delighted to see him in difficulties ; and though on the one hand
they were reluctant to give him the firm support that might have
gone far to silencing the magistrates, on the other their position
compelled them to show a little fight in face of common danger.
Therefore, early in February they half-heartedly advised the King
to proceed with the Edicts, to allow time for remonstrances and,
if need be, to hold a *lit de justice*.[44] Even Miromesnil concurred
in this advice, hoping to modify the Edicts at a later stage.[45]

Maurepas, too, who had so often criticized the Edicts in public,
found it expedient to follow suit. At first he had hoped to undermine Turgot by insisting that the clergy should be exempted from
the tax replacing the *corvées*. For he believed that upon this point
Turgot would refuse to give way and that, as a consequence, Louis
could be induced to reject the Edict. But after a determined
resistance Turgot made the concession.[46] Maurepas now tried
other means of defeating the reforms. Still professing his intention of allowing Louis to arrive at his own decisions he caused the
Edicts to be submitted to Miromesnil for detailed comments, and
succeeded in giving the Keeper of the Seals the confidence to make
these as disparaging as possible.[47] Once again the measure suppressing the *corvées* was singled out for special condemnation.
Louis, however, gave Turgot a fair hearing. He allowed him to
compose an answer to the objections that Miromesnil had raised.
On the evening of 4 February the King received the two *mémoires*.
He had read them twice when Maurepas called to see him at ten
o'clock the next morning. He said that he wanted to read them once
again, and then his conscience would decide.[48]

The famous dialogue formed by Miromesnil's comments and
Turgot's replies left little to be said on either side.[49] Miromesnil,
like all Turgot's detractors, praised the good intentions of the Edict
in question, and yet deemed it impracticable. This done, he out-
lined the history of the *corvées*, emphasized their necessity, and
attempted to justify Orry and Trudaine for preferring them to a
money tax. The real argument begins, however, when Miromesnil
discredits Turgot's contention that the *corvées* were, from the
administrator's point of view, appallingly inefficient. Turgot's
retort was, '. . . it is usually impossible for the best-inten-
tioned and the most active official to prevent abuses. I speak
from my own experience of the province that I administered.' And
he went on to explain at length the technical difficulties of building
roads under the régime of the *corvées*, and to mention his own

reforms at Limoges, where, he claims, he built more roads in ten years than had his predecessors in thirty-five.

Miromesnil had next contradicted the assertion that it was the proprietors alone who really gained from the construction of good highways. Turgot was ready to admit that the peasant did indeed derive some benefit; but the comfort of walking upon well-paved roads hardly compensated him for the hours of toil he had been forced to devote to their making. The argument led to a more serious debate upon privilege in general. Miromesnil had glibly suggested that the privileged classes had, when all things were considered, no real advantage over the *taillables*. Turgot seized upon the opening and gave a table of facts. First, the noble could culti-vate four *charrues* free from tax, a concession which in the environs of Paris was worth no less than 2,000 *livres* annually. Next, the noble paid nothing at all on his woods, meadows, vineyards, parks, and ponds. Thirdly, on the greater part of his income—that is to say, his revenue from *rentes seigneuriales*, feudal tithes, and profits of fiefs—he was assessed only for the *vingtième*, and not for the *taille*. Fourthly, on all his lands which he leased to tenants he paid only one-third or one-half of the usual rate of *taille*, (i.e., *taille d'exploita-tion*). Fifthly, in practice he gained further exemptions from the *capitation*, for he had the privilege of being assessed apart at a relatively moderate rate. Sixthly, if he had *métayers* on his estates, he usually arranged matters so that these tenants paid all the *taille*. Seventhly, unlike the *taillables*, he was free entirely from the *contrainte solidaire*. And lastly, he was exempt from all the additional taxes that were levied upon the commoners in time of war.

But Miromesnil's more weighty argument was that to abolish privilege was to endanger the constitution, the military greatness of the nation, and the whole social fabric of the kingdom. The nobles were exempt from taxation, he contended, because to their care was entrusted the defence of the realm. These assertions raised fundamental questions, and Turgot therefore thought it advisable to go back to first principles. ' What is a tax ? ' he asked. ' Is it a burden imposed by force upon the weak ? ' If so, then government would rest upon no other principle than that of might, and the Prince would then be regarded as a public enemy. ' This ', he went on, ' is not the conception of paternal government founded upon a natural constitution by which the monarch is raised above all for the good of all. . . . The expenses of government, having for their object the interest of all, should be borne by every one, and the more a man enjoys the advantages of society, the more he ought to hold himself honoured in contributing to those expenses. . . .' Privileges were thus destructive of the principles of political right. They were also to be condemned on the grounds of expediency. Not only did they deprive the Treasury of revenue which was necessary for the good governance of the realm, but they had also given rise to a pernicious and chaotic fiscal system. In an endeavour to make good the loss of income caused by privilege, the Government had extended indirect impositions, and had also taxed the tenants and *métayers* of the privileged classes ; and no one could deny that from these practices innumerable abuses had arisen.

' Does it follow ', Turgot continued, ' that all privilege must be abolished ? ' No. That was impossible, for obviously the clergy and the nobles could never be subjected to the *taille personnelle* which was a tax originally imposed on serfs ; nor had he any intention of abolishing at one stroke the old constitution which, he would admit, could be reformed only by degrees ; but it was quite ridiculous to maintain that this constitution gave to the nobility freedom from all financial obligations. In many provinces the nobles paid the *taille réelle*, and everywhere they were assessed for the *capitation* and the *vingtième*. Whatever may have been the position of the seigneurs in the early Middle Ages, it was obvious to every one that the times had changed. For several centuries they had ceased to perform military service in return for land, and, if they continued to serve in the army, they were paid for their trouble. The army had become a profession. Its cost had become a heavy liability upon the funds of the State, indeed a burden which was much too heavy, for—and Saint-Germain would agree—there were far too many lucrative military offices which were the preserve of the nobles, and many of the holders were thoroughly inefficient. Privilege from taxation had not conduced to the military greatness of the French aristocracy. In other European countries where the nobles possessed no privileges there was no lack of military excellence in the army, and even in France itself, in Languedoc, Provence, and Dauphiné, the nobles who paid the *taille* were ' no less brave, nor less attached to the service of the King ', than those of other provinces where privilege obtained. Miromesnil had also commented upon the detailed provisions of the Edict. He had maintained that the *vingtième*, owing to its chaotic assessments, was an unsatisfactory basis for the new tax. Turgot agreed ; the incidence of this imposition was most inequitable. But the charge was not a sound argument against the reform of the *corvées*, but rather an admission that the *vingtième* also ought to be reformed. Miromesnil's final suggestion was that Turgot should extend his reform of the *corvées* at Limoges to the kingdom at large. To this Turgot replied : ' That . . . would be a very bad measure, very difficult to plan and slow in execution—a measure which would leave the burden on the *taillables* and which, at this particular moment, would add to all these difficulties that of sacrificing the King's authority to the premature clamours of the Parlements.'

(6)

The Edicts were submitted to the Parlement on Thursday 7 February.[50] That suppressing the *Caisse de Poissy* was registered immediately. A number of the magistrates spoke in favour of the remaining Edicts ; but the majority were resolute against them. Conti was true to his word ; he attended every session of the Parlement, and he sat upon the committee appointed to compose remonstrances.[51] At any moment he might have withdrawn his opposition had the Ministers pronounced wholeheartedly in Turgot's favour ; but, encouraged by Miromesnil's stubborn resistance to Turgot in Council, he felt assured of success, and was convinced that Maurepas, who continued petulantly to censure the Edicts in public, would desert the Comptroller-General. He knew only too well that among the other Ministers only Malesherbes was prepared to give Turgot any encouragement. Indeed, it was at this time that Malesherbes submitted to Louis a *mémoire* advising him not to yield to the attacks of the magistrates, and denouncing as a most dangerous practice the leadership of the Parlement by a Prince of the Blood. What a shame, commented Véri, that a man who could take this line should actually speak of leaving the Ministry ! [52]

While the remonstrances were being prepared, Conti urged the magistrates to condemn Boncerf's *Inconvénients des droits féodaux*, a work ' which was little known until he drew it out of obscurity '. The author was a clerk in the Finances, and it was rumoured that the Comptroller, who as a fact was endeavouring to withdraw the brochure from circulation,[53] had arranged for its appearance in order to win the favour of the masses for revolutionary reforms.[54] Actually Boncerf's work was extraordinarily moderate both in its suggestions and in the form of their presentation ; it emphasized the difficulties and waste of effort in collecting a multiplicity of trivial feudal dues ; and it described the cumbersome machinery required for this purpose—the archives, the stacks of legal documents, the crowds of receivers and collectors, the complicated accounts, and the endless and costly litigation. Boncerf was really out to show that it was in the interest of the seigneurs to abolish feudalism, and he went on to propose that the King should take the initiative. These were the opinions that the magistrates now condemned as being subversive of the laws and customs of the kingdom, of the sacred and inalienable rights of the Crown, and destructive of Society and the constitution, declaring that there existed in the State *un agent caché* who, exalted by an enthusiasm for false systems, was attempting to pull down the whole social fabric.[55]

Boncerf's work was condemned to the flames on 24 February.

Turgot received the author at Versailles, had him covered by the royal protection, and prevailed upon Louis to silence the magistrates and to forbid them to take action against writings concerned with the administration.[56]   As a result the brochure quickly ran into several editions, was translated into many tongues, and, according to Stormont, ' bids fair for making as much noise . . . as Sacheverel's sermons'.[57]   Already yet another pamphlet war had begun, and Turgot's partisans again rushed into print.   One work, *Sur les finances*, advocated the abolition of the *ferme générale*. The remonstrances against the guilds drawn up by the Parlement in 1582 were published without comment and widely circulated.[58] Sainte-Croix's *Essai sur la liberté du commerce et de l'industrie*, which had been published six months earlier, now achieved a sudden popularity.   Baudeau and Roubaud were once again eager to enter the fray, until Turgot himself gently restrained them. On the other side, Lacroix had produced his *Mémoire . . . sur l'existence . . . des Six Corps*, the main theme of which was that Louis was a well-meaning King unfortunately advised by doctrinaires.   A similar idea is to be found in Linguet's *Réflexions des Six Corps*, which went on to predict that the abolition of apprenticeship would lead to a decline of morals among the young.   Other *mémoires*, too, which came chiefly from the pens of lawyers, indulged in gloomy and alarming prophecies—the depopulation of the countryside, the increase in the price of food and a fall in wages, the flooding of the markets with worthless trash, and the nation's sudden lapse into sartorial indecency.   The Ministry took fright and, in suppressing many hostile writings, was prepared to make a greater show of authority than Turgot, who was content merely to request his partisans to refrain from scurrilous and provocative attacks upon the clergy, nobility, financiers, and magistrates.   But Turgot was compromised ; and even Métra, usually so favourable to his administration, now accused him and the economists of intolerance.[59]

The remonstrances of the Parlement against the Edicts were received by Louis on 4 March.   Like the *arrêt* condemning Boncerf's pamphlet, they were a denunciation of Turgot's so-called system.   ' A new system has been fashioned ', the magistrates complained, ' and it has been announced by writings and dissertations which are erroneous in principle and neglectful of facts.   It is only too well known that the partisans of these novelties unveil their system only by degrees, and seek to induce the Government to take the first steps along a path the end of which they keep concealed.   They lead it farther than it realizes, against the wishes even of the King, who is a friend of the laws, and who in the most august ceremony has recently sworn before the altar to be their protector and their strength, and to rule according to them.' [60]   From beginning to end the remonstrances were nothing but vague sophisms and declamatory generalities. ' The first rule of justice ', they continued, ' is to conserve for each individual that which belongs to him.   This is a fundamental and a natural right, a right of man and of civil government, and a rule of justice which requires not only the maintenance of the rights of property, but also those attached to persons, those deriving from the prerogatives of birth and station.   From this principle of right and equity it follows that any system which, in the name of humanity and the public good, tends . . . to establish among men an equality of duties and to destroy fundamental distinctions, will soon lead to disorder . . . in civil society. . . .' Such was the tenor of the remonstrances.   And even when on rare occasions the magistrates condescended to come down to facts, they did so with a scant respect for truth.   They boldly contended that the *corvées* occupied the peasants at the most for merely eight days in the year, and then only during the seasons when work was slack ; they defiantly insisted that the price of grain had risen under the régime of free trade, when actually it had fallen appreciably ; [61] and they attributed to Turgot opinions and intentions which were certainly not his.   Horace Walpole described the resistance of the Parlement as being more scandalous than the deeds of a tyrannical and capricious depotism.   ' These lying magistrates ', he added, ' are opposed to happiness of several million men.'

On 6 March Louis answered curtly, ' My Parlement must respect my wishes. . . .'   The following day he sent a full reply composed by Miromesnil and corrected by his own hand.   ' I have examined with great care the remonstrances of my Parlement,' he said ; ' they contain nothing which was unforeseen and no reflections which were not considered. . . . There is no question of an humiliating tax, but merely one of a small imposition to which every one ought to be honoured to contribute.' [62]   Next day the magistrates composed new remonstrances.   These angered Louis, for it was implied that he had not read the original ones for himself.[63]   Shortly afterwards Louis convened a Council of State to discuss the position.   All the Ministers, with the exception of Turgot and Malesherbes, advised the King to give way to the Parlement.   Before the Council met, Maurepas took great pains to attempt to dissuade Louis from holding a *lit de justice*.   But the King ignored him.   ' He is so much hurt ', reported Stormont, ' with the ascendant M. Turgot has upon this occasion (for which, however, he has nobody to thank but himself), that he talks of asking leave to retire to Pontchartrain.   If he had opposed the Edicts at first, his judgement would have turned the scale, but he wished to take a middle way, and was probably in the hopes that Turgot would find himself entangled and be forced to relinquish his projects without his (Maurepas's) appearing to interfere.   He has . . . a great deal of that timid indolence which in some minds is an incurable disease and seems to be one of those men whom no experience can teach that half-measures are no measures at all.' [64]

Despite this timidity upon the part of the Ministers, Louis decided to hold a *lit de justice* upon 12 March. Before the day came secret agents, who were probably Conti's men, once again attempted to cause a shortage of bread in Paris, this time by inciting the bakers' journeymen and apprentices to leave their masters. On the night of the 11th Malesherbes was wakened by a courier who brought the news that Conti was going to Versailles to make a last frantic attempt to intimidate Louis, and thus to defeat the Edicts. Malesherbes conferred with Maurepas, who straightway went to warn the King. For even Maurepas could not stand by and watch a Prince of the Blood acquire predominance in the affairs of state. Malesherbes and Maurepas had decided to advise the King that Conti should be heard and yet ignored, and that after the *lit de justice* he should be forbidden to appear in the Parlement. When informed of this last decision, Turgot expressed the opinion that a measure so harsh was quite unnecessary ; Conti would quickly lose his popularity even among his magisterial following, and he would soon become an object of scorn and derision among the masses. [65]

The *lit de justice* of 12 March was held at Versailles with the usual solemnity. [66] Miromesnil spoke on behalf of the King, repeating, as was required of him, the views expressed in Turgot's preamble. D'Aligre was the first to reply. He called attention to the tears of the capital and the afflictions of the nobles, and these he contrasted with the universal happiness prevailing at the beginning of the reign. He denounced the tax to replace the *corvées* as ' a perpetual and arbitrary imposition upon the poor and the nobility ' ; he prophesied famine under a régime of free trade, the ruin of the roads, financial disaster, social dissension, and industrial anarchy ; and he contended that government was being conducted upon a system incapable of execution. The Edict suppressing the *corvées* was then read. Next, Seguier spoke. He suggested that the burdens of the *corvées* should be lessened by calling upon the troops to take a share in road-building. [67] But his chief purpose was to call upon the King to listen to the advice of the notables of the realm, his august brothers, the Princes of the Blood, the Ministers of his Council, and the Peers of France, for it was through them that the nation proclaimed its wishes. Seguier spoke upon all the Edicts in turn. His speech upon the guilds was an eloquent plea for ancient constitutional ideals. He regarded the State as the mediaeval *communitas communitatum*, in which the guilds, the clergy, the nobility, the legal corporations, the universities, and the financial companies formed not only the natural police of the kingdom, but also the means of social and civic life.   To him the communities were republics serving the interest of the individual upon the one hand and upon the other those of the realm at large.   At the conclusion of this harangue the women of the Court gave loud applause, and all of them averred that the magistrate had spoken not like a man, but like a god.   But a few miles away the populace of Paris were expectantly waiting for the signal to celebrate the abolition of the crafts.[68]

When all the Edicts had been registered, Louis said to the Parlement, ' You have heard the Edicts which my love for my subjects has led me to promulgate.   I except them to be obeyed.'   Once again then Turgot had triumphed.   Maurepas, however, did not resign, for, as Stormont had always predicted, when it came to the point his wife, ' who loves the sunshine of the Court ', would persuade him to remain.[69]   It was not long before he began to regain his lost ascendancy.   He successfully opposed Turgot's efforts to introduce d'Angivillers into the Ministry.   Turgot's move was an exceptionally wise one, for d'Angivillers was not only his personal friend, but also a man who had much influence with Louis.   Yet Turgot's designs served in the long run only to increase the suspicions and hostility of Maurepas.   Stormont, still keeping a careful eye on the happenings at Versailles, quickly detected the turn events were taking : ' M. de Maurepas will not only remain where he is, but probably be more alert than he has been of late, watch the growth of Turgot's credit and throw secret obstacles in his way.' [70]

CHAPTER XVI

TURGOT'S FALL AND RETREAT

(1)

THROUGHOUT the crisis there had been no slackening of administrative effort. The very man who was being vilified as an impractical visionary continued to display the painstaking of the most meticulous of civil servants. In collaboration with Sartine he was issuing new regulations for the *Compagnie des Indes*.[1] He was abolishing the tax-farm in the Pays de Gex.[2] He was organizing the *caisse d'escompte*. He was arranging loans at a low rate of interest for the Estates of Provence and Languedoc.[3] He was clearing up the confusion caused by the fire of 10 January which destroyed the *Cour des aides* and all its records.[4] He was ordering the destruction of rabbits on the royal *capitaineries*. He was planning road-works and supplies of trees for the highways.[5] He continued to encourage agriculture and to take further precautions against the cattle plague. He was giving bounties to new industries and gratifications to inventors;[6] and 'he was collecting information with a view to abolishing the guilds in the provinces. Several of his decrees extended freedom of trade. Always prepared to appeal to sectional interests in the hope that the value of free trade might gain a wider recognition, he allowed the glass-makers of Normandy to sell freely their wares in Paris and in other privileged localities.[7] Then again, much to their joy, he permitted the inhabitants of Saint-Brieuc, Binic, and Portrieux to export the Breton draperies direct to French America.[8] Other measures were of general application. Towards the end of April he reduced further the duties upon suet.[9] But a more noteworthy decree—one anxiously awaited by the vine-growers of the Midi [10]—was that of 6 April freeing the wine trade. The preamble of the Edict describes the multiplicity of local monopolies, some of which dated from the fifteenth century. At Bordeaux it was forbidden to consume any wines except those produced in the *sénéchaussée*, and no vintner could sell retail unless he were a burgess of the town. The wines of Languedoc were not permitted to descend the Garonne before St. Martin's day and those of Périgord, Angenois, Quercy, and Haute Guienne not until 25 December.   Other towns, while complaining of these regulations, had established similar restrictions of their own.   At Marseilles it was forbidden to captains of ships to purchase wine other than that produced within a specified area round the town. The remainder of the preamble is an economic treatise upon free trade.[11]   But the Edict failed to satisfy various interests which had thoroughly approved of free trade in grain.   Although registered immediately by the magistrates of Toulouse and Dauphiné, it was rejected by the Parlement of Bordeaux and when, after Turgot's fall, this court finally accepted the measure it was only after its provisions had been considerably modified. The Edict produced astounding results : it soon led to an export trade to the value of 60,000,000 *livres* a year.[12]

On the day that the Wine Edict was promulgated Turgot read to the Council, at the King's request, a *mémoire* on French foreign policy.   The Court of Spain, in view of a quarrel with Portugal and England, had attempted to ascertain what help could be expected from France under the provisions of the Family Compact. The occasion, according to many, was propitious for a forceful policy against the English.   Vergennes was in favour of preserving peace, but nevertheless feared that if the American colonies obtained independence, the English might be tempted to make good their loss at the expense of France.   Louis, who was receiving bewildering counsel, desired a thorough discussion of the problem ; and that is why Turgot had been asked to submit his views.   Less pessimistic than Vergennes, he believed that though it was most likely that the Americans would be successful, England would not attack the French possessions unless provoked by Spain, who might be disposed to place too great confidence in the armies of the Bourbon States.   The best policy for France was openly to disclaim all idea of war, first because aggression was in itself unjust, secondly because it would place too great a strain upon the finances, and lastly because intervention might lead to a reconciliation between England and her colonies.   His advice was that France, while refraining from sending troops, should supply the Americans legitimately with arms, concentrate upon improving her own navy and army, and wait upon events.[13]

Such, in brief, is the record of Turgot's achievements at the time when every effort was being made to undermine him.   Véri, writing in March, makes an interesting comment : ' If M. Turgot had quitted the Ministry three months ago he would have had the reputation of being only a visionary, because at that moment lists of his projects, many of which were extravagances, were being circulated.   The falsity of these imputations and the justice of his plans to promote the public good have now been realized.' [14]

What Véri means is that any one who could look dispassionately upon Turgot's administration would readily admit that he was moving slowly and surely. With him there was now no real danger that a utopian zeal would lead him to embark on schemes which were administratively impossible. He was merely moving too fast for those who did not want to move at all. The pace that he wished to set was determined by his own abilities and by the administrative machine that he handled. There is no evidence that in this respect he was guilty of any grave miscalculations. The accusation, made by his enemies and frequently repeated by historians, that he failed to prepare men's minds for his reforms is quite beside the point. Actually there was really no question of preparing men's minds in the sense of coaxing them gradually to discern the light of reason. There was no question, because those very minds that were hostile to him would have resented the preparation which would have appeared, and indeed did appear to them, more revolutionary than his moderate measures of reform. Ideas do not triumph by their mere quality according to a law of gradual dissemination which it is dangerous to violate. Nor can constant reiteration of these ideas in a rational form gain for them acceptance in a world moved by forces of a different kind—though Turgot himself at times seemed to think that it could. In reality the only minds that could be prepared were those that needed no anterior appeal, but were already receptive—receptive, that is to say, not of the abstract principles upon which reforms were based, but of the particular benefits flowing from them. It was only by supplying the demand for reforms that Turgot could prepare men's minds. Yet to do this was also to create a determined opposition. His two most popular reforms, the suppression of the guilds and the abolition of the *corvées*, were precisely those that heightened the conflict. That these reforms were applauded by the masses there is not the slightest doubt. On the night of the *lit de justice* Paris was illuminated and there were great rejoicings and demonstrations among the working population.[15] For once the magistrates were unpopular. In the provinces the peasants sang :

> Je n'irons plus aux chemins,
> Comme à la galère,
> Travailler soir et matin,
> Sans aucun salaire.

And soon they were demanding the abolition of the feudal dues. ' The provinces ', wrote Véri, ' felt that Turgot was their support ; but ', he adds, ' their voices did not reach the King who believed that every one without exception hated the Comptroller-General.'[16]

2

Turgot's opponents renewed their efforts to bring about his downfall. The day after the *lit de justice* the magistrates reiterated their protests, and made much of two incidents which seemed to justify their forebodings, the first the *jacquerie* upon the Marquis de Vibray's estates, which they attributed to a reading of Boncerf's brochure, the second, the brutal attack upon one of the Duc de Mortemart's relatives while he was hunting.[17] Shortly afterwards the Parlement denounced a work, *Le Parfait Monarque*, which, having eulogized Joseph II, went on to advocate a popular rebellion against the vested interests at the Court. Seguier, in leading the attack, associated these doctrines with Turgot's policy and, when the Comptroller wrote to him vehemently answering the insinuation, the magistrates complained of effrontery to one of their officials.[18]

Meanwhile a whole crop of libels made an appearance. One of the most scurrilous, *Les Mannéquins du gouvernement français*, which came from the pen of Monsieur, portrayed Louis and his adviser as the dupes of the charlatan, Turgot.[19] Another, *Les Étonnements des Chartreux*, ridiculed the Ministers. A third, the *Prophétie Turgotine*, written by the Chevalier de Lisle, singled out Turgot as a visionary and an encyclopaedist who would overthrow the monarchy, the aristocracy, and the Church. A fourth, *Les Trois Maries*, libelled Mme d'Enville, Mme Blondel, and Mme Du Marchai. All these, and many more besides, circulated freely, and the composition of scurrilous literature became more than ordinarily the occupation of the Court.[20] Whether Louis himself read these libels we do not know, but Maurepas certainly did, and now began to work in earnest for Turgot's disgrace. His task was made all the easier by the efforts of two intriguers, the one, Pezay, who was still plying Louis with his secret correspondence, the other d'Oigny, the *intendant général des postes*. It was to Pezay that Maurepas gave the copies of Turgot's budget for 1776, on the understanding that he should obtain the advice of experts and pass on the information to the King. As we have seen, one of the ' auditors ' was Necker, who seriously questioned the claims that Turgot was making. Mme Marmontel believed that Necker's report had brought about Turgot's downfall ; and so did Morellet, who for several years refused to visit the Necker's house,[21] but Du Pont holds that since Louis suspected an intrigue, the move produced no immediate effect.[22] Probably it was d'Oigny's machinations that first shook Louis's faith in the Comptroller-General. A forged correspondence between Turgot and a friend was brought to his notice. At first the letters contained no offensive matter, but later, when it was felt that Louis was convinced of their authenticity, the forgers began to attribute to Turgot bitter comments upon the King and Queen. Louis consulted Maurepas, who gave as his opinion that the correspondence was genuine. At the same time other letters were intercepted in the post, and any containing accusations against Turgot were also placed before the King.[23]

Yet these intrigues alone were not sufficient to bring about Turgot's dismissal. It had taken Louis some little time to decide to part with Abbé Terray, and it was most unlikely that he would make up his mind immediately to send Turgot a-packing. And much as Maurepas might want to be rid of his colleague, it was not his intention to appear too eager, for he was always sensitive to the danger that were he to come out into the open, he himself might be the victim of a sudden reaction upon the part of Louis. He preferred to retain his wonted pose of remaining aloofly and non-committally wise, and, by gentle insinuations, to help events to turn Louis's mind in a direction in which it would have been difficult to force it by argument. Merely by refraining from defending Turgot, and merely by confirming Louis's growing suspicions with a word here and there, he was bound in the long run to achieve his object. For everything that came to Louis's ears—facts endlessly distorted, fortuitous happenings which in normal times would have had little significance, the fatuous lies concocted by Turgot's detractors—all came to assume a unity and to take on the character of incontrovertible evidence, some of which, it must be admitted, deceived even Maurepas. One incident in particular gave plausibility to the growing case against the Comptroller. Delacroix, one of his nominees in the Finances, was discovered to be guilty of corruption. Louis said to Turgot : ' Your departmental chief, Delacroix, is a rogue. He employs your name . . . to sell offices for his own profit.' Turgot, who was taken by surprise, and who believed that here was yet another malicious invention, defended his subordinate with great fervour and appealed to the King to punish Delacroix's calumniators. But Louis pulled from his pocket a bundle of papers which the accusers had lodged with the Queen and, turning his back upon Turgot said, ' I love neither rogues nor those who uphold them.' [24]

Another scandal, the *affaire Chanvallon*, was even more serious, for it concerned the Chevalier Turgot. The Chevalier had been appointed Governor of Guyane, a French colony which in 1763 Choiseul had attempted to transform into a centre for the defence of French America, in order to compensate the strategic weakness incurred by the loss of Canada. The emigrants who had been poured into this pestilential and famine-stricken region had died like flies, and the intendant Chanvallon was made the scapegoat of the disaster. In 1764 the Chevalier Turgot had been sent out

to arrest Chanvallon. But while he was in Guyane he dis-
embarked other emigrants who, contrary to his advice, had been
sent out by the Government. In turn he, too, was made the
scapegoat of Choiseul's ill-planned measures and was dismissed
from office. Chanvallon was even less fortunate : he was forced
to pay out of his own pocket for Masses for the souls of the
deceased emigrants, to found a hospital in the colony, and to under-
go detention at Mont-Saint-Michel. In 1775 he appealed against
the sentence upon the technical point that evidence favourable to
him had not been heard. Sartine and Turgot examined the affair,
and their finding was that the trial had been legally conducted.
Exactly one year later Sartine, without informing Turgot, lodged
with Louis a dossier of papers, asking that the case should be
heard in secret before fresh commissioners. Louis informed
Turgot, who immediately suspected, and this time quite rightly,
that here was yet another intrigue to diminish his credit.[25]

Véri, before leaving for the country, had advised him to write
frequently to the King in defence of his policy, and thus to
discredit his enemies.[26] He took this counsel, and it is in one of
these letters, one dated 30 April, which Soulavie found among
the King's papers at the Tuileries, that we may read of his efforts
to expose his calumniators. Having first of all denounced d'Oigny's
vile plot and having warned the King of the dangers of trusting
to information obtained from the *cabinet noir*, he went on to
discuss the *affaire Chanvallon*. He explained that evidence could
not possibly have been suppressed, and then proceeded to inquire
into the motives that had led Sartine to reopen the inquiry.
' Last year ', he wrote, ' the arrival of M. de Malesherbes at the
Ministry and the favours Your Majesty bestowed upon me, gave
no hope of my being overthrown. . . . This year the (impending)
retreat of M. Malesherbes, the more decided union of all parties
against me, my absolute isolation, the enmity of M. Miromesnil,
which is common knowledge, and his influence over M. de
Maurepas—all show that I hang by a thread only. It is necessary
(for them) to break that strand by arranging secretly a new plot
which revives an old affair long forgotten. . . . These are the
reasons why the conduct of M. Sartine in 1776 is so different from
his conduct in 1775. Your Majesty has done me the honour to
tell me that it is neither a question of my own behaviour nor even
of my brother's. Admittedly ! These gentlemen are too adroit
to announce at first their project in its entirety. They know their
trade too well.' Turgot went on to describe the plot in detail,
and to show that it was neither for the love of justice, nor for the
peace of mind of the unhappy Chanvallon that the matter had been
raised, but out of hatred for himself ; and he concluded : ' As for
the rest, Sire, I have been able very easily to explain clearly this

intrigue, which will serve to let you know these men a little.
. . . I shall inform M. de Maurepas and I shall make him feel
the indecency of this subterfuge. I shall demand from M. de
Sartine that M. Chanvallon's request shall be taken before the
original commissioners to see if there is any ground for action. I
am sure that M. de Sartine seeing himself exposed will return to
the right path.' [27]

But by this time yet another protracted affair was taking a
course which was dangerous to Turgot. On 22 January the
decision had been taken in the Council to recall the Comte de
Guines, who, contrary to instructions, had informed the English
Court that France would give neither direct nor even indirect
assistance to the English colonies. Malesherbes had convinced
the Queen of the urgency of this move, but Vergennes had been
afraid to carry out instructions for fear he should displease her.
Turgot and Malesherbes exhorted their Sovereign to act upon the
decision, but, when a week passed by and nothing happened, they
feared that some intrigue had caused Louis and Marie-Antoinette
to change their minds. Turgot wrote a letter to the King imploring him to act at once and, on going to learn the answer, found
that Louis stood by his original intention.[28] But the Queen,
evidently under the influence of the Choiseulistes, was making
difficulties. She had insisted—and Louis had agreed—that no
successor to Guines should be appointed, on the ground that the
Ambassador would justify his conduct publicly on his return.
This challenge upon the part of the Choiseulistes placed the
Ministry in a quandary, because to take it up meant the disclosure
of diplomatic secrets. Turgot's suggestion was that the matter
should be thrashed out and Guines's dispatches read in the hearing
of the King, the Queen, Malesherbes, Vergennes, and himself.
In no way did he resent the Queen's share in political affairs. All
that he wished to do was to save her from becoming the dupe of
political adventurers. But on 9 February the Queen talked for
an hour with Choiseul at the Opera, and later declared against
Turgot's plan, being convinced, it seems, that the recall of the
Ambassador was a plot engineered by him and his accessory,
Malesherbes, to regain the favour of the Comte de Maurepas.[29]

When Guines returned from London on 25 February he received a warm reception from the Choiseulistes, who continued to
clamour for a public inquiry, in hopes of embarrassing Maurepas's
Ministry. This demand met with no success, and it is probable
that the Queen could not bring herself to favour it wholeheartedly.[30]
It is even likely that at this point she bore no real grudge against
Turgot and Malesherbes. Véri, in his entry for 4 March, where
he is obviously citing information received from Abbé de Vermond, states that Marie-Antoinette admired Turgot's courage and

honesty and despised thoroughly the crafty Maurepas, who once again had been attempting to bargain with her.[31] But a few days later, just before leaving to spend the spring-time in the provinces, Véri heard that the Queen had been saying in public that she gave Turgot only a fortnight more in office. Véri suspected that Maurepas had been busy, and sounded him upon the matter, but receiving an evasive answer, left at once for his abbaye Saint-Satur.[32] What had probably happened in the meantime is that which Mercy relates to Marie-Thérèse in a letter of 13 April, in which he announces his intention of doing his utmost to keep Marie-Antoinette clear of intrigue. ' I have discovered,' he wrote, ' and have made it known to the Queen, that the Comtesse de Polignac is obviously won over by the Comte de Maurepas and is acting with him. My evidence with regard to this goes so far as to prove that the Comtesse de Polignac has attempted . . . to persuade the Queen that it would be in her interest to prevail upon the King to appoint the Comte de Maurepas prime minister.' [33] Mercy's efforts, however, were unavailing, and it is without doubt that the Choiseulistes and their allies at the Court succeeded ultimately in turning the Queen against the Comptroller. Mairobert's account of Marie-Antoinette's words to Louis after 'her cold reception at the Opera is probably true : ' I would like to see you there, Sire, with your Saint-Germain and your Turgot. I believe that you would be rudely hooted.' [34] Nevertheless it is most unlikely that she played a decisive part in bringing about Turgot's downfall. Though she had become in some measure the agent of the Choiseulistes, she was never a party to the whole of their design, but merely to the lesser aim of obtaining satisfaction for the Comte de Guines. Nor did she fall easily into the snare set by Maurepas, who wanted her assistance in order that he himself remaining in the background might later throw upon her the blame for Turgot's dismissal.[35] She had learned to be wary of Maurepas's movements ; [36] and he, finding the Queen an unwilling accomplice, in the end dispensed with her aid.

    Events, it must be admitted, did not run altogether in Maurepas's favour. His wife, whose wishes he always respected, was not at all anxious to see Turgot overthrown, and was inopportunely demanding the recall of d'Aiguillon. Again, even though the Comptroller might be disgraced, a satisfactory successor must be found, or else the fruits of victory might be lost. It was with the greatest caution that Maurepas made his final moves. Rather than attempt openly to dislodge Turgot, he thought it advisable first to expedite Malesherbes's departure, thinking that Turgot might then resign. In the King's presence he assumed an air of injured innocence. ' Here are two men ', he said, 'whom I have given to you. . . . The one, Malesherbes, leaves you in time of difficulty; the other, Turgot, threatens to resign if you do not follow his advice on all occasions.' [37] For a long while Malesherbes had talked of going and, much to Turgot's consternation, after the *lit de justice* wanted to retire immediately. His departure had been fixed for Whitsuntide, all promises to relieve him of administrative detail and all Turgot's entreaties having failed to make him change his mind. As early as the end of April, Maurepas was trying to persuade Louis to appoint a successor at once.[38] Already he had made an agreement with Marie-Antoinette that together they would secure the Household for Sartine. But some time later Maurepas endeavoured to revise the bargain, and proposed Amelot, his own nephew, for the office, believing that Marie-Antoinette would be satisfied if a dukedom were given to the Comte de Guines. The Queen was angry. She accused Maurepas of breaking faith, and told him that she would have no haggling in having justice done to Guines.[39] She soon gave proof of her assertion. She caused Louis, who consulted no Minister on the matter, to give the Ambassador a dukedom and to write to him an honourable letter, which she herself revised three times, expressing the greatest satisfaction with his conduct.[40]

Maurepas's manoeuvre to advance Amelot meant that Turgot would be isolated in the Ministry and that his plans for the reform of the Household—to say nothing of other schemes he was preparing—could not possibly be carried out. Upon hearing what Maurepas was doing (he was not informed officially but learned of it from the public), he wrote straightway, on 30 April, to Véri, imploring him to return. ' Oh, if you were only here, at least you would prevail upon them (M. and Mme de Maurepas) to make a reasonable choice—as would be that of M. Fourqueux. I dare not tell you all. Change your plans for your journey and return. But I can tell you that it concerns the honour of your friends, the peace and glory of the King, and the welfare of more than twenty million men during all his reign and perhaps for centuries, for we know what roots evil pushes down into this unfortunate land and what it takes to pull them up. . . .' Yet perhaps, he added playfully, the Abbé Véri, like a true rustic, only wanted rain for his fields. Véri did not return. He hated more than ever being the focus of ministerial intrigues; but, he subsequently confessed, he would have returned immediately had he foreseen that Maurepas, in working for Turgot's downfall, would make such headway. Turgot, who would have liked him as a successor to Malesherbes, later rebuked him for showing no enthusiasm to enter the Ministry. Yet while he would have accepted responsibilities had he been invited, he was not disposed to intrigue his own way into office. Nor at this stage could he have done so, for Maurepas was beginning to regard him as Turgot's disciple and political agent.[41]

On 30 April, Turgot wrote another letter, his second [42] of that date to the King. He first complains of the cruel silence with which Louis had received him on the previous Sunday and also of Louis's failure to reply to earlier letters,[43] in which he had intimated that he could no longer carry on unless he were given full support. ' I cannot conceive, Sire,' he continued, ' that from levity of heart you will consent to sacrifice all your reign and the welfare of your people : it would be necessary to think that Your Majesty had not believed a single word I had said or written. . . . Sire, it was my opinion that Your Majesty, having a love of justice and goodness graven in his heart, merited to be served with affection. I gave myself up to such service ; and I have seen my recompense in your happiness and in that of your people. . . . What is my reward to-day ? Your Majesty surely sees how impossible it is for me to resist those who hinder me . . . and yet Your Majesty gives me neither help nor consolation. Sire, I have not merited this treatment. . . .' At this point Turgot warns Louis of the dangers to the royal authority, contending that ' the Parlements are already more impassioned, more audacious, more linked with cabals of the Court,' than in 1770. This done, he denounces Maurepas for listening to Miromesnil, who, fearing that Véri might succeed Malesherbes, had suggested that the incapable Amelot should have the Household. Nor is this all. He openly accuses Maurepas of attempting to bring about his dismissal. ' I would not be astonished ', he writes, ' to learn that your confidence had changed, since M. de Maurepas, who tells every one he fears my systems, will undoubtedly have told Your Majesty. He has certainly informed M. de Malesherbes . . . that, if he had kept the Abbé Terray, receipts at present would balance expenditure, which would be true if the Abbé Terray had imposed 20 millions of taxes or had defaulted to the extent of that sum. I wish for your sake, Sire, that he has not communicated to you this way of thinking.' Turgot now goes on to attribute Maurepas's manoeuvres to weakness of character—his inability to keep a course, his deference to his wife's opinions, his petty fears, and his susceptibility to the murmurs at the Court. ' My own character,' he continues ' which is firmer than his, must naturally place him in the shade. My external timidity perhaps gave him, especially at first, some consolation ; but I have reason to believe that quite soon he came to fear that I would obtain Your Majesty's confidence independently of him.' [44] Then, having explained that he would not have spoken thus of Maurepas were he not convinced that the King and his authority were imperilled, he again implores Louis to be firm and unflinching ; and it is here that occurs a famous passage which, until the discovery of Véri's diary, was the only part of the letter to be known.[45] ' Do not forget, Sire,'—so the passage runs—' that it was weakness that placed the head of Charles I on the block; it was weakness that made Charles IX cruel; it was weakness that led to the formation of the League under Henry III, that made Louis XIII and makes the King of Portugal today crowned slaves; it was weakness that led to all the unhappiness of the last reign.' Turgot finally answers his accusers: ' You have been told that I am hot-headed and flighty: it hardly seems to me that all I tell you resembles the words of a fool; to me it seems that even the measures I have introduced, in spite of the outcries and resistance to which they have led, have succeeded precisely as I announced.'

Véri, while admitting that Turgot's habit of speaking the truth, even when it was unpleasant, was in itself highly laudable and usually efficacious, holds that Maurepas would have been perfectly justified in pressing for the dismissal of a Minister who thus denounced his colleagues to their master. But Véri has no wish to make out a case for Maurepas. On the contrary, he explains that, as Maurepas was determined to dismiss Turgot before the letters were written, Turgot had no other course than to make this frantic effort to enlighten the King.[46]

Louis maintained a disconcerting silence. On 10 May he interviewed Clugny, the intendant of Bordeaux. That same day Turgot wrote to Véri: ' Well, my friend, all is said and done. Your old friend has used such energy and such art to come by his object that he decided the King this morning. He has just announced to Malesherbes that the King will send for him this evening or to-morrow to resign, and he has announced to him Amelot as his successor. I have reason to believe that he has been working for a long time in a masterly fashion to ruin your two friends. He is counting with reason upon my resignation, and I know . . . he has spoken to M. de Clugny. In a few days' time I was to have placed before the King a plan of reform for the Royal Household: it will surely not be adopted, and I will ask for my liberty. I shall part with the regret of seeing a good dream disappear, of seeing a young King, who deserves a better fate, and a kingdom lost entirely by one who ought to have saved it. But I shall depart without shame and without remorse, and I shall see how I can make my leisure useful.' [47]

It was Mme Blondel who had advised Turgot to resign. But later Mme d'Enville implored him to remain to the bitter end. Much earlier—actually in March—he had told Véri that he would never give in, because he believed that truth was always likely to triumph over lies and intrigue.[48] So, after writing to Véri, he journeyed to Versailles to see the King. ' What do you want ? '

said Louis. ' I have not the time to see you.' The next day, Saturday 11 May, he went again to Versailles. Louis was hunting. He called later, but Louis was dressing. He left intending to return the following day.[49] But on 12 May the old Minister Bertin carried to him the King's demand to resign his office.[50] That same day Malesherbes handed in his resignation. ' You are a happy man,' said Louis ; ' would that I could also leave my post.' [51] In December 1792 Louis was on trial before the Convention. Malesherbes had volunteered to defend him. One wonders, did they remember and did they regret their failure to uphold Turgot sixteen years before ? Did they reflect upon what might have happened had they chosen to do so ?

'What you, my friend, might have foreseen has happened,' wrote Turgot to Véri on 14 May. Then, having denounced Maurepas for leaving the young King to the flux and reflux of the cabals, he gently reprimands Véri for failing to return and to strive for office. ' Good-bye, my friend,' he added. 'I will pardon you if you come to see me.' [52] Four days later, on 18 May, he wrote his farewell letter to the King, having received permission through the intercession of the Comte d'Angivillers. It is a dignified and noble letter. It contains no petulant accusations against Maurepas and the Ministers, for these were now certainly uncalled for. All that he complained of was that Louis had dismissed him in such a cruel fashion and had denied him a hearing ; and once again he asked that he should be given the chance to answer any charges that might be made against him. Then for the future he wished the King well. ' All I wish, Sire, is that you may always believe that my vision was wrong, and that I pointed out to you chimerical dangers. I hope that time will not justify me, that your reign will be as happy and as tranquil for you and your people as your principles of justice and your concern for the public good once promised.' [53] To these words Louis made no reply. Yet again, one wonders, did he ever reflect upon them at a later time ?

<h2 style="text-align:center">3</h2>

In his last letter to the King, Turgot had pleaded for assistance for a number of his following, yet in vain, for the Government, acting now in deference to the wishes of the victorious interests, soon began a purge of Turgot's nominees. Du Pont, Roubaud, and Baudeau were exiled during the course of the summer of 1776, and the physiocratic journal, the *Nouvelles Éphémérides*, was summarily suppressed. Albert was once again hounded out of office, and Lenoir was reinstated as lieutenant of the police. During that same summer Turgot's work was rapidly destroyed. The Dutch bankers refused to make the loan that he had negotiated.

The shareholders of the *caisse d'escompte* withheld subscriptions and clamoured for the return of the money already subscribed. To meet the deficiencies thus created, Clugny resorted to a loan in life annuities to the value of 30,000,000 *livres* and organized a lottery, both of which measures meant the end of debt conversion.[54] Quite soon many of the old fiscal abuses were re-established. *Croupes* and pensions on the revenues were, even by July, beginning to multiply, there being among the recipients the friends of Maurepas, Pezay, Clugny, and Saint-Germain.[55] Other reforms were also suspended. The measure abolishing the *droit d'aubaine* was never executed, and Malesherbes's commission which was inquiring into *lettres de cachet* was ordered to cease its sessions.[56] In August, Clugny, ignoring the advice of the majority of the intendants, reimposed the *corvées*, which henceforward were exacted in the greater part of France until finally abolished by the National Convention. That same month the guilds were re-established. They, too, survived until the Revolution—until 4 August 1789—though actually their regulations were often ignored by the masses, whose prescriptive freedom of trade the Government never dared attack.[57] Another of Turgot's measures —that declaring liberty of commerce in grain—was completely rescinded in September 1776; nearly one year later a corn company was instituted, and the Parlement of Paris resumed its house to house searches.[58]

It was with great sadness that Turgot watched this destruction of his work. When the guilds and the *corvées* were restored, he was prompted to begin a letter to Maurepas accusing him of having betrayed the nation, but he never completed it, and the fragment remains merely a witness to one of the few moments when he lost his usual equanimity.[59] For, strange as it may seem, he remained placable and forgiving, and, as Condorcet tells us, he would have been serenely happy but for the spectacle of misery around him. He accepted failure, and quickly settled down to pursuits that had always been dear to him—literature, science, and the companionship of his friends.[60] To Caillard he wrote: ' Leisure and complete liberty form the principal *produit net* of my two years in office.' [61]

Having spent the summer of 1776 at La Roche-Guyon, Liancourt, Tremblay, and Montigny, he took a house in Paris. He attended regularly the Académie des Inscriptions, of which he was president in 1778.[62] He resumed a vast and interesting private correspondence. In his letters to Caillard he discusses literature and music; in those to Condorcet he mentions his studies in electricity and magnetism, physics and astronomy; but most memorable of all are his commentaries upon the political events of his day, which are contained in his correspondence with

Du Pont. It was not the diplomatic manoeuvres of Central and Eastern Europe that interested him most, or even the domestic affairs of France, but the momentous struggle in North America, which he discusses again in a letter to Dr. Price.[63] Though he regretted the decision of the French Government to aid the Americans, he sympathized with the colonists. But whether, in the event of victory, they would establish a state upon principles of justice and equity, he often doubted, for he surmised that separatist traditions and sectional interests, and also the hold of religion in the puritan colonies, might prove too powerful. Above all he feared that the Americans would blindly perpetuate the fiscal follies of the Europe of that day. Therefore he took it upon himself to enlighten his friend Franklin, the American representative in France, upon the true principles of taxation and of economic science. It was for Franklin's instruction that he composed in 1777 a *Mémoire sur l'impôt*,[64] which is virtually a résumé of physiocratic thought. He also began a work called *Réflexions sur la situation des Américains unis*, but, most unfortunately, neither the fragments that he wrote nor the notes from which he was writing have been handed down to us.[65]

Turgot's peaceful retirement was marred by long attacks of gout, a disease from which he had suffered since 1760. With advancing years his illnesses had become more prolonged. Of the twenty months that he had spent in the Ministry no fewer than seven had been passed in bed; and now during the winter of 1779–80 his health began to give cause for really grave concern. Not until the middle of April 1780 was he able to walk, and then only with the aid of crutches. The summer saw a slight improvement, but in the early part of 1781 he suffered more than ever, and after a long and painful illness died at eleven o'clock in the evening of 18 March at his own house in the rue de Bourbon, his best friends, Mme Blondel, the Duchesse d'Enville, and Du Pont de Nemours, being with him to the end.

CHAPTER XVII

TURGOT'S POLITICAL THEORIES

(1)

DURING those last five years spent in retreat Turgot had made no deliberate attempt to justify himself in the eyes of posterity, but on one occasion he was prompted to reply to a correspondent in England who had sent him a treatise by Dr. Price in which the author had maintained that Turgot's failure was the result of his disregard for the opinion of the country. ' Sir,' he answered, ' please accept first of all my thanks for the trouble you have taken in sending to me the last part of Dr. Price's *Observations*.[1] I already know this work ; when this section appeared I read it with as much pleasure as the first. I should, and I do, feel highly flattered at the esteem that he professes for me. He is misinformed, however, when he thinks that my dismissal was occasioned by my lack of regard for the public. He has imagined apparently that the Parlement was the interpreter of political opinion when it opposed my Edicts. But that there is very little truth in this is evident when it is remembered that this body dared not print its remonstrances. When a publisher from Holland procured the manuscript (I do not know how) and printed it, the Parlement took every precaution to prevent the entry of copies into France. The Edicts for the suppression of the *corvées* and the guilds were received with joy in all the provinces and by the masses in the towns. If they have been revoked, it is not because the public has desired their revocation ; on the contrary, they were acceptable to the public : it is because M. de Maurepas believed it to be in his interest to convince the King that there were insurmountable obstacles to the execution of these measures and that all I had proposed was impracticable.

'The outcries that have risen against me here were never raised in the provinces. The courtiers who feared a reform of expenditure, the financiers who feared economies in the collection (of indirect taxation), the intriguing magistrates angered at having to deal with a Minister who employed the ways of reason

and authority—all these factions were foolishly roused by several
Ministers, and above all by M. de Maurepas, who feared that the
King would have confidence directly and independently in me.
He therefore employed every device to excite opposition from all
sides against me, with a view to convincing the King that I was
the unpopular figure of which Dr. Price speaks, and one who did
not know how to keep in touch with opinion. I myself am not
overmuch disturbed by this reputation given me by the scandals
and the intrigues of the Court, and if your friend, Dr. Price,
had reproached me alone for this reputation, I would not have
troubled to make this explanation ; but I do not wish the public
to hold such a poor opinion of our nation as is displayed in the
assertion that my simple and obvious principles (with which
Dr. Price agrees) have caused the uproar of our people.' [2]

That letter calls for comment not so much because in it Turgot
attributes his downfall to the intrigues of Maurepas and his
fellow-Ministers as because it suggests that his faith in a monarchy ruling in the interests of the masses remained unshaken.
He still believed that, if the King would only keep firm and
follow the counsels of enlightened advisers, the aristocracy might
be overawed and the Parlements deprived of their popular
following. As far as it went, that opinion was politically sound.
To abolish the *corvées* and the guilds in the face of magisterial
and aristocratic opposition was not to force the conflict between
the claims of national efficiency and those of privilege to the
point of revolution, and such a measure involved a far lesser call
upon the resources of despotism than had Maupeou's *coup d'état*,
which, after all, had been a dangerous and daring move, and one
that might have led to civil war. It is even extremely doubtful
whether the more disgruntled factions could have organized a
subversive movement like the grain riots of 1775, so favourable
were the masses towards these particular reforms ; and had by
any chance they succeeded, it would have been a relatively easy
task for the military to restore law and order. To this extent,
then, Turgot was perfectly right in believing that, although he
himself had been removed by a palace intrigue, his policy and
his methods had not been proved a failure.

But, if he had remained in office to make a more thorough-
going attack upon the privileged classes, he might have found
himself confronted with an armed aristocracy—the *émigrés* to be ;
and then he would have been called upon to deal with a situation
which he had never really anticipated ; for, although his ideas
and methods were to some degree dictatorial, he never explored
the ways and means of establishing a form of dictatorship. He
saw vaguely that strong government might prevail if, by some
strange good fortune, the monarch were to rule in the interests

of the peasantry, the middle and the lesser *bourgeoisie*, and the masses in Paris, but he never conceived of such a design in terms of revolutionary politics. Only in an indeterminate and tenuous fashion, and trusting to a rapid dissemination of the ideas of enlightened despotism which he thought might infect the greater part of the aristocracy itself, did he contemplate a monarchical rule based upon the lower social orders of the realm. If he sometimes had fears that enlightenment might not easily spread among the privileged classes, he was not prompted to ponder deeply upon the facts that aroused those fears, and he never grasped fully that new ideas, while gaining strength in one quarter, would in another call forth a reiteration of the old and, what is more, a determination to uphold them. Nor did he realize—so firm was his belief that ideas derive their power from their sheer quality—that the organizing of opinion for action is of greater political importance than its intrinsic worth. Therefore he had no real plan for marshalling the popular forces to which he appealed; he merely hoped (and, as we have seen, with some justification when it was only a question of abolishing the guilds and the *corvées*) that under the prevailing political conditions the jubilation of the masses would make for the advantage of the reforming monarchy; yet never did he contemplate the occasion when the privileged classes might no longer retreat in face of popular legislation, but rally and fight until the bitter end.

It is because he was lacking in a political programme to meet such a contingency that Turgot may be called an utopian and a doctrinaire. The more usual verdict pronounces him a visionary for other reasons, though these are never very lucid as to the facts upon which they are based or very satisfactory as to the interpretation of the history of his times. First of all there seems to be a notion that because a man holds theories which form a system he must, by the very nature of things, be incapable of carrying them into practice. Where Turgot is concerned, the knowledge of his failure leads to a particular readiness to make this unwarrantable assumption. Turgot, the man of theory, is placed therefore in a simple causal relationship to his downfall, it being supposed that here is exhibited the infallible working of an historical law. And all this is done without a searching inquiry into facts and their meaning, and without any attempt to prove, or even to state definitely, the assumptions made. That Turgot was a speculative man may be readily conceded. But it does not follow that his ideas were the idle extravagances of the man of the study or those of the charlatan and dilettante. His critics, indeed, are the first to point out that most of his theories were later translated into practice—and the implication is—unfortunately (as though it could have been otherwise) in times of general up-heaval. Nor can it be said that he himself was so artless as to think that the whole range of his speculations could be given immediate application; and it would be quite preposterous, as we have already shown, to charge him with failing to consider his theories in relation to the administrative resources at his disposal. As intendant, and also as Comptroller-General, he kept his projects within the limits prescribed by the inadequacy of the bureaucratic system. Of no single reform can it be said that he planned it without reference to detail or without careful consideration of the means to carry it into execution; and on every occasion he was meticulous in ascertaining the facts of the problem before attempting the solution. No civil servant could have been more painstaking and no man less likely to be the victim of hastily planned and carelessly executed projects. The last thing that can be said of his measures is that they were paper reforms concocted without reference to economic and administrative fact.

But his detractors have interwoven with these charges another accusation, which is again a garbled version of the facts, and the result of ambiguous historical thinking. It is said that Turgot attempted to impose his reforms upon an unwilling public which he was far too hasty and too impatient to prepare. Yet very little attempt is made either to inquire into the precise nature of these reforms or to ascertain the degree of his haste; still less to consider the character of the minds that he ought to have prepared or the means by which he could have done so. Instead the vague suggestion is made that there is in history, this time, a law of gradual development (though its precise nature is never demonstrated) which somehow imposes a penalty upon those who violate it; and at this point Turgot, the hasty reformer, is placed in yet another simple causal relationship with his downfall. But, as our study has shown time and time again, his reforms, in spite of the revolutionary principles implicit in them, were extraordinarily moderate in scope and never harsh in application, since he went out of his way to indemnify those interests which he found it necessary to expropriate. Nor can it be seriously contended that he was unduly hasty in the sense of introducing measures which, though moderate in themselves and carefully planned, would best have been introduced at longer intervals; for there is no reason to suppose that the attitude of those who raised the outcry would have been vastly different had he taken five or ten years to launch his projects, instead of only two. The character of the opposition was such that it would have attempted to remove him in any event. It mattered little whether an attempt were made to abolish the *corvées* and the guilds in 1776 or 1786, for those who defended these institutions were in no way enlightened conservatives with the genuine belief that a gradual movement towards reform was preferable to more rapid measures ; nor were they a body who were open to conviction, but a caste intent upon defending their interest and privileges, and they were acting in 1776—though with less political intensity and fervour—substantially in the same manner as they were to act again in 1789.

But with regard to that larger public outside the privileged classes, it would be preposterous to maintain that he introduced reforms too precipitately. As the facts have shown, the masses, though unable to appreciate the theoretical basis of his work, were ready to accept his chief reforms, particularly those mitigating the burden of indirect taxation and those abolishing the guilds and *corvées*. Where free trade was concerned, the existence of sectional interests and the prevailing fears of famine and high prices combined to make reform more difficult. Only by a carefully balanced programme which would appeal to and placate particularist opinion, and only by taking precautions which would allay popular apprehension while a free-grain trade attained adequate dimensions, could Turgot hope to attain his ends. Yet this is precisely what he did. There was never a question of his moving too hastily : with much truth it may be said that free trade was a reform which by its very nature must be introduced in large instalments : it was rather a question of devising means of meeting special difficulties caused by failing harvests, of appealing to economic interests to pull the same way, until such a time as free trade itself would, in its material results, proclaim its value, which no amount of theory could ever demonstrate. All this Turgot perceived with exceptional clarity ; that at times he also thought that ideas in a written form can exert a profound influence upon opinion did not detract from his belief that to prepare the country for reform a reforming programme must be launched. Yet here precisely lay the difficulty : it was never easy to initiate reforms which would have a popular appeal. Relatively trivial adjustments in the finances might pass without much notice ; but the moment aristocratic privilege was infringed, even though never seriously menaced, there was an uproar at the law courts and at Versailles.

To infer that one more fortunate than Turgot in the social graces could have succeeded in coaxing the aristocracy to give way in the interests of the nation, is to forget the nature of politics at the French Court. Yet such an inference, which gives a superficial plausibility to those ill-considered verdicts that pronounce Turgot a visionary, is often made, much trouble being taken to say that he was gauche, domineering, politically artless, and that his character was calculated to arouse an unnecessary opposition. Now, we have readily admitted that he was arrogant and opinionated, and that he was quite incapable of forming the usual kind of connexion at Versailles. But our narrative has shown that he was neither so artless as is frequently assumed nor entirely without political weapons, and that this very man who was so maladroit when judged by the ordinary standards of the time was amazingly successful in maintaining himself in power. His constant appeal to the King's conscience and sense of justice was so effective that his enemies found it extremely difficult to dislodge him. Their most spectacular attempt—the Flour War of 1775—ended in a downright failure, and at the time served only to increase his credit. Nor did he neglect entirely the more conventional means of increasing his political resources. As we have seen, he tried always to ingratiate himself with the Queen and, in order to detach her from her circle, he employed the services of the Abbé de Vermond and Mercy-Argenteau; while in managing Maurepas he relied considerably upon the mediations of the Abbé de Véri.

But it was his personal credit with Louis which was of paramount importance; and, after all, he acquired by direct means the support which ordinarily was the result of devious and crooked journeys to obtain the royal favour. His political agents, Vermond and Véri, were only moderately successful, the former because as time went on it was hardly humanly possible to keep the Queen clear from the influence of the Choiseulistes (as Maurepas himself was always to find); the latter partly because he refused to return to Paris at a vital moment, but more so because other intrigues had rendered Maurepas less and less amenable to his artful persuasion. At the beginning of 1776 the general outcry against Turgot's administration combined with the manoeuvres of individuals like d'Oigny, Pezay, Miromesnil, Sartine, and the Prince de Conti had caused Maurepas to work for the Comptroller's dismissal, and no Minister could possibly have defended himself against such overwhelming odds. In the long run his political resources proved insufficient, or rather simply disappeared; but while they lasted they were certainly the only ones that could have been efficacious for carrying out a policy of reform. That they were inadequate no one can deny, but it is quite unreasonable to infer that had they been called upon to support a more moderate and more cautious policy they might have proved more durable; for while it is admitted that his later measures intensified the attack from the vested interests, that intensification was by no means proportionate to the provocation, but was a complex and incalculable process. The conflict between reform and privilege was confused with other issues of a more normal character—the efforts of the Choiseulistes to overthrow Maurepas, the intrigues of the *dévots* to restore religious intolerance, and the designs of the magistracy to win back their proud position as champions of liberties and to reassert their constitutional claims. Turgot was attacked not altogether for what he did, not altogether for what he might do, but because by undermining him the factions and political adventurers might hope to gain their ends. This being so, it is hard to believe that had he himself shown more moderation his enemies themselves would have been more moderate. Turgot was the victim not so much of his own actions as of a political system which capriciously victimized the King's Ministers, even in defiance of all the wiles they cared to employ to maintain themselves in power.

Because Turgot fell in this fashion, the full consequences implicit in that struggle between social reform and aristocratic privilege remained hidden for the time. Louis had surrendered to the privileged classes after a mere opening skirmish. Had he chosen by any strange fortune to continue his support of Turgot's administration, he would have been compelled to attempt the transformation of the monarchy of the *ancien régime* into an institution of a vastly different nature from what it was. And to do this would have meant either a form of dictatorship based upon the existing military resources, or, what was ultimately needed (since the greater part of the Army was a stronghold of privilege), an appeal to the numerical strength of the masses. That one or other of these two courses must be followed, Turgot seems vaguely to have realized. Or perhaps it would be truer to say that, perceiving only dimly the logic of events and reflecting very little upon political probabilities, he thought that a small degree of both methods might be combined. Yet while such a policy was immediately practical (when, for example, he designed popular legislation calculated to deprive the magistracy of their pose as demagogues), it was insufficient to overcome that growing hostility of the Parlements, the Church, and the nobility. To lead the masses against an old order which was determined to defend itself needed something more than a mere programme of social reform designed to provoke the applause of the nation. What was needed was a new constitution. Yet that, too, Turgot realized—but once again, for all the sternly practical proposals he had to offer, without a sufficient grasp of the meaning of the events of his day.

(2)

Turgot's views upon the constitution (a matter upon which he had reflected for fifteen years) [3] are contained in the *Mémoire sur les muncipalités*, a work from the pen of Du Pont, whom he requested to make a summary of the ideas and proposals they had discussed together.[4] He had intended to present this outline to the King and, if its general principles met with approval, to develop them into a detailed plan for reform;[5] but he fell from favour before obtaining Louis's sanction to proceed with this work, and never elaborated the picture of his suggested constitution. Nothing of consequence is lost, however, for the political ideas contained in the *Mémoire* show that he hardly understood the whole range of the problems of the age, and therefore a wealth of detail, while being evidence of his supremely practical turn of mind, must necessarily have been in the strictest sense utopian, like that, for example, which is to be found in James Harrington's *Oceana*.

The opening paragraphs of the *Mémoire* characteristically appeal to first principles which, expressed in simple language calculated to be understood by Louis, are those of the sensational philosophy of Locke. The authority of history (or more strictly that of history as commonly misunderstood) is summarily dismissed. Better it were to ponder well upon the natural interests of mankind, and upon the self-evident principles of justice which are revealed to man in the form of knowledge produced by sensation and by the mind's immediate awareness. Such knowledge, unlike the laborious learning of the historian, is easily and quickly grasped, and so free from black-letter scholarship as to be in its entirety within the comprehension of single mind. Indeed, Louis himself was already the master of it when he chose to make the end of government the good of all; and if he continued to rule upon this principle, he would avoid the errors of his ancestors, who had issued laws in ignorance. But essential as this form of knowledge is as a starting-point for government, it alone is not enough. In order to rule wisely, the legislator 'must know, and must know in sufficient detail, the condition, the needs, and the resources' of the nation. Under the existing constitution of the realm this second form of knowledge was not to be obtained; and while it remained hidden to the King, no matter what urge he might have to govern for the common benefit of his people, his good intentions could never issue in successful action. No matter what lofty conception of social justice the King might hold as a private person, he could never act adequately in a public capacity while the nerve-system of the body politic remained numbed and incapable, as it were, of transmitting sensations to the governmental mind. The passage in which these ideas are expressed forms an illuminating commentary upon Turgot's own career as a harassed intendant and Comptroller-General. A knowledge of the country—so runs the *Mémoire*—is a thing which ' under present conditions

Your Majesty cannot hope to come by, which your Ministers cannot arrive at, which the intendants of the provinces cannot acquire, and which even the subdelegates can obtain only very imperfectly for the small regions committed to their charge. As a consequence there arises an infinite number of abuses in the allocation, assessment, and collection of taxation, and these, falling upon the common classes, render them unhappy and excite among them the greatest outcries. . . . The root of the evil, Sire, is that your nation has no constitution. It is a realm composed of different social orders which have no real unity and of a people who have very few social ties. It is a country where, in consequence, each man is concerned with his private interest only, where hardly any one takes the trouble to fulfil his duties or to recognize his relationships with his fellows, with the result that there prevails a perpetual conflict of competing and particularist interests which reason and common enlightenment have never regulated. Therefore Your Majesty is obliged to decide everything himself or by means of his delegates. . . . You are called upon to legislate upon all matters, and nearly always upon trivial details, whereas you might govern like God by general laws if the component parts of your empire recognized their social relationships and had them organized.' Government was looked upon as hostile and law as the will of the mighty, there being no reason for obedience save the futility of resistance. Every individual attempted to deceive the agents of the royal administration and to throw social burdens upon his neighbours, with the result that impositions were levied only by means of an inquisitorial tyranny, the King, as it were, being engaged in a perpetual warfare with his people. It was true that all this applied rather to the *pays d'élections* than to the *pays d'états* where there indeed existed a form of constitution; but the local assemblies represented social orders with particularist aims; and nothing therefore was to be gained by extending these institutions to the kingdom at large. What was needed was a form of organization which would sink separatist interests in common endeavour. To suggest the nature of a constitution which would achieve this aim is the purpose of the *Mémoire sur les municipalités*.

The first proposal—one upon which considerable stress is laid—is for a system of public education; and it is put forward with an easy optimism which knows no bounds. The existing educational institutions, the establishments for grammarians, geometricians, physicians, painters, theologians, and lawyers, are criticized as being narrowly technical and academic, and entirely inadequate as training-schools for citizens. It is therefore proposed that a Council of Public Instruction should be established to draw up a curriculum of social education, to provide a schoolmaster for every parish, and to arrange for text-books to be written on the duties of citizenship. More advanced education, again in civics, was to be provided in the colleges and universities, from which, it is to be presumed, would be drawn the teachers and the civil servants, such opportunities for higher studies being open to all possessed of talent. Within ten years—this is the claim made in the *Mémoire*—the nation ' would not be recognizable ', for children of ten would be men and women and ready to take their places as active citizens.

In the meantime the adult population could also be trained to co-operate in the work of government. For this purpose a hierarchy of assemblies was to be established. In every village (which was a smaller unit than the parish or the *collecte*) a body was to be set up to control assessments for taxation, poor relief, and public works. These assemblies were to be composed partly of landowners enjoying a yearly income of 600 *livres* and over, and partly of representatives of the lesser proprietors chosen from among groups of ' fractional ' citizens whose incomes added up to 600 *livres*. Those landowners, however, who had incomes of 1,200 *livres* were to have two voices in the assemblies ; those with 1,800 *livres* were to have three, and those with 2,400 *livres* four—the principle being that every 600 *livres* of income from landed property should be represented by one vote.[6] Hence people outside the landowning classes, the labourers proper and the landless artisans, who so frequently moved from one region to another, were not to have a share in the government of the village. As a consequence, each assembly was not likely to be very large or tumultuous, it being estimated that normally there would be five or six persons sitting in their own right, and perhaps as many more as representatives.

Alongside of these village assemblies there were to be established a series of chambers in the towns, replacing the ancient municipal governments, most of which were hereditary oligarchies ; but no suggestion was made that the urban franchise should be thrown open to the masses, and it was wealth again that was to be represented. Buildings in the towns, it was argued, were as the fields to the village, and upon physiocratic calculations it was contended that the equivalent of an annual rural income of 600 *livres* was an urban ground-value of 18,000 *livres*. The contention, of course, is purely arbitrary, and the economic arguments upon which it is based have not much interest. What Turgot had in mind was the establishing of relatively small municipal assemblies in which the majority of the members would be the representatives of fractional citizens.[7] In the very large towns there were also to be a series of parochial assemblies upon which should fall the task of making taxation registers, provision for poor relief, and also arrangements for lesser public works. But these smaller bodies were not to elect the members of the municipal authority: instead the councillors were to be chosen by the King from a list of men who possessed full citizen status.[8]

Such, then, were the village and the urban assemblies. Turgot next provided for a series of provincial assemblies. Again wishing to avoid the unwieldy and tumultuous bodies that would result if each village and town were to send a representative, he proposed that the provincial chambers should be elected indirectly. He therefore provided for intermediate assemblies in the *élections* or cantons, and these were to be composed of paid representatives of the towns and the villages, it being stipulated that these delegates were to exercise votes in proportion to the number of voices they represented. Such intermediate bodies, however, were not to remain solely electoral chambers: they were to have the tasks of determining the quotas of taxation imposed upon the villages, of allotting the *moins-imposé*, and of hearing disputed assessments. These duties, it was assumed, would occupy the assemblies of the *élections* for two weekly sessions in every year, in one of which they were to elect the representatives to the provincial chambers.

Now, the assemblies of this next rank would at the most be composed of thirty members, each of whom would exercise a voting power proportionate to the wealth he represented. They were to meet twice a year. In one session of a week's duration they were to allot the imposition upon the *élections*; in a second session of three weeks they were to allocate the *moins-imposé*, draw up and arrange taxation for public works, and elect representatives to the Grand or Royal Municipality. This final assembly was therefore to contain quite a small body of provincial delegates. But it was also to include the King's Ministers, who were to have the right to vote, and it was hoped that the King himself would usually preside over its sessions. Its functions were to be similar to those of the lesser assemblies; it was to allot taxation and the *moins-imposé* upon the provinces, to draw up general plans for the building of the highways and works of national interest, and to co-operate with the King in a policy of reform.

These assemblies were not to replace but merely to co-operate with the existing institutions. That principle is stated quite clearly in a brief discussion of the relationship of the Grand Municipality to the royal authority. '. . . The municipal assemblies from the first rank to the last are municipal assemblies only and are not in any way Estates. They would give information . . . and provide the necessary knowledge for the levy of taxation necessary for meeting the needs of the localities; but they would have no authority to oppose the indispensable and courageous operations that the reform of your finances require. They would have all the advantages of Estates but none of their disadvantages—the struggles, the intrigues, the corporative spirit, the animosities and the prejudices of the separate social orders.' From these words it is also evident that Turgot did not intend that the assemblies should exercise any control over the executive, or that these bodies should have any positive share in legislation. They were to form merely an elected civil service which would supply information to the bureaucracy and in some measure relieve it of much of the detail of administration. To say, as some have done, that these bodies were designed to remedy the excessive centralization of the government of the *ancien régime* is to miss the point, if it is inferred that they were fashioned primarily to promote decentralization. Their real function, even where it involves a decentralization of administrative detail, is to make more perfect the existing centralization; they are intended to fortify, as it were, the weak paper links in the governmental system by supplying an organization of personal contacts. The whole *Mémoire* is, indeed, written from the administrator's point of view, and its general character is sternly practical. As a reading will suggest, there is a constant urge upon the part of the writer to work out the detail upon which he has obviously pondered well. There is nothing fantastic about the proposed constitution. Apart from the initial difficulty of persuading Louis to adopt the principles, to set the machinery working would seem a relatively easy task, so few were the burdens imposed upon it and so moderate the demands upon human intelligence.[9]

But even supposing that the King had been favourable, it is doubtful whether the constitution would have worked. It is most likely that the privileged classes would have refused to co-operate in serving on bodies which obliterated social distinctions. To meet this difficulty Turgot had no real political resources—no design, that is to say, to call into existence the popular forces capable of overcoming the aristocracy. Like his contemporary, Rousseau, he always feared that to establish machinery to represent the will of the community was merely to establish a form of tyranny and to perpetuate and to magnify those factious interests so characteristic of the mediaeval estates. In both writers there is a strong disposition to vest authority in a single man, the legislator, especially in the initial stages of a new form of state. Only in this way, it seems to them, can the transition be effected from the mediaeval and corporative state to that which has an individualistic basis.[10]

Turgot did indeed realize that his political proposals would

affect in the long run the monarchical constitution of the kingdom, but he never tells us exactly what he imagined the final
result would be.   In a vague way he contemplated a monarchy
limited no longer by privilege and prescriptive rights, but by the
will of the middle and the lower classes, whose interests he
assumed to be identical, the kingship thus transformed being
infinitely more powerful in spite of its new limitations.   The
monarchy that he contemplated was not merely an executive
power to be continually held in check from a constant tendency
to error and disregard for the popular will ; rather he always
assumed that the kingship, having chosen to rule in the interests
of the masses, would exercise fully both the legislative and the
executive authority, in which functions it would be aided rather
than controlled by a series of assemblies facilitating the work of
legislation and exercising a subordinate executive power in a
strictly limited field.   All the while he is thinking of a spontaneous and perfect harmony between the intentions of the
monarchy and popular requirements.   In other words, he is
really assuming the accomplishment of a peaceful revolution.

    Yet at times he would also seem to question this assumption.
Two years after his dismissal from office, when discussing with
Véri the experimental provincial assembly established in Berry,
he made some remarks which are full of interest, difficult as it is
to grasp exactly his meaning.   He was explaining to Véri his own
plan and was comparing it with Necker's, and at the same time
he was telling his friend why he had not persisted in pressing
Louis to adopt his own ideas.   ' Whatever checks ', he went on
to say, ' one might at first place upon the assemblies, there is no
doubt that as a result of their being estab'' 'ed in every province
and consequently of the intercourse (that would grow up) between
them, they would acquire a degree of force which would modify
considerably the monarchical constitution existing at present.
As a private citizen I was not alarmed at this prospect, but as a
King's Minister I was most scrupulous not to abuse the King's
confidence in me by curtailing the royal authority.   It was not
that I was without the design, but I wished to wait until the
King was older, more experienced and mature, and better able
to judge for himself than through the eyes of others.   I wished
to give him time to study the problem and to convince himself
by his own reflections of the necessity of sacrificing a portion of
his power in order to establish the rule of justice that he owes
his people.

    ' I did not wish to have the reputation of having abused his
confidence and youthful inexperience in forcing upon him such
sacrifices.   I permitted myself without reproach only those
innovations which, though useful to society, did not detract

from the royal authority. But '—and it is at this point that he criticizes Necker's plan on the grounds that it might lead to abolition of the monarchy altogether—' this present innovation, if it is followed up, might end by changing the monarchical constitution (entirely). Thirty provincial assemblies can easily come to an understanding in times of trouble, feebleness, and minority. In an instant they can form a congress which, like that in America, would have the support of the whole nation. If the military forces then turn against the monarchy there would be a legitimate civil war, and republican principles would take the place of the monarchical constitution.

' Therefore my own plan was not to have in each province a single assembly. Nor again did I plan to compose them of three separate social orders.[11] . . . In multiplying the number of assemblies and in giving them so little importance I did not fear the vexatious consequences that the monarchy might experience (if assemblies upon Necker's plan were established).' [12]

A number of phrases are obscure. To some extent this arises from Véri's hurried expression, which is seldom so clear as one could wish. But the ambiguities are those of thought as well of language, though it is hard to determine which are which.[13] Again, it should be kept in mind that Turgot was not expressing the whole range of his opinions; his main argument (or rather the insinuation) was that those very people who had overthrown him, alleging that his systems made for anarchy, were now introducing, if they were really so concerned as they professed to be about the royal authority, a truly dangerous experiment. Nevertheless the following ideas stand out fairly clearly: as a private citizen Turgot was prepared to welcome a considerable modification in the monarchical constitution; as a Minister he was not disposed to take great risks; and, in spite of his concluding words that he did not fear any disastrous consequences from the plan that he sponsored, he suggests earlier that even this scheme, designed to reduce that risk to a minimum, might be asking the young King to sacrifice too much. One feels, however, that in the expression of his political opinions he is usually emphasizing the conditions he wishes to avoid, rather than proclaiming boldly and clearly the changes he wanted. Most of all he contemplated with abhorrence the establishment of any political machinery which was likely to become the instrument of separatist interests and the battle-ground of conflicts then existing; and it was precisely from this angle that he criticized the American constitutions in a letter to Dr. Price, in which he suggested that his municipal administration might be adopted to advantage by the States of America. It might almost be said that while he was ready to appeal to the people, like

Rousseau, he profoundly distrusted the immediate response, for he feared that neither the people themselves, still less the people who represented them, could really express what they ought to desire.[14]

Worst of all, in his opinion, would be an appeal to the States-General or to any body modelled upon them. When in the early part of 1776 a project for convening the Estates had been mooted in the Council, Turgot and Malesherbes were resolutely opposed to it on the ground that such an expedient would be to restrict the royal authority in the interests of the privileged and at the same time to engender violent conflicts.[15] In some degree, then, he understood the history of his own times—for he feared those very things that came to pass in 1789. But what he did not anticipate—and if he did, he certainly could not contemplate the possibility with equanimity—was that the Third Estate might declare itself a National Assembly. Yet only in this way—only by an act of revolution—could any considerable range of Turgot's economic and social reforms, or even his imponderable political ideas—or even Rousseau's—be translated into practice.

CHAPTER XVIII

TURGOT'S PHILOSOPHICAL AND ECONOMIC
THOUGHT

(1)

As a social philosopher and political economist, Turgot has been frequently studied and much admired, but mainly for those thoughts which his panegyrists themselves considered admirable. In a selective reading of his works they discovered the prediction and justification of their own society ; for England, in particular, he was a prophet, only less venerable and less inspired than Adam Smith ; while in America he was gratefully remembered as the genius who foretold and gave his blessing to the Day of Independence. Culling the choicest thoughts from his works, the liberals of the nineteenth century treasured the words of one of the founders of their creed, believing that if indeed he was only a visionary, he was nevertheless the most respectable of prophets. His antagonists, too,—or rather the antagonists of his admirers : Louis Blanc, for example, and the socialists of 1848—were by necessity also selective in their reading of his works. To them he was the first philosopher of the age of modern capitalism, pronouncing the iron law of wages as the decree of Providence, and thereby showing his readiness to commit the labouring classes to everlasting degradation.

This habit of studying almost exclusively those of Turgot's prophecies which were apparently fulfilled has persisted, with the result that many of his opinions have been given insufficient emphasis, misrepresented, and sometimes neglected entirely. The historians of political economy in particular, intent upon finding in his ideas the source of later concepts, and intent also upon fitting them into their schemes of the evolution of economic thought, have handed over the man with his theories thus distorted to the general historian, who therefore becomes ever more disposed to pronounce him a visionary, utopian reformer. Some have gone so far as to regard him as a man of the nineteenth century who had the misfortune to be born fifty or sixty years too soon, and it has even been claimed for him that he ' persuaded his own century and governed the next '.[1] The aphorism has little depth of meaning. Mornet, in his *Les Origines intellectuelles de la Révolution française*,[2] has exposed Taine's legend of the magic influence of the thinkers in bringing about the events of 1789. And that which holds good of the *philosophes* is also true of Turgot and the political economists; neither he nor the physiocrats influenced to any appreciable extent the opinions of the nation; if they would seem to, then it was because they had in mind a practical programme of reforms parts of which coincided with the actual demands of the struggling classes within the kingdom. ' The things actually discussed ', writes Mornet, ' were the evils experienced in a particular province at a given moment, the reforms applicable in any given locality, epidemics among animals, disease among crops, methods of cultivation, improvements in milling.' [3] Neither Turgot nor the *économistes* did much to call forth or to stimulate such discussion : rather they themselves were products of the conditions that provoked it ; and the elaborate theories they expounded were merely an adornment of practical demands and common sense. Nor did Turgot govern the age that followed. To claim that he did is to attribute to the written word that which should be sought in the minutiae of economic change and political event. Or even to suggest that his opinions governed the next century in the sense that they merely anticipated its dominating ideas, is again to misunderstand him and to neglect essentials of his thought.

The study of a man's theories necessitates a willingness to listen to all that he has to say, a constant eye upon the institutions about which he is speaking, and an attempt to discover his fundamental assumptions. When all these conditions are observed, our idea of Turgot's philosophical and economic thought takes a somewhat different form from the traditional view ; [4] and it will be found that, though he vaguely discerned in the social history of his age the struggling birth of a new era, his vision of the nineteenth century was so much clouded by a profound impression of his own that it really remained much less precise than is commonly assumed. To do justice to the quality and niceties of thought, to see it not as a chapter in political economy but as the mental equipment of an administrator, he must be studied in his environment and placed where he belongs.

(2)

In the *Recherches sur les causes de progrès et de la décadence des sciences et des arts*, in the two *discours* to the *Sorbinistes*, and also in the *Plan de deux discours sur l'histoire universelle*,[5] all of which were written before his twenty-fifth year, Turgot had proclaimed his belief in progress and in the perfectibility of man. In the span of human time, in the ages that had passed, and those that were to come, he discerned a process of causation. To him the past explained the present : the present and the past together made the future. By thus emphasizing the twofold antecedent of the future, and by giving to the past a deeper meaning than did his contemporaries, he avoided much of the simplicity of eighteenth-century empiricism. The past to Montesquieu had meant largely the constant influence upon the human race of a few physical factors varying in place but not in time ; and his knowledge of historical event provided rather the adornment of his philosophy than the source of his ideas. Other thinkers, in particular d'Holbach and Helvétius, ignored the past almost completely and postulated that, if the human race were to make progress, then its records must be burned, for history was a storehouse of the follies of mankind and its authority a restraining force upon the human mind. The same to a lesser degree is true even of Voltaire ; in spite of his vast knowledge of historical event, he could discern in the story of mankind merely occasional and unsustained advances which, in part the result of favourable circumstances and in part the achievements of men of genius, relieved a gloomy chronicle of suffering, clerical bondage, and unenlightened government ; and though he yearned for progress and for the rule of reason, he could never believe that their nature might be discovered in the records of the human race. But to Turgot progress was at once the inevitable outcome of historical development and also the product of the human will acting with a knowledge of the past. History was not a dull, unchanging theme with accidental variations : it was not a lament for the abject failures of the race ; it told chiefly of man's triumphs, the study of which was vital for an understanding of the world. Only in the archives could man discover what was progress and how to provide for its speedy and complete attainment. In other words, history proved the existence, the direction, and the possibility of greater progress, even though it might also demonstrate that the march of progress was frequently impeded by the stupidity of man.

In thus discerning in the past a valuable store of experience for the human race, Turgot gave to sensational philosophy a richer and in some ways a less ambiguous meaning than that with which Locke and many of his followers had endowed it. In departing from Descartes's insistence upon *a priori* or innate ideas, Locke had conceived of knowledge as resulting from a mind which, like a photographic plate, was capable of receiving and registering sensations, and which possessed also the ability to rationalize experience. But Locke—and this is true also of many of Turgot's contemporaries who took as their starting-point the *Essay concerning human understanding*—tended to appeal exclusively to immediate experience, to contemporary facts, and, in so doing, they invariably made experience speak in predetermined phrases. Turgot, with his rare insight and knowledge of past event, though not entirely free from this dogmatism of his contemporaries, was much more disposed than they to allow the facts of history, above all those of economic history, to determine his sociological ideas.[6]

' All ages ', wrote Turgot, ' are linked with each by a chain of causes and effects.' [7] Through experience as afforded by the physical universe, by education and literature, by the laws, customs and institutions of society, each individual mind and the character of each successive generation take their form. But that process by which one age inherits the environment of its predecessor is not a mechanical and monotonous repetition : ' natural phenomena only are subject to constant laws and are enclosed in circles of revolutions which remain always similar.' [8] Whereas in nature every species perishes only to be reborn (each successive generation of animals and plants merely renewing their own kind), in the history of the human race the exercise of reason and volition enables man to change the cycle, and, unlike animals and plants, to reconstruct in part his environment, his achievements being handed down by language and books, and by the laws and institutions that he fashions.

Yet it is not only its triumphs which an age bequeaths to its successor, but also its failures. ' In the writings of men ', says Turgot, ' I look for the progress of human understanding, and I find almost nothing else than the history of error.' [9] And, strangely enough, during more modern times, when men might have been expected to possess the ability to inquire into, to select from, and to improve upon his environment, so heavy had been the shackles of custom and unenlightened rule, that less progress had been made than in remoter ages when, at the dawn of civilization, man had been unconsciously adjusting himself and reacting mechanically to his surroundings, discovering of necessity the primitive arts and power of speech. In the dim past progress was not so much the result of man's understanding and volition as the inevitable outcome of an unreasoned response to his physical environment. Such progress made in these early times had varied infinitely, since the races in their search for food had necessarily to scatter, and thus each had been subjected to separate geographical control. But everywhere the direction of progress inculcated by man's reaction to his physical surroundings was the same : ' nature led men to the same truths ' ; yet along the route thus traced for them the races marched at an uneven and uncertain pace. Progress was anthropological; the human mind throughout the world had a potentiality for progression; but ' from the infinite variety of circumstances was born the unequal progress of the nations '.[10]

This notion that society is influenced by geographical factors had been elaborated in 1748 by Montesquieu in his *L'Esprit des lois*, a work which Turgot studied while at the Séminaire de Saint-Sulpice.[11] Yet, while recognizing the power of these physical controls in the history of civilization, especially in the distant past, Turgot, in common with Voltaire, refused to admit their paramount importance in more recent times. History was much more subtle; its course was determined not by temperature, by contours, and by rainfall, but by the human mind in all its complex workings and by the elaborate consequences of seemingly simple things. To give one example: the mechanical skill and the knowledge involved in making lenses for spectacles had made possible the invention of the telescope, without which Newton could never have revolutionized man's knowledge of physics. Chance, too, played a part in determining the history of the world. If Columbus and Newton had died in infancy, the discovery of America and of planetary motions might not have been made until two hundred years later. No less important were political events and the prevailing conditions of government. Themselves in part the product of a variety of causes, they in turn gave rise to variable results. Only a reading, however, of Turgot's early essays in history can convey fully the powers of his analysis. Yet though at times he describes historical processes in terms which suggest that they are too elusive and complicated for human control, nevertheless there runs through his thought a prevailing optimism that a knowledge of the past enables mankind to construct a better future. If, as Montesquieu and the Abbé Dubos had contended, history were determined almost entirely by a few physical conditions, then, argued Turgot, there could be little hope of rectifying the human errors of past centuries, and philosophy would logically conclude that whatever is is right and imprescriptible.[12]

Even in the Middle Ages, so frequently despised by the liberals of his day, Turgot discovered contributions to progress. Though the barbarians had destroyed the old order, they had gradually evolved a system of police and government.[13] Feudalism, for all its shortcomings, was preferable to anarchy; towns grew beneath the protection afforded by the princes; the Church encouraged men to cultivate the arts of peace; and numerous discoveries, which remained hidden to the ancients, increased man's material comforts and wordly riches.[14] In more recent times strong government had been imposed throughout the whole of Europe, and the worth of religious toleration, even though persecution lingered, had at least been demonstrated to the world. And if throughout these ages mankind had committed stupendous and costly errors, and if, at first sight, evil had predominated over good, there was the consolation that the sins of ignorance were transient, while the modicum of good remained the inalienable heritage of man. Nor were injustice, hardship, and suffering altogether outside the scheme of progress : since man had experienced these he learned what to avoid, so that out of his vicissitudes was born renewed endeavour. Man, said Turgot, on one occasion, must make a thousand errors to arrive at the truth.[15] For all these reasons progress was not a smoothly running stream, but a series of cascades.[16]

To Turgot, then, knowledge and progress were practically coterminous : ignorance and wrong were one and the same thing.[17] The more recent the history of a race the more was its progress a matter of volition, and the more, therefore, was it necessary to discover the fundamental principles that lay beneath the working of the world.[18] Man must study the ways of God, no longer an immanent Deity, but a First Cause ; he must learn from knowledge and experience to adjust himself to the natural laws of the universe, not solely by a crude process of trial and error, but by a thorough scrutiny of the social, economic, and physical phenomena that he saw around him.

In common with contemporary followers of Locke, Turgot assumes a harmony in nature. Though he was never so thoroughly utilitarian as Helvétius, whose work *De l'esprit* he criticized fiercely, and though he was not a materialist to the same degree as d'Holbach, he nevertheless shares with them the assumption that the self-interests of men are, if enlightened, naturally identified almost completely. Of course, he never contended—in fact, he expressly denied—that the springs of action were exclusively egoistical ; [19] and in the main he accepted Rousseau's theory of the natural goodness of man ; but he always assumed that the individual when regulating his conduct in accordance with the laws of nature, whether these were the dictates of conscience or the precepts revealed by economic and sociological fact, would find himself in harmony with his fellows. Therefore, although, like Adam Smith and Bentham, he also saw the necessity of an artificial identification of interests by governmental action, his philosophical theories led him to pronounce for a diminution of the State's activity in many directions, though, of course, this did not prevent him from demanding an increase in others, especially in the early stages of the rule of reason.

2

To his great dismay, Turgot found that the institutions of eighteenth-century France evinced a complete disregard for natural laws. Above all, he deplored the prevailing economic system. Much more forcibly than his contemporaries he realized that commercial regulations and the excessive burden of taxation together restricted the vital flow of capital throughout the kingdom. This is the main theme of his most noted work, the *Réflexions sur la formation et la distribution des richesses*, and it runs throughout his official correspondence, where it is elaborated and vividly illustrated.

In his penetrating study of social history he discerned that the growth of capital constituted economic progress. Capital, he maintains, first made its appearance during the earliest days of settled agriculture, and originated out of the necessity of the primitive husbandman to exchange part of his produce for commodities which he himself could not provide. No farm had been entirely self-sufficing. For one thing, landed property had, from the earliest times, been unequally distributed, and for another, few heritages had been suitable for growing all productions. But an even more important condition giving rise to barter and exchange, and therefore to capital, was that nature did not furnish all things ready for consumption. Some form of specialized labour, and a class of artisans who exchanged their labour for the products of the soil, must therefore have existed in the distant past. Their skill was recompensed out of the superfluity of agricultural wealth, and they derived their livelihood from a fund of riches which remained when the husbandmen had fed their families and had made provision for the next year's sowing.[20] Turgot thus arrives at a twofold division of society : the agriculturalists, or *laboureurs*, and the artisans, or *ouvriers*. Of these two classes the former is pre-eminent, not necessarily in dignity and honour, but in so far as it is the agriculturalists who employ the craftsmen and provide their wages. The artificer has no possessions but his skill and tools ; he must sell his labour if he is to live ; and, since he competes with others to find employment, his wage will tend always to that minimum which provides sheer subsistence. The husbandman, on the other hand, derives from the soil products and riches over and above those that satisfy the simplest needs ; his earnings are determined, not by competition or by traditional rates of wages, but by the fertility of the land he farms, and by the measures that he takes to cause the earth to yield in plenty. Nature is kind to him, affording him gifts over and above the rewards of his physical exertions, and it is with these gifts that he can buy the skill and labour of other members of society.[21]

There is a danger at this point, if the *Réflexions* only is studied, of misconstruing Turgot's economic thought. In this particular work he is stating primarily a theory of wealth, and not of wages ; here he is attempting to show that the nation's riches are derived in the first instance from the products of the soil. Elsewhere he explains the factors that govern wages. In a letter to David Hume, written in 1767,[22] he clearly states that the reward of labour is determined by the relation between its supply and demand— ' a principle ', he adds, ' which fixes the price of every commodity possessing a commercial value.' A wage or price thus determined is the *current value* of the commodity or service ; but material goods and labour have another value—a *fundamental price*; and by that term is meant, not the value in exchange, but the limit below which a price or wage cannot go. For articles in commerce that level is determined by costs of production ; once that price is reached it is no longer profitable to make or cultivate the commodity in question. Similarly, the *fundamental price* of labour is the wage below which no man will work ; once that level is attained, the artisan or the agricultural day-labourer will emigrate to sell his skill in other markets, or become a burden on the parish. Yet never for one moment did Turgot believe that the prevailing rate of wages would be the *fundamental price* of labour, or that this *fundamental price* of labour would represent a starvation wage. The phrase ' level of subsistence ' does not carry with Turgot its later, nineteenth-century meaning ; it in no way implies an immutable condition of poverty and wretchedness for the working classes, but a standard of life continually improving.[23]

Turgot's optimism has its origin in his study of economic fact. In the half-century preceding the Revolution there was much prosperity among the *bourgeoisie*, who, affecting the manners and the culture of the ancient aristocracy of France, expended fortunes derived from land and industry in the building of new houses and in luxury in general. Wages were rising throughout the whole of France and, although in many trades and in many provinces this rise was less considerable than that of prices, there was a growing class of artisans who enjoyed prosperity.[24] Yet another striking fact—one which fostered a belief that the vast natural resources of the backward provinces of France might be similarly developed— was the agricultural progress of parts of Normandy and Picardy, regions of *la grande culture*, where 20 per cent. of the land was cultivated *à l'anglaise*.[25] Finally, although a rise in population had actually begun,[26] there was no reason to suppose that the number of mouths to be fed would increase more rapidly than supplies of food.[27]

But to return to the *Réflexions*. Like the Physiocrats, Turgot terms the agriculturalists the *classe productrice*, since it is they who create initially the nation's wealth. It is at this point, however, that he modifies the doctrines of the early Physiocrats. First of all, instead of naming the artisans the *classe stérile*, he designates them as the *classe stipendiée*, thereby affording them a greater dignity, and thereby recognizing that, even though their wages are paid out of income from the land, their labours contribute nevertheless to the nation's wealth. Yet more important than this departure in nomenclature is that he recognizes in society another class, which he names *disponible*—a class, that is to say, which derives its income, not from its physical exertions, but from its ownership of land. In remoter ages this group had not existed separately from the actual cultivators of the soil, but since 'all lands eventually found a master', and since all men could not obtain heritages, there came into being a class of proprietors who need not work themselves, but who could pay landless men to cultivate their fields. It was impossible, he adds, for any other condition to have come about; from the earliest times a series of historical contingencies, displaying the nature of an economic law, determined an inequality in property; one man was more grasping than his neighbour; another displayed more forethought and intelligence; a third possessed the most fertile stretches; a fourth inherited from several owners.[28] 'What would society be without this inequality of conditions?' he had written to Mme Graffigny in 1751. 'Every one would be reduced to what is barely necessary.'[29]

In drawing that distinction between the proprietors and the landless wage-earners in agriculture, and in emphasizing the affinity of the latter with the artisans, Turgot displays his penetrating analysis of the economic evolution of the age. The agricultural wage-earners, like the artificers, could never under normal circumstances amass much wealth, and although their standard of living was bound to improve, usually they would earn only enough to meet this increase in their immediate wants. The proprietors alone received a real superfluity of wealth; for after they had paid their wage-bill and had met other expenses of production, there remained a residue which nature gave them as an outright gift. It is this profit that Turgot, in common with the Physiocrats, terms the *revenu* or *produit net des terres*. It enabled its recipients to live upon the work of others, to devote their time to social services, to take up office in the Church, commissions in the army, and places in administration.

Turgot next describes the methods by which the *classe disponible* may provide for the cultivation of the land; first by the employment of day-workers; secondly by the labour of slaves or serfs; thirdly by *colonage partiaire* or *métayage*; and finally by leasing the land to farmers at a money rent. It is the last two that he examines at greater length. In his day *métayage* prevailed in most of the provinces of France. Here the *revenu* from land was lowest; here the tenant received, for the most part, merely a reward which was really little different from an ordinary wage; here the amount of capital in the land was trifling. In great contrast to these regions were those where *la grande culture* obtained, and where the estates of the landowners were cultivated by substantial farmers. 'This method of leasehold tenure', he continues, 'has come into being where husbandmen are rich enough to make the necessary outlay for cultivation; and, since these farmers can afford to put more labour on the land and to manure their fields, the result is a prodigious increase in production and in the profits of the soil. In Picardy, in Normandy, in the environs of Paris, and in the greater part of the provinces of the north of France, the land is cultivated by tenant farmers. In the provinces of the Midi *métayers* work the land, and so it happens that the northern provinces are incomparably richer and better cultivated than those of the Midi.' [30]

Nevertheless Turgot looked upon *métayage* as a stage in agricultural progress—as a form of tenure which, under a natural working of economic laws, must necessarily pass away. Its unfortunate survival in eighteenth-century France he attributed partly to the persistence of social habits, but mainly to the fiscal system that drained the supply of agrarian capital from the countryside. Only in the vicinity of the larger towns had the stimulus of markets been sufficient to counteract the effects of the crushing burden of taxation.[31] Under a more favourable fiscal régime than that of France, the *métayers*, amassing little by little a fund of capital, would gradually improve their farms, ultimately contracting to pay a money rent and to provide stock, seed, and implements of their own. In England *métayage* had long ago passed away, and in Scotland lingered only in outlying regions; but in France that economic evolution must necessarily be slow; for while the fiscal administration remained unreformed the burden of taxation—at least as far as the *taille* was concerned—owing to the method of assessment, fell with greater force upon the regions of *petite culture* than upon the provinces where the land was farmed by leasehold tenants.[32]

It was Turgot who was the first to demonstrate clearly that the distinguishing feature between *la grande* and *la petite culture* was the variation in the amount of capital employed in cultivation.[33] Quesnay in the *Encyclopédie* had contended that the difference between these two types of farming was that whereas horses were employed for ploughing on the *grosses fermes*, the *métayers* and small peasant proprietors usually worked their fields by means of oxen. The assertion gave rise to a long discussion; *mémoires* appeared in publications; pamphlets were composed and printed, and the Societies of Agriculture debated Quesnay's proposition. But the dispute hardly produced much more than a host of instances in support of the theory, and ponderous statements of facts which belied it. Turgot had obviously followed the debate with interest, and in his *Mémoire sur la surcharge* devoted twenty-six paragraphs [34] to the problem. Admitting that as a general rule horse-ploughing was one of the chief characteristics of *la grande culture*, he went on to contend that the real distinction between *la grande* and *la petite culture* was much more subtle. 'The farmers in the north,' he explains, 'are *entrepreneurs* in agriculture, and have, like middlemen in other kinds of industry, considerable capital, which they invest in the exploitation of the land. If the landowner does not wish to renew a lease, the tenant takes another farm, to which he transfers his capital. . . . The landowner, on his side, offers the lease to other farmers, and the competition among these tenants to acquire it gives to the farm a *current leasing price* . . . which is a constant value arising from the nature and fertility of the soil independently of the tenant who may happen to acquire it. . . . It is evident that this leasing value, and this uniformity of cultivation which gives all land of equal fertility an equal and uniform value, arise from the existence of a class of wealthy men who have not only their labour, but also their riches, to devote to agriculture; who need not earn their living by the sweat of their brows as do the day-workers, but who are in a position to employ capital to finance lucrative concerns much in the same way as the shipowners of Nantes and Bordeaux employ their wealth in commerce overseas. Where such farms exist, where there is a constant fund of capital circulating and flowing into agricultural enterprise, here is *la grande culture*; here, moreover, the profits of the land are calculable and easy to assess for taxation; but in the regions of *la petite culture* the *métayer* is simply a wage-earner, a menial to whom the landowner gives a portion of the harvest instead of wages.[35]

Having described the capitalist classes in agriculture, Turgot proceeds to examine those in industry and commerce, and to trace the relationships between agrarian and industrial organization. Just as he demonstrates the affinity of the artisan, the agricultural day-worker, and even the *métayer*, so now he draws attention to the similarity between merchant-manufacturers and industrial masters on the one hand and the landowners and tenant farmers on the other, all of whom derive their wealth from the employment of capital in their varied enterprises. Between producers and consumers of agricultural and industrial commodities, he discerns a class of middle-men traders whose activities cause capital to pulse through the tissues of society. 'The twofold interest', he writes, ' of the producer and consumer, the one to find a buyer, the other a vendor, and in doing this to avoid the waste of valuable time, must have led a third to place himself between them.' In that respect all merchants, from the pedlar with his handful of wares to the overseas trader with his fleet of ships, had much in common. Within that class, numerous subdivisions might be traced. Two main groups, however, were outstanding—the *détaillant*, whose activities were confined to local markets; the *négociant*, whose speculations extended to distant provinces and perhaps to all the great emporiums of the world. But one and all, the middlemen caused capital to flow more rapidly in channels always growing deeper and branching out in new directions—a service, adds Turgot, ' which is useful and productive, which animates the labours of society, which sustains the life and activity of the nation, and which, therefore, may be aptly compared to the circulation of blood in the body of an animal.'

Turgot went on to assert a profound truth of economic history when he pointed out that the development of commercial capital stimulates the growth of that in industry and agriculture. Only under the vitalizing influence of commercial capital did land begin to yield a considerable surplus and the crafts begin to furnish articles for a wider market. He knew only too well that for centuries the poorer classes engaged in agriculture had lived from hand to mouth and, though not entirely without agrarian capital, could hardly be expected to increase it. Where, indeed, the *grosses fermes* had come into existence, the impetus to agricultural development had been imparted by the wealth that the *bourgeoisie* had amassed in trading enterprise. This argument—and it is one which is not fully developed in the *Réflexions*—would seem to contradict the earlier contention that the soil is the unique source of wealth, and that capital arises from the *superfluity* or the *produit net* of land. But actually there is no inconsistency; for it is always implied that the store of wealth accumulated by the merchant and industrialist is provided in the first instance by the workers of the soil. If the agriculturalist produced only enough to feed himself, then the artisan must starve, and the merchant, even though his bags were full of gold, must also starve until the agriculturalist were rich enough to buy his coin. When the *bourgeois* trader sinks his capital in land, and when his commercial ventures create a demand for the productions of the soil, he is merely returning a fund of wealth to the place from which it came.[36]

There remains yet another group of capitalists whose place in economy Turgot examined, again with great powers of analysis. Within the *classe disponible* he recognized a growing body of men whose wealth was derived, not immediately from ownership of land, but from interest upon loans made to the farmers and land-owners, industrialists, and merchants, and, he might have added, also to the Government. The precious metals that this class possessed, he explained, were one of many forms of capital, and, like land, agricultural stock, and buildings, and like workshops, tools, and merchandise, had their origin in the *superfluity* of the productions of the soil. And though they had come ' to represent all other kinds of wealth ', as a result of the necessity of using the less bulky articles of value for the purpose of barter in primitive society, these precious metals must always have been an actual part of merchandise ; they were not solely an index or a mere sign of value, but were in themselves things of value.[37]

The increase in precious metals, itself the result of the growing complexity of economic life, had in turn made economy ever less primitive, first by leading to a progressive division of labour, then by conducing to the formation of those classes with capital and those without, and finally by bringing into existence a group of people whose wealth consisted not of land and stock, or of work-shops and merchandise, but of money and shares which earned their possessors a rate of interest.[38] Like all other capitalist classes, the financiers promoted the circulation of capital, and in the past their influence upon economy would have been considerably greater if it had not been for the usury laws of Church and State. To a refutation of the principles upon which these laws were based Turgot devotes several paragraphs of the *Réflexions*,[39] and he was again to discuss the matter more fully in 1770 in his *Mémoire au conseil sur les prêts à intérêt*,[40] submitted when in the town of Angoulême a number of debtors instituted criminal proceedings in the municipal court against their creditors, the bankers. It was futile, he argued, that civil and religious laws should fix the rate of interest. To lend and borrow money was a contract entered into freely by two parties, each of whom hoped to gain from the transaction. The lender did not necessarily take advantage of the borrower, as the schoolmen had contended : actually it was the lender who ran the greatest risk of loss and, as a general rule, it was the borrower who stood to make the greatest profit by in-vesting the capital in trade or agriculture. It was, he concluded, as legitimate to lease one's money as to lend one's fields. Nor was there any purpose in fixing by legislation the rate of interest, for the price of money, like that of leases, was largely determined by the laws of supply and demand.

Turgot now sums up the methods of employing capital. They are five in number : the purchase of landed property with a view to cultivating it or leasing it to farmers ; the renting of land and the purchase of stock and implements for agricultural enterprise ;

the acquisition of buildings, materials, and tools for manufacture ; investment in finished goods and other requirements for commercial speculation ; and finally, the making of loans to other people who are prepared to employ the money borrowed in any of the first four undertakings mentioned. The return of money in these five forms of investment varies obviously according to numerous conditions ; but, as a general rule, it will be found that the fifth will show the lowest profits, for no one will borrow unless he can expect an income which is greater than the rate of interest to which he is committed.[41] But no matter what the venture—whether it be financial, commercial, industrial, or agrarian—all profits derive ultimately from the soil, and all capital, therefore—ploughs, stocks, seeds, looms, factories, raw materials, and so forth—is the gift of nature to mankind. ' Not only can there exist no *revenu* other than the *produit net des terres*,' writes Turgot, ' but it is even the soil that has furnished all types of capital which compose the outlay in agriculture and in trade. The land gave without effort on the part of man the first advances indispensable for the first exploitations ; all the rest are the accumulated saving of the centuries. . . . This saving has been made, not only out of the incomes of the landowners, but also out of the wages earned by members of the labouring classes. It is even true to say that, although the proprietors have enjoyed a greater superfluity of wealth than other classes, they have saved less, because, having more leisure, they have had more wants to satisfy ; they look upon their fortunes as assured ; they think more of enjoying than increasing them ; luxury is their lot. But the labouring farmers, and above all the middlemen in other ventures, most of whom receive incomes in proportion to their outlay, their skill, and their industry, although, strictly speaking, not in receipt of *revenu*, acquire a superfluity above the necessity for subsistence, and since they are bent upon increasing their material possessions, and since their labours distract them from a life of elegance and expensive pleasures, they save profits to invest in their enterprises, thereby increasing them. The greater number of the middlemen in agriculture borrow little, and nearly all of them cultivate their domains themselves. The middlemen in other industries, wishing to render their fortunes secure, are obliged to own (or at least by habit do possess) their own capital, for those who trade on borrowed money run considerable risk of failure. But although capital is formed in part by the savings of the toiling classes, nevertheless these profits come always from the land, since all are paid either out of *revenu* or out of the expenses that produce it. . . .' [42]

This is a rarely quoted passage of the *Réflexions*, yet for an understanding of Turgot's thought it is among the most important.

It ties him to his century; it reflects his environment, a society of peasant proprietors, of small tenant farmers, and of small-scale industry. He was writing for an agricultural age, and, in so far as he had any conception of a final stage to which progress was tending, he contemplated an economic order in which the bulk of capital would still be in the hands of relatively small agricultural-ists and of small traders, and, if at all he anticipated an increase in the number of day-workers, then it was with an optimistic outlook, for, during the eighteenth century in France, a daily wage was often preferable to the precarious joys of peasant ownership.

3

Turgot's economic thought, then, was not so much a prophecy as a penetrating analysis of the economic conditions of his day, and therefore the proposals he offered were essentially practical remedies for the economic maladies that he had diagnosed. The *Réflexions* may be regarded as an outline of Turgot's political economy; it proclaims two principles upon which he based his proposals of reform : first, that land is the unique source of wealth; and secondly, that a flourishing economy depends upon an unrestricted flow of capital. Arguing from these doctrines, which in essentials he shared with the Physiocrats, he launched a fierce attack upon the nation's fiscal system.

Taxation to the Physiocrats was an unfortunate necessity. Since all wealth came ultimately from land, the expenses of the State were a charge upon the landowners, and if impositions happened to consume the greater part of the *produit net des terres*, then they restricted seriously the returning flow of capital to the soil and consequently production. Excessive fiscal burdens defeated their own ends ; and the best way, therefore, to increase the income of the State was to tax in moderation. This common-place is to be found in the bulk of the economic literature of the *ancien régime* ; but it was the Physiocrats who first ventured to give a scientific exposition of this obvious economic truth. The main principles had been enunciated in Cantillon's *Essai sur la nature du commerce en général*,[43] and had been developed by Quesnay in his articles in the *Encyclopédie*. But the most com-prehensive exposition was the latter's *Analyse du tableau économi-que*, 1760—a work which possessed the advantage of simplicity, the *tableau* itself demonstrating by means of conveniently chosen figures how, if agriculture is to flourish, its two main obstacles, luxury and taxation, must be considerably curtailed.[44]

Though he departed in matters of detail from Quesnay's pre-cepts, Turgot took every occasion in his official correspondence to propagate physiocratic doctrines and to advocate the *impôt*

unique or single tax levied upon proprietors of real estate. Of all
the vexatious forms of taxation to be encountered in eighteenth-
century France, he believed that the levy of duties upon articles
of consumption was by far the most pernicious. For one thing,
it defeated its own intention. 'People have thought', he wrote
on one occasion, 'that the towns can be made to pay taxation by
being subjected to *droits d'entrée*, but in reality it is the productive
class in the countryside around that ultimately pays. The incomes of the town-dwellers are limited ; they can pay taxes only
by reducing their consumption, or by paying less for the products
of the soil.' [45] In other words, if the urban classes are obliged,
owing to taxation, to reduce consumption, the demand for agricultural products will be decreased, and consequently the profits
that the agriculturalists receive will necessarily diminish.

But although all taxation automatically falls upon the owners of
the land, it does not follow that its method of levy is immaterial.
During his debate with Miromesnil on the project for suppressing
the *corvées*, it was put to him that if economic laws in general, and
in particular that regulating the incidence of taxation, worked
in spite of the administrative methods that ignored them, and if,
as the Physiocrats were so fond of saying, the burden of taxation
must, by the very nature of things, fell upon the proprietors of
land, then it was not of real importance whether the fiscal system
were reformed or not. Turgot's reply on this occasion brings
out the practical value in physiocratic doctrine : it was true, he
answered, that no matter how taxation was imposed, it still remained
a charge upon the land ; but that was no reason for ignoring
economic laws. Try as it would the Government could not place
a tax on trade and industry ; yet, in attempting to do so, it might
create, and had created, a condition of administrative chaos, and a
fiscal system which was wasteful, corrupt, and disastrous to the
kingdom. [46] Not only had there grown up a class of 'fiscal
feudatories ', as he called the financiers, who had bought the right
to manage and who ate away the revenues of the State, but there
was a perpetual conflict between the Prince and his people, the
Government meting out excessive and brutal punishments to
transgressors who were never easy to discover, and the citizen
having every incentive to practise frauds in which he might
reasonably hope to escape detection. [47] More serious still were the
restrictions that indirect taxation placed upon agricultural and
industrial expansion. Tolls and customs barriers, especially in
remoter regions like Limousin and Angoumois, tended to confine
the exchange of goods to local markets ; and even in the more
prosperous parts the French merchant was often placed at a disadvantage with the foreign trader, who in spite of the tariffs
levied at the ports, could under-sell the natives, whose com-

modities might easily have been doubled in price as a result of the tolls levied at frequent intervals along the internal trade routes.[48]

Colbert—for it was he who developed impositions on consumption—had favoured indirect taxation, on the score that all subjects would contribute to the State in proportion to their incomes available for spending.   While Turgot was prepared to admit an element of truth in this reasoning, he strongly maintained that the apparent advantage of Colbert's policy was nullified by two considerations.   In the first place there existed no logical basis, or at least no applicable rule, for determining at what rates different commodities should be taxed—whether, for example, a given weight of salt should be subjected to a higher charge than a given measure of wheat.   To fix them arbitrarily would be to favour one producer and unduly penalize another.[49]   In the second place—and this is an even more serious objection, strange as it may seem to modern ears—it was unjust to tax any single commodity at a level rate, the reason being that costs of production varied widely from place to place.   Where the yield of corn, for instance, was low, the cost of production in proportion to the selling price was high.   Hence to tax indirectly the producer, whose costs were heavy, at the same rate as him whose soil was fertile, was to commit a grave injustice ; and no system of indirect taxation, however elaborate it might be, could possibly provide for the multiplicity of adjustments in rates of taxation that would place all producers on an equal footing.   This argument, which obviously carries less force to-day, reflects the conditions that Turgot knew—the enormous variations in agricultural yield and the heavy burden of taxation which magnified every injustice of assessment.

Much of Turgot's criticism of indirect taxation was equally valid of the *taille*, the *capitation*, and the *vingtième*.   All three were levied upon industry as well as upon the land, and the royal officials and parochial collectors expended much useless energy in collecting ridiculously small sums, the urban workers and those engaged in cottage industries often paying as little as two *livres* annually.   Even those with higher incomes from industry and trade paid very little tax.   In the towns the *taille* had always been levied at a moderate rate, and the receipts from the *capitation* and the *vingtième* had gradually diminished, for the officials could rarely discover the exact profits made by merchants, and little or no attempt had been made to bring the taxation rolls up to date.[50]   By the year 1786, when Necker made his famous survey of the finances, the total revenue from the *taille* and the *vingtième* of industry was almost trifling.[51]   This very difficulty of levying direct taxes upon industry and commerce was, in Turgot's opinion, sufficient reason for their abolition.[52]

Turgot's further argument that a tax which failed to take into
account the costs of production was exceedingly unjust held
good also of the *taille personnelle* ; and it held true again of the
clerical and seigneurial tithes which were taken as a percentage
of total yield, and not as a proportion of clear profit.   It is no
wonder, then, that while Turgot lauded Vauban's proposals to
abolish the multiplicity of existing taxes, he opposed the substitution of the *dixme royale*.[53]   Both the tithe and the *taille
personnelle* were particularly heavy in those regions of *la petite
culture* where costs of production in proportion to the yield from
land were relatively high.   It was not uncommon for the tithe,
for instance, though levied only at one-twelfth, to amount to
two-thirds of the real profits from the soil.[54]   As a general rule,
however, it was the *taille personnelle* which was the more pernicious
imposition ; for not only was it levied at a higher rate, but it
fell upon a greater number of agricultural productions, some of
which—beasts of labour, hay, and roots for example—were
hardly profits, but again costs of productions.   'It is not all
real wealth', wrote Turgot, 'that should be subject to taxation ;
it is necessary for that wealth to be *disponible*, that is to say, it
must not be required for the production of the next year's
crops.'[55]   So far he was in perfect agreement with Quesnay
and the Physiocrats ; but when he came to consider the relative
merits of a single tax administered similarly to the *vingtième* and
an imposition like the *taille réelle*, he departed from the teaching
of his master, bringing his practical experience to bear upon
the issue.   Quesnay and the Elder Mirabeau favoured the form
of the *vingtième*, provided exemptions and privileges were abolished.   But Turgot, while admitting that such a tax was sound
in theory, contended that from the administrator's standpoint
it was most imperfect.   Had leasehold tenure been prevalent in
France there would have been nothing to say against it, for the
value of leases would have afforded a reliable indication of the
net profits of the domains ;[56] but in two-thirds of the kingdom
leasehold was the exception, and, as Turgot realized from experience in Limousin, it was a colossal and irritating task to determine
the profits made by a race of small proprietors and *métayers* who
habitually concealed their business affairs.   Quesnay had naïvely
spoken of requiring the landowners and farmers to make, under
pain of increased assessments, faithful declarations of their
incomes.   Turgot, with the knowledge of Tourny's difficulties
in introducing the *taille tarifée* in Limousin, fully realized the
impracticability of Quesnay's suggestion.[57]   To apply this
method to a tax like the *vingtième* was particularly unwise.   For,
unlike the *taille*, an imposition the total of which was fixed beforehand and divided in stages first among the *généralités*, and finally

among individuals within the parishes, there being every incentive for a man to tell tales about his neighbour's affairs, the *vingtième* was assessed as a proportion of profit, and therefore it was the Treasury, and not his fellow-parishioners, that stood to lose if a man failed to reveal his profits. Hence Turgot favoured a land tax retaining one of the chief characteristics of the *taille* : it must be an *impôt de quotité*—that is to say, an imposition the total of which was determined prior to assessment.[58]

In order to simplify the administration of such an imposition, he proposed to tax only the landowners, and not the tenants and *métayers*. ' To require a tenant to pay a tax ', he argued, ' is to do nothing else than to increase his expenses by a corresponding amount, and these additional costs he must necessarily recover, like all his outlay, from the *produit net* ; hence the portion (*i.e.*, the rent) that he gives to the landowner will be diminished by a sum equivalent to his taxes.'[59] This argument was not based upon theory alone. In Limousin and other parts of France it was frequently stipulated, in the agreements between landlord and tenant, that the proprietor should meet the expenses of taxation, although in law it was the tenant who was responsible for the major part.[60]

Quesnay had failed to draw this conclusion which was implicit in his doctrines. He had spoken of taxing the farmers and *métayers* and, in spite of his pronouncement for the *impôt unique*, of assessing even the day-workers, artisans, and traders. In other ways, too, he was somewhat inconsistent. Though he had recognized that beasts of labour were part of agrarian capital, and therefore should be exempt from tax, he was content to levy impositions upon houses, barns, and stables. But Turgot insisted that these agricultural buildings were also forms of capital ; and he went on to give this principle an even wider application in proposing that meadows for grazing beasts of labour should be exempt from taxes.[61]

Turgot's ideal in taxation was a single imposition somewhat of the nature of the *taille réelle* of the *pays d'états*, but levied only on the landowners, privileged and non-privileged alike, and assessed upon the basis of an accurate land register or *cadastre* which indicated the average net annual profits of every domain. He had considered the whole problem not only from the angle of economic theory, but also from that of the administration. Never for one moment did he think that the whole programme could be given immediate application ; [62] nor did he fail to see the difficulties even in giving the scheme piecemeal execution. Although he pronounced for a single tax on landowners, he fully realized that the greater part of the soil was in the hands of small peasant proprietors, and that therefore the making of a *cadastre* would require considerable administrative effort. But, as we have seen repeatedly, he always had in mind administrative reforms and plans to develop not only the civil service, but also to call forth local co-operation.

(4)

Although Adam Smith could write, ' The labour of farmers and country labourers is more productive than that of merchants, artificers, and manufacturers ', to the majority of Englishmen of the time physiocratic theories were too sharply in contrast with the facts and ideals of English economic life to gain unqualified acceptance, or even to be understood.[63] Adam Smith, for example, in criticizing the Physiocrats, to some degree misrepresents their theories and ignores their assumptions. When he pointed out that manufactured goods were part of the nation's wealth, contending that ' a small quantity of manufactured produce purchases a great quantity of rude produce ',[64] he was denying a statement which the Physiocrats never made, or was at least refuting an assertion out of its context ; and when he called attention, as did David Hume in his criticism of Turgot's theories, to the example of Holland, a kingdom which ' draws a great part of its subsistence from other countries—live cattle from Holstein and Jutland, and corn from almost all the different countries of Europe ', he was not so much exposing a fallacy in physiocratic theory as showing that his mind was moving on a different level from that of the French economists. Adam Smith placed considerable emphasis upon foreign trade and exchange of goods ; but Turgot and the Physiocrats, while contending that countries should abolish their tariff walls, believed that the real wealth of the nation was in its natural resources. When Graslin, like Smith and Hume, also cited the example of Holland, Turgot's reply was that a nation was not coterminous with a political unit, but was a self-sufficing economic area in which agriculture and industry existed side by side, affording reciprocal benefits. In his estimation Holland lacked those qualities that made for permanence and stability ; the Dutch were a political community of shopkeepers, and their country a mere emporium for the hinterland of northern Europe. ' Other nations ', he remarks, ' pay the taxes of this republic.' [65]

To appreciate such assumptions, and also to recognize the limits to the vision of the Physiocrats, are forms of criticism of much more historical value than to judge their doctrines in the light of modern economic theory. Oncken's statement that their theory of wealth and taxation still awaits scientific refutation or Higgs's view that they were in error when the identified wealth with material objects and value with the cost of production are comments, even if true, of little interest. It is much more important to recognize that the Physiocrats never contemplated an economic organization based upon a highly complex division of labour, or a world economy in which the nations of Europe would draw much of their revenue from the exertions of poorly-paid natives in other lands.[66] In the nineteenth century it would have been ridiculous to propound the theory—for such would be the logical conclusion of physiocratic doctrine if applied to a later age—that the Indian and South African landowner should pay directly the greater part of English taxation, or that the American wheat-grower of the middle west should contribute to the upkeep of the British Navy. But the physiocratic proposal to levy the whole of French taxation on the soil that supplied food and raw materials was not extravagant in an age when imported products were exceedingly small in volume and when there was no reason to assume an impending economic revolution. Considered not as a theory in isolation, but as the basis for proposals for practical reforms, physiocratic thought—at least when expounded by an administrator like Turgot—was particularly appropriate to the age.

Although the examination of physiocratic theory in the light of later doctrines is really a superfluous exercise, nevertheless, because it has frequently been performed, it has given rise to various misconceptions. Higgs's remark, for example, that the Physiocrats confused wealth with material objects and value with costs of production,[67] is not strictly true. Without exception the Physiocrats recognized that wealth transcended the bounds of material goods, that any natural product when mixed with labour increased in value, and that a commodity—a work of art, for example—might have a value out of all proportion to that of the materials embodied in it. Nor did they contend (as Higgs supposes) that the cost of production was determined solely by the price of raw material and by the cost of subsistence of the artisans who worked upon it. Invariably they recognized that the expenses of production depended also upon other factors—upon the outlay on capital improvements and interest on money—and that wages were determined not by the cost of subsistence, but by supply and demand. Actually, the Physiocrats employed the term *value* in two different senses. More narrowly they meant by it the price that a commodity would fetch in the market, and they anticipated in a general way, though they never elaborated, the theory of marginal values. More widely the term had another meaning which cannot be adequately conveyed in a single word ; when they spoke of commodities and services as being valuable, they did not mean their market or their current price, but their part in increasing the nation's wealth. A work of art, for example, might have a high value in exchange; but it would have no 'productive' value unless it were sold abroad, and the money thus realized invested in raw materials, implements, or stock for the production of further wealth. Again, when the Physiocrat spoke of industry as being *stérile*, he did not mean that the craftsman and the artisan had no share at all in the production of the nation's wealth. Far from it; their contribution was a threefold process: as consumers of agricultural products they created a demand which was necessary to sustain a flourishing husbandry; as producers they were creative, for they imparted to the raw materials they fashioned a value as capital; and finally, in performing vital tasks in economic life, they allowed the agriculturalist to devote whole-time attention to his fields. The labours of the artisan and craftsman were unproductive only in the sense that they had no share in the initial process of amassing wealth, in the extraction of raw materials from the earth.

(5)

Nevertheless Turgot himself accused the Physiocrats of being much too fond of saying that industry was sterile and of forgetting too frequently Gournay's denunciations of the restrictions on trade and industry. Professing to be the disciple of both, he held that Gournay, arguing from the principle of economic self-interest, arrived at similar conclusions as Quesnay, who approached the problem of economics from another angle.[68] Gournay had maintained that it was futile for the Central Government to place restrictions upon manufactures, to favour one industry at the expense of another, or to allow towns and guilds to perpetuate monopolies. Turgot sums up Gournay's teaching in three axioms. First: 'Give to all branches of commerce that precious liberty which the prejudices of centuries of ignorance, the support that Government has given to particular interests, the desire for false perfection, have caused them to lose.' Secondly: 'Free the labour of all members of the State with a view to stimulating competition, from which necessarily results perfection in manufacture and a price the most advantageous to the buyer.'[69] Thirdly: 'Give to the buyer the maximum amount of choice by opening to the seller all markets for his goods—a course which is the only means of assuring work its reward and production its expansion.'[70] 'My principles in this matter', he wrote to Dr. Tucker, 'are absolute freedom to import without preference for the vessels of this or that nation, and without any dues of entry; freedom equally absolute to export in every kind of vessel, without any export duty even in times of scarcity; freedom within the country to sell to whom one chooses, without being required to take grain to the public market and without interference of anyone to fix the price of corn and bread. These principles I would extend to all kinds of merchandise, and this, as you are aware, is quite opposed to the practices of your government and of ours.' [71]

But although he spoke in unqualified terms of the desirability of freedom in foreign commerce, he was primarily interested in the abolition of restrictions upon trade and industry within the country, and he invariably makes it clear that he contemplated an overseas commerce confined chiefly to luxuries and to a few raw materials not produced in France. For where food and staple commodities were concerned, the cost of transport would always be exceedingly high in proportion to their value, and therefore it was only on those occasions when there were excessively high prices in France that the English merchants would take corn, for example, to the French ports. Moreover, as Turgot contemplated an improvement of roads and internal waterways, and none at all in shipping, and as it was common knowledge that prices varied from province to province as much as between nation and nation, free trade, he believed, would stimulate internal rather than foreign commerce. Finally, even though a nation might, owing to the possession of extremely favourable material resources, be able to sell a staple commodity cheaply outside its boundaries, it could not develop a large export trade unless it were prepared to import goods to the value of those it sold abroad; and, as the purchase of luxuries was unlikely to restore the balance, it would have to be prepared to forfeit one staple industry to favour another. No nation, assumed Turgot, was prepared to do this.[72]

Hence it was the abolition of restrictions on internal trade and commerce that Turgot had chiefly in mind, and above all those on the grain trade, in attacking which he worked out his principles more fully than elsewhere. First of all he exposes the popular fallacy that hoarding grain is the cause of famine. Merchants store, he argues, only in order to sell again; they preserve the abundance of one year to eke out the dearth of the next; and, if given complete freedom, they naturally sink much of their capital into the construction of large granaries, where grain may be safely and economically preserved. Furthermore, they transfer the glut of one region to make good the scarcity of another; and it is this free movement of grain which at once encourages storage, and yet at the same time renders it a less lengthy, and therefore a less costly, process. Similarly, the increase of granaries facilitates circulation. This storage and the free movement of grain are interdependent factors, and together they ' level, as it were, both time and place, and maintain the price of grain at a rate which is uniform and constant '.[73] This stabilization of prices, he states in a letter to Terray, benefits both producers and consumers.   In support of this contention he gives two tables,[74] the one reflecting conditions in France under a régime of restriction and of an undeveloped corn trade, the other illustrating the position in England, where internal trade was free and the corn trade relatively highly capitalized. He shows, on the one hand, that in England the producer received over a number of years a higher price for his grain than the farmer in France; and, on the other, that over that same period the consumers in England not only paid less for their grain than those in France, but also were never called upon to meet famine prices in times of mediocre harvests.[75] ' One sees ', he had written elsewhere, ' a famine nearly every two years in France, whereas in England, where the corn trade is not only free but also encouraged, there has hardly been a famine these last eighty years.' [76] Whereas in London prices showed remarkable stability, in Paris, and still more in the provincial towns like Limoges, the corn markets displayed violent fluctuations from season to season and from year to year.   During the winter of 1740–41 the price of wheat per *setier* in Paris remained from October to the following February at over 40 *livres*, touching 45 *livres* 6 *sols* in November.   Meanwhile, at Angoulême the price throughout these winter months was always below 17 *livres*.   Under a régime of free trade, merchants would have been rewarded handsomely had they transported grain by land from the cheaper markets to the capital, and they could have made a fortune had they brought in supplies from England; but so primitive and so local was the grain trade, so lacking in large concerns working over considerable areas, that only very few supplies, which came chiefly from the northern provinces, were rushed to Paris, these serving merely to reduce the November price by a trivial amount.

To all these arguments the Abbé Terray took exception, contending that the consumer, although possibly benefiting from steady prices, would in the long run pay a greater average sum for his grain, and that it was not the producer who would gain from the better sale of productions, but the landlords, who would raise the farmer's rent.   For the sake of argument Turgot was ready to concede that the average price of grain might rise; but, he went on to explain, this increase would be apparent rather than real, for it would be necessarily accompanied by an improvement in the purchasing power of the industrial community, a prosperous agriculture stimulating the demand for manufactured products.   That demand in turn would lead to a rise in the wages of the artisans.   As a consequence the wage-earning classes need never fear a gradual increase of prices;

what exposed them to hardships and privations was the rapid increase in the cost of bread occasioned by a seasonal dearth of grain. Consider, adds Turgot, the conditions in Limoges : here, in times of plenty, the price of grain is low—much lower than at Angoulême, which, being a seaport, possesses the rudiments of a grain trade—here, in Limoges, wages are extremely low, much lower than at Angoulême. But when prices begin to soar, they are always higher in Limoges than in the seaport towns. The wage earner of Limoges is consequently at a double disadvantage : he must pay a higher price for his bread than the labourer in Angoulême ; and he must meet that payment with a lower wage. The advantage of free trade to the producer was equally pronounced. It was true that the rents paid by leasehold farmers must necessarily rise, but only at intervals of nine years, for this was the usual duration of leases in the greater part of France. During the intervening years the farmers would reap the reward that came from the better average price of grains ; they would be in a position to amass a store of capital ; and out of this they could defray the costs of improvements in their land and stock. High rents were a sign of agrarian prosperity : low rents obtained in France precisely in those regions, like La Marche and Limousin, where the husbandmen were poor. The interests of landowners and their tenants were identical ; both classes would share in the inestimable benefits deriving from free trade, the former being able every nine years to raise his rents in view of the competition among the farmers to lease domains, the latter receiving the increasing profits during the period that they held the leases. *Métayage*, with its wretched tenantry, would disappear ; capital would flow into husbandry ; surplus capital would return automatically to industry ; and thus a fresh and ever-increasing demand would be created for the productions of the soil. Famine and starvation would be horrors of the past ; and all classes in the realm—landowners, tenants and day-labourers, manufacturers, artisans, and wage-earners—would participate in the prosperity of the nation.

The greatest of all follies was the belief that a grain board could control efficiently the supplies of corn. Even though the royal officials were paragons of probity—which was a most unwarrantable assumption in view of the happenings of the past—they could never hope to grasp the complexities of economic life ; they could never assess demand, or estimate supplies ; and they could never appreciate the numerous factors that at a given time determine prices. The funds at their disposal must always be inadequate : for to trade efficiently in grain required a store of capital ten times greater than the normal income of the State. ' Why attempt ', asks Turgot, ' to regulate a process which, left

to itself, is automatic ?   The price of food, the nation's wealth,
the price of labour, the growth of population are all linked
together; they establish themselves in equilibrium according
to a natural process of adjustment; and this adjustment is
always made when commerce and competition are entirely
free.' [77]

BIBLIOGRAPHY

I. TURGOT'S WORKS

Three editions of Turgot's works have been published : (1) DU PONT DE
NEMOURS, *Œuvres de M. Turgot, précédées et accompagnées de mémoires et de
notes sur sa vie, son administration et ses ouvrages.* 9 vols. 1808-11. The
first volume reproduces, with a few changes, Du Pont's *Mémoires sur la vie et
les ouvrages de M. Turgot,* 1782 (Philadelphia). (2) DAIRE ET DUSSARD. *Œuvres de Turgot, nouvelle édition* . . . *avec les notes de M. Du Pont de Nemours,
augmentée de lettres inédites* . . . *et précédée d'une notice sur la vie et les ouvrages
de Turgot.* 2 vols. 1844. The additons include Turgot's letters, chiefly on
literary topics, to his secretary, Caillard. (3) SCHELLE, G. *Œuvres de Turgot
et documents le concernant.* 5 vols. 1913-23. This edition, which contains bio-
graphical and historical introductions to each volume, adds to the earlier
collections many documents taken from the papers of the Turgot family at
Lantheuil, from the *Archives Nationales,* and from several of the departmental
archives. It includes also : extracts from several documents, since lost,
quoted by d'Hugues (see below) ; three hundred letters written by Turgot to
Du Pont (these, which were obtained from the Dupont family in the United
States of America, probably represent one-third of those which Turgot sent to
his friend) ; letters from Henri (see below) and from the *Œuvres* of Condorcet,
from Burton's *Letters of Eminent Persons Addressed to David Hume* (1849), and
from the *Journal de l'abbé de Véri,* part of which (up to January 1781) has since
been published by Baron Jehan de Witte (see below). Schelle has also included
in his edition extracts from other documents, from contemporary memoirs,
periodicals, and other works. In my references I have frequently cited these
originals when I might more easily have given a page reference to the *Œuvres.*
I have done this in order to make clear the prime authorities upon which my
statements are based. Contemporary sources are often at variance on important
issues : where I have chosen one and rejected another, I wish to show that the
choice, which may be disputed, is my own responsibility. Another reason for
following this method is that, since Schelle sometimes quotes extracts from these
authorities without giving page references, the reader may more easily refer to
the originals. Where the since-published *Journal de l'abbé de Véri* is concerned,
my practice has obviously much to recommend it.

II. MANUSCRIPTS

(1) Archives Nationales, chiefly series H 1503, H 1510, F^{11} 223, F^{11} 155,
K 879, K 899. More detailed mention of manuscripts in these and in other
series will be found in the notes.

(2) British Museum, Additional Manuscripts. These include :

    (a) Letter of Turgot to Miromesnil, 11 April 1775 (Eg. 27 f. 77).

    (b) Letter of Turgot to Dr. Darut, 17 Dec. 1779 (Eg. 27 f. 78).

    (c) Copy of a letter of Turgot to a correspondent in England, 1777
(35,839, f. 377).

(3) British Record Office, State Papers Foreign, 78/287-306, 323, 324,
these being the Dispatches of Lord Stormont, English Ambassador at Paris.

III. Published Documents

Archives Parlementaires. Série I. Vols. ii and iii. 1869–72.

ARNETH, A. D', and GEFFROY, M. A. Correspondance secrète entre Marie-Thérèse at le Comte de Mercy-Argenteau. 3 vols. 1874.

BOISLISLE, A. DE (a) Correspondance des contrôleurs généraux des finances avec les intendants des provinces. 3 vols. 1874–97.

BOISSONNADE, P. Cahiers de doléance de la sénéchaussée d'Angoulême. 1907.

Bulletin de la Société archéologique et historique de la Corrèze. Vols. i and ix. 1878, 1886.

Bulletin de la Société archéologique et historique de la Charente. Vol. xi. 1889.

Bulletin de la Société archéologique et historique du Limousin. Vols. li, lii, and lxi. 1902, 1903, 1911.

Choix de documents historiques du Limousin. Archives historiques de la Marche et du Limousin. Ed. A. Leroux. Vols. iii, iv, and vi. 1887–93.

DEFFAND, MME DU. (a) Correspondance complète . . . avec la duchesse de Choiseul etc. Édition Lévy. 3 vols. 1866.

—— (b) Lettres de la Marquise du Deffand à Horace Walpole, 1766–80. Ed. Paget Toynbee. 3 vols. 1912.

Documents limousins des Archives de Bordeaux et autres villes. Ed. A. Leroux. 1912.

FLAMMERMONT and TOURNEUX. (a) Remontrances du Parlement de Paris au XVIIIᵉ siècle. 3 vols. 1888–98.

GUIBERT, L. Cahiers du Limousin et de la Marche en 1789. 1889.

HENRI, C. Correspondance inédite de Condorcet et de Turgot. 1882.

Historical Manuscripts Commission Reports. (The Ninth Report, Appendix, 481 (Morrison MSS.), cites two letters of Turgot, one dated 1 Feb. 1775, to an unknown person, the other of 20 April 1775, to Du Muy.

HUGUES, G. D'. (a) États généraux de 1789. Cahiers du Bas-Limousin. 1892.

Introduction à l'inventaire des Archives hospitalières. Série A–D. Ed. A. Leroux. 1884.

ISAMBERT, JOURDAIN, and DECRUSY. Recueil des anciennes lois françaises. Vols. xxii and xxiii. 1822–9.

KNIES, C. Carl Friedrichs von Baden brieflicher Verkehr mit Mirabeau und Du Pont. 2 vols. 1892.

LESPINASSE, MLLE DE. Lettres inédites. Published by C. Henri. 1887.

MIROMESNIL, HUE DE. Correspondance politique et administrative. Published by P. Le Verdier. 5 vols. 1899–1903.

PIGEONNEAU and DE FOVILLE. L'Administration d'agriculture au contrôle général des finances, 1785–7. 1882.

PROUST, A. Archives de l'Ouest. 5 vols. 1867–9.

VIGNON, E. J. M. Études historiques sur l'administration des vois publiques. 4 vols. 1862–1881.

IV. Contemporary Periodicals

Encyclopédie ou Dictionnaire raisonné des sciences, des arts et métiers. 17 vols. 1751–65.

Éphémérides du citoyen ou Chronique de l'esprit national et Bibliothèque raisonnée des Sciences Morales et Politiques. 66 vols. 1765–72. (This publication was edited by Baudeau from November 1765 to May 1768, and from then onwards by Du Pont. The collection in the Bibliothèque Nationale is far from complete : that in the British Museum contains 63 vols.—i.e., all issues after the *Éphémérides* became a monthly publication. The volumes are numbered i to xii for each year.)

Nouvelles Éphémérides économiques ou Bibliothèque raisonnée de l'Histoire, de la Morale et de la Politique. (Edited by Baudeau.) Dec. 1774–Feb. 1776.

Gazette du commerce. April 1763, &c.

Journal de l'agriculture, du commerce et des finances. July 1765, &c.

Note.—A number of articles from these periodicals are mentioned in the next section.

V. Contemporary Memoirs and Works First Published Prior to 1789

Acte de bienfaisance du gouvernement (Éph. 1769. vi).
Argenson. Considérations sur le gouvernement ancien et présent de la France. 1767.
Allonville. Mémoires secrets de 1770 à 1830. Vol. i. 1838.
Bachaumont. Mémoires secrets pour servir à l'histoire de la République des lettres en France depuis 1762 jusqu'à nos jours. Continué par Pidansat de Mairobert et Moufle d'Angerville. (36 vols. 1784–9.) Vols. vii, viii, and ix.
Baudeau. (a) Chronique secrète. (Revue rétrospective. Série I. Vol. iii. 1834. 29–96, 262–96, 375–415.)
—— (b) Avis au peuple sur son premier besoin. (Éph. 1768. i, ii, iv, and v. Also apart. 1768.)
—— (c) Suites des Avis . . . sur la cherté du pain. (Éph. 1769. x.)
Besenval. Mémoires. (Barrière. Bibl. des mémoires. iv. 1846. First published in 1805. 4 vols.)
Boncerf. Les Inconvénients des droits féodaux. 1776.
Bougainville. Éloge de Michel-Étienne Turgot. 1759.
Butré. De la grande et la petite culture. (Éph. 1767. ix–xii.)
Cabanis. Essai sur les bêtes à laine relativement au Limousin. (Journ. d'agr. Sept.–Oct. 1767.)
Cahier du clergé du Bas-Limousin. 1789.
Cahier du clergé des sénéchaussées de Limoges et Saint-Yrieix. 1789.
Cahier de la noblesse du Bas-Limousin. 1789.
Cahier de la noblesse des sénéchaussées de Limoges et Saint-Yrieix. 1789.
Cahier du tiers état du Bas-Limousin. 1789.
Cahier du tiers état des sénéchaussées de Limoges et Saint-Yrieix. 1789.
Calendrier ecclésiastique et civil de Limoges. 1770–7.
Campan, Mme. Mémoires sur la vie privée de Marie-Antoinette. (Barrière. Bibl. des mémoires. Vol. x. 1846.)
Cantillon. Essai sur la nature du commerce en général. 1755.
Carlier. Considérations sur les moyens de rétablir en France les bonnes espèces de bêtes à laine. 1762.
Choiseul. Mémoires. Ed. P. Calmettes. 3rd edition. 1904.
Collection des comptes-rendus. 1788.
Condorcet. (a) Vie de Turgot. 1786.
—— (b) Lettres sur le commerce des grains. 1774.
—— (c) Oeuvres (édition Arago). 12 vols. 1847–9.
Coquereau. Mémoires de l'abbé Terrai avec une relation de l'émeute arrivée à Paris en 1775. 1776. (Part ii, 231–72, is known as the Relation Historique.)
Croÿ, Duc de. Journal inédit. Published by Cottin and de Grouchy. 4 vols. 1906–8.
Darigrand. L'Anti-financier. 1764.
Du Hausset, Mme. Mémoires. (Barrière. Bibl. des mém. iii. 1846.)
Du Pont de Nemours. (a) De l'exportation et de l'importation des grains. 1764.
—— (b) Lettre au sujet de la cherté du blé en Guyenne. 1764. (Also Gaz. du com. May 1764.)
—— (c) Lettre sur la différence qui se trouve entre la grande et la petite culture. 1765. (Also Gaz. du com. Oct. 1764.)
—— (d) De l'administration des chemins. 1767. (Also Éph. 1767. v.)
—— (e) Lettre de M. de . . . , Conseiller au Parlement de Rouen, a M. de M . . . , Premier Président. 1768.
—— (f) Observations et réponses sur le commerce des grains et des farines. 1769.
—— (g) Observations sur les effets de la liberté du commerce des grains et sur ceux des prohibitions. 1770.
—— (h) Mémoire sur les municipalités. (See note 4, Ch. XVII.)
—— (i) Analyse historique de la législation des grains depuis 1692. 1789.

Du Pont de Nemours. (j) L'Enfance et la Jeunesse de Du Pont de Nemours racontées par lui même. (1906.)
—— (k) Mémoires sur la vie et les ouvrages de M. Turgot. (See above section I.)
—— (l) Lettre à M. N . . . , ingénieur des Ponts et Chaussées. (Éph. 1769. viii.)
—— (m) Observations sur les effets de la liberté du commerce des grains. Exemple du mauvais effet des règlement contraires a la liberté en Limousin. (Éph. 1770. vi.)
—— (n) Police établie pour les ateliers de charité dans la généralité de Limoges. (Éph. 1772. ii.)
—— (o) Lettres à l'auteur de l'essai sur la richesse et sur l'impôt. (Éph. 1768. ii.)
—— (p) Lettre sur la classe stérile. (Gaz. du com. Feb. 1766.)
—— (q) Vie de Poivre.
Du Puy. Éloge de Turgot. Mémoire de l'Académie des Inscriptions et Belles-Lettres. xlv. 1783.
Encyclopédie méthodique. 1782, &c.
Éphémérides de Limoges. 1765. (Only one number was published.)
État des défrichements et des desséchements. (Éph. 1770. vii.)
Galiani. Correspondance. Ed. Perey and Maugras. 2 vols. 1881.
Georgel. Mémoires pour servir a l'histoire des événements de la fin du XVIIIe siècle. 6 vols. 2nd edition. 1820.
Graslin. Essai analytique sur la richesse et sur l'impôt. 1767.
Grimm, Raynal, &c. Correspondance littéraire, philosophique, et critique. 20 vols. 1877-87.
Guyot and Merlin. Répétoire universel et raisonné de jurisprudence. 17 vols. 1784-5.
Halifax. An essay on taxation, 1693. Somers Tracts. xi. 1814.
Hardy. " Mes loisirs." 1764-73. Journal. (Part published by Tourneux and Vitrac. 1912.)
Journal historique de la révolution opérée dans la constitution de la monarchie française par M. de Maupeou. Journal Historique du rétablissement de la magistrature, pour servir de suite à celui de la révolution opérée dans la constitution de la monarchie française. 7 vols. 1774-6.
La Michodière (Messance). Recherches sur la population. 1766.
La Motte. Memoirs of the Countess de Valois de la Motte, translated by herself. 1789.
Lavoisier. Oeuvres. 6 vols. 1864-93. Vol. v.
Lauzun. (a) Memoirs. Broadway Library Edition. Tr. C. K. Scott. 1928.
—— (b) Mémoires. Ed. G. d'Heylli. 1880.
Lettre qui contient l'exemple d'une correction pastorale et bienfaisante. (Éph. 1767. v.)
Lettre de M. B., gentilhomme limousin. (Éph. 1767. vii.)
Lettre sur les émeutes populaires que cause la cherté des grains. (Éph. 1768. xii.)
Lettre de M. le Curé de Mondréville. (Éph. 1770. v.)
Letrosne. (a) De l'administration provinciale et de la réforme de l'impôt. 1779.
—— (b) Lettre sur l'entière liberté du commerce des grains. (Éph. 1767. xi.)
—— (c) La Liberté du commerce des grains, toujours utile et jamais nuisible. 1765.
Linguet. (a) Le Pain et le blé. 1774.
—— (b) Annales politiques, civiles et littéraires. 19 vols. 1777-92.
Marmontel. (a) Mémoires. Ed. M. Tourneux. 3 vols. 1891.
—— (b) Memoirs of Marmontel written by himself. Nichols edition. 2 vols. 1985.
Massac. Mémoire sur la qualité et l'emploi des engrais. (Journ. d'agr. July and Aug. 1767.)

Maupeouana, recueil des écrits patriotiques . . . 1775.

M.D.T.R. Essai sur le bien public et observations sur les mémoires concernant la vie et les ouvrages de M. Turgot. 1783.

Mémoire sur l'état des paroisses d'Azat-le-Ris et autres circonvoisines. (Éph. 1768. i.)

Mémoire économique. (Éph. 1770. ii.)

MÉTRA. Correspondance secrète, politique et littéraire . . . depuis la mort de Loius XV. 18 vols. 1787–90.

MIRABEAU. (a) Philosophie rurale. 1763.
—— (b) Théorie de l'impôt. 1760.
—— (c) Traité de la population. 2 vols. 1758.
—— (d) Mémoire sur les états provinciaux. 1758.
—— (e) Mémoires. Edited L. de Montigny. 8 vols. 1834–5.

MOREAU DE BEAUMONT. Mémoires concernant les impositions et droits en Europe. 3 vols. 1768.

MOREAU (J. N.). Mes souvenirs. Ed. Hermelin. 2 vols. 1898–1901.

MORELLET. Mémoires inédits. 2 vols. 1823.

Moutre économique. (Éph. 1769. vi.)

MUSNIER. Essai d'une méthode générale propre a étendre les connaissances des voyageurs . . . 2 vols. 1779.

NECKER. L'Administration des finances. Vol. i. 1784.

NORVINS. Mémorial de J. de Norvins. Ed. Lanzac de Laborie. 3 vols.

PALMER. A four months' tour through France. 2 vols. 1776.

POTHIER. (a) Traité du droit de domaine de propriété. 2 vols. 1776–7.
—— (b) Traité du droit de possession. 2 vols. 1771–2.

PRICE, DR. Additional observations on Civil Liberty. Part iii. 1777.

Procès-verbal de l'Assemblée générale du clergé de France, tenue . . . en 1775. 1777.

Protection sagement accordée par l'autorité à la liberté du commerce. (Éph. 1770. iv.)

QUESNAY. (a) Analyse du Tableau Économique. 1760.
—— (b) Grains, Fermiers. (Articles in the Encyclopédie, vii, 1757.)
—— (c) Impôts. (Revue d'histoire des doctrines économiques et sociales. 1908.)
—— (d) Œuvres économiques et philosophiques. Ed. Oncken. 1888.

Relation historique. (See Coquereau.)

Recueil des principales lois relatives au commerce des grains en France. 1769.

Remontrances de la Cour des aides de Paris. 1775.

ROSIER. De la fermentation des vins. 1770.

SAINT-HILAIRE. Mémoire sur les communaux. (Journ. d'agr. July 1767.)

SAINT-LAURENT. (a) Mémoire : quelques importants points de la culture des terres. (Éph. de Limoges. 1765.)
—— (b) Lettre . . . aux auteurs. (Journ. d'agr. July 1767.)
—— (c) Mémoire sur . . . le vin. (Journ. d'agr. June 1767.)

SAINT-MAUR. Essai sur les monnaies. 1746.

SAINT-PÉRAVY. Les effets de l'impôt indirect. 1768. (Also Éph. 1768. xii. 1769. i and ii.)

SAINT-PIERRE. (a) Projet de taille tarifée. 1723.
—— (b) Œuvres de morale et de politique. vol. xvi. 1741.

SAINT-SIMON. Mémoires. Ed. A. de Boislisle. 2 vols. 1904.

SALLIER. Annales françaises . . . 1774–89. 2nd edition. 1813.

SAVARY DES BRÛLONS. (a) Dictionnaire universel de commerce. 3 vols. 1723–30.
—— (b) Universal Dictionary of Trade and Commerce. Tr. Postlewaight. 2 vols. 1751–5.

SEGUIER. Speech pronounced in the Parliament of Paris in consequence of . . . Abbé Raynal's Political and Philosophical History. Tr. O. B. 1781.

SÉNAC DE MEILHAN. Du gouvernement, des mœurs et des conditions en France avant la Révolution (1795). Ed. M. de Lescure. 1862.

SOULAVIE. Mémoires historiques et politiques du règne de Louis XVI. 6 vols. 1801.

Tableau de l'exportation du bled. (Éph. 1768. iv.)
TERRAY. Mémoires. (See Coquereau.)
THICKNESSE. A year's journey through France. 2 vols. 1778.
TREILHARD. (a) Mémoire : de l'industrie et des richesses. (Éph. 1768. i.)
—— (b) Lettres aux auteurs. (Éph. 1772. ii.)
TURBILLY. Mémoire sur les défrichements. 1760.
Un Citoyen français. M. Turgot à M. Necher. 1780.
VÉRI, L'ABBÉ DE. Journal, publié avec une introduction et des notes par le
    Baron Jehan de Witte. 2 vols. 1928.
VOLTAIRE. Oeuvres complètes. Édition Garnier. 52 vols. 1883–5.
WEBER. Mémoires concernant Marie-Antoinette. (Barriére. Bibl. des mém.
    vii. 1846.)
YOUNG. (a) Travels in France. Ed. C. Maxwell. 1929.
—— (b) Travels in France. Second edition. 2 vols. 1794.
—— (c) Letters concerning the present state of the French Nation. 1769.

VI. TURGOT

ANGELESCU, D. Après l'expérience de Law. La lettre de Turgot sur le
    papier-monnaie. 1928.
BARNARD, J. M. Sketch of Anne Robert Jacques Turgot. With a translation
    of his letter to Dr. Price. 1899.
BATBIE, A. Turgot, philosophe, économiste et administrateur. 1861.
BAUDRILLART, M. Turgot. Revue des Deux Mondes. 15 Sept. 1846.
BOUCHET, A. Éloge de Turgot. Académie française. 1846.
BOUDET, H. Discours sur Turgot. Bulletin de la Société Royale d'Agriculture,
    des Sciences et des Arts. Jan. 1822.
CADET, F. Turgot, 1727–81. 1873.
CARRÉ, H. (a) Turgot et le Rappel des Parlements. La Révolution française.
    Vol. xliii. 1902.
CONDORCET. See Section V (a).
DU PONT DE NEMOURS. See Section V (k).
DU PUY. See Section V.
FEILBOGEN, S. Smith und Turgot. Ein Beitrag zur Geschichte und Theorie
    der Nationalökonomie. 1892.
FONCIN, P. Essai sur le ministère de Turgot. 1877.
FENGLER, O. Die Wirtschaftspolitik Turgots und seiner Zeitgenossen im
    Lichte der Wirtschaft des Ancien Régime. 1912.
GERLIER, E. Voltaire, Turgot et les franchises du pays de Gex. 1883.
GOMEL, C. Les Causes financières de la Révolution . . . Les ministères de
    Turgot et de Necker. 1862.
HODGSON, W. B. Turgot : his Life, Times and Opinions. 1870.
HUGUES, G. D'. (b) L'Essai sur l'administration de Turgot dans la généralité
    de Limoges. 1859.
LAFONT, J. Les Idées économiques de Turgot. 1912.
LARCY, M. DE. Louis XVI et Turgot. Correspondant. 26 août 1866.
LAVERGNE, L. DE. Turgot. Les Économistes français du XVIIIᵉ siècle.
    1870.
LODGE, E. Sully, Colbert and Turgot. 1931.
LOMÉNIE, L. DE. Le Marquis, le bailli et Turgot. Programme administrative
    de Turgot. (Les Mirabeau. ii, 393–434.) 1879.
MARION, M. (a) Turgot et les grandes remontrances de la cour des aides, 1775.
    Vierteljahrschrift für Social and Wirtschaftsgeschichte. Leipzic. 1903.
MASTIER, A. Turgot, sa vie et sa doctrine. 1862.
MAXWELL, C. Life and Work of Turgot. History. Vol. xviii. 1933–4.
M.D.T.R. See Section V.
MONTJEAN. Biographie de Turgot. Dictionnaire d'économie politique.
MONTYON, A. DE. Turgot. Particularités et observations sur les ministres des
    finances de France, 1660–1791. 1812.
MORLEY, J. Turgot. Critical Miscellanies, 1877.
NEYMARCK, A. Turgot et ses doctrines. 2 vols. 1885.

NOURISSON, J. Trois Révolutionnaires. Turgot, Necker, Bailly. 1886.
PARTOUNAU DU PUYNODE, M. Turgot. Études sur les principaux économistes. 1868.
RENAUD, G. Les Prophètes de la Monarchie. 1870.
RENAN, E. Turgot. Revue de Paris. 1 juillet 1901.
RIAUX, M. F. Turgot. Dictionnaire des sciences philosophiques. Vol. vi.
ROBINEAU, L. Turgot : Administration et œuvres économiques. 1889.
SAY, L. (a) Turgot. Tr. Masson. 1887.
—— (b) Turgot. 2nd edition. 1891.
SCHELLE, G. Turgot. 1909.
SÉE, H. La notion des classes sociales chez Turgot. (Ch. IV of See (a). See Section VIII.)
—— La doctrine politique et sociale de Turgot. (Ch. III of Pt. IV of Sée (d). See Section VIII.)
SHEPHERD, R. P. Turgot and the Six Edicts. Columbia University Publications. Studies in History, Economics, and Public Law. Vol. xviii. No. 2. 1903.
STEPHENS, W. W. The Life and Writings of Turgot. 1895.
TISSOT, M. (a) Turgot, sa vie et ses ouvrages. 1875.
—— (b) Étude sur Turgot. 1878.
WHITE, A. D. Turgot. Seven Great Statesmen. 1910.

VII. LIMOUSIN AND ANGOUMOIS. THE *GÉNÉRALITÉ* OF LIMOGES

BOISSONNADE, P. La province d'Angoumois au XVIIIe siècle. Bull. de la Soc. arch. et hist. de la Charente. Vol. xi. 1889.
CLAPIER, B. Le métayage, particulièrement en Limousin. 1899.
FAGE, R. La vie à Tulle au XVIIe et XVIIIe siècle. 1901.
GUIBERT, L. (a) La famille limousine d'autrefois. 1883.
—— (b) Livres de raisons, registres de famille et journaux individuels limousins et marchois. 1888.
—— (c) Nouveau recueil de registres domestiques limousins et marchois. 1895.
LAFARGE, R. L'Agriculture en Limousin et l'intendance de Turgot. 1902.
LEROUX, A. (a) La Société d'agriculture de la généralité de Limoges. Bull. de la Soc. agr. du Limousin. 1902.
—— (b) Les Dernières Années de la Société d'agriculture de Limoges, 1786–1790. Bull. de la Soc. arch. et hist. du Limousin. li. 1902.
—— (c) Histoire de la porcelaine de Limoges. 2 vols. 1904.
LEYMARIE, A. Histoire du Limousin. La bourgeoisie. 1845.
MOULÉ and RAILLIET. Turgot et l'École Vétérinaire de Limoges. 1902.
SAUZET. Du métayage en Limousin. 1897.

VIII. GENERAL

AFANASSIEV, G. Le Commerce des céréales en France au XVIIIe siècle. Tr. Boyer. 1893.
ARDASCHEFF, P. Les Intendants sous le règne de Louis XVI. Tr. Jousserandot. 3 vols. 1909.
AULARD, F. La Révolution française et la féodalité. 1919.
AVENEL, G. D'. Histoire économique de la propriété, des salaires, des denrées et de tous les prix en général depuis l'an 1200 jusqu'en l'an 1800. 6 vols. 1894–1912.
BABEAU, A. (a) Le Village sous l'ancien régime. 1878.
—— (b) La Province sous l'ancien régime. 2 vols. 1894.
—— (c) La Ville sous l'ancien régime. 1880.
—— (d) La Vie rurale dans l'ancienne France. 1885.
—— (e) Les Préambules des ordonnances royales et l'opinion publique. 1896.
Biographie universelle. 45 vols. 1842–1865.
BIOLLAY, L. Le Pacte de Famine. 1885.
BLOCH, M. (a) Les Divisions régionales de la France. 1913.
—— (b) L'Assistance et l'État en France à la veille de la Révolution. 1909.

Boissy d'Anglas, F. A. de. Essai sur la vie, les écrits et les opinions de M. de Malesherbes. 3 vols. 1819–21.
Bord, G. Le Pacte de Famine. Revue de la Révolution. Vol. ii. 1883.
Boscheron des Portes. Histoire du Parlement de Bordeaux. 2 vols. 1877.
Brette, A. Les Limites et les divisions territoriales de la France en 1789. 1907.
Bridge, J. C. S. A History of France. Vol. v. France in 1515. 1936.
Broc, H. de. La France sous l'ancien régime. 2 vols. 1887–9.
Bruntière, F. Études critiques sur l'histoire . . . 2ᵉ Série. Malesherbes. 1889.
Burton, J. H. (a) Life and Correspondence of David Hume. 2 vols. 1846.
—— (b) Letters of Eminent Persons Addressed to David Hume. 1849.
Cahen, L. Les Querelles religieuses et parlementaires sous Louis XV. 1913.
—— (b) Le Pacte de famine et les spéculations sur les blés. Revue historique. 1926.
Cambridge Modern History. Vol. viii. Chapters I, II, III, V, and XXIV.
Capron and Plessis. Vie privée du Prince de Conti. 1907.
Carcassonne, E. Montesquieu et le problème de la constitution française au XVIIIᵉ siècle. 1927.
Carré, H. (b) La Noblesse de France et l'opinion publique au XVIIIᵉ siècle. 1920.
—— (c) La Fin des Parlements. 1912.
Champion, E. La France d'après les cahiers de 1789. 1911
Chérest, A. La Chute de l'ancien régime. 3 vols. 1884–6.
Chéruel, A. Dictionnaire historique des institutions, des mœurs et coutumes de la France. 8th edition. 2 vols. 1910.
Clapham, J. H. The Economic Development of France and Germany. 1928.
Clément, P. M. de Silhouette, Bouret, les derniers fermiers généraux. 1878.
Clerget, P. Les Industries de la soie en France. 1925.
Cobban, A. Rousseau and the Modern State. 1934.
Coulaudon, A. Chazerat, denier intendant de la généralité d'Auvergne, 1774–89. 1932.
Denis, H. Histoire des systèmes économiques et socialistes. Vol. i. 1904.
Droz, F. Histoire du règne de Louis XVI. 3 vols. 1839–42.
Dumas, F. La Généralité de Tours au XVIIIᵉ siècle. Administration de l'intendant Du Cluzel, 1766–83. 1894.
Esmein, A. Cours élémentaire de droit français. 1901.
Fagniez, G. L'Économie sociale de la France sous Henri IV. 1897.
Fay, B. L'Esprit révolutionnaire en France et aux États Unis au XVIIIᵉ siècle. 1924.
Fay, C. R. Great Britain from Adam Smith to the Present Day. 1929.
Flammermont, J. (b) Le Chancellier Maupeou et les Parlements. 1883.
Funck-Brentano, F. (a) L'Ancien Régime en France. 1926.
—— (b) The Old Régime in France. Tr. H. Wilson. 1929.
—— (c) Les Lettres de cachet d'après les documents. Revue des deux Mondes. 15 Oct. 1892.
Gasquet, A. Précis des institutions politiques et sociales de l'ancienne France. 2 vols. 1885.
Gide and Rist. Histoire des doctrines économiques depuis les physiocrates jusq'à nos jours. 1909.
Girard, R. L'Abbé Terray et la liberté du commerce des grains. Bibl. de la Faculté des Lettres de l'Univ. de Paris. Série 2. No. 3. 1924.
Glasson, E. (a) Le Parlement de Paris : son rôle politique depuis le règne de Charles VII. 2 vols. 1901.
—— (b) Histoire du droit et des institutions politiques, civiles et judiciares de l'Angleterre comparés au droit et aux institutions de la France. 6 vols. 1881–3.
Godard, C. Les Pouvoirs des intendants sous Louis XIV. 1901.
Guyot, Y. (a) Quesnay et la Physiocratie. 1896.
—— (b) The French Corn Laws. Tr. Probyn. 1888.
Hanotaux, G. Tableau de la France en 1614. 1898.

HASBACH, W. Adam Smith's Lectures. Pol. Sci. Quart. Vol. xii. 1897.
HENNET, L. Les Milices et les troupes provinciales. 1884.
HIGGS, H. The Physiocrats. 1897.
JOBEZ, A. La France sous Louis XVI. 3 vols. 1877–93.
KARIÉW, N. Les Paysans en France dans le dernier quartier du XVIIIᵉ siècle. 1899.
KNOWLES, L. New Light on the Economic Causes of the French Revolution. Economic Journal. Vol. xxix. 1919.
KOVALEWSKY, M. La France économique et sociale à la veille de la Révolution. 2 vols. 1909–11.
La Grande Encyclopédie. 31 vols. 1885–1901.
LA ROCHETERIE, M. DE. Histoire de Marie-Antoinette. 2 vols. 1890.
LAVERGNE, L. DE. (a) Les Assemblées provinciales sous Louis XVI. 2nd edition. 1879.
—— (b) Les Économistes français du XVIIIᵉ siècle. 1870.
LAVISSE, E. Histoire de France. Vols. viii and ix. 1911.
LEGRAND, M. Sénac de Meilhan et l'intendance de Hainaut sous Louis XVI. 1868.
LEMAIRE, A. Les Lois fondamontales de la monarchie française. 1907.
LETACONNOUX, J. Les Voies de communication en France au XVIIIᵉ siècle. Vierteljahrschrift für Social und Wirtschaftsgeschichte. 1909.
LEVASSEUR, E. (a) Histoire des classes ouvrières et de l'industrie en France avant 1789. 2nd edition. 2 vols. 1900–1.
—— (b) Histoire de la population française. 3 vols. 1889–92.
—— (c) Des progrès de l'agriculture française dans la seconde moitié du XVIIIᵉ siècle. Revue d'économie politique. 1898.
L'HÉRITIER, M. L'Intendant Tourny. 2 vols. 1920.
LIPSON, E. The Economic History of England. Vols. ii and iii. 1934.
LOMÉNIE, L. DE. Les Mirabeau. 5 vols. 1879–91.
LOUTCHISKY, J. La Propriété paysanne en France à la veille de la Révolution. 1912.
LUÇAY, H. DE. Des origines du pouvoir ministériel en France. Les secrétaires d'état depuis leur institution jusqu'à la mort de Louis XV. 1881.
LUCHAIRE, A. Manuel des institutions françaises. 1892.
MACDONALD, J. A History of France. 3 vols. 1915.
MARION, M. (b) Les Impôts directs sous l'ancien régime. 1910.
—— (c) Dictionnaire des institutions en France au XVIIᵉ et XVIIIᵉ siècles. 1923.
—— (d) La Chalotais et le duc d'Aguillon. 1898.
MARTIN, M. Petite histoire financière de l'ancien régime. 1922.
MAUGRAS, G. La Disgrace du duc et de la duchesse de Choiseul. 1903.
MORNET, D. Les Origines intellectuelles de la Révolution française. 1933.
NOLHAC, P. DE. Études sur la Cour de France. La reine Marie-Antoinette. 1899.
PAGÈS, G. La Monarchie d'ancien régime en France. 1928.
PALGRAVE, R. Dictionary of Political Economy. 3 vols. 1925–6.
PAULTRE, C. La ' Taille tarifée ' de l'Abbé de Saint-Pierre et l'Administration de la taille. 1903.
PIÉTRI, F. La Réforme de l'état au XVIIIᵉ siècle. 1935.
RENOUVIN, P. Les Assemblées provinciales de 1787. 1921.
ROCQUAIN, F. L'Esprit révolutionnaire avant la Révolution. 1878.
—— (b) The Revolutionary Spirit preceding the Revolution. Tr. J. D. Hunting. 1891.
ROUSTAN, M. Les Philosophes et la société française au XVIIIᵉ siècle. 1906.
—— (b) Pioneers of the French Revolution. Tr. F. Whyte. 1926.
SAGNAC, P. Les Cahiers de 1789 et leur valeur. Revue d'histoire moderne. 1906–7.
—— (b) La Propriété foncière au XVIIIᵉ siècle. Revue d'histoire moderne. 1901.
SAY, L. (c) Dictionnaire d'économie politique. 3 vols. 1891–7.
—— (d) David Hume. 1888.

SAY, L. (e) Vincent de Gournay. 1897.
SAIT, E. The Manorial System and the French Revolution. Pol. Sci. Quart. Vol. xxiii. 1908.
SCHELLE, G. (b) Du Pont de Nemours et l'école physiocratique. 1888.
—— (c) Vincent de Gournay. 1890.
SÉE, H. (a) La Vie économique et les classes sociales en France au XVIIIᵉ siècle. 1924.
—— (b) Une Enquête sur la vaine pâture et le droit de parcours. Revue du dix-huitième siècle. 1913.
—— (c) La France économique et sociale au XVIIIᵉ siècle. 1925.
—— (d) L'Évolution de la pensée politique en France au XVIIIᵉ siècle. 1925.
—— (e) Les Idées politiques en France au XVIIIᵉ siècle. 1920.
—— (f) L'Évolution commerciale et industrielle de la France sous l'ancien régime. 1925.
SÉGUR, P. M. DE. Le Royaume de la rue Saint-Honoré. Madame Geoffrin et sa fille. 1897.
—— (b) Au couchant de la monarchie. 2 vols. 1910.
—— (c) Marie-Antoinette. Tr. Watt. 1927.
SEMICHON, E. Les Reformes sous Louis XVI. 1876.
STOURM, R. Les Finances de l'ancien régime et de la Révolution. 2 vols. 1885.
SOREL, A. L'Europe et la Révolution française. Vol. i. 1902.
TAINE, H. A. The Ancient Régime. Tr. J. Durand. 1876.
TARLÉ, E. L'Industrie dans les compagnes en France à la fin de l'ancien régime. Published in Bibl. d'hist. mod. Vol. xi and also apart. 1910.
THOMPSON, J. M. Lectures on Foreign History. 1925.
TOCQUEVILLE, A. DE. The State of Society in France before the Revolution. Tr. H. Reeve. 1873.
VAISSIÈRE, P. DE. Gentilshommes campagnards de l'ancienne France. 1903.
VIOLLET, P. (a) Le Roi et ses ministres pendant les trois derniers siècles de la monarchie. 1912.
—— (b) Histoire des institutions politiques et administratives de la France.
WEBSTER, N. Louis XVI and Marie-Antoinette before the Revolution. 1936.
WEULERSSE, G. Le Mouvement physiocratique en France. 1756-70. 2 vols. 1910.

NOTES

ABBREVIATIONS

Add. MSS.—Additional Manuscripts in the British Museum.
A.N.—Archives Nationales.
A.P.—Archives Parlementaires.
D.P.—Du Pont de Nemours, *Mémoires sur la vie et les ouvrages de M. Turgot.*
   (Unless otherwise stated references are given to the edition of 1811.)
Éph.—*Éphémérides du citoyen.*
H.M.C.—Reports of Historical Manuscripts Commission.
Œuv.—*Œuvres de Turgot*, edited by G. Schelle.
Œuv., D.P.—*Œuvres de Turgot*, edited by Du Pont de Nemours.
Reg.—*Nouveaux extraits du Registre des assemblées de la Société d'Agriculture de Limoges. Choix de documents historiques du Limousin*, vol. iii.
Stormont.—Dispatches of Lord Stormont (see Bibliography, Section II).
   N.B.—In these notes works are referred to by the author's name, and, if more than one of his publications are cited in the Bibliography, also by the letters (a), (b), (c) . . .

CHAPTER I

[1] Du Hausset, pp. 114–15.
[2] On this section see *Œuv.*, i, 8–20; D.P., pp. 3–7; Condorcet (a), pp. 1–3.
[3] Tr. by W. Forbes-Leith, 1896.
[4] Montyon, p. 172.
[5] Paris, 1739.
[6] Add.MSS. 28,543, ff. 247–59.
[7] Morellet, i, 12.
[8] D.P., pp. 418–19.
[9] Ibid., p. 30.
[10] See Véri, i, 340, 392–3, 409–10, 422–3; D.P., pp. 417–19; Condorcet (a) pp. 255–6; Montyon, pp. 169–70; Sénac de Meilhan, pp. 193–8; Marmontel (a), iii, 92–3.
[11] Véri, i, 449.
[12] On this section see *Œuv.*, i, 20–35.
[13] Morellet, i, 15, 12.
[14] Véri, i, 190–5.
[15] D.P., p. 10.
[16] *Œuv.*, i, 98–100.
[17] Ibid., pp. 194–235.
[18] Ibid., pp. 109–13.
[19] Ibid., pp. 143–51.
[20] *Œuv.*, D.P., ii, 1.
[21] See *Liste d'ouvrages à faire* (*Œuv.*, i, 115–16).
[22] *Œuv.*, i, 157–83.
[23] Ibid., pp. 185–93.
[24] Ibid., pp. 116–42.
[25] D.P., pp. 14–15.   See also *Œuv.*, i, 56–7.
[26] Ibid., pp. 28–9.
[27] Morellet, i, 31.

[28] 121 ff.

[29] D.P., p. 54.

[30] Though he was known as Turgot de Brucourt, he never possessed this particular estate. Later he bought the fief of Laune : hence his title, Baron de Laune.

[31] See Œuv., i, 48–55 and D.P., pp. 28–37.

[32] Condorcet (a), p. 14.

[33] See Rocquain, Ch. V.; Carcassonne, pp. 261–96 ; Lavisse, viii (ii), 237–44.

[34] See below, Ch. X.

[35] Condorcet (a), pp. 15–16. D'Allonville (i, 82) also makes this assertion.

[36] Œuv., i, 387–91.

[37] On this section see Œuv., i, 35–48, 64–76.

[38] See Roustan.

[39] Morellet, i, 140–1.

[40] Turgot also visited the salon of the Duchesse d'Enville, who, along with Mme Blondel, became a life-long friend.

[41] Loménie, ii, 416.

[42] Œuv., i, 57–60.

[43] (a) 201. For a discussion of this point see below, Note 64 to Ch. XVIII.

[44] See Schelle (c).

[45] Turgot acknowledged that he was the disciple of both Quesnay and Gournay (letter to Du Pont, Œuv., ii, 506–10).

[46] See below, Ch. XVIII.

[47] Œuv., iii, 422.

[48] Part of the Éloge appeared in the Mercure de France in August 1759.

[49] Le Conciliateur, a plea for toleration published anonymously in Rome in 1754 and again under Turgot's name in 1788, and accepted as authentic by Du Pont, is attributed by Schelle (Œuv., i, 391–3) to Brienne.

[50] See Œuv., i.

[51] Condorcet (a), p. 7.

[52] Corr., xii, 192.

[53] Cited by Schelle (Œuv., ii, 89).

CHAPTER II

[1] Œuv., ii, 81.

[2] Ibid., pp. 86–8.

[3] The best short account of the French monarchy is that by G. Pagès. For other works see Bibliography.

[4] Montesquieu recognized this in his Esprit des Lois. Had his study of politics remained as objective as he set out to make it, he would have been compelled to admit that the French monarchy was not so despotic as he supposes. All the same, absolutism in France was not tempered in the manner that Montesquieu desired : it was limited as the result of perpetual conflict, and not as the outcome of its harmonious working through the intermediary powers in the realm.

[5] On English politics in the eighteenth century see F. S. Oliver's The Endless Adventure and G. B. Namier's Structure of Politics at the Accession of George III.

[6] Lavisse, viii(ii), 365–8.

[7] Véri, i, 64–5. See also pp. 71, 120–1, 213.

[8] Mémoires des intendants, 1761 (A.N., H 1427/1–34 and in particular no. 25). See also Œuv., ii, 275.

[9] Proust, v. 322.

[10] See below, Ch. X.

[11] Tocqueville (Tr. Reeve), pp. xv. and 72.

[12] Ardascheff's great work errs, I think, in this respect as also do the studies of L'Héritier, Legrand, Dumas, d'Hugues and Coulaudon. Condorcet, (a), pp. 29–30, thoroughly appreciated the limits to the powers of the intendants.

[13] Éph. de Limoges, p. 53 ; Cal . . . de Limoges, 1770, 44, 1774, 35.

[14] Cahier de la noblesse . . . de Limoges . . . , pp. 24–8. Cf. Champion, pp. 78–9.

CHAPTER III

[1] See Bibliography, Section VII. For this chapter I am greatly indebted to Lafarge and also to Loutchisky.

[2] The following description is based upon Bernage, *Mém. sur la gén. de Limoges*, 1698 (A.N., H 1588/28 and Stowe MSS. 902); *Mém. sur la gén. de Limoges*, 1703 (A.N., K 1179/2); *Éph. de Limoges*, 1765; Cornuau, *Carte de . . . Limoges* (see note 41 to Ch. V).

[3] *Rapport de la population*, 1774 (A.N., H 1444).

[4] *Droit écrit* was nevertheless a customary code (see Bridge, v, 64).

[5] Lafarge, pp. 25–6.

[6] Tourny to Saint-Pierre (Saint-Pierre (b), p. 110).

[7] See note 59.

[8] Loutchisky's figures (*Tableau* XVII *et passim*) of the distribution of population among social classes, which are based upon the taxation rolls, are open to objections, for he counted domains and not persons. I have modified his figures in the light of information taken from Bernage, the *Éph. de Limoges*, the *Calendrier* and *Rapport au Conseil*, 1703 (A.N., K 1179/6).

[9] (b), i, 1–7.

[10] *Mém. des intendants*, 1745 (A.N., K 899/39); Cornuau, *Rapport*, 1780 (A.N., F¹²654); *Choix de docs.*, p. 224.

[11] See Tarlé's study of rural industry.

[12] *Œuv.*, ii, 479; *Éph. de Limoges*, pp. 114–22; Cornuau, op. cit.

[13] Young (b), i, 540.

[14] Cf. Bretagne described by Sée (a), pp. 144–8.

[15] *Rapport . . . 1703*, op. cit.

[16] Young (a), p. 302.

[17] Bernage, ff. 4–5, 11.

[18] Turgot, *Circ.* (ii) (see note 9 to Ch. IV). Cf. *Éph.*, 1767, vii, 7–8.

[19] Pothier (a), i, 5–6.

[20] Pothier (b), ii, 269. See Aulard, pp. 1–69.

[21] Musnier, i, 170.

[22] See list in Young (a), p. 332.

[23] *Œuv.*, iii, 247; Du Pont's note in *Œuv.*, D.P., vi, 61; A.N., H 1503/105.

[24] Figures based on Loutchisky, pp. 48, 108–118. Kowalewsky (i, 11, 56–7, 67–88, 123) has challenged these statistics, contending that the *Cahiers* of 1789 prove that the *bourgeoisie* and the nobility held by the far the greater part of the soil. His evidence is thoroughly unsatisfactory, and he fails to recognize that the peasants enjoyed a form of legal ownership and an economic possession of the land. See also Sait in *Pol. Sc. Quart.*, xxiii and Sagnac (b), pp. 169 ff.

[25] *Mém sur la culture des terres*, 1772 (A.N., H 1510/16). Loutchisky (54, 98–101) found that 2 per cent. of the taxpayers in Limousin and nearly 5 per cent. in Normandy were *métayers*, but he admits that in the rolls they figure in their capacity of small proprietors, and not of *métayers*. Contemporaries—Young, Musnier, Saint-Laurent, and Turgot himself—speak of the *métayers* as being very numerous in Limousin and in other regions of *la petite culture*. Young (a), p. 296, says ' *Métayage* is the tenure under which perhaps seven-eighths of the lands of France are held.' But he also speaks of one-third of the soil as being in the hands of peasant proprietors (b, i, 41) and one-sixth or one-seventh under tenant farmers (a, 296). What he probably means is that of the lands which were leased, and not owned, seven-eighths were in the hands of *métayers* and one-sixth or one-seventh in the hands of leaseholders. Had these fractions made a unit, his meaning would have been perfectly clear; but he explains himself further: certain domains were leased twice over, first to middlemen and by them to *métayers* (a, 296). Cf. *Œuv.*, ii, 454–5). All the same, Young under-estimates the amount of leasehold, being misled by the fact that farms were often called *métairies*, though actually leased at a money rent. Turgot (*Œuv.*, iii, 312), giving an impression after reading Saint-Maur's *Essai . . .*, pp. 28–61, mentions four-sevenths of the soil as being in the hands of *métayers*, but elsewhere (ii, 449) cites that figure for the proportion of land under *la petite culture*. Sauzet, working upon *livres de raison* of the *bourgeoisie* and

the nobility, has greatly over-estimated the number of *métayers* in Limousin, having failed to take into account the large amount of land owned by the peasants. (See Lafarge, pp. 36 ff.)

[26] Lafarge, p. 66, citing Musnier, i, 209.

[27] Loutchisky, pp. 48, 60–3, 111–17, 136 ; Lafarge, pp. 47–67.

[28] Lafarge, p. 62.

[29] *Œuv.*, ii, 449.

[30] Young (a), p. 282.

[31] Marcheval to Bertin, A.N., H 1503/223.

[32] *Mém. sur la culture des terres*, op. cit.   On ploughing see also Saint-Maur, p. 28 and Add. MSS. 12, 130 ff. 27–8.   The plough was really a kind of hoe. From watching this implement at work Tull " obtained his idea of horse-hoeing corn." (Young (a), p. 58).

[33] A.N., H 1503/32.

[34] Ibid.   Also H 1503/39, 104 ; *Mém. sur . . . Azat-le-ris (Éph.,* 1768, i, 63) ; Marcheval, op. cit. ; *Cahier de la noblesse de . . . Limoges,* op. cit,, pp. 4–5 ; *Éph. de Limoges,* p. 202 ; Turgot, *L' Avis sur l'imposition,* 1762–74 *(Œuv.,* D.P. *passim).*

[35] Bernage, f. 3.   Cf. *Œuv.*, iii, 317 and Malepeyre, *Mém.* (A.N., F^{14}105).

[36] *Œuv.*, ii, 90.

[37] Bernage, f. 4.

[38] *Œuv.*, ii, 92.

[39] Ibid, iii, 678 ff.

[40] *Choix de docs.*, iii, 260–1.

[41] See also *Mém. sur l'engrais des bœufs,* A.N., F^{10}222 (parts cited by Lafarge) ; Young (b), ii, 32–52.

[42] *Mém. sur la culture des terres,* op. cit. ; Cabanis *(Journal d'agr.)* ; Carlier, pp. 15–6 ; Young (b), i, 419.

[43] Lafarge, pp. 86–9.

[44] Bernage, f. 9.

[45] *Mém.,* 1745, op. cit.

[46] *Œuv.*, ii, 91–2.

[47] Young (a), p. 281.

[48] Malepeyre, op. cit. ; *Choix de docs.* (Beuvron, *Mém.*) vi, 209.

[49] Young (a), pp. 286–7.

[50] *Œuv.*, ii, 453.

[51] Young (a), p. 314.   See Lipson, iii, 142–3.

[52] Bread cost nearly twice as much in England (Young (a), pp. 314–15).

[53] Avenel, passim ; *Éph. de Limoges,* pp. 205–8.

[54] *Mém. sur les fêtes religieuses,* 1763 (A,N., H 1510/29).

[55] (a), pp. 332–3.

[56] Lafarge, pp. 92–128.   Cf. Kowalewsky, i, 306 ff.

[57] See below, Ch. IV, Section 6.

[58] Marcheval, op. cit.

[59] Quoted by d'Hugues (b), pp. 6–7.   For what they are worth the following estimates of population may be cited.   Bernage, 1698—500,000.   Vauban, 1707—585,000.   Add. MSS. 20, 822 f. 32, 1775—376,200.   *Rapport . . .* 1774 —571,175 (births multiplied by 25).   Necker, 1784—646,500 (births multiplied by 25¾).   Many accounts speak of a decline in population up to 1770. Probably Turgot's administration led to the return of exiles and to a greater increase in population than in other parts of France.   Cf. Levasseur (b), i, 213–88.

CHAPTER IV

[1] For financial administration, see Marion (b).

[2] See below, Ch. XI, Section 1.

[3] *Œuv.*, ii, 89–96.

[4] *Projet de taille tarifée* (submitted in 1716).   See Lavisse, viii(ii), 13–14 and for further detail Paultre's study.

[5] Saint-Pierre (a), pp. 22–48, 197–206. See also Treilhard, *Mém. sur la taille tarifée* (A.N., H 1503/106).

[6] *Bull. de la Soc. arch. du Lim.*, 1911, lxi, 604 ff.

[7] Saint-Pierre (b), xvi, 110.

[8] Six hundred parishes were surveyed in two years. (See Orry's correspondence with Tourny, 1738–9. A.N., G^7 45–57.)

[9] See *Méms.* cited by d'Hugues (b), p. 64. See also Turgot, *Circ. aux comm. des tailles*, 10 June, 1762 (ii). N.B.—There are two circulars of this date. The first is reproduced in the *Œuv.* (ii, 136–54) from *Œuv.*, D.P. (iv, 15–50), without date. A short extract of the second taken from D.P. (63–5) is to be found in the *Œuv.* (ii, 154–5). In the *Additions* (v, 668 ff.) Schelle gives the date of the first circular and long extracts of the second from the printed exemplars of these papers to be found in the *Archives Nationales* (K 899/35, 36). This second circular (35) is extremely valuable for understanding the *taille tarifée*, and, in my opinion, Schelle ought to have reproduced it in full. My references are to the original. Yet another circular (Angoulême, 4 Aug. 1762) is in the *Archives Nationales* (37). Schelle mentions it, but does not reproduce it.
It is interesting to note that Du Pont failed to find the second circular of 10 June for inclusion in his edition of the *Œuv.*

[10] A.N., G^7 45, 56.

[11] *Œuv.*, ii, 229.

[12] Ibid., pp. 97–8. The intendants were strongly opposed to the Ministry's ruling. (A.N., H 1427/1–34.)

[13] *Œuv.*, ii, 136 (*Circ.* i). See also below, Ch. XVIII, Section 3.

[14] *Œuv.*, ii, 94–5 and *Circ.*, ii, f. 4.

[15] *Circ.*, ii, f. 4.

[16] *Œuv.*, ii, 106–10.

[17] Ibid., 101–2, 111–15, 163–4.

[18] Cited by Schelle (*Œuv.*, ii, 11).

[19] *Œuv.*, ii, 103–5.

[20] Ibid., pp. 105–6.

[21] *Circ.*, ii, f. 2.

[22] *Choix de docs.*, iii, 349–50.

[23] *Circ.*, iii, f 1. In 1778 the forty-five commissioners were paid 14,200 *livres* (*Choix*, op. cit.).

[24] From this point onwards we have the extract of *Circ.*, ii, cited by Du Pont.

[25] *Circ.*, ii, f. 3.

[26] Ibid., ff. 4–10.

[27] Ibid., ff. 17–18 (Also *Circ.*, iii, ff. 1–2).

[28] Ibid., ff. 2, 16, 19, 21–2.

[29] Ibid., ff. 23–4.

[30] Ibid., f. 2.

[31] *Œuv.*, ii, 228–34.

[32] Treilhard, op. cit.

[33] *Œuv.*, ii, 409–11 (*Circ.*, 10 June 1765), and ii, 622–3 (*Circ.*, 1 June 1767). Lavisse (ix, 25–6) and Tissot (p. 19) are in error when they say that Turgot made a land register.

[34] Ibid., p. 616.

[35] Ibid., pp. 136–54, 177–9, and *Circ.*, iii f. 6.

[36] Ibid., pp. 444–5 and d'Hugues (b), pp. 86–90.

[37] Actually Loutchisky studied the *vingtième* rolls, but these were based upon the reformed *taille* rolls. Kowalewsky is in error when he says that the rolls do not include lands held in privilege. Turgot expressly instructed the commissioners to record these properties, (*Circ.*, iii, f. 14).

[38] *Circ.*, iii, f. 4.

[39] *Œuv.*, ii, 414–6.

[40] Ibid., p. 265.

[41] Ibid., pp. 412–4.

[42] Ibid., pp. 179–83.

[43] D.P., p. 108.

⁴⁴ *Circ.*, iii, f. 6 ; *Œuv.*, ii, 267 ff.

⁴⁵ Turgot, *Circ. aux curés*, 15 July 1766 (cited by Lafarge, p. 150, but not included in the *Œuv.* See Schelle's note, ii, 619).

⁴⁶ D.P., pp. 70–2. Also Du Pont's note, *Œuv.*, D.P., v, 364.

⁴⁷ See *Œuv.*, ii, 169–70, 174–6, 182–3, 248–9, 322–4, 619–21 ; v, 677–9 ; *Œuv.*, D.P., v, 379 ; D.P., pp. 103–4 ; Turgot, *Circ. aux curés*, 4 Aug. 1763 (A.N., H 1503/215).

⁴⁸ *Œuv.*, ii, 170–4.

⁴⁹ See above, p. 42.

⁵⁰ *Œuv.*, ii, 445–77.

⁵¹ 1767, v, 78–105, under the title *Des caractères de la grande et la petite culture.*

⁵² *Œuv.*, v, 680–2.

⁵³ L'Averdy to Turgot, 31 Dec. 1766 (A.N., H 1510, 3/190).

⁵⁴ *Œuv.*, ii, 156–60.

⁵⁵ A.P., ii, 8, 36.

⁵⁶ Kowalewsky cites Turgot's *Mém.* in support of his contention that the nobles held seven-twentieths of the soil. Turgot's meaning is that the nobility received seven-twentieths of the income of the land.

⁵⁷ Montyon, pp. 123–4.

⁵⁸ A.P., iii, 541, 544, 562.

CHAPTER V

¹ Marcheval, op. cit.

² A.N., F¹⁴154.

³ Tourny, *Ordonnance*, Sept. 1731 (A.N., H 1546).

⁴ See Luchaire, pp. 346–7.

⁵ Tourny, *Ord.*, Sept. 1732 (A.N., H 1546).

⁶ Vignon, iii, 78.

⁷ A.N., F¹⁴154 *passim.*

⁸ 23 Oct. 1744.

⁹ *Œuv.*, ii, 208, 211.

¹⁰ Ibid., pp. 121, 219, 221–2.

¹¹ Turgot, *Circ.* . . . 4 Aug. 1763, op. cit.

¹² *Œuv.*, ii, 336–7.

¹³ L'Abbé, D. . . , *Questions concernant l'administration des chemins*, 1776 (A.N., F¹⁴155/4).

¹⁴ *Œuv.*, ii, 342.

¹⁵ Du Pont (d), p. 25.

¹⁶ *Œuv.*, ii, 118–19.

¹⁷ March 1739 (A.N., H 1416).

¹⁸ Du Pont (d), pp. 54–8 ; *Œuv.*, ii, 216–17.

¹⁹ Du Pont (d), pp. 61–2.

²⁰ *Œuv.*, ii, 120. That very year Trudaine's department had been raided, the usual grant of 60,000 *livres* to Limoges being reduced by half.

²¹ Vignon, iii, 58–9.

²² The *élections* and *cour des aides* could claim that they were the only authorities competent to grant reductions on the *taille.*

²³ Turgot, op. cit. Du Pont (d) fails to make this point clear. Turgot, who read the work in manuscript, replied, ' In my opinion several alterations ought to be made . . . ' (*Œuv.*, ii, 517.) But Du Pont's knowledge of technical details of Turgot's reform was never complete.

²⁴ *Œuv.*, ii, 183 ff.

²⁵ L'Abbé D. . . , op. cit.

²⁶ *Œuv.*, ii, 197–209.

²⁷ Vignon, iii, 62 (summarized in *Œuv.*, ii, 218–19).

²⁸ D.P., pp. 73 ff.

²⁹ *Œuv.*, ii, 218–21.

³⁰ Ibid., p. 221.

³¹ Ibid., pp. 319–21 (28 Jan. 1763).

³² There is no documentary evidence on this point. But on several occasions Turgot negotiated with the magistracy (see pp. 51, 106–7, 111, 112, 117).

[33] *Œuv.*, ii, 338–43.

[34] Ibid., pp. 344–54.

[35] *Extr. du Reg. du Conseil*, 24 April 1765 (A.N., F¹⁴155/4). Vignon, ii, 198, cites an *arrêt* of Jan. 1766 (A.N., E 2428), but this is the second issued, and not the first.

[36] In all the *arrêts* the parishes are named. Hence it is possible to trace the scenes of the road-works from year to year. My figure for 1778 is taken from A.N., E 2530.

[37] Millière, *Mém. sur l'admin. des chemins dans la gén. de Limoges*, 1783 (A.N., F¹⁴155/4).

[38] A.P., ii, 7, 25.

[39] *Œuv.*, ii, 353; Vignon, iii, 183.

[40] *Mém. sur les corvées*, 1782 (A.N., F¹⁴155/2).

[41] Cornuau, *Carte de la gén. de Limoges*, 1783 (A.N., F¹⁴155/1). This map, made at Turgot's instigation (*Œuv.*, ii, 680, iii, 51), distinguishes the roads constructed under the *rachat de corvée* and those under the *ateliers de charité*.

[42] Trésaguet, *Mém. sur la construction et l'entretien des chemins . . . dans la gén. de Limoges depuis* 1764, 1775 (A.N., F¹⁴155/4). The first part describes Turgot's reform, and the second explains, with the aid of diagrams, Trésaguet's methods of building roads.

[43] (a), pp. 20–2.

[44] Vignon, iii, 183.

[45] Millière, op. cit.

[46] L'Abbé D . . . , op. cit. The *Cahiers* of 1789 (A.P., ii, 7, 25) complain of the increasing imposition.

[47] *Œuv.*, ii, 404, 425–9.

[48] Ibid., iii, 42–3.

[49] Ibid., ii, 612–14.

[50] Ibid., 611–12.

[51] Ibid., iii, 36–42.

[52] Ibid., pp. 42–3.

[53] He was not successful in building barracks in other towns (*Choix de docs.*, iii, 275).

[54] See Lafarge, pp. 153–63, Marion (c), pp. 376–9, and also Hennet's work on the *Milice*.

[55] For an incident see *Œuv.*, iii, 655–60.

[56] Ibid., iii, 597–611, 655–60 and also ii, 39–40, 597–8.

[57] Véri, i, 78, 216–18, 280–2, 284; Stormont, 30 Nov. 1774; *Œuv.*, iv, 263; Isambert, xxii, 87.

CHAPTER VI

[1] His administration overlapped to some degree that of the Comptroller.

[2] See studies by Sée (a, b, c), Levasseur (c), and Pigeonneau (docs.).

[3] In particular A.N., H 1503, 1510; 'Nouv. extr. du Registre de la Soc. d'Agr. de Limoges' (*Choix de docs., iii*); 'Del. du Bur. d'Agr. de Brive' (*Bull. de la Soc. Arch. de la Corrèze*, i). Lafarge has used these sources. I have studied them and also the *Œuv.* mainly with the object of determining Turgot's attitude to the Government's agricultural policy.

[4] Bertin to Intendants, 22 Aug. 1760 (A.N., F¹²149).

[5] Marcheval, op. cit.; *Reg.* (pp. 161–9).

[6] *Reg.* (pp. 169–70).

[7] Bertin to Marcheval 17 Sept. 1760 and 2 Feb. 1761 (A.N., H 1503/221, 218).

[8] For details of the constitution and membership see *Reg.* (pp. 176–7, 181–2), Sélébran to Bertin, 29 July 1763, *Reglement du Bur. de Brive*, *Arrêt du Conseil du 12 mai 1761*, *Résultat des ass. du Bur. d'Angoulême* (A.N., H 1503/108, 237, 32). Brive held its first session in May 1761: Angoulême in Nov. 1761. Young (a), p. 20, is in error when he attributes the foundation of the *bureau* of Angoulême 'to that distinguished patriot, Turgot'. On other societies see Sée (a), pp. 5–24.

[9] *Reg.* (pp. 190–2).

[10] A.N., H 1510, 3/200.

[11] *Œuv.*, ii, 225.

[12] *Reg.* (pp. 171–6, 185).

[13] *Œuv.*, ii, 225, v, 680; Bertin to L'Averdy, 1765 (A.N., H 1510, 3/217).

[14] A.N., H 1510, 3/202.

[15] Sée (a), p. 97.

[16] *Reg.* (p. 162). Turbilly, one of the founders of the Society of Agriculture of Paris, had gained a great reputation by transforming the *commune* of Villiers into one of the richest estates in Anjou.

[17] Ibid. (pp. 198, 216–17).

[18] *Relevé somm. des Reg. du Bur. d'Agr. de Brive*, 1763–4 (A.N., H 1503/105). Cf. *Reg.* (pp. 251–4).

[19] Sée (a), pp. 98, 107.

[20] *Éph.*, 1770, vii, 228 (Limoges–3628 *arpents*). By 1773 400,000 *arpents* had been reclaimed (Du Pont. See Knies, ii, 140).

[21] *Œuv.*, iii, 316. Cf. *Mém.* read to Society of La Rochelle (A.N., H 1510, 3/177): 'The problem in this region is much the same as that in Limousin: the lack of labour upon the land is everywhere noticeable, there being only ten men at work where there ought to be twenty.'

[22] Guyot et Merlin, xvii, 427–41; xii, 551–7 (cited by Sée (a), 25 ff.).

[23] This hesitancy finds expression in the writings of the Elder Mirabeau, a staunch Physiocrat yet friend of the people.

[24] *Reg.* (p. 239). The only extensive commons were in the heath districts of Bourganeuf (Lafarge, pp. 50–1). See also Sée (a), pp. 53–92.

[25] For the result of Bertin's inquiry, see Sée (b).

[26] *Reg.* (pp. 190–1).

[27] Ibid. (p. 239).

[28] Ibid. (p. 206); A.N., H 1510, 3/97.

[29] *Reg.* (pp. 207, 223).

[30] Ibid. (p. 226).

[31] Lafarge, p. 229.

[32] *Reg.* (p. 226–7); 'L'Épine, *Mém.* au Conseil, 1764' (*Bull. de la Soc. Arch. . . . du Limousin*, li, 124–5).

[33] *Œuv.*, ii, 469 ff.

[34] *Reg.* (p. 236).

[35] Turgot estimated the loss at one-third, (*Œuv.*, ii, 51 ff.).

[36] *Œuv.*, ii, 115–17.

[37] *Reg.* (pp. 188–9).

[38] D.P., p. 125.

[39] *Reg.* (pp. 197–8); A.N., H 1503/13, 22, 24, 48.

[40] D.P., p. 125.

[41] *Reg.* (pp. 223, 255, 262); *Dél . . . Brive* (pp. 564–5).

[42] *Œuv.*, iii, 76–7, 380. See also *Moutre économique* (*Eph.*, 1769, vi, 269–73).

[43] *Reg.* and *Dél . . . Brive, passim.*

[44] A.N., H 1503/36. Marcheval had earlier attempted to introduce 'hay-grass' from England and lucernes and sanfoins from Holland (Marcheval, op. cit., and A.N., H 1503/242).

[45] Cabanis, *Observations sur les mais* (A.N., H 1503/114).

[46] *Reg.* (p. 222).

[47] *Éph. de Limoges*, pp. 198–208.

[48] *Reg.* and *Relevé somm., passim.*

[49] Lafarge, pp. 208–9; *Éph.*, 1769, vi, 263–5.

[50] Fagniez, pp. 106–7.

[51] The bounty increased in stages to 10s. for every pound over 100 pounds.

[52] Lafarge, pp. 206–8.

[53] Probably that in *Éph. de Limoges*, pp. 191–4.

[54] *Reg.* (p. 223).

[55] *Compte des opérations du Bur. de Brive*, 1764–5 (A.N., H 1503/106) (cited in part by Lafarge, p. 203).

[56] *Reg.* (pp. 255, 250).

[57] *Œuv.*, iii, 27, 54; D.P., p. 127.

[58] *Œuv.*, ii, 252.
[59] *Reg.* (p. 267).
[60] L'Épine to Leclerc, 1780 (A.N., H 1503/179).
[61] Lafarge, p. 203.
[62] It was this that had prompted Turgot to reform the *moins-imposé*.
[63] *Œuv.*, ii, 324-5.
[64] D.P., pp. 104-5; *Reg.* (pp. 210, 239); Turgot to Cluzel, 23 July 1767 (*Choix de docs.*, vi, 385-7); Boisbedeuil to Bertin, Oct. 1762, and L'Épine to Bertin, 23 March 1762 (A.N., H 1503/24, 229). See also Moulé et Railliet and Lafarge, pp. 198-201.
[65] *Reg.* (pp. 257-9).
[66] *Œuv.*, ii, 678-80.
[67] *Résultat, op. cit.*; A.N., H 1503/106.
[68] Lafarge, pp, 195-8.
[69] *Relevé somm* . . . *Brive*, 1760-3 (A.N., H 1503/104); Sélébran, *Mém.* ibid. /102); *Reg.* (pp. 168, 222).
[70] *Prog. de Prix* (A.N., H 1503/207); L'Épine to Bertin, 6 Nov. 1767 (ibid. /178).
[71] For Montalembert's researches (Angoulême) see A.N., H 1503/58, 33.
[72] Note 70.
[73] See Ch. IV, Section 6.
[74] See Bibliography.
[75] See Bibliography.
[76] *Reg.* (p. 247).
[77] *Compte des opérations.*, op. cit.
[78] A.N., H 1510, 3/58.
[79] A.N., H 1503/202, 206, 204.
[80] Ibid./200 (L'Averdy to Bertin, 15 May 1766).
[81] Ibid./198.
[82] For subjects see *Reg.* (p. 247).
[83] A.N., H 1503/188 (MSS.). For other examples see H 1503/41, 49 and *Reg.* (p. 287).
[84] Ibid./187 (D'Aine to Bertin, 1777).
[85] *Reg.* (pp. 293 ff.). See also Leroux (b).
[86] *Résultat* . . . Angoulême, op. cit.
[87] (a), pp. 20-1.

CHAPTER VII

[1] Say (c), i, 1095, article on Galiani.
[2] Savary (b), article 'Grains.'
[3] Quoted by Lafarge, pp. 223-4.
[4] *Œuv.*, ii, 469-77.
[5] *Mercuriales et Forléaux de Limoges* (Lafarge, p. 72). See also Malepeyre, op. cit., and *Eph.*, 1767, vii, 6-31.
[6] Say (c), i, 337 (*Céréales*).
[7] Boislisle, i, 252.
[8] A.N., K 1179/8.
[9] Biollay, pp. 152-8, 260-2.
[10] *Œuv.*, ii, 122-8.
[11] Schelle (a), p. 48.
[12] For text, Isambert, xxii, 403. For L'Averdy's policy see Miromesnil, *Corr.*, v, 68-107, and also Girard, pp. 11-13.
[13] A.N., F^{11}223/2 (the intendant of Provence to Terray, 17 Nov. 1771). Bertin had hoped to fix the figure at 10 *livres.* (Biollay, pp. 111-12).
[14] A.N., F^{11}223 *passim*; *Eph.*, 1768, iv, 266-7.
[15] *Reg.* (p. 226).
[16] *Dél. du Bur. d'Agr. de Brive* (p. 571). See also *Œuv.*, iii, 113.
[17] *Œuv.*, iii, 572. See also *Eph.*, 1770, v, 12-24.
[18] Letrosne (c), pp. 59, 74. Roubaud (cited by Afanassiev, p. 160) holds that 2,000,000 *septiers* were exported within four years. Afanassiev (p. 233) states that all the seaports were closed to grain export by 1768; but Girard (pp. 20-1) contends that most of the land exits remained open, though his

evidence is a mere petition drawn up by a sectional interest, the deputies of the chambers of commerce (A.N., F²715). Girard also holds that figures of exports drawn up by the *bureaux des fermes* (A.N., F¹¹223) do not reveal the whole export because the farmers were not interested in levying a number of small dues not included in their *bail*. While this is true, these figures (which are admittedly incomplete in other ways) do, nevertheless, suggest a decrease in export as prices rose ; and it is significant that the Government ordered officials to purchase grain near places of export in order to force up prices, and thereby to render free export inoperative.

[19] *Œuv.*, iii, 20. The Parlements of Grenoble (Dauphiné), Province and Toulouse, and also the Estates of Languedoc and Brittany, upheld free trade (*Éph.*, 1768, vii, 96-105, 1769 ; i, 199-213 ; vii, 100-5, 256). See also Du Pont to the Margrave of Baden (Knies, ii, 142).

[20] *Œuv.*, ii, 469-70, 474-6.

[21] Biollay, pp. 127-58. Malisset was allowed to speculate for his own profit when the price of grain was below 12 *livres*. (Girard, pp. 13-15).

[22] Merchants entered the Limousin ' with their lives in their hands ' (*Éph.*, 1768, i, 68. See also xii, 96-119).

[23] *Œuv.*, ii, 53-4.

[24] Biollay, p. 154.

[25] *Œuv.*, iii, 21-8, 51 ff.

[26] Ibid, pp. 34-5.

[27] Ibid., pp. 491, 573.

[28] Véri, i, 66.

[29] Girard (pp. 32-3) contends that Terray's policy was to establish a just balance between the interest of producers and consumers.

[30] See Véri, i, 118.

[31] *Œuv.*, iii, 265-354. The second, third, and fourth letters were lost during Turgot's lifetime, and our knowledge of them is based on a *résumé* made by Du Pont, who tells us that these letters were lent by Turgot to Louis XVI. The fifth, sixth, and seventh were published (with alterations) by Du Pont in 1778, and these, together with the first, were included in *Œuv.*, D.P. Schelle's text of the four surviving letters is based on the originals (see *Œuv.*, iii, 265, 275).

[32] *Œuv.*, iii, 392-4.

[33] Ibid., p. 271.

[34] Ibid., pp. 398, 468.

[35] Text given in *Œuv.*, iii, 355-7.

[36] Véri, i, 117-19.

CHAPTER VIII

[1] Turgot, *L'Avis sur l'imposition*, 1766-71 (*Œuv.*, ii, iii, *passim.*). See also *Œuv.*, D.P. iv, 253 ; v, 204, 207, 226, 236, 253-4 ; vi, 70-7.

[2] Lafarge (table facing 70) ; *Œuv.*, iii, 111-29 (I have adjusted Turgot's figures to the Limoges measure).

[3] *Œuv.*, iii, 136, 383 ; *Œuv.*, D.P., vi, 70-6.

[4] *Œuv.*, D.P., v, 253-7.

[5] The road contractors (see above, Ch. V).

[6] *Œuv.*, iii, 114.

[7] Ibid., pp. 128-9.

[8] Ibid., pp. 363-8, 142-3 ; *Œuv.*, D.P., vi, 70-6.

[9] In the *Éph. du citoyen.*

[10] *Œuv.*, iii, 376-7.

[11] Ibid., pp. 136, 381, 384.

[12] *Œuv.*, D.P., vi, 38 (note).

[13] Ibid., v, 383 (note).

[14] 29 Jan. 1770 (A.N., F¹¹223/37). See also *Œuv.*, iii, 257.

[15] Turgot to Du Pont (*Œuv.*, iii, 372).

[16] Ibid., iii, 259-60.

[17] Ibid., p. 260.

18 Turgot to Du Pont (*Œuv.*, iii, 261–3).
19 Ibid., p. 263 (citing note from *Œuv.*, D.P., vi, 48).
20 Ibid., pp. 138–40 (see also *Éph.*, 1770, iv, 211–14).
21 Ibid., p. 50.
22 Orry to Tourny, 1736–7 (A.N., G⁷53, 54).
23 *Œuv.*, iii, 134.
24 Ibid., pp. 111–29; Lafarge, p. 255.
25 Parliament prolonged the prohibition of English export.
26 *Œuv.*, iii, 135.
27 Ibid., p. 137.
28 Turgot also encouraged individuals to use these ovens, the result being that the guild of bakers was forced to reduce prices by one-third. Citizens from Saint-Julien, five leagues away, used to carry their loaves to bake them at Limoges. (D.P., p. 99). For a contemporary account of the bread monopolies, see Baudeau (b, c).
29 *Œuv.*, iii, 433–59 (*Compte-rendu des opérations en* 1770 *et* 1771).
30 *Œuv.*, D.P., vi, 308.
31 *Œuv.*, iii, 310.
32 Ibid., pp. 462–8.
33 Ibid., p. 153.
34 Ibid., pp. 358, 361.
35 *Compte-rendu*, op. cit. *passim.*
36 *Œuv.*, iii, 360 ff., 460.
37 Ibid., p. 427.
38 A.N., G⁷53.
39 *Œuv.*, iii, 243–4.
40 Ibid., pp. 245–9.
41 *Œuv.*, D.P., vi, 59–61 (note).
42 The State did indeed maintain the *enfants-trouvés*. Turgot reformed these foundling hospitals in his *généralité*, his sub-delegate, Boisbedeuil, reorganizing that at Angoulême, where formerly hardly a child lived to reach the age of twenty (see *Reg*, (pp. 234, 237)).
43 *Reg.* (p. 283).
44 A.N., H 1546.
45 Letrosne, *Mém.*, A.N., H 1502.
46 *Œuv.*, iii, 125.
47 D.P., p. 92.
48 *Œuv.*, iii, 205–19.
49 Ibid., pp. 224, 210–11.
50 Ibid., p. 212.
51 ' Notes hist. sur Meymac ' (*Bull. de la Soc. Arch. de la Corrèze*, ix, 111 ff.).
52 *Œuv.*, iii, 223, 239.
53 Known as *marreaux* (*méreaux*).
54 ' Police établie pour les ateliers de charité ' (*Eph.*, 1772, ii, 195–206; *Œuv.*, iii, 229–32).
55 *Œuv.*, iii, 250–1.
56 Treilhard, Letter in *Éph.*, 1772, ii, 194–5.
57 See Ch. V, note 41.
58 *Œuv.*, iii, 443.
59 L'Abbé D . . . , op. cit.
60 *Œuv.*, iii, 125.
61 Ibid., p. 435.
62 Ibid., p. 215.
63 *Invent. des Arch. hospitalières* (A-D).
64 *Œuv.*, iii, 225.
65 Ibid., p. 217.
66 *Œuv.*, D.P., v, 422–4 (note).
67 *Œuv.*, iii, 432–3.
68 Ibid., p. 553.
69 Ibid., pp. 458–9.

Chapter IX

[1] *Œuv.*, iii, 661, 664–6, 675.

[2] Stormont, 4 May, 1774.

[3] Ibid., 4 and 5 May; Véri, i, 86–9.

[4] The phrase soon became widely known (see Stormont, 11 May).

[5] See Soulavie, ii, 42 ff.; Véri, i, 109; Arneth, ii, 10 (Mercy to Marie-Thérèse).

[6] Stormont, 18, 25 May, 8 June; Véri, i, 97–8, 108, 170–1. According to Moreau, Louis would fly in despair from the Council Room, but Véri (i, 228) tells us that the King never tired of the small committees that were organized at the beginning of the reign.

[7] Stormont, op. cit.; Véri, i, 94–5, 109, 126, 248–9.

[8] Stormont, 25 May.

[9] See Véri's comments (i, 153, 205–6, 240–3). See also Métra, i, 105, and Arneth, ii, 256–7 (Mercy).

[10] Arneth, ii, 291 (Marie-Thérèse).

[11] Véri, i, 298.

[12] Stormont, 11, 18, 25 May, 1, 8, 15, 18, 22 June; Véri, i, 110, 138–9, 241; Arneth, ii, 173 (Mercy, 15 June).

[13] On the day of the funeral the inns at Saint-Denis were full of drunkards (*Journ. Hist.*, vi, 8–9).

[14] Stormont, 15 June.

[15] Ibid., 11 May.

[16] Ibid., 1 June.

[17] Different versions of this letter are to be found in *Journ. Hist.*, vi, 10; Véri, i, 93; Stormont, 1 June. On Maurepas' appointment, see Stormont, op. cit., Véri, i, 94; *Journ. Hist.*, vi, 10, 19–20.

[18] Véri, i, 30–3.

[19] Stormont, 29 June. See also Marmontel (a), iii, 87–8. Du Pont (Knies, ii, 351).

[20] *Œuv.*, pp. 452–3.

[21] At first Véri (i, 94, 96) pictures Maurepas in a kindly light and praises him for his masterly moderation and for his genuine design to teach Louis the art of government. But later (after July—see i, 112, 162), though still convinced that Maurepas was acting in good faith, he criticizes him for failing to protect the King from the intrigues at the Court. Later still (i, 244–7, 250–1, 268, 282–3), Véri became hostile to him, and in the end (i, 368–9, 394, 411–12, 445–9) could find nothing to say in his favour.

[22] See Véri, i, 134, 170–1, 188–9. Georgel (i, 371–2) believed that Maurepas had but very little influence during the early days of the reign.

[23] Stormont, 22 June.

[24] Stormont (11, 18 May, 8 June) and Véri (i, 99–103) agree on this.

[25] Rochford to Stormont, 10 June; Stormont, 1 June; Véri, i, 76–7.

[26] Véri, i, 106–7.

[27] Stormont, 8 June.

[28] Véri, i, 110; Arneth, ii, 198 (Mercy).

[29] Stormont, 15 June.

[30] Baudeau (a), 273–8.

[31] Stormont, 15 June. Cf. Véri, i, 113.

[32] Montyon, p. 175 (cited Foncin, p. 41). Cf. Turgot's words to Du Pont (*Œuv.*, iv, 83).

[33] Métra's story (i, 67–8), that Louis suddenly decided upon Turgot after hearing him denounce Terray's impositions in the Council that he had attended in order to receive instructions before returning to his province, cannot be substantiated.

[34] Véri, i, 128–30, 143–4. Cf. Montyon, 165–85, and Morellet, i, 230–1.

[35] For contemporary comments on Turgot's appointment, see Foncin, 42–4 and *Œuv.*, iv, 74–8.

[36] Arneth, ii, 207. Véri maintains that the Queen had no influence upon the Ministerial changes of 1774 (i, 111).

[37] D.P., pp. 409–10.
[38] Œuv., iv, 80, 94.
[39] Ibid., p. 92.
[40] Ibid., pp. 7, 91–2. See also Véri, i, 172–4 and Du Pont (q).
[41] Foncin, 45 ; Œuv., iv, 90–1.
[42] Œuv., iv, 92–3. (See also Condorcet (a), 61).
[43] Ibid., pp. 87, 89.
[44] Ibid., p. 88.
[45] See Véri, i, 162, 169.
[46] D.P., pp. 131–4.
[47] For the naval reforms of Sartine and Castries, see Lavisse, ix, 60–5, 68–70.
[48] Stormont, 6, 13 July, 3 Aug. ; Véri, i, 113, 115, 129, 162.
[49] Véri, i, 97, 134. Later a small committee for financial affairs was in existence. (Véri, 14 Aug., i, 171).
[50] Ibid., p. 122 ; Stormont, 10, 31 Aug.
[51] Véri, i, 127, 157. Turgot pressed for Malesherbes.
[52] Ibid., p. 128.
[53] Ibid., p. 161. Véri frequently denounced to Maurepas the practice of opening the post (see i, 109, 248–9), and also the King's habit of employing informers (i, 274–5). Turgot believed that Maurepas could have abolished these abuses had he honestly made the effort (i, 334).
[54] 3 Aug. Cf. Véri, i, 161–2.
[55] Véri, i, 150–1, 154–5.
[56] Ibid., 159. See also pp. 162 and 176.
[57] This narrative, which I have shortened and rearranged, is from Véri, i, 182–7 (23, 24 Aug.). Véri's story is unfinished, for Cahier 13 of his Journal has been lost, the next beginning with 12 Sept. Cf. D'Allonville, i, 110.
[58] 29 Aug., 1774 (cited by Foncin, p. 49, and in Œuv., iv, 103). Véri, i, 156, 157, implies that Turgot was prepared to point out to Louis that he would be leaving a relatively secure and agreeable office for one which was precarious and difficult. Baudeau maintains that Turgot raised no objections to taking the Finances, and Condorcet (a, 63) goes so far as to say that he was glad to leave the Marine.
[59] See below, p. 278.
[60] Say (b, 93) notes : ' After having written the words contre la générosité de Votre Majesté, Turgot had traced the words et de la, when he checked himself and covered dela by des personnes.
[61] Œuv., iv, 109–13.
[62] For extracts from their correspondence see Foncin, pp. 51–2, and Œuv., iv, 19–20, 102 ff.
[63] Stormont, 31 Aug. ; Véri, i, 159.
[64] Coquereau, p. 230.
[65] Foncin, p. 51, citing Métra, i, 67.
[66] Arneth, ii, 241, 229. Mercy states (Arneth, ii, 237) that the Queen raised no objection to Turgot's appointment.
[67] For text see Œuv., iv, 106–7.
[68] Stormont writes (27 July) : ' M. Turgot's nomination was a most favourable circumstance for the old Parlement, and was considered as such by all that party.' See below, Ch. X, section 2.
Métra (i, 67) says, with some degree of truth, that Turgot's appointment was universally approved. But there is no evidence for Funck-Brentano's statement (b, 319, cf. 357) that the voice of public opinion brought Turgot, and later Malesherbes, into the Ministry against the wishes of Maurepas who enjoyed the King's confidence, unless it is Du Pont's assertion (Knies, ii, 350) that the public voice called Turgot to the Finances.

CHAPTER X

[1] On this section see Lavisse, viii (ii), 379–88, 391–403 ; Funck-Brentano (b), pp. 244–50 ; Carré (b, c) ; Flammermont (a, b) ; Marion (a) ; Rocquain (a, b) ; Carcassonne, pp. 379–467 ; Journ. Hist., i–v.

[2] Véri, i, 207–8.

[3] Ibid., p. 121.

[4] E.g. at Rennes, Aix, Lyons and Besançon.

[5] Véri exaggerates (i, 72–4, 121–4).

[6] Carré (a) was the first to challenge the traditional view, based upon Métra, i, 110, and others, that Turgot was opposed to the restoration of the Parlements. As Carré has shown, Georgel (i, 385), Soulavie (i, 195, 200, 237, 253) and Albertas (*Journal, Bibl. Nat.* MSS. *nouv. acq.* 4389, f.2052, f.2060, f. 2062)— all state that Turgot favoured the recall of the ancient magistracy. Carré has also reminded us that Voltaire's letters to Condorcet (*Œuv.*, Garnier, xlix, 539, 443), in putting forward the view that Turgot was the dupe of Maurepas and Miromesnil, assume that Turgot favoured the reversal of Maupeou's *coup d'état*. An equally weighty authority in Carré's opinion is the *Journal Historique* (vi, 185, 205), a promagisterial publication which makes quite clear that Turgot was invited to attend the committees that discussed the question of the Parlement because he had pronounced in favour of recall, Maurepas, it seems, having ignored those (Vergennes and Du Muy) who were prepared to speak for the existing *régime*.

Carré's view is substantiated by Turgot's letters to Du Pont, by Stormont's dispatches, and by Véri's *Journal*; but these authorities compel us to reject Carré's suggestion that Turgot was deceived by Maurepas and Miromesnil, who misrepresented to him their real intentions. Turgot was not deceived : he knew that they wanted to restore to the magistrates a large degree of their ancient powers without appearing to prejudice the Royal authority : and it was his policy to force them to provide guarantees for Louis's prerogative which they professed to uphold. That policy, though meeting with momentary success, ultimately failed ; but, as our narrative shows, Turgot took a more definite course than that described by Carré.

[7] Letters to Du Pont (*Œuv.*, iii, 398, 470, 471, 475, 477–8).

[8] Ibid., p. 469.

[9] Stormont, 31 Aug.

[10] Ibid., 13 July. For Miromesnil's negotiations with Maupeou, see Carré (a), pp. 194–5.

[11] Véri, i, 211, 214.

[12] Stormont, 10 Aug.

[13] Maurepas is supposed to have said, ' The King must be master of the Parlement, and yet no one must think it so.' (Lavisse, ix, 13–4) Carré takes the view that Maurepas and Miromesnil were not ' republicans ', and yet did not want to pass for absolutists. It would be truer to say, however, that they were not absolutists, and yet did not want to appear, in the King's eyes, as ' republicans '. Véri (i, 175) implies that Maurepas genuinely desired a compromise.

[14] Stormont, 6 July. Cf. Véri, i, 150.

[15] Véri, i, 155.

[16] Stormont hints that the magistrates were organizing displays of popular disapproval of the King and the Queen.

[17] Stormont, 24 Aug.

[18] Véri, i, 171.

[19] Ibid., p. 202. See also Moreau, ii, 104–5.

[20] Stormont, 21 Dec.

[21] Lavisse, ix, 17

[22] Cf. Véri, i, 204.

[23] *Procès-verbal du lit de justice du 12 novembre* 1774 (printed, Paris, 1774) See also Stormont, 14, 23 Nov. and Véri, i, 209–12. The *Enquêtes* and the *Requêtes*, formerly the scenes of many constitutional conflicts, were not restored.

[24] Stormont, 31 Aug.

[25] Ibid., 16 Nov.

[26] Ibid., 14, 30 Nov., 7 Dec.

[27] See Véri, i, 225–6, 232–5, and Stormont, 4, 11, 20 Jan. 1775.

[28] Lavisse, ix, 16 ; Foncin, p. 133.

[29] *Œuv.*, iv, 281.

CHAPTER XI

[1] For the organization of these councils see Marion (c), Viollet (a, b), Saint-Simon, iv–vii.

[2] Excluding the *Conseil de conscience*, which disappeared after the Regency, and the *Conseil de guerre* created by Brienne in 1787.

[3] Strictly speaking, the title of Minister belonged only to those who had entry to the *Conseil d'en haut*. The four Secretaries of State (Foreign Affairs, War, Marine, Household), the Chancellor and the Comptroller-General were not necessarily Ministers of State, and there were times when even the Minister for Foreign Affairs was not called to the Council. It was customary, however, to call these secretaries *Ministers*.

[4] The *conseillers d'état*, who should be distinguished from the even more numerous *conseillers du roi*—a title given freely to countless persons—were recruited principally from the intendants and masters of requests.

[5] Re-established in 1730 and in 1787 united to the *Conseil des finances*.

[6] Véri, i, 96–7. Even the *Conseil d'en haut* often took the form of a reading without discussion of items from a gazette, and it was not unusual for Ministers never to set eyes upon important dispatches. Louis XV sometimes signed contradictory orders. Maurepas's plans to stir the councils into greater activity, besides having the object of teaching the King his business, were designed to check the despotism of the departments of State (Véri, i, 134–5, 157–9).

[7] See Véri, i, 156–7.

[8] Véri (1782: part of his *Journal* not yet published, cited in *Œuv.*, iv, 122–3). See also Véri, i, 95–6, 134.

[9] Véri, i, 129–30, 156. Terray was appointed not because he possessed financial abilities, but because Maupeou hoped to find him a useful ally against Choiseul. (Coquereau, p. 9). See also Girard, pp. 28–30.

[10] See Foncin, pp. 57–77 and *Œuv.*, iv, 120–35.

[11] He later became Chief Inspector of Commerce.

[12] These remonstrances were printed, and gained wide circulation.

[13] In the eighteenth century the newer form of specialization according to types of business was slowly replacing that according to geographical areas (see Girard, pp. 36–7).

[14] Fargès once intendant of Bordeaux, had been dismissed by Terray for collaborating with the Parlement to render inoperative an *arrêt du conseil*. Turgot commented: ' . . . It is a great fault but one can pardon a poor intendant ' (*Œuv.*, iii, 418).

[15] Albert held his office by commission.

[16] Stormont, 31 Aug. 1774.

[17] *Coll. des comptes-rendus*, pp. 115 ff.

[18] Véri, i, 69, 113–15.

[19] D.P., p. 340.

[20] A very detailed and fairly accurate description of the French finances during the Seven Years' War is to be found in the Add. MSS., 38,468.

[21] *Coll. des comptes-rendus, passim.*

[22] A contemporary English source describes these as ' negotiable effects payable on demand and something of the nature of English bank notes '. (Stowe MSS. 88 f.9).

[23] *Journ. Hist.*, iv, 45 ; Moreau, ii, 34 ; Linguet (b), iii, 179, vi, 390.

[24] Véri, i, 69–70, 113, 141–3.

[25] Foncin, p. 79 (citing Weber, i, p. 83).

[26] 16 Nov. 1774.

[27] The *revenus casuels* (or *parties casuelles*) comprised the various dues on transfer of offices, and also the taxes imposed on office-holders.

[28] It is possible that he intended to substitute a tax for the customary gift.

[29] Foncin, pp. 78–89 ; *Œuv.*, iv, 20 ff.

[30] Stormont, 16 Nov. 1774 ; Véri, i, 201. Turgot's proposals included : a system of rationing and billeting at market rates ; the abolition of venal offices ; the reduction of excessive salaries and luxury ; the throwing open of army careers to talents (*Œuv.*, iv, 137–46).

[31] *Œuv.*, iv, 136-7.

[32] Ibid., p. 108.

[33] A fund for debt redemption established by Machault in 1749. Terray had suspended its activities, but dared not oust the Treasurer, Longchamp, whose wife was governess to the royal bastards (*Œuv.*, iv, 24-5, 129-31 ; Véri, i, 319, 321).

[34] See note 27.

[35] *Œuv.*, iv, 147. Du Pont (D.P., p. 167) erroneously states that Turgot abolished the office of Court Banker.

[36] Ibid., pp. 283-7, 291-5 ; D.P., pp. 248-50.

[37] *Œuv.*, iv, 288-90.

[38] Ibid., pp. 291-2 ; Lavisse, ix, 29. For other minor economies, see *Œuv.*, iv, 282, 290, 520-6, 652-3 ; v, 300.

[39] Véri, i, 270-1.

[40] Ibid., pp. 358-9, 367-9 ; Stormont, 4 Jan. 1775 ; Arneth, ii, 386-7 (Mercy).

[41] Arneth, ii, 249-50 (Mercy).

[42] Véri, i, 304.

[43] See Roustan, Ch. V, and Clément.

[44] E.g., Baudeau (a), Mirabeau (b), and Darigrand.

[45] The *ferme générale*, originated in 1680, was reorganized in 1726, after which date it remained substantially unchanged.

[46] In 1726 the value of the lease was only 80,000 *livres*.

[47] 16 Nov. 1774.

[48] *Œuv.*, iv, 12-13.

[49] The *croupier* advanced money and received profits, though he performed no administrative work. The pensioner received profits without even advancing money, the pension being the reward for influence in obtaining office for the farmer whose profits he shared.

[50] Coquereau, 241-5 (reproduced in *Œuv.*, iv, 154-6).

[51] *Œuv.*, iv, 150-4, 157-8. See also Foncin, pp. 90-4.

[52] Mlle de Lespinasse to Guibert, 30 Sept. 1774 (Foncin, p. 95) ; D.P., p. 176. (See *Œuv.*, iv, 108-9).

[53] Véri, i, 272 ; D.P., p. 177.

[54] Cited in *Œuv.*, iv, 22-3.

[55] D.P., p. 169-170. But Du Pont's figures exaggerate.

[56] See Marion (c), pp. 247-50.

[57] Véri, i, 139-141. The financiers had claimed that the monopoly would reduce smuggling.

[58] Cf. his letter to Du Pont (16 July 1771, *Œuv.*, iii, 490-2), in which he states that he would refuse to execute in Limoges Terray's project to increase the *gabelles*.

[59] *Œuv.*, iv, 159-64.

[60] More strictly the *domaine corporel*, composed of real property : the *domaine incorporel* was composed of pecuniary rights (*droits domaniaux*), which included *droits d'amortissement, de contrôle, de petit scel, de franc-fief*, &c.

[61] p. 411.

[62] Véri, i, 135-8. See also Mlle de Lespinasse, 19, 22, 30 Sept. 1774 (cited Foncin, pp. 110-12, and *Œuv.*, iv, 174, 176).

[63] *Œuv.*, iv, 176-7. The question whether a *régie* was preferable to a *ferme* was frequently debated. Montesquieu, having denounced the tax-farm, later admitted that where new taxes were concerned, the farmers reduced defaults and expenses of collection. Opinion came to favour the *régie*, and Necker, in deference to it, established a *régie générale* in 1780.

[64] These were *droits domaniaux* (see note 60). Terray, upon the advice of the more enlightened officials, had reformed the *hypothèques* in 1771.

[65] *Œuv.*, iv, 177 ; D.P., pp. 159-60.

[66] *Œuv.*, iv, 179.

[67] Ibid., pp. 364-78.

[68] Lavoisier, *Œuv.*, v, 693-702. Véri (i, 402-3) records that Americans

visited France in 1776 to learn the new processes. According to Bachaumont (vii, 338) and Métra (i, 339), Turgot's reform met with great opposition from Du Muy in Council.

⁶⁹ A financier said to Véri : ' Turgot will crush us . . . but at present I cannot complain : he has done no injustice against which we may rightfully protest ' (Dec. 1775, i, 381). See also i, 341.

⁷⁰ Métra, i, 68. The rumour was common enough when Bertin and L'Averdy were at the Finances. See News Letters, Liverpool Papers, Add. MSS., 38,201 ff., 261, 370.

⁷¹ Véri's language (i, 372) suggests that Turgot was planning a *régie générale*.

⁷² Véri, i, 371–3.

⁷³ Ibid, pp. 378–80.

⁷⁴ Ibid, p. 380.

⁷⁵ ' Those who are hostile to the Controller (and all those who live by plundering the revenue are so to a man) hold one uniform language, representing him as a visionary theorist.' (Stormont, 30 Nov. 1774. Cf. Véri, i, 341).

⁷⁶ Véri, i, 410.

⁷⁷ See below, pp. 278–9. Véri (i, 394) suggests that early in 1776 Turgot had shelved his more elaborate and more revolutionary reforms. For his projects, see Œuv., v, 316–7, citing D.P., pp. 334, 344.

⁷⁸ The reform of the *vingtième* of Paris had given rise to the attack.

⁷⁹ Œuv., iv, 334.

⁸⁰ D.P., pp. 193 ff.

⁸¹ Œuv., iv, 350–1.

⁸² Ibid., pp. 338–47. See also Véri, i, 226–7, and Turgot's letters to individual intendants (Œuv., iv, 347–8, 352–8).

⁸³ Ibid., pp. 338–347. Turgot had also sanctioned a *subvention territoriale* in the three *généralités* of Normandy to meet the cost of refunding the capital of various magisterial offices suppressed in the Parlement of Rouen (ibid., pp. 352–8).

⁸⁴ The *octrois* were originally revenues conceded to the towns and other communities. Later they were shared by the State and these bodies, the former receiving (in 1789) 46,000,000 *livres* out of 70,000,000. In 1681 the *octrois* of Paris were brought under the *ferme générale*. In 1758 further *octrois* (*droits reservés*) were conceded to the towns to enable them to make their *dons gratuits* to the Treasury.

⁸⁵ Œuv., iii, 555–9.

⁸⁶ Ibid., iv, 179–83.

⁸⁷ Ibid., pp. 183–4.

⁸⁸ Ibid., pp. 329–30.

⁸⁹ Ibid., pp. 184–5, 322–3, 325–8.

⁹⁰ See note 84.

⁹¹ Œuv., iv, 330–2.

⁹² Ibid., pp. 165–8.

⁹³ Ibid., pp. 170, 358, 360–2 ; v, 317–320. Mention of other measures which reduced indirect taxation will be found in Ch. XII and Ch. XIV.

⁹⁴ Œuv., v, 321, 326.

⁹⁵ Véri (i, 320) gives the figure of 2,000,000, having included the savings on the costs of the transport of money.

⁹⁶ D.P., p. 256.

⁹⁷ Œuv., iv, 26, 657, 664–6 ; v, 327. Véri (i, 381) states that the clergy were not altogether opposed to Turgot's finance.

⁹⁸ Œuv., iv, 654–5 ; v, 308–311. See also Véri, i, 321.

⁹⁹ Véri, i, 410.

¹⁰⁰ Œuv., v, 354–8.

¹⁰¹ Véri, ii, 26.

¹⁰² Œuv., v, 300–6.

¹⁰³ Véri, i, 372 ; ii, 26.

¹⁰⁴ Œuv., v, 2–3, 306–8.

¹⁰⁵ Véri, i, 373. See also 321 and 396.

Chapter XII

[1] *Œuv.*, iv, 34–6. See also Coquereau, 169–70 and Baudeau (a), pp. 292–3.

[2] See Biollay, pp. 168 ff., Afanassiev, pp. 169 ff., Girard, pp. 34–7 and Véri, i, 75–6.

[3] Véri, i, 117–18, 156. See also Girard, pp. 34–5.

[4] Véri, i, 150–1, 200–1 ; Arneth, ii, 221 (Mercy).

[5] For Bertin's observations on Turgot's project, see *Œuv.*, iv, 200. See also Baudeau (a), pp. 413–14.

[6] Véri, i, 200–1.

[7] *Œuv.*, iv, 201–10.

[8] Stormont, 14 Sept. 1774.

[9] *Œuv.*, iv, 210–12, 214–15.

[10] See above, pp. 109–10.

[11] *Œuv.*, iv, 38. On Galiani's ideas and his disputes with the Physiocrats, see Foncin, pp. 101–2.

[12] Stormont, 21 Dec. 1774. See also Véri, i, 224.

[13] *Œuv.*, iv, 217–20 ; Véri, i, 224.

[14] Coquereau, p. 235 (*Relation Historique*).

[15] See *Œuv.*, iv, 40–4, 185–94, and Foncin, pp. 74–5.

[16] Métra, i, 102 ; Knies, ii, 344 ff. ; Véri, i, 150 ff.

[17] *Œuv.*, iv, 222–3 ; Foncin, p. 108.

[18] It cannot be stressed too much that Turgot's legislation freeing the grain trade was not a measure introduced in face of hostile opinion.

[19] Véri, i, 283–4. For details of these writings see Foncin, pp. 170 ff.

[20] *Œuv.*, iv, 231, 395–404 ; Foncin, pp. 184–5.

[21] *Œuv.*, iv, 407–10. Métra (i, 339) reports that Turgot's object was to defeat speculators who were cornering the market.

[22] Coquereau, p. 256.

[23] *Œuv.*, iv, 404–6, 414–15.

[24] Véri, i, 282–3. Cf. Métra, i, 339–41.

[25] See Métra, i, 338 ; Coquereau, pp. 255–6 (*Lettre de Dijon*, 20 *avril*), Soulavie, ii, 290. (All cited by Foncin, pp. 186–8.) See also Turgot to Du Muy, 20 April 1775 (H.M.C. Ninth Report, Appendix, p. 481).

[26] Métra, i, 341 ; *Œuv.*, iv, 413 (Turgot to Véri, 30 April 1775, from Véri, i, 284).

[27] *Œuv.*, iv, 407–10, 499–515. For further details see below, pp. 199–200

[28] There are several contemporary descriptions of the corn riots—*Relation Historique* (Coquereau, pp. 231–72) ; Métra, i, 339 ff. ; Sénac du Meilhan, pp. 175 ff. ; Georgel, i, 423 ff. ; Soulavie, ii, 289 ff. ; Du Pont (Knies, i, 178–182, ii, 354–364) ; D.P., pp. 182 ff. ; Mercy (Arneth, ii, 331) ; Marmontel (a), iii, 95–6 ; Véri, i, 284 ff. (Véri was away at the time, but collected information upon his return) ; St Paul (who was deputizing for Stormont), 3, 6, 10 May. All agree in essentials (the more important variations are mentioned below). See also Foncin, pp. 194–216 and *Œuv.*, iv, 44–55, 415 ff.

[29] *Œuv.*, iv, 415–16.

[30] Métra, i, 342.

[31] *Œuv.*, iv, 416–7.

[32] Coquereau, p. 259.

[33] Véri, i, 289.

[34] Foncin, p. 198.

[35] Véri, i, 291–2.

[36] Ibid., Cf. D.P., p. 189.

[37] *Œuv.*, iv, 427.

[38] *Procès-verbal du lit de justice du 6 mai*, 1775 (Printed. Copy in Stormont Papers). See also *Œuv.*, iv, 420 ff.

[39] *Œuv.*, iv, 428–9. Louis admitted that his memory failed him in his first speech. Cf. St. Paul, 6 May, ' He began several times before he could continue.'

[40] Véri, i, 287, 288. For different versions see Weber, p. 84 and Coquereau, p. 264. Véri's is the nearest to that which Turgot himself gives in a letter to Vaines (see *Œuv.*, iv, 306).

[41] The price of bread in Paris, St Paul reports (3 May), was barely one-quarter above the normal. See also the *mercuriale* in *Œuv.*, iv, 45 and Du Pont (Knies, ii, 362).

[42] See Foncin, pp. 208, 215–16, citing Mirabeau(e), iii, x, 158 and Marmontel (a), iii, 96.

[43] Véri, i, 285. See also p. 287.

[44] Mme du Deffand (a), iii, 168. See Foncin, pp. 212–13.

[45] Mairobert was at this time writing the *Mémoires secrets* (Bachaumont).

[46] On the foregoing paragraphs see Bachaumont, viii, 45–6, 48, 54 ; Métra, ii, 17, 28 ; Soulavie, ii, 291 ; Arneth, ii, 331, 340, 341.

[47] *Œuv.*, iv, 431–2 (list taken from Funck-Brentano (c)).

[48] See Foncin, pp. 213–14. See also *Lettre royale aux archevêques et évêques* (9 May 1775) and Turgot's ' Instruction aux curés ' (*Œuv.*, iv, 436–442). The instruction contains the following words. ' When the people know who are the authors (of the revolt) they will behold them with horror . . . when they know the consequences they will fear these more than the famine itself.' The words were taken as a promise that the instigators of the riot would be exposed. Turgot was attacked for failing to keep it (see Marmontel, op. cit.)

[49] Bord (p. 445). The actual figure was 4,000,000 (D.P., p. 184).

[50] *Œuv.*, iii, 534–5.

[51] E.g. *Cahier* 23 (end of May 1775). See Véri, i, 287–8, 385–6.

[52] Knies, ii, 355 ff. (Cited in *Œuv.*, iv, 53). It is significant that Conti frequently speculated in the corn markets.

[53] Webster, pp. 91–5

[54] Cited Webster, pp. 80–1

[53] Webster, pp. 91–5.

[54] Cited Webster, pp. 80–1.

[55] *Œuv.*, iv, 473–5.

[56] St. Paul, 27 July 1775.

[57] *Œuv.*, iv, 393–4, 455–9, 462–6 ; v, 322–5.

[58] Ibid., pp. 491–9.

[59] St Paul, 17 May 1775.

[60] For these literary polemics, see Foncin, pp. 217–34.

[61] *Œuv.*, iv, 412–13 ; Foncin, pp. 223–31. See also Morellet, i, 236–8 ; Marmontel (a), iii, 100; Sénac de Meilhan, pp. 178, 208 ; Bachaumont, viii, 16–17, 18–19, 31, 76 ; Soulavie, ii, 302–5.

[62] Véri, i, 377–8 ; ii, 15–16, 43, 61–3, 72 (cf. Besenval, pp. 62–3 and Sénac de Meilhan, pp. 163–4). Véri suspected that Pezay was introduced to the King by Sartine, who certainly encouraged him. At a later date Sartine, to whom Véri pointed out the folly of what he had done, himself nearly became the victim of Pezay's intrigues. On this occasion the mischief-maker was disgraced. He died in exile in December 1777.

CHAPTER XIII

[1] 4 Jan. 1775. See also Véri, i, 347–8 and Foncin, pp. 134 ff.

[2] *Œuv.*, iv, 244–53.

[3] Ibid., pp. 253–7.

[4] Métra, i, 267–8 ; D.P., pp. 181.

[5] *Œuv.*, v, 34–5.

[6] Ibid., pp. 39–50.

[7] Ibid., pp. 50–8. (Stormont sent a copy to the English Government which was watching with great interest Turgot's fight against the cattle plague—22 Feb.)

[8] Ibid., pp. 34–87 ; Foncin, pp. 164 ff.

[9] St Paul, 21 June 1775.

[10] See *Œuv.*, v, 40–1, 67–8 and Foncin, pp. 316 ff.

[11] Ibid., iv, 248–9 ; v, 35–9, 65, 71–2, 82–9. See also Véri, i, 391.

[12] Ibid., v, 90 ; Véri, i, 348.

[13] Véri, i, 391.

[14] *Œuv.*, v, 29–30, 89–90.

[15] Ibid., pp. 77–80, 329–39.

16 One result of the epidemic was the loss of the hide trade to the English. Turgot permitted trade in hides which had been disinfected. His efforts in collaboration with Vergennes to persuade foreigners again to buy French hides met with no success.

17 *Œuv.*, v, 29–31.
18 Ibid., pp. 329–32.
19 Ibid., pp. 339–41. See also D.P., p. 329.
20 Ibid., iv, 265–8; v, 118–19, 422–3.
21 Ibid., iv., 349–50, 407–11, 499–515.
22 Ibid., pp. 264–5, 515–20; v, 426–7. See also Véri, i, 364–7.
23 On this section see *Œuv.*, iv, 237–44, 628–51; v, 91–8, 121–4, 133, 317, 321–2, 342–69, 428–9.
24 Bridge, v, 156–8; Marion (c), pp. 372–3. After 1719 a portion of the profits were still paid to the Colleges, which were able to increase the number of university scholarships.
25 Foncin, pp. 275–6.
26 *Œuv.*, iv, 378–92. See also D.P., pp. 234 ff.
27 Ibid., p. 655. See also St Paul, 27 Sept, 1775.
28 Ibid., p. 392, v, 326.
29 Véri, ii, 58; Métra, ii, 149–51; D.P., pp. 234–40.
30 Véri, i, 424.
31 Métra, op. cit. St Paul (11 Oct. 1775) states that 200 post-masters lost employment.
32 Foncin, pp. 280–1, citing Abbé Proyart.
33 St Paul, 2 Aug., 1 Nov. 1775. See also Véri, i, 329–30, and Mercy to Kaunitz (Arneth, ii, 366).
34 Véri, i, 334.

CHAPTER XIV

1 18 Dec. 1774.
2 Véri, i, 241.
3 Métra, i, 339–40. See also Arneth, ii, 312, 319, 331.
4 Véri, i, 250–1.
5 Ibid., pp. 297–8 (and see also pp. 152–3, 243). See further Ségur (b), i, 70.
6 Arneth, ii, 349–50 (Mercy).
7 Copies of their *mémoires* (printed) are to be found in the Stormont Papers.
8 Véri's account (i, 278–80) breaks off at this point, *Caheir* 21 being lost. For a full report of this affair, see Stormont, 11 Jan., 25 Jan., 12 April 1775
9 *Journ. Hist.*, vii, 201–2, 224–5, 248, 252–3, 271; Bachaumont, viii, 18, 37–8, 50–1, 70; St Paul, 7 June; Arneth, ii, 313–14, 318, 322, 345 (Mercy).
10 Métra, i, 298; Arneth, ii, 218–19.
11 Arneth, ii, 322–3 (Mercy to Marie-Thérèse, 20 April). Foncin, who cites this letter (p. 180), assumes that a compact was made between the Queen and Maurepas at this time. But actually no agreement was reached.
12 Véri, i, 294–5 (describing a conference between Maurepas, Vergennes and himself).
13 Ibid., pp. 296–9.
14 Bachaumont, viii, 72–4.
15 St Paul, 7 June.
16 Bachaumont, viii, 74.
17 Véri, i, 294–7, 307–11; St Paul, 24 May. Cf. Georgel, i, 406.
18 Arneth, ii, 343 (Marie-Antoinette), 346–7 (Mercy); St Paul, 14 June.
19 Véri, i, 336–7.
20 Arneth, ii, 362.
21 Ibid., pp. 356–8.
22 See Murray Keith's dispatches to Suffolk (S.P.F., 80/215, 216) and Mercy's letters to Marie-Thérèse (Arneth, ii, *passim*). See further Véri, i, 303.
23 Véri, i, 311.
24 Ibid., p. 308; St Paul, 21 June.

²⁵ Véri, i, 305–9, 324–5. See also Arneth, ii, 349; St Paul, 21 June; Bachaumont, viii, 85.

²⁶ Véri, i, 309–11, 337.

²⁷ Cf. Bachaumont, viii, 87–8 : 'Many diverse interests are growing to frustrate the return of Choiseul. M de Vergennes, who fears him because he recognizes his superior talents, would not view his recall with pleasure. M. le Comte du Muy . . . would be set against the return of the Duke who is inconstant, frivolous, superficial and partial. The Comptroller-General feels that all his projects of economy would go up in smoke if Choiseul came to power.'

²⁸ This interview was probably arranged by Besenval for the following day (Besenval, pp. 168–74), but the Queen had caused the meeting to take place earlier.

²⁹ Véri, i, 309–18. Besenval (pp. 173–4) did not know the whole story.

³⁰ St Paul, 12, 27 July.

³¹ Arneth, ii, 355.

³² Véri, i, 299–300.

³³ See speeches of 12, 21, 27 Nov. 1774 (printed copies of these are in the Stormont Papers). See also Véri, i, 218–19.

³⁴ Bachaumont, viii, 47.

³⁵ Foncin, pp. 221–2. For Turgot and the remonstrances, see Marion (a).

³⁶ 10 July (cited by Foncin, p. 266)

³⁷ Métra, ii, 69 ; Bachaumont, pp. 129–30.

³⁸ Stormont, discovering that the Spanish Ambassador took precedence over other foreign Ministers, arranged to take his leave before the *Sacre* and to be detained by pressing business.

³⁹ *Œuv.*, iv, 119–20. In 1772 the cost had been 7,000,000 *livres*. By 1775 prices had increased, and there were now the additional households of the Princes.

⁴⁰ Ibid., pp. 549–50; D.P., p. 215.

⁴¹ Foncin, p. 242.

⁴² Bachaumont, viii, 8 ; Véri, i, 269.

⁴³ Véri, i, 237.

⁴⁴ Foncin, p. 251.

⁴⁵ *Œuv.*, iv, 567 (citing D.P., p. 221).

⁴⁶ Véri, i, 252–3, 255–7, 383. St Paul reported (30 Aug. 1775) that the Protestants were ready to offer 20,000,000 *livres* in return for toleration.

⁴⁷ Véri, i, 253–5.

⁴⁸ *Œuv.*, iv, 551–3 (citing D.P., pp. 217 ff. and *Œuv.*, D.P., vii, p. 316).

⁴⁹ Foncin, p. 253.

⁵⁰ *Œuv.*, iv, 554.

⁵¹ D.P., pp. 219–20.

⁵² *Œuv.*, iv, 557–67.

⁵³ Véri, i, 384.

⁵⁴ Holder of the *Feuille des bénéfices*, an office of great political importance involving control of ecclesiastical appointments. Turgot and Véri urged Maurepas to support Brienne as successor to Laroche-Aymon. In the end they secured nomination of Marbeuf of Autun—their second choice (Véri, i, 189–200, 340).

⁵⁵ Foncin, pp. 297–9.

⁵⁶ Véri, i, 381.

⁵⁷ On these phrases see Foncin, pp. 177–8.

⁵⁸ Bachaumont, viii, 251

⁵⁹ Métra, ii, 141–2

⁶⁰ Bachaumont, viii, 153–66 *passim*. See also Véri, i, 357–8.

⁶¹ Bachaumont, viii, 141.

⁶² Métra, ii, 174 ; St Paul, 27 Sept. ; Véri, i, 357.

⁶³ Véri, i, 383.

⁶⁴ Stormont, 29 Nov. 1775.

⁶⁵ Véri, i, 358.

⁶⁶ Ibid., pp. 316, 318–19, 327–9, 331, 334, 335, 339 (see also pp. 394, 435–6).

⁶⁷ See Foncin, pp. 306–9, for extracts from their correspondence.
⁶⁸ Arneth, ii, 368–9.
⁶⁹ Arneth, ii, 368–9.
⁷⁰ Bachaumont, viii, 132.
⁷¹ Véri, i, 337.
⁷² Arneth, ii, 366 ff.
⁷³ Bachaumont, viii, 188.
⁷⁴ Arneth, ii, 367, 389 ; Véri, i, 354.   See also Foncin, pp. 309–10.
⁷⁵ Véri, i, 319, 337–9, 358, 367–8.   Besenval's own account, though less precise, agrees substantially with Véri's.
⁷⁶ Arneth, ii, 387.
⁷⁷ Véri, i, 358–9, 368–9.
⁷⁸ St Paul, 4 Oct.
⁷⁹ Foncin, p. 314 (citing Walpole, *Corr.* 3 Oct. 1775).
⁸⁰ Lauzun (a), pp. 115–42 *et passim.*
⁸¹ Rochford to St Paul, 13 Oct. ; St Paul, 11 Oct.
⁸² Véri, i, 369–70 ; Stormont, 25 Oct.
⁸³ Foncin, p. 345.   See also Besenval, pp. 215 ff.
⁸⁴ Véri, i, 369–70.   This account is substantiated by Turgot's letter of 30 April 1776 to the King (*Œuv.*, v, 453) and also by Stormont's dispatch of 1 Nov. 1775 reporting a conversation with Maurepas.   Georgel i, 408 ff., is in error when he says that Turgot experienced difficulty in persuading Maurepas. Foncin (p. 347) leaves the question open.
⁸⁵ Besenval, pp. 217–19.
⁸⁶ Stormont, 25 Oct.   See also Véri, i, 360–3.
⁸⁷ Véri, i, 370.
⁸⁸ Stormont, 25 Oct. and 1 Nov.
⁸⁹ Véri, i, 373–4, 408–9.
⁹⁰ *Œuv.*, v, 109–18, 434–5
⁹¹ Stormont, 1 Jan. 1776.   Stormont's dispatches contain a very detailed account of Saint-Germain's reforms.   See vols. 297–300 and the additional papers, 324.
⁹² The *mémoires* are lost, but we have summaries made by Du Pont (*Œuv.*, iv, 312–13).
⁹³ *Œuv.*, iv, 362, 483–90.
⁹⁴ Stormont, 3, 10 Jan.   See Véri, i, 371.
⁹⁵ Véri, i, 386–7.
⁹⁶ Stormont, 20 Dec. 1775.   Cf. Métra, ii, 296–7.
⁹⁷ Stormont, 3 Jan. 1776 ; Véri, i, 208, 300–2.
⁹⁸ *Œuv.*, iv, 306.
⁹⁹ See Foncin, pp. 312–13, 356–60.
¹⁰⁰ Véri, i, 341, 347.
¹⁰¹ Métra, ii, 174.
¹⁰² Arneth, ii, 410.

CHAPTER XV

¹ The figure fixed later was 10,000,000 *livres.*
² Stormont, 8 Dec. 1775.   See also 20 Dec. 1775 and 10 Jan. 1776
³ Véri, i, 392–6.   Véri argues that Turgot waited too long between announcing the reform of the *corvées* and drawing up the details for executing it.   But it was impossible for him to work secretly ; he had to prepare Louis for the reform and he had to employ the intendants in making investigations.
⁴ Ibid., pp. 406–7.
⁵ *Œuv.*, v, 148–62.
⁶ For a more detailed account of the provisions of the Six Edits, see Foncin, 374–402 and Shepherd's monograph.
⁷ *Œuv.*, v, 154–7.   For the text of the Declaration, see *Œuv.*, v, 218–19. The preamble describes the archaic regulations obtaining in Paris.
⁸ Ibid., pp. 157–8, 234–8.

⁹ Ibid., pp. 265–6 (citing article by Baudeau in *Nouv. Éph.*, 1776, ii). See also Bachaumont, ix, 111–12, 114.
¹⁰ Paris News Letter (Add. MSS., 38, 202, ff.303–4).
¹¹ *Œuv.*, v, 160–1, 260–6.
¹² Ibid., pp. 161–2, 267–9.
¹³ Ibid., pp. 260–1 (citing D.P.).
¹⁴ Ibid., pp. 629–32, 634, 640 ff.
¹⁵ Bachaumont, viii, 90, 94–5 ; *Œuv.*, iv, 632.
¹⁶ *Œuv.*, v, 159.
¹⁷ St Paul, 28 June 1775.
¹⁸ Véri (i, 419) gives the figure of 1,000,000 *livres* a year.
¹⁹ See Tarlé's study.
²⁰ *Œuv.*, v, 158–60, 238–48.
²¹ Condorcet (a), pp. 74 ff.
²² For text see *Œuv.*, v, 248–55.
²³ See Ch. XVIII, Section 2.
²⁴ *Œuv.*, iv, 234.
²⁵ Ibid., p. 236.
²⁶ Ibid., pp. 235–6 (Vignon, iii, no. 102.)
²⁷ Stormont, 4 Jan. 1775 ; Véri, i, 228.
²⁸ Véri, i, 227–8.
²⁹ *Œuv.*, iv, 528–9.
³⁰ Ibid., pp. 499–500, 530–1.
³¹ Stormont, 10 Jan. 1776.
³² *Œuv.*, iv, 235, 531–7.
³³ Ibid., 538–47 (Vignon, iii, no. 96).
³⁴ Véri, i, 258–9.
³⁵ See Foncin, 375–8, 403–5, 430–2 ; Vignon, iii, 111–116, 140, 218 ; *Œuv.*, v, 162.
³⁶ Foncin, p. 378 (citing Buffon, *Corr.* 6 Jan. 1776).
³⁷ *Œuv.*, v, 148–54, 200–13. Du Pont maintains that the figure of 10,000,000 *livres* was based upon the expert advice of the engineers. The *corvées*, according to Du Pont's own calculations, cost the *pays d'élections* 50,000,000 *livres* annually.
³⁸ Véri, i, 396 ff.
³⁹ See Bachaumont, ix, 44–5 ; Soulavie, iii, 89.
⁴⁰ Véri, i, 395, 406, 411–12.
⁴¹ Stormont, 10 Jan. 1776.
⁴² Véri, i, 391–2, 395, 396, 411–12.
⁴³ Stormont, 31 Jan. 7, Feb. 1776.
⁴⁴ Véri, i, 394–7.
⁴⁵ D.P., pp. 365–6. Véri endeavoured to discover the exact part played by Miromesnil throughout these struggles. He tells us that Malesherbes was always of the opinion that Miromesnil had a secret understanding with the magistrates, and that Maurepas's feebleness made his task relatively easy ; for Louis could hardly be expected to see through the intrigue to bring about Turgot's downfall. Turgot himself held a similar view. In 1782 Véri asked the Keeper of the Seals outright whether he consciously worked for Turgot's dismissal. Miromesnil's answer was that while he defended aristocracy and privilege on principle, he did not engineer a factious opposition. He believed that Turgot was bound to fall, and this he greatly regretted. He concluded, 'It was not I who brought about his disgrace.' But, as Véri points out, Miromesnil's policy of advancing the claims of the magistracy and of attempting to abolish the *Grand Conseil* was certainly one of the chief causes of Turgot's dismissal (see Véri, i, 420, 459–60 ; ii, 26–7, 31–2, 53–5, 64, 70–1).
⁴⁶ Condorcet (a), p. 69 ; Véri, i, 423.
⁴⁷ D.P., p. 365.
⁴⁸ Véri, i, 396–7.
⁴⁹ See *Œuv.*, v, 163–200. Long extracts in English are to be found in Shepherd, and also in Stephens.
⁵⁰ This was the occasion when a workman at the Palace said to Louis, ' I see

that only you and M. Turgot love the people.' (Véri, i, 406). This is probably the true version of the phrase usually attributed to Louis himself, ' Only M. Turgot and I love the people.' Louis repeated the workman's words to the Queen, who made them public, the phrase quickly acquiring its traditional form.

⁵¹ Stormont, 14, 21 Feb. 1776 ; Véri, i, 421.

⁵² Véri, i, 407, 408, 411.

⁵³ *Œuv.*, v, 270-1.

⁵⁴ Stormont, 28 Feb. and 6 March 1776. One of Conti's sayings in committee was that all he demanded of God was to die a gentleman and seigneur of his lands. See also Véri, i, 417, and Bachaumont, ix, 55, 56, 59.

⁵⁵ *Arrêt* . . . *du 23 fevrier*, 1776 (printed ; copy in the Stormont Papers).

⁵⁶ Stormont, 6 March.

⁵⁷ Stormont, 13 March.

⁵⁸ Véri, i, 418.

⁵⁹ Métra, ii, 405. For details of these pamphlets (taken chiefly from Bachaumont, ix) see Foncin, pp. 422-9.

⁶⁰ Vignon, iii, 145.

⁶¹ See Schelle's note (*Œuv.*, v, 9) citing figures from Garnier's translation of the *Wealth of Nations*.

⁶² Véri, i, 417, 419-20 ; Stormont, 13 March.

⁶³ Véri, i, 417-18. Actually Louis had read them twice.

⁶⁴ Stormont, 13 March.

⁶⁵ Véri, i, 418, 421.

⁶⁶ *Procès-verbal du lit de justice* . . . *du 12 mars*, 1776 (printed ; copy in the Stormont Papers). Extracts are given in *Œuv.*, v, 273 ff.

⁶⁷ Saint-Germain had made the same suggestion, and even Voltaire favoured it. (Foncin, p. 508).

⁶⁸ Véri, i, 423.

⁶⁹ Stormont, 6 March.

⁷⁰ Stormont, 20 March. The English Ambassador devotes much space in his dispatches to the conflict concerning the Six Edicts, for he feared it might ultimately lead to important changes in the Ministry. He refrains from expressing definite opinions about the edicts themselves, but the impression he gives is that, while he approved of their practical value, he was suspicious of their equalitarian principles. His aristocratic prejudices were certainly in conflict with his respect for common sense. Nor is his verdict of Turgot a clear one. At times he is ready to admit that the uncompromising vested interests and the political manoeuvres of the ministers rendered the most necessary reforms impossible : at others he tends to voice freely the charge that Turgot was a hasty and speculative man who pressed on recklessly heedless of all difficulties. Again, while criticizing Turgot for not preparing opinion, he asserts that his preambles were out of place, and that his patronage of the economists was most prudent. (See in particular the following dispatches : 1775—1, 8, 29 Nov., 20 Dec. ; 1776—10, 17 Jan., 14, 21, 28 Feb., 6 March (three dispatches), 13, 20 March).

CHAPTER XVI

¹ *Œuv.*, v, 312.

² Ibid., pp. 99-108. This reform is described at length in Foncin, pp. 327-34, 471 ff. and also by Gerlier.

³ *Œuv.*, v, 327, 354-7.

⁴ Ibid., p. 432.

⁵ Ibid., pp. 327-9, 424.

⁶ Ibid., pp. 329-41, 342-51.

⁷ Ibid., p. 345.

⁸ Ibid., p. 369 (see also Véri, i, 427).

⁹ Ibid., p. 269.

¹⁰ See Turgot to the Bishop of Cahors (*Œuv.*, v, 369-70). See also his letter of 16 Aug. 1775 to Véri (*Œuv.*, iv, 696). This letter shows that the decision to free the wine trade had been taken as early as Aug. 1775.

[11] For text, see *Œuv.*, v, 370–84.

[12] *Œuv.*, v, 384 (citing D.P., p. 381).

[13] Ibid., pp. 384–420. See also Véri, i, 421–2, 441–4.

[14] Véri, i, 413. Speaking of Gournay Turgot had said, ' This name, *homme à systèmes*, has become a kind of weapon in the mouths of those interested in maintaining abuses ' (*Œuv.*, iv, 6).

[15] Turgot's health was drunk at Bristol (Foncin, p. 507).

[16] Véri, i, 413. See also Véri's remarks (ii, 307, 405–6) when the Provincial Assembly of Berry was engaged in reforming the *corvées*. Du Pont told the margrave of Baden that Louis XVI had encountered more opposition in an attempt to relieve the people than had his grandfather in oppressing them. (*Œuv.*, v, 269).

[17] Métra, ii, 421 ; iii, 23–4.

[18] Foncin, p. 516. Turgot was also in conflict with the Parlements of Besançon, Bordeaux and Grenoble. See Du Tillet, Bishop of Orange, to Turgot (*Œuv.*, v, 298–300). See also Véri, i, 420.

[19] The King, the first mannequin, was controlled by Maurepas. Maurepas, the second, was governed by his wife. She in turn was under the influence of Véri, who was the agent of the sinister Turgot (see Soulavie, iii, 106–27).

[20] A full description of these libels (taken chiefly from Bachaumont, ix) is given by Foncin, pp. 506–18. See also *Œuv.*, v, 467–80.

[21] See Foncin, p. 522 (citing Marmontel (a), iii, 39 and Morellet, i, 162).

[22] See D.P., pp. 386 ff

[23] Ibid., p. 390. A year later Louis mentioned the finding of the letters to d'Angivillers. Joseph II expressed the opinion to Véri that those who employed the device of opening letters to obtain secret information would sooner or later be mis-informed by clever rogues (Véri, ii, 46–7). See also Véri, i, 413–4, ii, 15–16, 26.

[24] For further details of this affair, see Fonchin, pp. 524–6 (citing Fleury, *Mémoires*).

[25] *Œuv.*, v, 17–19.

[26] Véri, i, 414.

[27] *Œuv.*, v, 445–8.

[28] This letter is lost. Turgot admits in his second letter of 30 April to the King (*Œuv.*, v, 453) that he took the lead in the demand for Guines' recall.

[29] Véri, i, 388–90, 397–402, 416–17 ; Stormont, 6 March.

[30] Stormont, 6 March ; Véri, i, 416–17.

[31] Véri, i, 412–13.

[32] Ibid., p. 424. On returning after Turgot's fall, Véri attempted to piece together the story.

[33] Arneth, ii, 437.

[34] Bachaumont, ix, 90–1.

[35] Condorcet attributes to Maurepas such a design (to Voltaire, 12 June 1776, cited by Foncin, p. 529).

[36] Véri, ii, 11–12.

[37] *Œuv.*, v, 13 (citing D.P., pp. 393–4).

[38] Véri, i, 413, 429–30, 435. See also Turgot to Véri, 30 April 1776 (*Œuv.*, v, 439).

[39] Véri, ii, 11–12 ; St Paul, 29 June 1776.

[40] This letter, dated 10 May, is reproduced by Foncin, 527, n. 2. Foncin, however, gives this letter a false context. To explain this point it is necessary to discuss briefly the part played by Marie-Antoinette in bringing about Turgot's dismissal. Foncin takes his account almost at random from sources which are conflicting—Bachaumont, ix, Mercy's letter of 16 May to Marie-Thérèse (Arneth, ii, 446–9), which implicates the Queen, and Condorcet's letter of 12 June to Voltaire, which exonerates her almost completely. While accepting much of Condorcet's evidence, Foncin dogmatically states (p. 528) that the Queen was responsible more than anyone else for Turgot's dismissal, and in a footnote he explains that Condorcet was not in a position to know the truth. And yet he accepts Condorcet's word that the Queen refused in the last resort to bargain with Maurepas, and caused the letter of 10 May to be sent to Guines.

Foncin goes on to explain, suggesting that Maurepas was suddenly taking a new
line after this rebuff, the attempt to expedite Malesherbes's departure.   At
what date did Maurepas make this move ?   Had the Queen already secured
Turgot's dismissal ?   Was her quarrel with Maurepas an incident of no real
consequence ?   These are questions which Foncin never raises.

As we have seen, Maurepas had been attempting to expedite Malesherbes's
resignation ever since the beginning of April, and he had agreed with Marie-
Antoinette that Sartine should have the Household, but whether it was part of
that same bargain that Turgot should be disgraced there is no evidence to tell us.
By 30 April the news that Maurepas was proposing Amelot for the Household
was public.   Therefore, it must have been about this time that the Queen was
estranged from Maurepas.   Foncin (citing Mercy, Arneth, ii, 442) holds that
the Queen accepted Amelot, though we are not told at what point exactly she
gave way.   Nor is it really certain that she agreed to Amelot : it is very easy to
read too much into Mercy's account, which gives the impression that the writer
was not at all conversant with the inner story of the intrigue.   In fact, Mercy
admits that the Queen had evaded his searching and prying, and he was probably reporting in part the scandal which Maurepas found it convenient to make
public on this occasion.   Against Mercy's story must be set the Queen's own
remarks of 15 May : ' I confess to my dear mother that I am not ill-pleased at
these departures (of Turgot and Malesherbes), but I have not been involved in
them.' (Arneth, ii, 441).   And when Marie-Thérèse told her that the public
were attributing to her *petites menées* inappropriate to her position (Arneth, ii,
450), she protested her innocence a second time (ibid., p. 453).

Veri, who was at first inclined to believe that the Queen played an important
part (i, 431), later came to the conclusion that her share was very little, having
no doubt sounded Vermond and Maurepas upon the matter (i, 447).

[41] Véri, i, 429–34, 439.
[42] The first concerns the Chanvallon affair.   The original has been lost, and
our text is taken from Soulavie, iii, 426–30.   The original of the second is also
lost, and our text is from Véri, i, 450–7.
[43] Véri (i, 450, 457) speaks of two earlier letters, both of which he had glanced
at hurriedly.   He probably refers to the first letter of 30 April and another dated
26 Feb. concerning the appointment of the Provost of Merchants at Lyons (see
Œuv., v, 445).   Malesherbes, who had charge of Turgot's papers in 1781,
mentions four in all, but probably includes that of 18 May (see *Œuv.*, v, 442–5).
The reference to the cruel silence would seem to confirm Montyon's anecdote
(p. 183).   When, towards the end of April, Turgot read a *mémoire* (*Œuv.*, v,
358–68) concerning a dispute between the Chamber of Commerce of Lille
and the Customs Officers of Lyon, Louis listened impatiently and demanded
with disgust, ' Is that all ? '—' Yes, Sire.'—' So much the better,' added Louis,
turning his back.
[44] Cf. Turgot to Du Pont (*Œuv.*, v, 491) and Turgot's letter to a correspondent
in England, quoted in full below.
[45] Soulavie had read the letter when the King's papers were seized during
the Revolution.   In the *Mémoires* (ii, 55 ; iii, 165) he mentions this passage.
Extracts from Véri's text were published by Larcy in 1868 (see *Œuv.*, v, 444).
[46] Véri, i, 450, 457.   St Paul (15 May 1776) gathered from a conversation
with Maurepas that it was the dispute concerning Malesherbes's successor that
brought the matter to a head.
[47] Véri, i, 430–1.
[48] Ibid., p. 415.
[49] Moreau, ii, 254–5.
[50] Georgel (i, 425–6) implies that the final decision was not taken until that
morning—a fact true enough when it is remembered that at any moment Louis
was likely to change his mind.
[51] Bachaumont, ix, 133.
[52] Véri, i, 431–2.
[53] *Œuv.*, v, 456–9.
[54] Stormont, 21 Aug. 1776.
[55] Véri, ii, 15 (see also Turgot to Du Pont, *Œuv.*, v, 504).

[56] Véri, ii, 31.
[57] Ibid., p. 58.
[58] Turgot to Du Pont (*Œuv.*, v, 525).
[59] *Œuv.*, v, 21.
[60] Véri, ii, 63.
[61] *Œuv.*, v, 488.
[62] Here he was presented to Joseph II, who greatly admired him, and who confessed to Véri a deep regret at not being able to arrange an intimate conversation with the man whose doctrines he held himself (Véri, ii, 49–50).
[63] *Œuv.*, v, 532–40.
[64] Ibid., pp. 510–6.
[65] Ibid., p. 650.

<h3 align="center">CHAPTER XVII</h3>

[1] *Additional Observations on Civil Liberty*, London, 1777. Dr. Price had regretted that ' a want of due regard to that degree of public conviction which must influence in a despotic as well as in a free state should have deprived the world of those lights which must have resulted from the example of such administration ' (p. 151).
[2] 8 March 1777. Hardwicke Papers, CCCCXCI, f. 377.
[3] Turgot to Du Pont, 23 Sept. 1775 (*Œuv.*, iv, 676).
[4] Du Pont was working on the *Mémoire* at Chevannes in 1775 (see *Œuv.*, iv, 675–6). Turgot reserved the right to make alterations. A version of the *Mémoire* was published in the *Œuvres posthumes de Turgot* in 1787 along with a *Lettre à M. le comte de M.*, *Commentaire par un républicain*, and also a preface claiming that the text of the *Mémoire* was taken from Turgot's papers. Actually the version was Mirabeau's (being in want of money, he had included the additional matter to satisfy the publisher's demand for a greater bulk of material). Du Pont, though in possession of these facts, was content merely to announce in a letter to the *Journal de Paris* (3 July) that the text was not authentic, for at that time he was anxious not to offend Mirabeau. In 1778 Du Pont sent a copy of his own text to the Margrave of Baden. This version (first published by Knies, i, 244–83) differs from that which Du Pont revised for the *Œuvres*, but it probably gives a truer account of Turgot's opinions than does the text of 1809. See *Œuv.*, iv, 568–74. Schelle gives Knies's text and also the variants from the edition of 1809 (*Œuv.*, iv, 574–621).
[5] He hoped to inaugurate this reform in Oct. 1775, but the cattle plague and the corn riots caused him to postpone his projects until the following year (D.P., p. 198).
[6] The nobles and the clergy were to be excluded when the *taille* was in question, and the clergy again excluded when the *vingtième* and *capitation* were concerned. The effect of fiscal reform upon the constitution is discussed at length (pp. 592–8). It should be noticed that the seigneurs would have a large number of votes spread over several villages.
[7] In Paris, it was estimated, there were only forty people with property bringing in 18,000 livres *ground* rent.
[8] On this point the *Mémoire* is somewhat vague.
[9] Four provincial assemblies were established by Necker, though these differed from Turgot's in so far as the separate social orders were retained. It is probable that Louis would have accepted Turgot's plan had not Maurepas and the other Ministers decided to oppose it. (But cf. Soulavie, iii, 146–54.) When, in 1778, Necker and Maurepas established the Provincial Assembly of Berry, Véri remarked to Turgot that the very men who had opposed the scheme on the ground that it would arouse opposition were now ready to accept it, it being significant that no outcry had arisen. Turgot replied, ' It would have been acceptable in my time if those at Versailles had not raised difficulties ' (Véri, ii, 146–7).
[10] Cf. Cobban, p. 130. It may be noted here that the affinity between the thought of Turgot and that of Rousseau is rarely recognised, so strong is the tradition to contrast them. Although Turgot's position as an administrator and

an economist causes him to cast his ideas in a form which exaggerates his material-
ism, he always has in mind a philosophy of morals not greatly dissimilar from
that of Rousseau, whose works he admired (see his letter to Condorcet in which
he criticises Helvétius (*Œuv.*, iii, 636–41), and also his letter to Hume (ibid.,
ii, 658–62).

[11] Cf. *Œuv.*, v, 563 (letter to Du Pont).

[12] Véri, ii, 145–8. Cf. his words to Du Pont (*Œuv.*, iii, 488) : ' Do not think
I approve of republican constitutions. I do not believe that there has ever
existed a good one, and I am of the opinion of the economists, that a condition of
internal strife and a separation powers are worth nothing.'

[13] In translating Véri's words I have endeavoured to avoid clarifying (and
falsifying) his ideas.

[14] ' A general rule, my friend : it is the public alone that it is necessary to
instruct and convince. One can do this only by demonstrations which will convince the best minds, for the public that masters powerful men is in its turn
mastered by enlightened men ' (to Du Pont, *Œuv.*, iii, 482). In another letter
(*Œuv.*, iii, 491) he explains that it is waste of time to attempt to enlighten those
holding office—a course which many of the economists proposed.

[15] Véri, ii, 8.

<h2 style="text-align:center">CHAPTER XVIII</h2>

[1] Say (a), p. 28.

[2] This brilliant study is based upon an examination of the vast literature of
the *ancien régime*. See Mornet's Bibliography (pp. 505–48). For a brief
account of the controversies concerning the origins of the Revolution see
Roustan (introduction).

[3] Mornet, p. 476.

[4] The best study, in my opinion, of Turgot's economic thought is that by
Lafont.

[5] See above, p. 10.

[6] Turgot's arguments in his article ' Existence ' in the *Encyclopoedia* are,
it is true, closer to those of Descartes then to those of Locke. His relationship
to these two thinkers is a problem which does not admit of brief discussion.
But Turgot's thought was eclectic ; both Cartesian and Lockian ideas, which
have more in common than Locke himself admits, find a place in Turgot's
philosophy. Here, however, we are chiefly concerned with Turgot's elaboration of Locke's sensational psychology.

[7] *Tableau philosophique* . . . (*Œuv.*, i, 215).

[8] Ibid., p. 214.

[9] Ibid., p. 219.

[10] Ibid., pp. 217–19.

[11] Turgot had also studied Dubos (*Histoire critique* . . . 1734), who had
propounded a similar idea.

[12] *Recherches sur les causes des progrès* . . . (*Œuv.*, i, 116, 122, 140). See
also *Œuv.*, iii, 477 (letter to Du Pont).

[13] Ibid., p. 137.

[14] *Tableau philosophique* . . . (pp. 219–30). See also *Fragments* . . .
l'histoire universelle (i, 325).

[15] *Plan* . . . *l'histoire universelle* (i, 314).

[16] *Œuv.*, iii, 471 (to Du Pont).

[17] Ibid., p. 27 (to Du Pont).

[18] It will be noticed that Turgot's philosophy of history anticipates Comte's
conception of three stages in human development—the animistic, the speculative
and the scientific.

[19] See his letter to Condorcet (*Œuv.*, iii, 636–41).

[20] *Réflexions* . . . Sections i–iv. Schelle's text (ii, 533–601) follows that
which Turgot himself revised for the edition of 1770. The text in *Éph.* (1769,
xi, xii, 1770, i) was, much to Turgot's annoyance, drastically edited by Du Pont.
See *Œuv.*, iii, 373 and ii, 533–4.

[21] Ibid., sections v–vii.

[22] *Œuv.*, ii, 658–65.

[23] *Cinquième lettre sur les grains* (*Œuv.*, iii, 288).

[24] *Septième lettre* (ibid. p. 355). The masons in Paris and in other towns were receiving good wages. Young (a, 314–5) speaks of a 20 per cent. rise in wages and a 37 per cent. increase in prices over a period of twenty years. On this topic see Levasseur (a), ii, 839 ff., 972.

[25] Clapham, p. 17.

[26] Levasseur (b), i, 213–17.

[27] Véri's view (which was held also by Grimm and Galiani and which was probably very common) was that France was becoming exceedingly prosperous, and that, with her growing population and vast agricultural resources, she would soon be wealthier and more powerful than England (i, 82–5, 91, 167–8, 346 ff.). On the foregoing paragraphs it is interesting to compare Lipson, iii, 276–7. Having described labour conditions in England, Lipson adds : ' The important conclusion follows that it would be erroneous to apply to eighteenth-century England the theory of the *Iron Law* of wages, which was based upon the widely different conditions supposed to exist in eighteenth-century France. In this country wages were not ground down to a minimum level of subsistence, but the working classes laboured only sufficiently to maintain a traditional standard of life.' The same is true of France.

[28] *Réflexions* . . . Sections viii–xiii.

[29] *Œuv.*, i, 242.

[30] *Réflexions* . . . , Sections xiv–xxviii. See above, Ch. III, Section 2.

[31] *Mémoire sur la surcharge* . . . (*Œuv.*, ii, 451).

[32] *Sixième lettre* . . . (ibid., iii, 311).

[33] He had indeed been anticipated by Saint-Maur in the *Essai sur les monnaies* (pp. 28–37), a work from which he profited considerably.

[34] See Ch. IV, note 51.

[35] *Œuv.*, ii, 448–9.

[36] *Réflexions* . . ., Sections lxvii, lxviii.

[37] Ibid., Sections xxix–xliii (cf. Turgot's letter to Cicé, 1749, *Œuv.*, i, 143–51). Turgot goes on to explain that the value of money and of precious metals varies according to supply and demand (Section xlvi). In the seventh letter to Terray (*Œuv.*, iii, 335) he quotes figures from Saint-Maur to show that the increase of coin had led to a rise in prices and wages.

[38] *Réflexions* . . . , Sections xlvi–lix.

[39] Ibid., Sections lxxi–lxxiii.

[40] *Œuv.*, iii, 154–202.

[41] *Réflexions* . . . , Sections lxxxii–lxxxix.

[42] Ibid., Section xcix.

[43] Written between 1730 and 1734, the first French edition appearing in 1755. These fiscal theories had been anticipated in Halifax's *Essay on Taxation*, 1693.

[44] Mirabeau considered Quesnay's mathematical diagram (the *zic-zac*) an invention equal in importance to those of writing and money.

[45] *Plan d'un mémoire sur les impositions* . . . (*Œuv.*, ii, 299). This treatise was intended as a reply to Bertin's circular to intendants of 18 June 1763 (A.N., K 879/5. 6).

[46] *Œuv.*, v, 173.

[47] *Les effets de l'impôt indirect* (*Œuv.*, ii, 310).

[48] *Plan d'un mém.* . . (p. 310). See also *Mém. sur les douanes intérieures* (*Œuv.*, v, 358–61).

[49] *Prix proposé par la Société d'Agr. de Limoges*, op. cit.

[50] *Plan d'un mém* . . . (pp. 297–8).

[51] See Stourm's account of these taxes.

[52] *Observations sur un projet d'édit* . . . 1763 (*Œuv.*, ii, 256).

[53] *Plan d'un mém.* . . . (p. 304).

[54] Ibid., p. 303. See also *Notes sur l'article ' Impôts ' de Quesney* (*Œuv.*, ii, 318).

[55] *Observations sur le mém. de Graslin* (*Œuv.*, ii, 630).

[56] *Plan d'un mém.* . . (pp. 303–8).

[57] And so did other intendants (*Résumé des mém.* 1763-4. A.N., K 879/4. 5).

[58] *Plan d'un mém.* . . . (pp. 307-8). See also *Mém. pour Franklin,* 1777 (*Œuv.,* v, 513).

[59] *Prix proposé* . . . , op. cit.

[60] *Œuv.,* ii, 145. The tenant was responsible by law for the *taxe d'exploitation,* which amounted usually to two-thirds of the *taille.* Non-privileged land was subject also to the other third, which was known as the *taxe de propriété.* (See *Œuv.,* iii, 9).

[61] Ibid., p. 144. See above, p. 56.

[62] Ibid., p. 503 (letter to Hume, 1766).

[63] Quesnay's view ' is one from which English economists are far removed, for it is difficult to reconcile his principles with the ambition to monopolise the trade of the world.' (Letter to Hume, *Œuv,* ii, 495-6. See also Turgot to Dr. Price, ibid., v, 533).

[64] Bk. iv, Ch. XI. The relationship of Turgot's ideas to Adam Smith's and the influence of the one economist upon the other are problems not easily solved. Cannan, having criticized Du Pont's wild statement that ' everything that is true in this respectable and tedious work,' the *Wealth of Nations,* is to be found in Turgot's *Réflexions,* and that ' everything added by Smith is inaccurate ', concludes (Introduction to Smith's *Lectures on Jurisprudence,* 1896, 23 ff.) : ' Instead of Smith stealing from Turgot, the truth was that Turgot stole from Smith.' In support of this contention Cannan points out that Turgot's *Réflexions* appeared at first only in the *Éphémérides,* which had a very small circulation, and that the edition of 1770 was neither among Smith's books nor in the Advocates' Library at Edinburgh. Cannan also argues that the *Lectures* (1760-3) anticipate the *Wealth of Nations,* and that these works are vastly different from Turgot's. Against Cannan's view must be set Hasbach's (' Adam Smith's Lectures,' *Pol. Sci. Quart.,* xii), that before Smith went to France he worked within the limits of the Scotch moral philosophy (*political economy* being a mere subordinate subject of *police*), and that his associations with the Physiocrats produced the ' gaping chasm ' that exists between the *Lectures* and the *Wealth of Nations.*
Now, Cannan's evidence concerning Smith's library is not so convincing as appears at first sight. As Shepherd (pp. 26-8) has shown, Bonar did not complete the catalogue which Cannan cites. It is highly probable that Smith (like Tucker, to whom Turgot sent a copy) read the *Réflexions,* and it is quite likely (for Condorcet's evidence (a, p. 201) cannot be summarily dismissed) that the two economists corresponded after their meeting in 1764. Schelle (*Œuv.,* ii, 31-2, 66-7) does not rule out this possibility entirely, but he is inclined to believe that no correspondence passed between the two, and assumes that there was little or no borrowing of ideas upon the part of the one or the other.

[65] *Observations sur le mém. de Graslin* (pp. 474-5) ; *Mém. pour Franklin* (pp. 517 ff.). See also *Œuv.,* ii, 509-10 (letter to Du Pont). Many Frenchmen believed that their country struck a happy balance between England, which was rapidly becoming another Holland, and China, with her vast agricultural resources, her large population, and yet lack of trade.

[66] It should be noticed that Turgot believed that the colonies, having received the surplus population from the mother countries, would themselves become nations.

[67] Higgs, p. 124. Neymarck's criticism of the Physiocrats (pp. 125, 133) is also unconvincing.

[68] *Œuv.,* ii, 506-8 (letter to Du Pont). Batbie (p. 9) and Say (a, pp. 54-5) contend that Turgot derived his principles from Quesnay. Schelle (b, pp. 14-15, 246) avers that he was a follower of Gournay. But Lafont's conclusion (pp. 7-14, 203 ff.)—that he followed slavishly neither the one nor the other— is obviously the most satisfactory.

[69] Cf. the preamble to the Edict suppressing the guilds : ' God, by creating man with needs . . . has made the right of labour the right of every man ; and this is the first, the most sacred and the most imprescriptible of all ' (*Œuv.,* v, 242).

[70] *Éloge de Gournay* (*Œuv.,* i, 595-622).

[71] *Œuv.*, iii, 614–15.

[72] *Cinquième lettre* . . . (*Œuv.*, iii, 289–91).

[73] *Septième lettre* . . . (ibid., p. 323). According to Letrosne's estimate' (c, p. 21), the amount of grain that rotted or was devoured by rats was ten times that exported.

[74] These tables have no statistical value; but they illustrate conclusions which Turgot drew from a study of market quotations.

[75] *Quatrième lettre* . . . (*Œuv.*, iii, 277–85).

[76] *Circ. aux officiers de police des villes*, 1766 (*Œuv.*, ii, 471). He also argued that prices in England would have been yet more stable but for the corn laws (cf. Prothero, Ch. XII).

[77] *Œuv.*, iii, 299, 301–13, 320–8, 334, 344 (*Lettres sur les grains*). See also iv, 224–5.

INDEX